ACTION IN ELEMENTARY SOCIAL STUDIES

David W. Van Cleaf

Washburn University
Topeka, Kansas

Allyn and Bacon
Boston • London • Toronto • Sydney • Tokyo • Singapore

Library of Congress Cataloging-in-Publication Data

Van Cleaf, David W.
    Action in elementary social studies / David W. Van Cleaf.
      p.   cm.
    Includes bibliographical references.
    ISBN 0-13-013210-1
    1. Social sciences—Study and teaching (Elementary)—United States. 2. Lesson planning—United States.
3. Education, Elementary—United States—Activity programs.   I. Title.
LB1584.V34   1991
372.83′044—dc20

90-36490
CIP

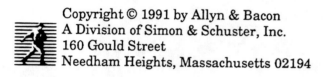
Copyright © 1991 by Allyn & Bacon
A Division of Simon & Schuster, Inc.
160 Gould Street
Needham Heights, Massachusetts 02194

ISBN 0-13-013210-1

Printed in the United States of America

98 97 96 95 94 93 92   10 9 8 7 6 5 4 3 2

TO
Rosemary Van Cleaf
Kara M. Van Cleaf

Contents

Preface   ix

PART I *The Foundations of Social Studies*   1

    Chapter 1 **The Current Status: Controversy, Uncertainty, and Conflicting Purposes**   1

        Introduction   2
        Controversy and Conflicting Views   4
        Three Traditions in Social Studies   12
        Other Conflicts   16
        Summary   18

    Chapter 2 **The Social Studies Curriculum**   23

        Introduction   24
        Curriculum Organization   24
        Scope and Sequence   27
        Curriculum Subject Matter   36
        Summary   46

PART II *Planning Effective Instruction*   49

    Chapter 3 **Characteristics of Effective Teaching**   49

        Introduction   50

Complexities of Classrooms 50
Characteristics of Effective Teachers 51
Suggestions 60
Summary 65

Chapter 4 **Planning Lessons and Units** *67*
Introduction 68
The Importance of Planning 68
Elements of Effective Planning 70
Lesson Planning Models 75
Unit Plans 82
Summary 86

Chapter 5 **Personalizing Instruction** *95*
Introduction 96
Dimensions of Individual Differences 97
Personalizing Instruction: Principles and Strategies 107
Summary 115

Chapter 6 **The Evaluation Process** *117*
Introduction 118
The Purposes of Evaluation 119
The Vocabulary of Evaluation 121
Limitations of Evaluation 123
Suggestions for Measuring Achievement 127
Affective and Subjective Suggestions 128
Summary 138

PART III *Teaching Elementary Social Studies* **141**

Chapter 7 **Methods for Teaching Map Skills** *141*
Introduction 142
Map Skills and Activities 144
Cautions 164
Summary 164

Chapter 8   Methods for Teaching Graphing Skills   *167*

Introduction   168
Developmental Stages   168
Constructing Four Types of Graphs   174
Getting the Most from Graphs   186
Summary   186

Chapter 9   Teaching Content Through Inquiry   *189*

Introduction   190
Inquiry Steps   191
Examples of Inquiry Activities   194
Analysis of Inquiry Examples   204
Summary   205

Chapter 10   Concept Attainment Teaching Strategies   *213*

Introduction   214
Elements of Concepts   215
Benefits of Concept Teaching   216
Beyond Concepts: Generalizations   218
Strategies for Teaching Concepts   219
Summary   230

Chapter 11   Effective Questioning and Discussion Strategies   *233*

Introduction   234
Purposes   235
Types and Taxonomies   238
Research on Questioning   242
Improving Classroom Questions   243
Discussions   248
Summary   252

Chapter 12   Interactive Teaching Strategies: Role Playing, Simulations, and Games   *255*

Introduction   256
Role Playing   257
Simulations   264

Games   269

Computer Software   271

Summary   275

Chapter 13 Character Development   *285*

Introduction   286

Terminology   287

Theoretical Perspectives of Moral Development   288

Encouraging Moral Development   293

Summary   304

PART IV *Related and Supporting Themes*   **307**

Chapter 14 Reading and Social Studies   *307*

Introduction   308

Today's Textbooks   308

Readability   312

Improving Reading in Social Studies   314

Writing and Social Studies   326

Summary   328

Chapter 15 Supporting Themes   *331*

Introduction   332

Multicultural Education   332

Global Education   339

Law-Related Education   343

Computers and Social Studies   346

Critical Thinking   350

Summary   356

References   *359*

Index   *365*

Preface

For a number of years social studies was accorded marginal status in many elementary schools. Reading, math, and language arts received considerably greater emphasis. However, we are beginning to realize that to maintain our prominence in the international community, the primary subjects included in social studies must assume more importance in the school day. As a result, social studies is witnessing a renaissance.

The teacher is the central figure in this renaissance. If children are to develop into the types of adults capable of contributing to our country's preeminence, they must be provided numerous opportunities to become active participants in social studies. Teachers will need to utilize a challenging variety of child-centered instructional strategies. The variety of child-centered strategies appearing in this text will enable teachers to meet the challenge.

PURPOSES OF THIS TEXT

This text is based on three assumptions. First, current practices, which focus on teacher talk and student seat work, are overused and provide limited results. To be effective, social studies teachers will need to utilize an extensive variety of instructional strategies. Second, children must become actively involved in learning if they are to achieve the level of understanding necessary to function effectively as adults. Children are not passive recipients of information; they actively construct a knowledge of their world. Social studies instruction must include numerous provisions for actively involving children. Third, effective citizenship is critical to the survival of a democratic society. Our children must develop character traits that will enable them to function as effective, responsible citizens. They must learn about active citizenship skills and responsibilities rather than accepting roles as passive citizens.

The principles of developmental psychology provide the guidelines necessary for actively involving children. These principles are an underlying thread running throughout this text.

AUDIENCE

This text was written for individuals studying to become elementary teachers. A conscious effort was made to provide a balance of ideas appropriate for primary and intermediate grades. It will help preservice teachers learn how to teach social studies in creative, exciting, and child-centered ways.

Although the primary audience is preservice elementary teachers, the text will help in-service teachers expand their repertoire of instructional strategies. It may also be adapted for individuals interested in becoming middle-school teachers.

ORGANIZATION

The text is divided into four parts. Parts I and II provide the reader with the foundations of effective social studies teaching. Parts III and IV focus on teaching methods.

Part I includes the first two chapters. These chapters describe the status of social studies and the nature of the social studies curriculum.

Part II emphasizes principles of effective teaching and planning. The four chapters in Part II describe the characteristics of effective teachers, alternative means of planning instruction, suggestions for personalizing social studies instruction, and the importance of evaluation in the instructional process.

Part III includes descriptions of child-centered teaching strategies. The map-reading and graph-reading chapters present suggestions for actively teaching these skills in developmentally appropriate ways. Suggestions to help teachers use inquiry, concept attainment, discussions, questioning, role playing, games, simulations, and character development are also presented in Part III.

Part IV contains two chapters that describe six related topics and themes. Chapter 14 presents numerous ideas that can be used to integrate reading and social studies skills. The last chapter describes five themes related to social studies: multicultural education, global education, law-related education, computers in education, and critical thinking.

Social studies is one of the least-liked subjects in the elementary school. It is rated low by both children and teachers. The suggestions provided in this book provide a foundation for actively involving children in social studies. These suggestions will also help teachers become more creative and more effective. As a result of children and teachers engaging in a variety of creative, child-centered activities, the perceptions of social studies will improve. Rather than dreading social studies, social studies will become the highlight of each child's day.

ACKNOWLEDGMENTS

This text reflects the contributions of respected colleagues, secretaries, and students. I wish to thank Jan Norris, Natalie Pearson, and Roseanna Sterbenz for providing insights from the practitioner perspective. Review support was provided by five of my colleagues. Jerry Gray, Mary Shoop, Lyle Baker, Daniel Harden, and Rita Martin reviewed portions of the text. The secretarial support provided by Claudette Mason, Shanna Walker, Colleen Myers, Therese Collins, and Eileen Redmond is gratefully acknowledged. I also wish to thank the Prentice-Hall reviewers: Dr. JoAnne Buggey, Curriculum and Instruction Dept., University of Minnesota; Dr. Charles M. Godwin, Center for Curriculum and Instruction, University of Nebraska; and William M. Watkins, Educational Studies, University of Utah. Most important, I wish to thank all of my former students and two social studies mentors, F. Wm. Sesow and Charles Godwin.

ACTION
IN ELEMENTARY
SOCIAL STUDIES

Pro-life and pro-choice demonstrators hold signs on the steps of the Supreme Court building in Washington, D.C. on July 3, 1989 after the court ruled on the Missouri abortion case.

Source: Photograph courtesy of AP/Wide World Photos.

chapter 1

The Current Status: Controversy, Uncertainty, and Conflicting Purposes

I hate social studies!

(Carla, grade three)

AS YOU READ...

- define social studies
- determine your psychological and philosophical preferences
- identify major issues affecting social studies
- describe how the conflicts affect children and teachers
- begin considering how you will teach social studies in your classroom

INTRODUCTION

When asked to identify their least-liked subjects, children rate social studies as one of their least favorites. They dislike social studies because the content and teaching methods are usually considered boring and not seen as relevant to their lives.

Teachers are the key to improving social studies instruction. They must improve the learning climate and actively involve children if they hope to improve children's attitudes toward social studies. They must also take a more active role in determining the topics included in their social studies program.

Teaching social studies in the elementary school should be one of your most exciting teaching opportunities, and it should be one of the most exciting learning opportunities for your children. Because of the rich nature of the topic, the relationships with children's daily lives and the endless possibilities of making the lessons creative and challenging, social studies should be everyone's favorite subject. Children should look forward to school because of your social studies instruction.

For a variety of reasons, however, social studies is not well liked by children. Nor is social studies taught well by many teachers. This chapter describes major problems affecting social studies instruction in our nation's elementary schools.

As You Begin

Take a few minutes to complete the following activity. Your responses will serve as a foundation for reflection and personal analysis throughout the chapter. You will be asked to reconsider this activity in several other chapters, so please keep your responses in a convenient place.

1. Assume that you have been asked to write a eulogy for someone you would consider a typical "good person." Please *list* the characteristics of that person and the types of information you might include in the eulogy.
2. Now that you have identified the characteristics of a typical "good person," brainstorm a list of goals for elementary schools that would contribute to the preparation of a society of good people.

A Definition

Social studies is generally considered to be the study of people and their relationship to their environment. The environment includes the physical world, the social world, and the spiritual world—past, present, and future. While the spiritual world affects human behavior, public schools usually exclude aspects of the spiritual world in their social studies programs.

Socialization and Social Studies

Every society and every culture has a major responsibility to socialize its young. Children must learn skills and conventions that will enable them eventually to assume their roles as adults. The socialization process is a long, complex process that begins at birth and continues well beyond the elementary school years. The responsibility to socialize the young is shared by our schools. Within the elementary school, social studies assumes major responsibility for helping children learn how the world affects their behavior, how to work effectively with others, and how to function within the role of citizen. Children must become well socialized if they are to function harmoniously in their physical, social, and spiritual worlds.

The socialization process has many challenges and conflicts. Erikson (1963) described various stages through which people proceed as they resolve these challenges and conflicts. During the preschool and early elementary school years most psychologically healthy children are in the latter part of the initiative-versus-guilt stage. Elementary children then enter the industry-versus-inferiority stage.

Children enjoy social studies when they have opportunities to actively investigate.

Photograph by Ken Karp.

Children in the initiative stage must be encouraged to try new behaviors, ask questions, and explore their world. This should occur with adult guidance and encouragement, but without fear of excessive adult reprisals. Social studies teachers working with young children must recognize this need and provide many opportunities for children to explore actively their social world. Primary-grade children should have many opportunities to engage in creative dramatics activities, take field trips, observe people in various situations, and analyze social phenomena.

These types of active exploration provide the foundation for many citizenship skills. The ability to inquire, think critically, seek information from a variety of resources, and interact effectively with others emerge from enriching opportunities to exercise initiative.

However, typical teaching practices require children to work alone on worksheets. In these situations children are expected to learn specific information contained in reading or worksheet assignments. Children are not encouraged to ask questions or to inquire. Rather than nurturing children's need for initiative, children are expected to act as passive learners. Consequently, social studies is uninteresting and may not contribute to the children's socialization.

Children's major challenge during Erikson's industry stage is to make considerable progress toward learning the basic skills of society. The three R's, social skills, religious doctrines, physical skills, and information about the society and culture are learned during this stage. As children master these challenges they develop a healthy belief that they will be able to make positive, industrious contributions as adults.

Elementary social studies programs can contribute to children's developing sense of industry. Teachers must ensure that social studies lessons are based on concepts necessary for children's later success as adults. Trivial topics present in many social studies textbooks should be avoided. Teachers can also contribute to children's growing sense of industry by designing lessons that actively involve the children. Decision-making skills, social participation skills, pride in children's heritage, study skills, and social studies concepts must be included if children are to develop a positive sense of industry.

While there isn't much controversy regarding the school's primary function, namely socializing the child, there is considerable controversy regarding the means of accomplishing this function. Experts and laypersons disagree about what children should be taught and how they should be taught. Disagreement and turmoil have resulted in a decreased emphasis on social studies, a reliance on the use of questionable practices, and a relatively boring approach to teaching social studies.

CONTROVERSY AND CONFLICTING VIEWS

Children should be excited about the prospects of becoming productive, contributing adult members of their society. They have a vested interest and motivation to learn about their world. They should therefore love social studies. The following sections briefly describe the foundations of many of the conflicts affecting social studies. As you consider these sections, please examine the conflicting perspectives and try to develop a personal focus for yourself as a social studies teacher.

Much of the current controversy in education and social studies relates to conflicting views of psychology and philosophy. There are two primary psychological views of people and how they learn. There are also several prevailing philosophies in American education, each emphasizing a somewhat different perspective. The following sections will help you understand the conflicting views of psychology and philosophy and how they affect social studies.

Two Psychological Views

Should learning and development be measured objectively or subjectively? Are schools responsible for the quantity of knowledge learned or the quality of the thought process? Should schools be characterized as teacher-directed or child-centered? Should schools transmit knowledge efficiently or should schools help children discover knowledge? Do children have an inner "self" over which they endeavor to exercise greater control, or are children shaped by the environment, unable to alter their behaviors? These are questions related to the two contrasting psychological views described in this section.

Behaviorism. Behaviorism is a field of psychology that views human behavior as a direct function of the environment. According to behaviorists, learning is defined in terms of the quantity, or amount, of information and behaviors acquired.

The environment is the primary factor in shaping an individual's behavior and learning. Individuals are viewed as passive agents; they are molded and shaped by the environment rather than through self-initiated efforts. Behaviors that are reinforced by the environment are strengthened whereas behaviors that are not reinforced are weakened and eventually extinguished.

Behavioristic principles minimize the role of an internal locus of control. Individuals act and behave because of environmental influences, not an inner self. Self-discipline emerges when children have mastered behavioral rules well enough to apply appropriate behaviors in a variety of situations.

The role of educators is to identify specific learning outcomes and then arrange learning experiences so learners acquire the outcomes as quickly and efficiently as possible. Behavioristic learning environments are characterized as teacher-directed. Teachers arrange instruction in such a way that specific skills, behaviors, and knowledge are identified and taught to children. The lecture method is the most notable example of teacher-directed instruction—instruction is direct and efficient. Teachers reinforce children for performing the correct responses as a means of strengthening desired behaviors. Active learning practices like inquiry are not usually considered compatible with behaviorism.

The following example illustrates the behavioristic approach. In a lesson about good citizenship a behavioristic teacher would begin by stating the definition and providing supporting information. Children would then have an opportunity to practice the information taught by the teacher. As children practice the information the teacher would monitor children's progress, reinforcing and redirecting children when necessary.

A traditional teacher-directed lesson. Effective teachers use a variety of teacher-directed and child-centered lessons.

Photograph by Kenneth P. Davis.

Mastery learning models, such as those advocated by Benjamin Bloom (1984) and Madeline Hunter (1982), are closely aligned with behaviorism. *Direct instruction* is another term often used to describe this type of teaching.

The most notable educational effects of behavioristic psychology include teaching for mastery rather than understanding and using passive rather than active teaching activities. Other notable aspects of behavioristic practices include an increased use of objective tests and an emphasis on efficiency in the teaching-learning process. This efficiency has had a devastating impact on social studies. Children are deprived of opportunities to investigate, inquire, and critically examine social phenomenon because such procedures take additional time.

Cognitive Developmental Psychology. Cognitive developmental psychology is referred to by several related terms such as *cognitive psychology* and *developmental psychology.* This view is exemplified by the writings of Piaget, Kohlberg, Elkind, and Feuerstein.

Major assumptions of cognitive developmental psychology differ markedly from behaviorism. This view assumes that there is an autonomous inner self that exerts control over the learning process. The environment is important, but each person processes, filters, and responds to the environment in unique personal ways.

People are viewed as active, adaptive organisms that learn from their interactions with the environment. Many of these interactions are initiated by the individual. As individuals interact with the environment they adapt and develop more complex cognitive abilities.

Learning is viewed in terms of the quality of thought rather than the amount of knowledge acquired. As children learn they develop more sophisticated ways of processing information. Piaget's stages of cognitive development illustrate how children's thinking develops.

Self-discipline is developed within an individual. As children interact with others they discover ways to improve their self-discipline.

Examples of child-centered learning include the use of language experience stories, manipulatives, inquiry, discovery, moral dilemmas, classroom meetings, creative dramatics, role playing, and learning centers. The teacher's role is one of identifying learning outcomes, selecting appropriate activities, and then helping children interact with the materials and activities in a way that will help youngsters learn the desired information.

The following citizenship lesson illustrates the cognitive developmental approach. The teacher might begin with a discussion in which the children describe people who are good and bad citizens. The children would then reconsider the points made in the discussion and develop a list of characteristics of good and bad citizenship. Children could then develop posters advocating behaviors associated with good citizenship. In this type of lesson the children learn about citizenship in personally meaningful ways; the teacher acts as a guide.

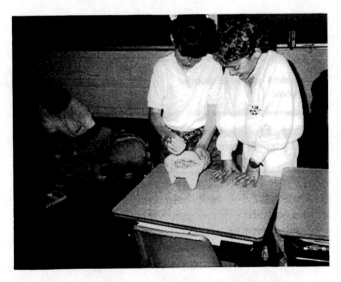

Artifacts help children develop a better understanding of social studies concepts.
Photograph by David W. Van Cleaf.

Child-centered learning has been effective in many areas of education. Child-centered learning has helped youngsters improve in areas such as moral development, logic, language, reading, self-discipline, composition, science, mathematics, and social studies.

More effort and training are required to use child-centered teaching techniques. Teachers must have clear educational goals, understand each child's capabilities, and then organize interactive activities that will lead each child toward the intended outcomes. More importantly, teachers must believe that children will learn and perform well when involved in child-centered learning.

Table 1–1 outlines major differences between behavioristic and cognitive developmental approaches described in this portion of the chapter. The comparisons should help you review the differences and clarify your own views.

Table 1–1 A Comparison of Two Psychological Views

PSYCHOLOGICAL VIEW	THEORETICAL PERSPECTIVES	TEACHING METHODS
Behaviorism:	Behavior shaped by environment	Teacher-directed cues
	Focus on quantity of knowledge/ behavior acquired	Reinforce, punish, extinguish
	Minimizes internal "self"	Technology of teaching
		Mastery learning
		Assertive discipline
Cognitive Developmental:	Learning is a function of development and interaction between individual and environment	Child-centered
	Considers quality of thought process	Interaction with manipulatives
	Autonomous, inner self	Inquiry & discovery learning
	Individuals are active and adaptive learners	Instruction based on developmental needs

The activity in Appendix 1–1 will help you understand the differences between behavioristic and cognitive developmental teaching practices. Seven stem sentences are presented, which represent selected social studies goals for children. Each stem sentence is followed by four possible ways to develop the goal. Two of the possible responses represent behavioristic teaching practices and two represent cognitive developmental teaching practices.

Please reexamine the eulogy you were asked to write earlier. Also, look carefully at the elementary school goals contributing to the development of "good people." Do your eulogy and goals tend to represent the behavioristic or cognitive developmental perspective? Do you have a better understanding of your views? Do you need to modify your eulogy and list of goals?

Educational programs built upon both psychological views are effective. Behavioristic practices help children learn lower-level skills and factual information. Problem-solving skills and understanding of democratic principles are nurtured more effectively through cognitive developmental practices. Unfortunately, too many current practices are primarily behavioristic and therefore contribute to uninspiring social studies lessons.

Contrasting Educational Philosophies

Psychologists examine the origins and development of learning and behavior. Philosophers are concerned with purpose and meaning. Each teacher has a philosophy that affects decisions regarding what to teach, what not to teach, how to teach, and how to manage children. Similarly, school districts have philosophy statements affecting teaching practices and the curriculum. The public and special-interest groups also have philosophical perspectives, and friction often results from conflicts between the philosophical perspectives of the school and its various constituencies.

Elementary social studies practices are affected by conflicts among groups with differing philosophical perspectives. For example, most school districts and teachers recognize the need to teach values to children. Some educators believe values should be inculcated; other educators favor developing values through a process of analysis. The controversy regarding values becomes more controversial because some groups do not want the schools to teach values.

An understanding of differing philosophical perspectives will help you gain a better understanding of the conflicts in elementary social studies education. You will then be better prepared to understand and defend your practices.

There are four prevailing philosophies of education relevant to elementary education. They are: realism, idealism, pragmatism, and existentialism. For the purposes of this text and usefulness in elementary social studies, the four philosophies are combined under two headings: a classical perspective, which includes the traditional philosophies of realism and idealism, and a progressive perspective, which includes the philosophies of pragmatism and existentialism.

A Classical Perspective. Idealism and realism are educational philosophies that have several similarities affecting elementary social studies. They maintain that reality is objective and essentially unchanging. Reality, the way the world exists, is objectively knowable and is not based on the subjective views of individuals. Further, what was real and moral thousands of years ago is valid today. Reality is as absolute today as in the past. Reality and morality are not subject to change, nor are they subject to personal interpretation. The adult's responsibility is to transmit the real and correct notion of reality to children.

The content of a classical educational curriculum emphasizes development of traditional basic skills and knowledge. Schools should emphasize instruction in traditional subjects as a means of transmitting the knowledge and wisdom of the culture to children. Values, morality, and reality can be transmitted through the study of great books, enduring ideas, and heroes from the past.

Teaching practices tend to be traditional. The teacher and curriculum materials should, for the most part, convey ideas and knowledge to children using teacher-directed methods. As children listen to teachers and participate in learning activities they acquire the skills, knowledge, and morality necessary for rational thought and behavior. The back-to-basics movement, a return to an emphasis on studying classical literature and classical languages, and a traditional college preparatory core curriculum reflect the classical view.

A Progressive Perspective. A progressive perspective includes aspects from two somewhat similar educational philosophies—pragmatism and existentialism. These two philosophies view reality as subjective and relative. Knowledge, the nature of reality, and one's understanding of reality develop as a result of experiences with the environment. Because individuals are different and their interactions with the environment are different, each person develops a somewhat different view of reality.

A person's conceptualization of reality is said to be actively constructed rather than copied. A camera analogy may help illustrate this. According to the classical perspective, knowledge is objective and educators must transmit objective knowledge to children. This is like taking pictures of the world with a camera and then transmitting those images to children. According to a progressive perspective, knowledge and reality are not copied; they are constructed. Painters construct images on canvas that represent their subjective view of the thing being painted. No two artists will paint the same object in the same way because each has constructed a different view of the world.

Values, like knowledge, are relative. While the classical view assumes that values are universal and based on irrefutable moral principles, the progressive view denies their universal existence and asserts that values vary according to time, place, and culture.

Values are also seen as situational. What may be right in one instance may be wrong in another. In a classical program, children learn the universal, absolute values. Conversely, children in a progressive program would have opportunities to discover and examine society's values. By examining society's values children will learn to make socially appropriate value responses as situations dictate.

The ability to analyze and solve problems is deemed more important than the acquisition of information. This is another distinction between the classical and progressive views. The classical view advocates teaching a set of information for mastery. The progressive view advocates engaging children in active learning in which information is used to solve problems. John Dewey epitomized the progressive view. He maintained that learners need to learn how to function in society and solve problems if they are to become contributing members of a democratic society. Knowledge is useless if it cannot be used.

The premise of the progressive view is helping each child develop according to personal needs, interests, and abilities. Greater emphasis is placed on the *way* people learn (the process of learning) than on the content of their learning. This is done through active child involvement in projects and activities. As children interact with projects and activities they extract knowledge and skills that become useful for their present situation. The knowledge and skills also become the basis for more sophisticated learning. Teaching strategies such as inquiry, discovery, child investigations, moral dilemmas, discussions, role playing, and values clarification actively involve children in the learning process and enable them to construct knowledge.

It is time to consider again the points in your eulogy and your goals for an elementary program. Are you more closely aligned with a classical philosophy, a progressive philosophy, or do you have a philosophy that includes aspects of classical and progressive views? Table 1–2 illustrates major differences between the two views. Refer to it as you reconsider your own philosophical perspective.

Table 1–2 A Comparison of Two Philosophical Views

PHILOSOPHICAL VIEW	PHILOSOPHICAL TENETS	CLASSROOM EMPHASIS
Classical:	Objective nature of reality	Teach correct values
	Reality is unchanging	Traditional basic skills and content
	Values are universal and irrefutable	Great Books
	Wisdom and knowledge of past must be transmitted to new generations	Teacher-directed
		Focus on traditional academic subjects
Progressive:	Subjective and personal nature of reality	Discovery learning
	Knowledge is constructed and reconstructed	Examine and develop a set of values
	Values are relative	Emphasis on solving socially practical problems

As an elementary social studies teacher you will likely be confronted with demands to adhere to goals and practices emerging from both philosophical perspectives. If your teaching decisions are based on conscious thought you will be able to communicate your purposes and gain support for your efforts.

Psychology and Philosophy Reconsidered

Each psychological view and philosophical view share many of the same ends— well-educated, capable adult citizens. But they differ on how to achieve those ends. Consider these views and then consider your own.

Many state legislatures and school districts are responding to the criticisms of the schools by adopting a more classical curriculum. Many are also emphasizing the use of greater control over student learning by using behavioristic principles. As you prepare to teach you need to understand the climate of the community and its effects on the schools. However, you must also understand how elementary school children learn. They need opportunities to explore, discover, manipulate, and practice newly learned abilities in creative, active ways.

THREE TRADITIONS IN SOCIAL STUDIES

Just as people have different philosophies of education and predispositions to a psychological perspective of learning, social studies educators have different views of the nature of social studies. Barr, Barth, and Shermis (1977) described three views, or traditions, of social studies. The three traditions, summarized in Table 1–3, are described in the following sections according to three topics: their purposes, their content emphasis, and the instructional methods they employ. The first tradition exemplifies a classical philosophy. The second and third views are similar in several ways and reflect a progressive view.

Social Studies as Citizenship Transmission

Citizenship transmission is the most prevalent approach to teaching social studies. It reflects a classical philosophy and a reliance on teacher-directed learning.

The *purposes* of programs based on this tradition are to transmit the fundamental beliefs and values of a culture to the young. A major assumption is that adults know what children must learn and have a responsibility to make children "loyal believers."

Many people are concerned that schools are not teaching the traditional notions of character and want the schools to reassert the emphasis on character development. To accomplish this goal they call for a greater emphasis on a citizenship transmission approach.

The *content* of the citizenship transmission tradition emerges from a set of principles, information, and behaviors that adults assume to be correct and necessary. Learning about our past, taking pride in our traditions, accepting responsibility, behaving appropriately, and respecting authority are included in the content of the citizenship transmission tradition. Children are not encouraged to question content presented by teachers or textbooks, nor are they encouraged to question adults and other authority figures.

One might ask how a tradition of citizenship transmission encourages change and growth. This is a status quo type of curriculum because it tends to impart content from the past as a means of shaping present behavior. While concern for future behavior is evident, children are being prepared to perpetuate currently accepted traditions and behaviors.

Table 1–3 The Three Social Studies Traditions

	1. Social Studies Taught as Citizenship Transmission	2. Social Studies Taught as Social Science	3. Social Studies Taught as Reflective Inquiry
Purpose	Citizenship is best promoted by inculcating right values as a framework for making decisions.	Citizenship is best promoted by decision making based on mastery of social science concepts, processes, and problems	Citizenship is best promoted through a process of inquiry in which knowledge is derived from what citizens need to know to make decisions and solve problems.
Method	*Transmission:* Transmission of concepts and values by such techniques as textbook, recitation, lecture, question and answer sessions, and structured problem-solving exercises.	*Discovery:* Each of the social sciences has its own method of gathering and verifying knowledge. Students should discover and apply the method that is appropriate to each social science.	*Reflective Inquiry:* Decision making is structured and disciplined through a reflective inquiry process which aims at identifying problems and responding to conflicts by means of testing insights.
Content	Content is selected by an authority interpreted by the teacher and has the function of illustrating values, beliefs, and attitudes.	Proper content is the structure, concepts, problems, and processes of both the separate and the integrated social science disciplines.	Analysis of individual citizen's values yields needs and interests which, in turn, form the basis for student self-selection of problems. Problems, therefore, constitute the content for reflection.

Reprinted with permission of the National Council for the Social Studies.
Source: Barr, R.D., Barth, J.L., and Shermis, S.S. (1977). *Defining the social studies,* p. 67. Arlington, VA: National Council for the Social Studies.

The *methods* employed to transmit citizenship are primarily teacher-directed. Teachers identify the ideal citizen and then direct children's learning and behaviors in such a way as to move children toward the ideal. This is essentially a process of inculcation—expectations are clear and taught to children in direct, unambiguous ways.

Social Studies Taught as a Social Science Tradition

As children mature their world changes and the problems they encounter change. When they become adults they will be required to resolve issues that others have not previously confronted. To respond effectively to the challenges of a dynamic, changing world, educators from a social science tradition maintain that problem-solving skills are necessary. Traditional responses to problems may not be appropriate for future dilemmas; therefore citizens need skills to resolve future conflicts.

The *purpose* of social studies instruction from this perspective is to help children learn the content and principles of the social sciences. The social sciences include sociology, psychology, anthropology, economics, political science, geography, and history. Programs within this tradition also attempt to help children learn the methods by which social scientists acquire knowledge. By training children to think and study the world like social scientists, educators hope to develop citizens who are capable of examining the world and making appropriate decisions.

The *content* of this tradition emerges from the various social sciences. Children learn about human behavior and citizenship by examining concepts and principles from the major social sciences. Further, children learn these concepts and principles by looking at the world as social scientists. They learn content, but they also learn how to think about and study their world.

The *method* of instruction in the social science tradition is inquiry. Social science inquiry and investigation techniques become the primary instructional approach. An emphasis is placed on the process of learning as well as on the acquisition of knowledge from the social science disciplines. Unquestioning acceptance of belief systems is not encouraged.

Social Studies Taught as Reflective Inquiry

Similar to the preceding tradition, the emphasis of the reflective inquiry tradition is on inquiry and problem solving. However, while the social science tradition typically presents problems and learning opportunities from the social science disciplines, the reflective inquiry tradition draws problems and topics from situations personally affecting children.

Because personal issues are related to the social world, they are also tied to the political world. These personal issues therefore take on social-political perspectives that become the focus of the social studies program. Teachers help youngsters identify and examine issues and then help them consider the wider political and social implications.

The *purpose* of the reflective inquiry tradition is to help students learn how to make decisions about issues and problems affecting them. As adults they will be asked to vote for leaders, support positions, and protect their rights. They may be faced with proposed changes in zoning ordinances or they may be asked to support measures that will alter the economic base of their community. They may also be faced with the prospects of ethnically different neighbors or having a child with a disease such as AIDS attending school with their own children. This social studies tradition attempts to help prepare students to make appropriate decisions as adults. This is encouraged by engaging children in decision-making activities about personal, social, and political issues.

The *content* in the reflective inquiry tradition is not the typical content contained in textbooks. Rather, this tradition encourages children to learn the process of rational decision making. Of course, children learn content information as they resolve problems, but the importance of this information is secondary to the development of rational decision-making skills.

Five primary skills are involved in reflective inquiry. They include literacy, using information from a variety of sources, identifying and solving problems, interpreting information, and being able to identify and respond to value issues.

The *method* is inquiry. Children inquire about problems real to them and thereby develop better inquiry skills. Teaching strategies that enhance inquiry learning include values clarification, creative dramatics, role playing, small group work, moral dilemmas, classroom meetings, simulations, and cooperative learning.

Children should study many printed materials in social studies.

Photograph by Carmine L. Galasso.

Social studies programs are not limited to these three traditions. A model advocated by a National Council for the Social Studies (NCSS) task force is described in Chapter 2. A global education view is described in Chapter 15. An additional view, built upon ten primary themes, is not described in this text. Information about this view of the curriculum is described in an article by Kniep in the October 1989 issue of *Social Education*.

Please refer to your eulogy and the goals you identified regarding the elementary school's role in the development of a "good person." With which tradition are you most closely aligned? As you encounter issues in social studies education you should be prepared to understand the views of others, your own views, and the probable effects of the issues on your classroom practices and your children's preparation for the future.

OTHER CONFLICTS

In addition to conflicts emerging from differing psychological views, philosophical views, and competing traditions, social studies programs are affected by a myriad of other factors. Several of the more important factors affecting elementary social studies include classroom control, the relative importance of other subjects, the hurried child phenomenon, and the poor definition of social studies. Each of these factors is briefly described in this section.

Classroom Control

As a classroom teacher you will be responsible for a large group of students who are heterogeneously grouped. Some of your students will not be able to read the text; others will be excellent readers and readily bored with the traditional social studies teaching approach. Some of your students will be highly motivated about their school work; others will be highly motivated about anything but their school work. Some students will have traveled widely and will be aware of the world; others will have traveled little. Additional differences in your students will include intelligence, success orientation, ethnic background, and value structures.

Teachers must establish control and effectively manage the diverse needs and challenges of their students. Early in the year they need to be relatively teacher directed. Later they "loosen up" and exercise less direct control and more indirect control.

Some teachers prefer to maintain a rigid control structure throughout the year. Managing large groups of children is difficult, but it appears easier if youngsters are provided few opportunities to become active in the classroom. To maintain control these teachers may lecture too much, give out extensive reading assignments, assign additional problems, and hand out numerous worksheets. Each of these activities is appropriate in certain situations, but using them to manage the diversity of children is inappropriate.

In this type of situation teachers are using instructional activities inappropriately as control techniques. Consequently, learning and enjoyment suffer. The negative attitudes most children have of social studies result, in part, from teachers misusing instructional materials to control children.

Teachers are leaders, and leaders in any situation must establish control of their group. As effective leaders establish control and begin to assess the abilities and needs of their members they begin to alter their methods of control. They don't abdicate their responsibility to exercise control; they modify the means of control. They utilize ways to involve children actively.

Emphasis on Reading, Math, and Language Arts

Elementary schools and teachers usually feel pressured to teach basic reading, writing, and math skills. With an increasing emphasis on these subjects, other subjects are essentially "crowded out" of the school day. Social studies, science, music and art receive less emphasis because of their perceived lack of importance.

Teachers and schools are frequently judged by students' achievement scores. Most of the achievement tests emphasize reading, language arts, and math skills. With test scores of one school being compared to the scores of other schools, teachers get a powerful message: emphasize reading, language arts, and math.

Good social studies teachers use and teach reading, language arts, and math skills as integral parts of social studies. After all, children don't read about reading and they don't write about writing. They read and write about content from the social and physical sciences. Social studies teachers must make a stronger argument supporting the integration of basic skill instruction through the social studies so that social studies does not remain in the curriculum as an afterthought.

Hymes (1981) described conflicts within programs for young children by noting competition between the three R's and the three L's. The three L's are Love of one's self, Love of others, and Love of learning. Every school should strive to emphasize the three L's as they help children learn the three R's. Today's schools are placing too much emphasis on narrowly conceived reading, writing, and math skills. Aspects of social studies contributing to the three L's are ignored.

Your eulogy probably did not include the individual's reading rate, the speed with which basic math facts could be completed, or the levels of academic achievement. These skills are important, but if children cannot use these skills to solve the problems faced by adults, elementary education has failed. Social studies is important!

Hurried Child Phenomenon

David Elkind (1981b) wrote an enlightening book identifying the ways our society hurries children. The hurrying that Elkind described leads to increased stress, frustration, and burnout.

We live in a scientific, technologically advanced society. We have produced means of growing food more quickly and more efficiently. Technology has been used to cure a number of major diseases. We can manage business and adult employees efficiently. The science, technology, and efficiency that have been applied to many aspects of our world are now being applied to children in their homes. In some instances, parents are attempting to teach infants and toddlers how to read. Other parents are enrolling children in preschools in hopes of providing their children with higher levels of academic achievement.

The schools, too, are hurrying children. Kindergartens have become first grades. Young children are expected to learn skills that are beyond the limits of their developmental levels. Society expects teachers to teach information at earlier ages and as efficiently as possible.

As schools attempt to apply the principles of scientific efficiency to children they forget that children need time to grow and develop. Children have their own developmental needs, which are based on their individual biological clocks. As Rousseau (reprinted 1974) stated many years ago:

> Nature means children to be children before they become men. If we deviate from this order, we produce a forced fruit, without taste, maturity, or power of lasting; we make young philosophers and old children. (p. 28)

Goodlad (1983) noted that schools are being criticized for not teaching the basics. He also stated that schools are spending most of their time teaching the basics. In other words, schools are being criticized for not doing what they spend most of their time emphasizing. Yet many of the critics are pressuring schools to spend more time teaching the basics. Schools may be hurrying our children too quickly and not meeting their needs. They may be producing what Rousseau called a "forced fruit."

Poor Definition

Although a definition of social studies has been presented, there is little agreement regarding the focus and goals of elementary social studies programs. The conflicting views of social studies relate to psychological and philosophical perspectives. The conflicting views also relate to the three traditions described by Barr, Barth, and Shermis (1977). Project SPAN (1982) stated that with so many conflicting views, social studies lacks a clear rationale. Because educators cannot agree on a clear definition and focus for social studies they are unable to promote social studies. They are unable to convince others of the importance of social studies.

SUMMARY

Social studies is important. We are living in a period marking the end of the cold war era. The people of Eastern Europe are demanding greater freedom. Without an effective social studies program, we may be erecting walls of ignorance and prejudice for our children. We may be contributing to our children's ultimate lack of freedom.

As the title of this chapter implies, social studies is embroiled in controversy and uncertainty. The field is hampered by conflicting philosophies of education and psychological views of learning. Social studies is also limited by different views of what social studies should do. Finally, social studies is affected by pragmatic challenges of classroom management and the mood of the community. As a result of these controversies and uncertainties, social studies is in a state of turmoil. The discipline is often treated as an unimportant subject in the elementary school curriculum. When social studies lessons are taught, they are often boring and taught poorly. The result is that children do not like social studies and they often do not learn concepts pertinent to becoming effective citizens.

These challenges and uncertainties make social studies an exciting subject. While there are conflicts regarding what to teach and how to teach, these clouded issues have a silver lining. Social studies teachers have more freedom to make professional decisions regarding social studies instruction. They have considerable freedom regarding what they teach and how they are allowed to teach.

These uncertainties and challenges provide you with opportunities to develop your creativity and flexibility. You can try new activities, use different materials, and challenge children in creative, active ways.

However, as you strive to become more creative and flexible, you must act responsibly. You must be able to justify your actions. An understanding of your own views and the current issues affecting social studies will enable you to utilize a variety of alternatives that will make social studies the best part of each child's school day.

SUGGESTED ACTIVITIES

1. Interview an elementary-school teacher to determine the following: psychological view, philosophical view, degree to which the teacher enjoys teaching social studies, amount of time per week allocated to teaching social studies, major reasons for teaching social studies, and major difficulties encountered when teaching social studies.

2. Interview several elementary-school children to determine the following: their favorite and least favorite subjects, what they like and dislike about social studies, how much time their teacher spends on social studies, and what they would recommend to improve social studies.

3. Obtain a curriculum guide from a local school district. Examine it to determine the district's philosophy, preferred teaching practices, view of citizenship, and concept of the school's role in the socialization process.

4. Examine a teacher's guide from the Distar reading program. Is it an example of behavioristic or cognitive developmental psychology? Should social studies be taught this way?

5. Reconsider the goals you identified in the eulogy activity. How do your goals contribute to your becoming an effective social studies teacher?

APPENDIX 1–1 Behavioristic and Cognitive Developmental Teaching Practices

DIRECTIONS: Please identify the two behavioristic and the two cognitive developmental teaching practices for each of the following social studies goal statements.

1. To help children learn to cooperate with other children, teachers should:
   a. establish rules and teach the rules to children.
   b. allow children to work and play together often.
   c. reward children when they cooperate.
   d. ask leading questions that will get children to think of alternative ways of acting.

2. To help children become more responsible (self-discipline), teachers should:
   a. establish classrooms that offer desirable and responsible choices for children.
   b. help children examine the effects of their behavior.
   c. teach self-discipline skills to children in easily learned steps.
   d. reward children when they act in responsible ways.

3. To help children learn academic skills, teachers should:
   a. provide activities and problems that require children to use more difficult skills.
   b. present skills and information in such a way as to have children respond often and correctly.
   c. provide experiences that will broaden the background for academic learning.
   d. decide what children should learn, cue the behavior, and reward children for correct answers.

4. To help children become better citizens, teachers should:
   a. reward children when they act like good citizens.
   b. provide many opportunities for children to work and play with others.
   c. establish citizenship rules and teach those rules to the children.
   d. allow children to help establish citizenship rules.

5. To help children organize and use information to solve problems, teachers should:
   a. provide opportunities for children to evaluate information to see if it is needed to solve a problem.
   b. give children activities that lead them in a step-by-step process through solutions of problems.
   c. tell children when and how to use particular problem-solving skills.
   d. work together with children on problems that are meaningful to them.

6. To help children develop positive self-concepts, teachers should:
   a. reward children when they are successful in meeting the teacher's standards.
   b. provide children with activities that help them learn to control and make sense out of their world.

     c. help children select and successfully complete activities.

     d. teach skills and information that will lead to success.

7. To motivate children, teachers should:

     a. base learning activities on experiences real to the child.

     b. reward children with praise and tokens.

     c. provide self-correcting materials that acknowledge correct responses.

     d. ask questions that encourage children to consider options beyond their current focus.

Behaviorist responses are listed here. The other responses are cognitive developmental. 1. a & c; 2. c & d; 3. b & d; 4. a & c; 5. b & c; 6. a & d; 7. b & c.

Source: Van Cleaf, D.W. (1979). Reprinted with permission of the author. *A comparison of parents' attitudes with those of kindergarten teachers and principals concerning kindergarten objectives and preferences relating to behaviorist and cognitive transactionist methods.* Unpublished doctoral dissertation, University of Nebraska.

The Washington Monument during the August 27, 1983 march on Washington, D.C.

Photograph taken by Marc Anderson.

The Declaration of Independence.

The Lincoln Memorial, Washington, D.C.

Photograph taken by Eugene Gordon.

chapter 2

The Social Studies Curriculum

Today's social studies curriculum needs to be reevaluated
and presented in a different way to students.

(Megan Taylor, social studies methods student)

AS YOU READ...

- define the following terms: curriculum, scope, sequence
- illustrate the expanding environment and the spiral curricula
- develop an argument supporting the teacher's need to adapt the curriculum
- identify the focus of the major social sciences included in the elementary social studies curriculum
- describe the importance of concepts

*Used with permission.

INTRODUCTION

The term *curriculum* has been defined in several ways, but for the most part curriculum refers to a school's plan delineating its educational intentions at the classroom level. The curriculum is a blueprint that teachers follow as they plan lessons.

This chapter introduces you to the general nature of the curriculum so you can develop an understanding of its influences in your classroom. This chapter also describes the scope and sequence of the social studies curriculum. The final portion of the chapter describes concepts and the importance of a conceptual approach for social studies instruction.

CURRICULUM ORGANIZATION

The influences affecting the curriculum result in an assortment of formally written documents as well as an informal, hidden curriculum. This section describes the nature of the formal curriculum and the hidden curriculum.

The Formal Curriculum

The formal curriculum is a school district's formally written and adopted educational plan. A well-organized district curriculum has several levels of planning. The levels range from a general philosophy statement at the school district level to rather specific curriculum guides at the classroom level.

Good curriculum guides usually describe the scope, or extent, of the subject matter and skills to be taught in a given grade level. They also identify objectives, suggested activities, teaching strategies, and materials. The objectives and subject matter are arranged into a series of lessons that provide direction for teachers as they plan for instruction.

A well-designed formal curriculum is parallel and consistent from the district's philosophy statement through to the specific objectives and learning activities described in each curriculum guide. District-level planners, administrators, and teachers should ensure that the majority of the activities occurring in the district's classrooms contribute to the district's curriculum.

This is the ideal situation. Unfortunately, too many districts end their responsibility in the curriculum development process once they have identified specific courses and grade-level responsibilities. Such districts then expect teachers to make decisions about what to teach. They provide teachers with textbooks that essentially become the curriculum guides. As a result, many districts and teachers abdicate aspects of their decision-making responsibilities. By closely following the text they are allowing the textbook publisher to make curriculum decisions on their behalf. When this occurs there may be little parallel between the district's philosophy and classroom practices.

The Hidden Curriculum

As mentioned earlier, the curriculum is the school district's formally adopted educational plan. There should be a high correlation between the district's philosophy and actual classroom practices, and it is at this point that difficulties occur. For example, most school districts indicate that they want students to become active participants in the democratic process. However, most classrooms and most lessons do not support this outcome. They treat students as passive recipients of information presented by the teacher or the text. The pervasive message is to accept information and not ask questions.

This illustrates the concept of the "hidden curriculum," which consists of everything indirectly taught in classrooms not delineated in the school's formal curriculum. Quite often it includes the values of both the educators and those of the community.

For example, a school district that hires primarily conservative, white, middle-class teachers has a hidden curriculum based on conservative, white, middle-class values. Values related to time, the future, the nature of human existence, and individual work receive a middle-class emphasis. Districts striving to achieve racial and ethnic balance through the hiring process are making statements about the nature of their schools, which will eventually result in modifications in the hidden curriculum.

Teachers who rely on the use of the textbook as the primary instructional agent convey a hidden message that is quite different from the message conveyed in classrooms in which children question and inquire. The message conveyed in textbook-dominated classrooms is that the information is static and must be acquired and accepted by children. In an active-inquiry environment, children learn to inquire, solve problems, and think critically.

The hidden curriculum appears to be responsible for many of the complaints parents and the public have with the schools. Parents and community groups recognize the subtle influences teachers exert on children. They readily challenge educational practices that appear to conflict with their personal or religious value structures. Censorship, evolution, celebrations of religious holidays, and situational ethics are examples of parental and community concerns.

The hidden curriculum is subtle and may have a greater impact on children than the formal curriculum. As a teacher, you must be aware of the formal curriculum as well as the subtleties of the hidden curriculum existing in your district, your building, and your classroom. Take time to examine your philosophy of education, your views regarding the way children learn, and your idea of an ideal citizen.

Teachers should monitor the progress of children participating in cooperative learning activities.
Photograph by David W. Van Cleaf.

The Teacher's Role

Elkind (1981a) described a weakness in elementary social studies education related to curriculum development. Curriculum materials are frequently developed by subject-matter experts who have little understanding of the practical aspects of teaching. Teachers then have difficulty utilizing the materials in their classrooms because the materials are not designed for the developmental needs of their children.

The teacher's role in the curriculum is to act as a mediator. That is, the teacher must arrange learning activities, learning materials, and instructional settings so students can obtain maximum educational benefits. Teachers must consider the goals and objectives outlined in the curriculum guide and simultaneously consider the needs, abilities, and interests of their students. Teachers must ask themselves: Are these goals and objectives appropriate for my students? Do I need to modify the goals and objectives? Do I need to teach any prerequisite objectives? Are the suggested materials and activities listed in the curriculum guide appropriate for my students? How can I modify the lesson? How can I ensure that the lesson will be interesting for the children?

These questions will help you consider the relationship between the curriculum and your students. You then must make professional decisions regarding your methods of implementing the lessons outlined in the curriculum guide. You must mediate between the curriculum and your students.

Figure 2–1 illustrates the relationships among the teacher, students and the curriculum. The teacher's role is one of linking students with curriculum materials. The teacher is a decision-maker who selects and adapts information and materials appropriate for the students. The teacher is somewhat like a convex lens focusing instruction for the children.

District-level curriculum plans and classroom-level curriculum guides are *only* guides. They should not be considered as mandates forcing teachers to teach specific information in predetermined ways. Teachers are professionals hired to

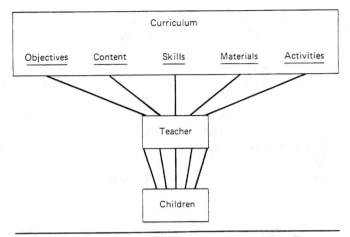

Teachers must know the curriculum and make conscious decisions. These decisions should be based on the needs of their children and the goals of the school district.

Figure 2–1 The Teacher's Role as Mediator

Source: Van Cleaf, D.W. (1986). *Teaching elementary social studies: Supplemental materials.* Unpublished manuscript, Washburn University, Topeka. Adapted and reprinted with permission of the author.

make instructional decisions. The curriculum only provides direction and suggestions. The needs, interests, and abilities of your students must be considered, and your own interests and abilities must be considered as you make instructional decisions. You must be an active mediator.

SCOPE AND SEQUENCE

Well-developed curricula outline the range of subject matter, skills, and values for each subject. This is referred to as the *scope* of the curriculum. Once the scope of the curriculum is determined, the subject matter, skills, and values must be arranged in some fashion. The order in which the curriculum is arranged is referred to as the *sequence* of the curriculum.

Articulation is another curriculum term. Articulation refers to the manner in which curriculum subject matter is integrated and expanded upon from grade level to grade level and from subject to subject.

Social studies textbooks include scope and sequence charts. Usually found in the front of the teacher's guides, the scope and sequence charts outline the scope of the information included in the text and the manner in which it is sequenced through the text. The text's scope and sequence will also illustrate the scope and sequence for other grade levels in the series.

Scope of the Social Studies

A report by the National Council for the Social Studies Task Force on Scope and Sequence (NCSS Task Force 1989) recommended organizing the social studies curriculum into three areas: subject matter knowledge, democratic values and beliefs, and skills. These categories are briefly described below.

Knowledge. Subject matter knowledge is one important aspect of a social studies program. Children must learn information so they have an intellectual basis from which to make reasoned decisions. Through formal learning experiences and informal day-to-day encounters with the world, youngsters acquire factual information. As children attempt to understand factual information they organize groups of related facts into concepts. As concepts become more complex and sophisticated, they merge and overlap with other concepts to form generalizations. Facts, concepts, and generalizations form the basis of the subject matter in social studies programs.

Social studies knowledge usually emerges from the social science disciplines. History, geography, political science, economics, anthropology, sociology, and psychology are social sciences from which social studies content is derived. Social studies knowledge may also be derived from law, humanities, and science. The contributions of each social science is described in a later section of the chapter.

Democratic Values and Beliefs. Democratic values and beliefs are attitudinal aspects of learning. Children must learn about their country, what it represents, and how they can contribute to its vitality. Children must also develop a sense of pride in their country and its core values.

Our democratic values and beliefs emerged from historical encounters and conflicts. Major documents reflecting democratic values and beliefs include the Declaration of Independence and the United States Constitution. Our democratic values include justice, equality, responsibility, rule of law, freedom, diversity, privacy, and international human rights. These values are tied to democratic processes, which include due process, equal protection, and civic participation. An extensive list of American democratic values appears in Table 2–1.

As we socialize children we are responsible for helping them develop an appreciation of core social values. We must help them develop commitment to those values. Further, we must help them become proud of their country and committed to helping it become better. However, we must ensure that we do not indoctrinate them to the point that they cease to question. A vibrant democratic society needs individuals who will challenge questionable practices.

Skills. The third aspect of the social studies curriculum is skills. The NCSS Task Force defined skills as "the ability to do something proficiently in repeated performances. Skills are processes that enable students to link knowledge with beliefs that lead to action" (1989, p. 378). Social studies skills emphasize and relate primarily to obtaining information, solving problems, and interacting with others. The basic skill categories, outlined by the NCSS Task Force, are listed following Table 2–1 and Table 2–2. A comprehensive list of the skills appears in Table 2–2.

Table 2–1 American Democratic Values

A. RIGHTS OF THE INDIVIDUAL

Right to life
Right to liberty
Right to dignity
Right to security
Right to equality of opportunity
Right to justice
Right to privacy
Right to private ownership of property

B. FREEDOMS OF THE INDIVIDUAL

Freedom to participate in the political process
Freedom to worship
Freedom of thought
Freedom of conscience
Freedom of assembly
Freedom of inquiry
Freedom of expression

C. RESPONSIBILITIES OF THE INDIVIDUAL

To respect human life
To respect the rights of others
To be tolerant
To be honest
To be compassionate
To demonstrate self-control
To participate in the democratic process
To work for the common good
To respect the property of others

D. BELIEFS CONCERNING SOCIETAL CONDITIONS AND GOVERNMENTAL RESPONSIBILITIES

Societies need laws that are accepted by the majority of the people
Dissenting minorities are protected

Source: NCSS Task Force (October 1989). In search of a scope and sequence for social studies. *Social Education, 53,* p. 383. Reprinted with permission of the National Council for the Social Studies.

Table 2–2   Essential Skills for Social Studies

Suggested strength of instructional effort:

▬ (thin line)	Minimum or none
▬ (medium)	Some
■ (bold short)	Major
■ (bold)	Intense

I. Skills Related to Acquiring Information

A. Reading Skills

Grade bands: K–3   4–6   7–9   10–12

1. Comprehension
   - Read to get literal meaning
   - Use chapter and section headings, topic sentences, and summary sentences to select main ideas
   - Differentiate main and subordinate ideas
   - Select passages that are pertinent to the topic studied
   - Interpret what is read by drawing inferences
   - Detect cause and effect relationships
   - Distinguish between the fact and opinion; recognize propaganda
   - Recognize author bias
   - Use picture clues and picture captions to aid comprehension
   - Use literature to enrich meaning
   - Read for a variety of purposes: critically, analytically, to predict outcomes, to answer a question, to form an opinion, to skim for facts
   - Read various forms of printed material: books, magazines, newspapers, directories, schedules, journals

2. Vocabulary
   - Use usual word attack skills: sight recognition, phonetic analysis, structural analysis
   - Use context clues to gain meaning
   - Use appropriate sources to gain meaning of essential terms and vocabulary: glossary, dictionary, text, word lists
   - Recognize and understand an increasing number of social studies terms

3. Rate of Reading
   - Adjust speed of reading to suit purpose
   - Adjust rate of reading to difficulty of the material

B. Study Skills

1. Find Information
   - Use various parts of a book (index, table of contents, etc.)
   - Use key words, letters on volumes, index, and cross references to find information
   - Evaluate sources of information—print, visual, electronic
   - Use appropriate source of information
   - Use the community as a resource

2. Arrange Information in Usable Forms
   - Make outline of topic
   - Prepare summaries
   - Make timelines
   - Take notes
   - Keep records
   - Use italics, marginal notes, and footnotes
   - Listen for information
   - Follow directions
   - Write reports and research papers
   - Prepare a bibliography

C. Reference and Information-Search Skills

1. The Library
   - Use card catalog to locate books
   - Use *Readers' Guide to Periodical Literature* and other indexes
   - Use COMCATS (Computer Catalog Service)
   - Use public library telephone information service

2. Special References
   - Almanacs
   - Encyclopedias
   - Dictionary
   - Indexes
   - Government publications
   - Microfiche
   - Periodicals
   - News sources: newspapers, news magazines, TV, radio, videotapes, artifacts

3. Maps, Globes, Graphics
   - Use map- and globe-reading skills
     - Orient a map and note directions
     - Locate places on map and globe
     - Use scale and compute distances
     - Interpret map symbols and visualize what they mean
     - Compare maps and make inferences
     - Express relative location
   - Interpret graphs
   - Detect bias in visual material
   - Interpret social and political messages of cartoons
   - Interpret history through artifacts

4. Community Resources
   - Use sources of information in the community
   - Conduct interviews of individuals in the community
   - Use community newspapers

D. Technical Skills Unique to Electronic Devices

1. Computer
   - Operate a computer using prepared instructional or reference programs
   - Operate a computer to enter and retrieve information gathered from a variety of sources

2. Telephone and Television Information Networks
   - Ability to access information through networks

Source: NCSS Task Force on Scope and Sequence (October 1989). In search of a scope and sequence for social studies. *Social Education, 53,* pp. 386–387. Reprinted with permission of the National Council for the Social Studies.

Table 2–2   Essential Skills for Social Studies (*continued*)

II. Skills Related to Organizing and Using Information
A. Thinking Skills

1. Classify Information
- Identify relevant factual material
- Sense relationship between items of factual information
- Group data in categories according to appropriate criteria
- Place in proper sequence:
  (1) order of occurrence
  (2) order of importance
- Place data in tabular form: charts, graphs, illustrations

2. Interpret Information
- State relationships between categories of information
- Note cause and effect relationships
- Draw inferences from factual material
- Predict likely outcomes based on factual information
- Recognize the value dimension of interpreting factual material
- Recognize instances in which more than one interpretation of factual material is valid

3. Analyze Information
- Form a simple organization of key ideas related to a topic
- Separate a topic into major components according to appropriate criteria
- Examine critically relationships between and among elements of a topic
- Detect bias in data presented in various forms: graphics, tabular, visual, print
- Compare and contrast credibility of differing accounts of the same event

4. Summarize Information
- Extract significant ideas from supporting, illustrative details
- Combine critical concepts into a statement of conclusions based on information
- Restate major ideas of a complex topic in concise form
- Form opinion based on critical examination of relevant information
- State hypotheses for further study

5. Synthesize Information
- Propose a new plan of operation, create a new system, or devise a futuristic scheme based on available information
- Reinterpret events in terms of what *might* have happened, and show the likely effects on subsequent events
- Present visually (chart, graph, diagram, model, etc.) information extracted from print
- Prepare a research paper that requires a creative solution to a problem
- Communicate orally and in writing

6. Evaluate Information
- Determine whether or not the information is pertinent to the topic
- Estimate the adequacy of the information
- Test the validity of the information, using such criteria as source, objectivity, technical correctness, currency

B. Decision-Making Skills
- Identify a situation in which a decision is required
- Secure needed factual information relevant to making the decision
- Recognize the values implicit in the situation and the issues that flow from them
- Identify alternative courses of action and predict likely consequences of each
- Make decision based on the data obtained
- Take action to implement the decision

C. Metacognitive Skills
- Select an appropriate strategy to solve a problem
- Self-monitor one's thinking process

III. Skills Related to Interpersonal Relationships and Social Participation
A. Personal Skills
- Express personal convictions
- Communicate own beliefs, feelings, and convictions
- Adjust own behavior to fit the dynamics of various groups and situations
- Recognize the mutual relationship between human beings in satisfying one another's needs

B. Group Interaction Skills
- Contribute to the development of a supportive climate in groups
- Participate in making rules and guidelines for group life
- Serve as a leader or follower
- Assist in setting goals for the group
- Participate in delegating duties, organizing, planning, making decisions, and taking action in a group setting
- Participate in persuading, compromising, debating, and negotiating in the resolution of conflicts and differences

C. Social and Political Participation Skills
- Keep informed on issues that affect society
- Identify situations in which social action is required
- Work individually or with others to decide on an appropriate course of action
- Work to influence those in positions of social power to strive for extensions of freedom, social justice, and human rights
- Accept and fulfill social responsibilities associated with citizenship in a free society

Source: NCSS Task Force on Scope and Sequence (October 1989). In search of a scope and sequence for social studies. *Social Education, 53,* pp. 386–387. Reprinted with permission of the National Council for the Social Studies.

Skill Categories

Skills related to acquiring information:

- reading skills
- study skills
- reference and information search skills
- technical skills unique to the use of electronic devices

Skills related to organizing and using information:

- intellectual skills
- decision-making skills

Skills related to interpersonal relationships and social participation:

- personal skills
- group interaction skills
- social and political participation skills*

The comprehensive list of skills appearing in Table 2–2 also indicates the degree of emphasis recommended for each skill during the elementary years. Most of these skills are developed in each of the elementary school subjects. Concerned elementary teachers recognize this shared responsibility and willingly reinforce these skills in a variety of instructional settings.

Sequencing Social Studies

Several methods are used to sequence elementary school curriculums. Table 2–3 illustrates a variety of sequencing formats. Explanations in the following sections will refer to Table 2–3.

Table 2–3 Sample Curriculum Sequences

Sequence Format	Examples
Simple to Complex	Math, Map Reading, Graphing
Part to Whole	Phonics
Familiar to Unfamiliar	Social Studies (expanding environment)
Concrete to Abstract	Social Studies (spiral curriculum)
Chronological Order	History
Usefulness	Sex Education
Topics	Preschool Unit Approach, Current Events

*Source: NCSS Task Force on Scope and Sequence (October 1989). In search of a scope and sequence for social studies, *Social Education*, 53, p. 378. Reprinted with permission of the National Council for the Social Studies.

Two major scope and sequence structures are common in elementary social studies programs. The most traditional is the expanding environment curriculum. The second is the spiral curriculum. Many social studies programs are beginning to integrate the two methods as they attempt to develop more comprehensive programs. Each curriculum integrates aspects of the other methods described in Table 2–3. Hence, a good expanding environment or spiral social studies program will develop simple skills prior to moving to more complex skills, begin instruction at the concrete level, follow chronological order when appropriate, and allow deviations for useful, timely topics.

Expanding Environment Curriculum. The expanding environment curriculum format has been the primary means of organizing most elementary school social studies programs. It continues to be a dominant force in today's elementary social studies curriculum. Its basic premise is that children should consider social studies topics related to their familiarity with the world. The subject matter of an expanding environment curriculum proceeds from topics with which children are familiar and proceeds, from grade level to grade level, to subject matter representing progressively more distant environments. Thus, in kindergarten and first grade, children study information about themselves and their families. As children mature, their sphere of influence and their understanding of the environment expand to more distant social environments.

In grades two and three, children might study neighborhoods and communities. Grades four, five, and six expand areas of study to progressively more distant environments. The expanding environment sequence in these grades usually proceeds from the study of the students' home state and other states in fourth grade, to the study of the United States (and sometimes its neighbors) in fifth grade, to the study of other countries in sixth grade.

The expanding environment curriculum may be illustrated by using a series of concentric circles. Figure 2–2 illustrates the concentric circle notion using two sequences, one from a textbook series, the other from the NCSS Task Force (1989). The progression from environments near the children to more distant environments is similar for each sequence; however, the specific topics for each grade level differ. This indicates that there is flexibility in the arrangement of the social studies curriculum. An example of this flexibility is a trend in several western states to substitute the study of the Pacific Rim in lieu of a traditional area.

The expanding environment curriculum is based on fairly good logic. As children develop, their world expands and they become more capable of understanding more distant places and more abstract information. This curriculum assures that children study progressively more complex social arrangements, moving through the grade levels from family to the world.

However, there are several criticisms. Elementary school children are, for the most part, preoperational or concrete operational thinkers. They are not capable of abstract, formal operational thought. Assuming that children are ready to consider more distant places may be inappropriate. For example, the expanding

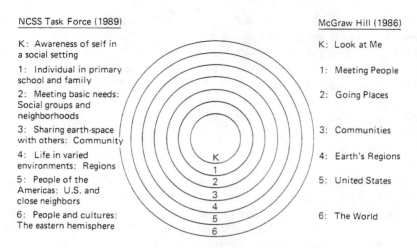

NCSS Task Force (1989)

K: Awareness of self in
a social setting

1: Individual in primary
school and family

2: Meeting basic needs:
Social groups and
neighborhoods

3: Sharing earth-space
with others: Community

4: Life in varied
environments: Regions

5: People of the
Americas: U.S. and
close neighbors

6: People and cultures:
The eastern hemisphere

McGraw Hill (1986)

K: Look at Me

1: Meeting People

2: Going Places

3: Communities

4: Earth's Regions

5: United States

6: The World

Figure 2–2 Two Expanding Environment Curriculum Sequences

Source: NCSS Task Force on Scope and Sequence (October 1989). In search of a scope and sequence for social studies. *Social Education, 53*, pp. 376–387. Reprinted with permission of the National Council for the Social Studies.

Source: McGraw-Hill (1986). Our nation, our world—The success series (2nd ed.), pp. xii–xvi, *The World* (Teachers Edition) by Leonard Martelli and others. Reprinted with permission of Macmillan/McGraw-Hill School Publishing Company.

environment curriculum often requires sixth-grade students to learn about the history of Western civilization. Textbook presentations of such topics are relatively abstract and may therefore be inappropriate for these youngsters.

Another criticism of the expanding environment curriculum is built on the assumption that today's children are being exposed to more distant environments through travel and the media. This criticism assumes that because children are exposed to a greater variety of environments at an earlier age, the traditional grade-level divisions in the expanding environment curriculum are no longer tenable.

The media confronts children with information and pictures from more distant environments. In one television news program children might see athletes competing in one country, soldiers fighting in another, and political demonstrations in yet another.

The expanding environment curriculum continues to be promising if utilized appropriately. Moving to the study of more distant environments through succeeding grade levels provides students and teachers with a conceptual focus. However, teachers must relate each topic to their students' concrete levels of understanding. Teachers can effectively utilize the expanding environment curriculum by approaching the curriculum with an attitude of flexibility and a commitment to personalizing the curriculum for their students.

Spiral Curriculum. In a spiral curriculum, essential concepts are identified and taught at each grade level. Each concept is spiralled through the curriculum and taught at a more sophisticated level as children progress from year to year. Instruction related to each concept should be relatively basic and concrete at the lower grades and progress to more sophisticated levels as students proceed through the grades.

Taba (1967) proposed a spiral curriculum for elementary social studies. Taba's spiral curriculum included a list of main ideas and concepts that would be taught each year.

Taba encouraged teachers to select appropriate content and factual information that would contribute to the main ideas and concepts at each grade level. She stated that "specific facts (for example, population statistics) serve to develop the main ideas. They are rarely important on their own account,..." (p. 8). The curriculum should outline the major concepts, but teachers should make conscious decisions regarding what subject matter to include and exclude. The content and facts selected for instruction should contribute to the main idea, not replace it.

Figure 2–3 illustrates the spiral curriculum for the concept *the American economic system*. The content is from the Texas mandated curriculum guidelines (Texas Education Agency, 1987).

Figure 2–3 An Economic Spiral Curriculum

Source: Concepts from Texas Education Agency (1987). *Essential Elements,* chapter 75. In *The State Board of Education rules for curriculum.* Austin: Texas Education Agency. The figure does not appear in the original publication.

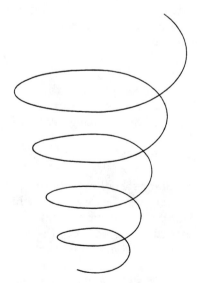

6. Interdependence, work, economic systems, competition (world)

5. Economic activity, conservation transportation, communication, price, changes in work (U.S.A.)

4. Independence, production, resources (state)

3. Community needs, division of labor, property, resources (community)

2. Goods, services, income, interdependence (community)

1. Work, exchange, scarcity, necessities (met by personnel in school and families)

K. Economic wants (family)

The spiral curriculum has promise, but it also has several limitations. First, identifying the major conceptual themes for a K–12 social studies curriculum is a challenging task that few school districts are willing to support. Further, the groups (elementary, middle school, and high school teachers; subject matter experts; parents; administrators) that would contribute to the identification of appropriate concepts are diverse; seeking consensus would likely inhibit the process.

Integrating Expanding Environment and Spiral Curricula. The two curriculum approaches are now being integrated in many textbook series. General topics, concepts or themes are identified and spiralled through the grade levels. The content of each grade level series then reflects an expanding environment influence. The Texas curriculum has integrated the two approaches. A closer examination of Figure 2–3 reveals that while the concepts are presented at more complex levels in each higher grade, the subject matter focus parallels the expanding environment model. Kindergarten children consider content related to self and family; older children are exposed to content from more distant environments.

There is no "one best" curriculum. Each has strengths and limitations. Your task is to examine the curriculum and then adapt it to meet the goals of your school district and the needs of your students.

CURRICULUM SUBJECT MATTER

Humans have been studying their world since the beginning of time. Eventually they began to group observations and information about the world into categories, which have gradually developed into the academic disciplines. Information about the social world became the social science disciplines. The term *social studies* is comprised of subject matter from the social science disciplines.

The social studies curriculum is designed to help children learn about their world, and the subject matter of the curriculum is selected from the social sciences. Each of the social sciences has organized information into categories. These categories are called *concepts and generalizations*.

The Social Sciences

In the elementary school most of the content for social studies is related to three of the social sciences: history, citizenship education (political science), and geography. Concepts and content from the other social sciences are often integrated into the curriculum to enhance the study of history, citizenship education, and geography. This section of the chapter briefly describes each of the social sciences playing a role in elementary social studies. The next section describes the three major components in greater detail.

In 1983, Wayne Herman reported the results of efforts to identify key concepts and goals within the social science disciplines contributing to social studies. The following description of the social sciences includes statements about important subject matter headings.*

Anthropology. Anthropology is a discipline in which human beings and their origins and customs are studied. Anthropology examines aspects of culture that include lifestyles, artifacts, rituals, arts, tools, ideas, etc. The subject matter statements that Herman identified included the following:

1. Explains the universality of culture; identifies specific cultural universals with trait variation.
2. Describes cultural complexity and continuity, the dynamics of cultural change, and adaptation to the environment (both physical and social); describes the changes that occur in that environment; explains the idea of cultural ecology.
3. Identifies language as the most important aspect of culture; defines speech communities; explains how language and thought patterns influence each other; lists ways in which all languages express abstract thoughts.
4. Categorizes all modern humans as *Homo sapiens*; explains that type variations are minor, whether races are viewed geographically, typologically, biologically, or psychologically.
5. Identifies and is sensitive to cultural nuances (p. 95).

Citizenship Education. While citizenship education is not a social science, it is an integral aspect of social studies programs. The subject matter and concepts identified by Herman parallel many of the democratic values and beliefs outlined by the NCSS Task Force. Citizenship education will be developed more thoroughly later. The subject matter statements identified by Herman include the following:

1. Practices democratic principles when engaged in group processes: respect for individual; one man–one vote; being open to opposing viewpoints; majority rule but not running roughshod over the minority; representative government, etc.
2. Uses decision-making skills: identification and internalization of problem culminating in a rational decision of which the decision-maker is conscious; states probable consequences of alternatives; becomes advocate for a chosen position.

*Source: Herman, W.L. (February 1983). What should be taught where? *Social Education*, 47(2) pp. 94–99. Reprinted with permission of the National Council for the Social Studies.

*Note: Numbered subheadings in each of the following categories have been reprinted with permission from the National Council for the Social Studies.

3. Identifies social, economic, and political systems (including their evolution and interrelationships) and their processes.
4. Employs basic communication processes: reading, listening, speaking, writing.
5. Gathers, organizes, interprets, analyzes, and evaluates information about government, politics, and citizenship.
6. Works with others in problem-solving (involves communication, perspective-taking, group skills) in order to reach individual and group goals (p. 75).

Economics. This social science discipline is concerned with the manner in which goods and services are produced, distributed, and consumed. Economics also examines the nature and distribution of wealth. Many elementary social studies textbooks integrate economic concepts under topics such as needs, wants, goods, and services. Additional information regarding the nature of economics identified by Herman includes:

1. Distinguishes basic economic concepts and principles that give one the capacity to think about economic issues.
2. Describes how our economic system works; scarcity and opportunity cost; productivity, specialization, income, employment, labor unions, price of a good or service, etc.
3. Applies economic concepts and principles in problem-solving contexts: defines criteria, identifies alternatives, weighs alternatives, makes decisions (p. 96).

Geography. Geography is the study of the natural features of the earth's surface, features constructed by humans, and relationships between the environment and ways humans adapt to their world. Geography is a major social science discipline in the elementary school and will be discussed in more detail later. Herman provided the following statements to describe the concepts and goals of geography.

1. Describes and appreciates the relationships between the physical and cultural worlds (human–land relationships including environmentalism and conservation).
2. Explains with examples the interdependence of nations (economic and social).
3. Explains how people and places (regions) differ from one another at various scales—local, national, world; describes area differentiation.
4. Identifies problems resulting from physical and economic factors including population distribution and density.
5. Applies geographic concepts and principles to contemporary social, economic, and political problems; uses skills of observation, mapping, analysis (p. 96).

History. History is the mainstay of most elementary social studies programs. History should help children develop an understanding and appreciation of their heritage and traditions. Children should then be able to compare the progress of their nation with other nations. Herman's subject matter and concepts elaborate on these points. Statements describing history include:

1. Uses a process of inquiry.
2. Logically analyzes contemporary circumstances (problems and otherwise) by investigations of origins and development of those circumstances and from other data.
3. Identifies point of view, bias, and historical interpretation.
4. Uses analytical reasoning from data-useful methodology in "real world" activities.
5. Gains skills in reading and writing (p. 97).

Political Science. This social science examines the process of governance and types of governments. In most elementary schools, content from political science is integrated into citizenship education. Herman's subject matter and concept statements related to political science include:

1. Explains aspirations of democratic governmental process, its dependence upon enlightened participation, and its significance in fostering individual potentialities and rights.
2. Acquires information and skills necessary to participate in political life as responsible citizens.
3. Studies the past and describes ways in which the past is relevant to contemporary life.
4. Explains that social problems are not subject to black-and-white solutions but inevitably require making decisions on the basis of carefully weighing conflicting attitudes and evidence.
5. Practices attitudes of social commitment and tolerance (p. 98).

Psychology. This is a social science that receives minor emphasis in elementary social studies. However, skillful teachers may integrate aspects of psychology into topics being studied and help children examine additional, enriching perspectives. The subject matter and concept statements identified by Herman are:

1. Critiques a question about human activity with regard to how testable the question is; determines what limitations are necessary to bring the terms used in the question into an experiment; and recognizes an activity as an experiment, and from the results identifies limitations and generalizations.
2. Uses language skills for effective communication.
3. Describes the applications of some psychological principles to everyday human problems (p. 98).

Sociology. Sociology is concerned with the study of people living together in groups. Group behaviors, group characteristics, and social institutions are included in sociology. Like psychology, sociology is not emphasized in elementary social studies curriculums, yet considerations of sociology concepts may enrich instruction. Herman listed subject matter and goals of sociology, but he also included aspects of psychology. Herman's heading was social psychology essentially because of the need to help children develop positive interpersonal relationships. Sociology statements include:

1. Identifies factors that contribute to self-concept.
2. Explains that all behavior is learned; describes how patterns are transmitted within the family; states plural causes of behavior.
3. Identifies principles of the behavior of small groups.
4. Explains the interrelationship among social roles, social behavior, social systems.
5. Describes reasons why interdependency of human relationships is vital for need and support.
6. Lists and appreciates similarities and differences of people (p. 98).

These are the main social sciences contributing to the elementary social studies curriculum. There are several other innovations in the social studies curriculum that Herman and others identified as curriculum topics. Such topics include career education, consumer education, death and dying, energy education, future studies, global education, legal education, multicultural education, philosophy, religious studies, and urban studies. Several of these topics will be described in the last chapter. The subject matter and concepts of these other topics are either integrated into the three primary social studies disciplines or are not appropriate for most elementary-grade children.

History, Citizenship Education, and Geography

History, citizenship education, and geography constitute the primary focus of the elementary school curriculum. Each is described more thoroughly in this section.

History. The goals of history involve the process of studying history as well as considering the historical antecedents of contemporary circumstances. Bennett (1986) indicated that the study of history should help children understand and appreciate their heritage. Bennett also noted that the study of historical facts was important, but more importantly, children should understand how the facts are related.

Traditional approaches treat history as a chronological study of the past. We begin studying the history of a country, people, or event beginning at some point in the distant past and then examining a series of events occurring along a chronological sequence from past to present. Recent studies have begun examining the appropriateness of traditional methods of teaching history in the elementary school. While the findings are not conclusive, they raise questions and offer new directions for elementary teachers. Levstik (1986) examined recent studies regarding children's abilities to learn historical information. Levstik offered the following two insights.

First, current teaching practices are unsuccessful. Levstik suggested including more emphasis on people and events as a means of improving instruction. Children should study the past by examining artifacts, visiting historical sites, reading diaries, biographies, and autobiographies, listening to speakers and reading (or listening to) interesting literature. As children examine these materials they should be asked to relate the materials to their own lives as a means of getting intellectually and emotionally involved with history.

Second, Levstik suggested identifying historical topics that interest children and then organizing instruction around those topics. Topics that do not interest children should be eliminated. Children are interested in their personal and family histories, the historical changes in toys and sports technology, inventions and lifestyle changes resulting from inventions, and holidays. Significant events, such as major battles, and interesting eras, such as the wild West, also capture children's interests. By making the study of history relevant and interesting, children will learn more and develop a better appreciation of their heritage.

Hallam (1969) suggested that history instruction should be based on topics concretely related to children's lives. Topics include transportation, lifestyles, housing, family life, occupations, and leisure-time activities. According to Hallam, children have a concrete understanding of these topics and can relate their understanding of them to the historical events they study. As a result, history becomes more meaningful.

Bennett encouraged teachers to develop history lessons around legends and heroes. Legends include Paul Bunyan and Johnny Appleseed. Heroes include Sacajawea, Harriet Beecher Stowe, Emily Dickinson, Benjamin Banneker, George Washington Carver, and Nathan Hale. Learning about legends and heroes from the past can make history exciting and memorable. Exciting history lessons occur when children have opportunities to study heroes. The events, lifestyles, and contributions are exciting.

Thornton and Vukelich (1988) reviewed a number of studies about children's concepts of history and historical time. They identified several suggestions for elementary social studies teachers. First, children as young as six are capable of learning simple historical concepts. The social studies curriculum should therefore systematically contribute to the development of these concepts. Second, children's understanding of historical time follows a developmental sequence, therefore, historical topics should be integrated into the curriculum to reinforce this sequence.

History is included in the elementary school curriculum; thus you will be required to teach history. History can be an exciting subject to study if you maintain students' enthusiasm and their interest in their heritage. You must ensure that history instruction is exciting and related to students' developmental needs and interests.

You must look for ways to go well beyond the traditional methods of teaching history. Examples of exciting history teaching activities include:

1. *Change Chart.* Compare the period being studied with children's lives. Use the concepts identified by Hallam (1969) as the topics for comparison.
2. *Family History.* Children can develop accounts of family history and include places lived, biographical sketches of interesting family members, occupations, family size, and family trees.
3. *This-n-That.* A local television reporter has a weekly five-minute segment on points of historical interest. Children may develop videotape "This-n-That" presentations describing historical information about a house, church, public building, business, or person.
4. *Tall Tales.* Read tall tales to children and have them identify historical fact and fiction.
5. *Minority Contribution Scrapbook.* Children can develop a scrapbook containing contributions of women and minorities.
6. *Investigative Reporters.* Kindergarten and primary-grade children have difficulty reading and writing well enough to participate in oral history activities. However, by providing tape recorders, young children can become "reporters" and interview people about past events and human-interest stories.

Citizenship Education. Citizenship education is a term that incorporates political science, government, and law education. The term is also synonymous with the term *civics.*

Your eulogy in Chapter 1 described the characteristics of a good person. Many of those characteristics exemplify aspects of good citizenship. Good citizens are good neighbors. They take care of themselves, treat others with kindness and respect, offer assistance, and contribute to the well-being of society. Good citizens are responsible, contributing members of society. However, a democratic society requires more of its citizens. Citizens in a democratic society must assume an active role in participatory governance. In our society, rules are made for the mutual benefit of all people. In a democracy like ours, people exercise ultimate control over the law, a concept referred to as "rule of law." If local, state, and national governing bodies are to remain representative and responsible to all citizens, then citizens must exercise their participatory responsibilities.

The challenge of citizenship education is a twofold challenge. First, children must learn about their heritage and its rich traditions and customs. Children must also learn the fundamentals of the political system so they can function within the system to make necessary changes. Children should take pride in their country and its traditions. Without this pride, their commitment may be less intense.

However, a citizenship education that is limited to this emphasis ultimately undermines the long-term vitality of the democratic process. Thus, teachers have a second challenge: to teach their students how to examine critically the policies and practices of their elected officials. Students must learn how to voice their opinions and hold officials accountable. Students must learn how to work toward improving society through the democratic structure. Not only must they learn about these skills but they must commit themselves to acting on their beliefs. Without action, we may become a country of nice neighbors, but under the control of a powerful minority.

Children must learn about their freedoms as well as the responsibilities of democratic citizenship. They need to learn how to participate in public life, to understand and appreciate democratic processes, and to acquire the information and skills necessary to contribute to the democratic processes.

Sample citizenship education activities include:

1. *Current Events Discussions.* Designate a regular time when children can present and discuss current events. For example, set aside the first few minutes of each day and require students to bring in topics. Discuss the issues and encourage students to examine the issues critically.
2. *Current Events Debates.* Select controversial events and allow students to research and present conflicting views.
3. *Bill of Rights Review.* Select one of the rights contained in the Bill of Rights and discuss related current events.
4. *Election Time Line.* Develop a time line of events leading up to election day.
5. *Election Symbols.* Examine the emotional symbols used by politicians and the effects the symbols have on voter attitudes (red, white, and blue color schemes; flags in the background; use of value terms such as *liberal* and *conservative*).
6. *Role Models.* Compare good and poor role models in government.
7. *Participation in community-service projects* (trash recycling, food drives, adopt a family for the holidays, etc.).

Geography. Geography examines how people adapt to the physical environment. There are five basic themes in geography (Geographic Education National Implementation Project, 1987).

The first theme is *location.* Concepts related to this theme include the position of things on the earth, describing the locations of places, and identifying reasons for the locations of items and places. Children's activities may include locating their homes, schools, and churches on maps.

The second theme is *place.* Concepts included in this theme are the physical characteristics, human characteristics, and ways to describe places. Children demonstrate these skills when they identify major land features in their environment and point out routes taken to and from school.

The third theme is *relationships between places.* Concepts within this theme include the ways people depend on the environment, how they adapt to the environment, and how technology affects the environment. Encouraging children

Children should use globes to discover many geography concepts.
Photograph by Ken Karp.

to consider the effects of seasons and geographic locations on lifestyles helps develop this theme.

The fourth theme is *movement*. Concepts within this theme include interdependence, links between places, and patterns of movement. Providing opportunities to consider transportation changes and the effects on local businesses illustrate a way to develop this skill.

The fifth theme is *regions*. Concepts include characteristics of regions and changes within regions. Locating natural and political boundaries, examining regional customs, and identifying regional products exemplify activities related to this theme.

Geography is much more than learning the locations of specific places such as cities, states, countries, continents, and hemispheres. Children need to learn about their world. They need to learn how the world affects both their lives and the lives of others in distant places. The weather affects how we live and dress, natural resources affect our economic endeavors, landforms affect leisure-time activities, political subdivisions affect our form of government and need for defense. Learning the locations of specific places may enable children to perform well on games, but this alone will not prepare children to analyze and resolve complex issues affecting their lives.

As with history and citizenship education, geography must be taught in ways that are exciting and developmentally appropriate for children. Students should learn about geographic concepts by examining their familiar environments and by considering concrete relationships between their environments and their lifestyles. With a concrete basis well established, students will be ready to explore more abstract relationships and more distant lands.

Sample geography activities include:

1. *Shelter Comparisons.* Compare shelters used in the past with the natural resources available for their construction.
2. *Trail Adaptations.* Examine geographic features along a transportation route, such as the Oregon Trail, and describe how people had to adapt to environmental changes.
3. *City Geography.* Consider geographical features affecting your community. How do the features inhibit development in some areas and enhance it in other areas?
4. *Ideal Vacations.* Describe and illustrate ideal vacation spots. Include descriptions of geographic concepts such as landforms, climate, weather, natural resources, and recreational options.

The social sciences are the foundation of social studies. History and geography are the primary social sciences contained within the scope of the elementary school curriculum. Citizenship education is the third area of emphasis. Subject matter, skills, and democratic values and beliefs from the social sciences are then sequenced through the elementary school curriculum.

Concepts

The scope and sequence of an elementary school curriculum should be organized around concepts. Therefore, a discussion of the curriculum would be incomplete without a section on concepts. The nature of concepts and the importance of concepts are briefly described in this section. Chapter 10 elaborates on concepts and describes teaching strategies that will nurture concept development.

The human mind is somewhat like a large, fluid filing system. As individuals interact in the world they acquire information about their world, compare it to previously learned information, and retain it in a mental file for future use. As information about the world is filed away in memory, we tend to combine information into related categories. Jean Piaget referred to these categories as *schemes* and *mental structures*.

Social studies educators use the term *concept* rather than schemes and mental structures (reading educators are currently using the term *schema*). Concepts emerge from subject matter and experience.

Generalizations are defined as the relationship between two or more concepts. As children develop more sophisticated understandings of concepts they begin to see relationships between concepts. The relationships between the concepts *poverty* and *crime* results in a generalization about the probability of encountering higher crime rates in areas with higher poverty levels. Similarly, generalizations have emerged from the concepts of *supply* and *demand*. Before children can understand complex generalizations they need well-developed understandings of the underlying concepts.

The social science disciplines have identified key generalizations. The disciplines have also identified concepts supporting the generalizations. These generalizations and concepts have emerged from information (content, facts, experiences) that people in the disciplines have collected. The relationships among facts, content, experiences, concepts, and generalizations are illustrated in Figure 2–4.

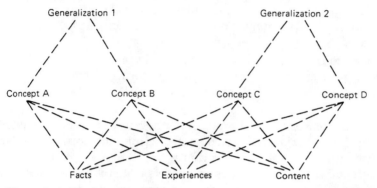

Figure 2–4 The Nature of Concepts

Elementary social studies programs should promote the development of concepts. Prepared with excellent conceptual understandings, children will be better able to consider the complex relationships in their world.

Facts have been the foundation of too many social studies programs. But facts are quickly forgotten if they are not related to an appropriate conceptual understanding. Organizing instruction with a conceptual focus will enhance learning. If your curriculum guide fails to identify a conceptual focus for a lesson, you will need to provide one for your children.

SUMMARY

This chapter introduced the formal and hidden curriculum. It also described two major curriculum organization structures in elementary social studies programs—the expanding environment curriculum and the spiral curriculum. Each is present in many elementary social studies programs, and an increasing number of programs are integrating the two curriculum formats.

This chapter also described the social sciences as they contribute to the elementary social studies curriculum. History, citizenship education, and geography receive major emphasis in the elementary curriculum.

Concepts should be the basis of a social studies program. The importance of concepts was introduced in the discussion of the spiral curriculum and reinforced in the description of the social sciences. The relationship among facts, content, experiences, concepts, and generalizations was explained in the final section of the chapter. Effective elementary programs develop a sound conceptual basis so children can ultimately develop generalizations.

A recurring message in this chapter encouraged you to adapt the curriculum to meet the needs of your students. You must understand the nature of the curriculum to be effective, and you must be capable of altering and adapting the curriculum to provide the best instruction for your students. An inerrant or infallible view of the curriculum will restrict your ability to provide instruction at a level necessary for your students.

SUGGESTED ACTIVITIES

1. Examine a scope and sequence chart in the teacher's edition of one of the social studies textbook series. These charts are usually located in an area of the library containing curriculum materials. Complete the following questions:
   a. What major topics are repeated at each grade level?
   b. What skills and subject matter areas are emphasized?
   c. How are the topics sequenced through the text?
   d. Is there a logical relationship of the scope and sequence between the grade levels?
2. Locate and read a journal article about the social studies curriculum. Summarize the main points and determine the degree to which the author supports ideas presented in this chapter.
3. Compare several elementary social studies textbooks. Do they use an expanding environment or a spiral curriculum?
4. As you compare the textbooks for the above activity, determine the extent to which history, citizenship education, and geography are integrated into the series.

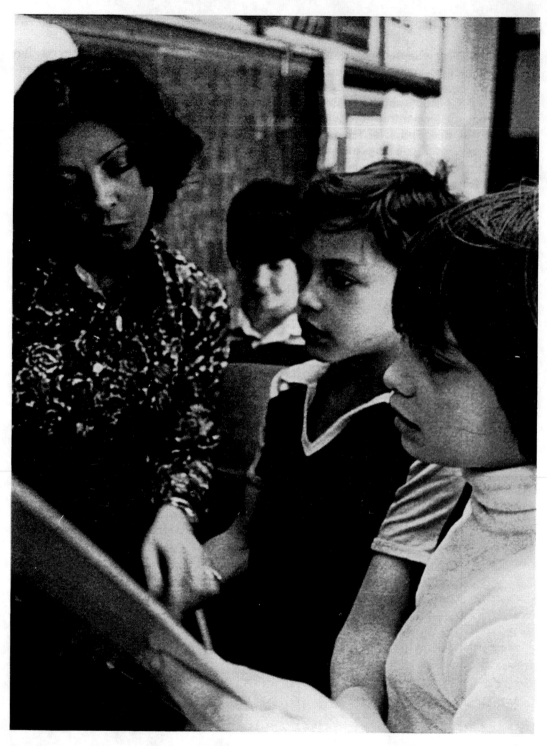

Students benefit from small-group instruction.

Photograph by Carmine L. Galasso.

chapter 3

Characteristics of Effective Teaching

Deciding what to instruct and nurture and how to instruct and nurture are decisions made by each of us in our classrooms.

(Joyce & Weil, 1986, p. 496)*

AS YOU READ...

- describe the complexities of classrooms
- identify and describe characteristics of effective teaching
- develop a rationale for becoming an omnivore
- develop an argument supporting the use of the following practices in your development: a professional development plan, instructional planning, and reflection

**Source:* Joyce, B., & Weil, M. (1986). *Models of teaching* (3rd ed.). Englewood Cliffs, NJ: Prentice Hall. Reprinted with permission of Prentice Hall, Inc.

INTRODUCTION

Teachers are confronted with a myriad of challenges. They must organize instruction, manage time, and respond to the varying needs of their students. Few professions require their members to deal with the array of challenges that teachers must manage. Yet effective teachers manage the complexities of classrooms well while fostering active learning.

This chapter describes the characteristics of effective teaching. As you read the chapter you should consider how you can develop greater levels of expertise. Also consider the challenges of actively involving children in exciting social studies activities.

COMPLEXITIES OF CLASSROOMS

Classrooms are dynamic, complex places. They have a life of their own and change from day to day. Doyle (1980) described the essence of classroom complexities by identifying six characteristics of classrooms. His characteristics include immediacy, publicness, multidimensionality, unpredictability, history, and simultaneity. The following description of these complexities introduces you to the challenges you will encounter. The characteristics of effective teachers, described in the following sections of the chapter, provide you with a foundation for responding to these challenges as you strive to become an effective social studies teacher.

Effective teachers often have a variety of different activities in progress at one time.
Photograph by David W. Van Cleaf.

Immediacy refers to the need for quick teacher responsiveness to student behavior. Teachers make more than 1,000 decisions a day. Effective teachers respond quickly and appropriately.

Publicness refers to the idea that a teacher's responses to a student are viewed by the other students in the classroom. Does the teacher respond warmly or harshly? Does the teacher allow misbehavior or is this a no-nonsense teacher? Does the teacher provide constructive help? Children quickly identify the level of the teacher's expectations and the way the teacher will respond.

Multidimensionality means that many activities occur in classrooms. Classrooms are complex settings with many goals, many tasks, numerous agendas, and many responsibilities.

Unpredictability refers to the likelihood and frequent occurrence of unanticipated disruptions. The school nurse may need to weigh children, there may be an unscheduled fire drill, something tragic may have happened to one of your students, or the electricity may fail. Effective teachers can adapt quickly without frustrating their students or themselves.

History is the fifth characteristic. How teachers deal with students early in the year sets a precedent for the way the students expect them to respond throughout the year. Effective teachers recognize this and spend time at the beginning of the year structuring youngsters' expectations.

Simultaneity is the final characteristic. A variety of activities occur in classrooms at the same time. Several skill groups may be working on different assignments, the teacher may be working with one group, several students in another group may need help, and others may be creating a disturbance. It is as if the teacher is a central computer receiving input from a variety of external terminals...simultaneously.

Managing groups of children while helping them learn is one of the most challenging jobs in our society. Knowledge of the subjects taught in the elementary school is necessary, but is not enough. Effective elementary teachers are multidimensional individuals. They are intelligent, motivating, and capable of working well with children.

Excellent teachers work hard before their students arrive. They work hard while their students are in school, and they work hard after their students leave each day. Excellent teachers work hard because they know that excellence requires hard work. Mediocrity requires only some work. Poor teaching requires little more than being present. Excellent teachers work hard because they realize that they must be prepared to manage the complexities of life in their classrooms.

CHARACTERISTICS OF EFFECTIVE TEACHERS

This is an exciting time to be in education. There are reforms demanding all sorts of changes to improve education. Some of the reforms are based on myopic, idiosyncratic views; others are grounded in long-term social needs. Some of the proposed reforms are based on results of empirical findings, using data gleaned from observations of effective teachers and schools. Other reforms derive from philosophical perspectives.

This section of the chapter describes recent findings related to effective teaching. The first part examines research-based characteristics of effective teaching. The second part proposes an expanded view of effective teaching. The third part describes the personal dimensions of effective teachers.

Research-Based Characteristics of Effective Teachers

The process of teaching has been extensively studied during the past several decades. As a result of these studies several descriptions of effective teaching have emerged. Berliner (1984) described categories of effective teaching practices that are helpful for organizing research findings into more readily understood topics. Berliner's categories describe processes of teaching, which include planning considerations, positive learning environments, teaching practices, and evaluation practices. Characteristics of effective teaching related to these categories are described in the following sections. As you read about these characteristics please compare them to a list of characteristics developed by a group of teachers (see Table 3–1).

Table 3–1 Teacher Perceptions of an Effective Teacher

CHARACTERISTICS BASED ON PERSONALITY

sense of humor	enjoys children	creative
spontaneous	concern for children	personable
motivated	persistent	exciting
stamina		trustworthy

CHARACTERISTICS DEVELOPED THROUGH PROFESSIONAL TRAINING

presents lessons in a variety of ways	knowledge of content
relates content to children's levels	rapport with children
an advocate for children	rapport with parents
maintains positive control	rapport with public
has a well-run classroom	innovative
knowledge of one's capabilities	nurtures creativity
adapts to children's needs	evaluates children
evaluates self	

CHARACTERISTICS BASED ON PERSONALITY AND TRAINING

professional ethics	good listener	organized
continues to improve	entertaining	patient
high expectations	flexible	understanding
positive role model	mature/professional	fair/consistent
communicates well		maintains composure

Planning. Effective teachers are well prepared when they enter the classroom. They spend a considerable amount of time preparing for instruction. If teaching were described in terms of an iceberg, planning might be viewed as that portion of the iceberg lying beneath the surface of the water. Effective teaching that on the surface appears polished and effortless requires extensive planning. Although the casual observer does not see the planning process, the results of planning are evident. Unfortunately, the results of ineffective planning are also evident.

Brophy and Good (1986) identified three concepts related to planning. Each of these concepts contributes to increased academic achievement.

1. *Content Pacing.* When children are exposed to more instruction, they tend to learn more. Pacing refers to the amount of content covered and the rate at which teachers and children proceed through the curriculum. Some teachers move quickly through the curriculum while others proceed slowly. For the most part, children achieve more when more content is taught.

However, this creates a problem for social studies instruction, for social studies textbooks often contain too much information. When pacing is rapid, students cover large amounts of material, but at superficial levels. Pacing in social studies needs to be adapted so students skip unimportant topics and cover more important topics in greater depth.

2. *Engaged Time.* Engaged time refers to the amount of time allocated for instruction. Teachers must plan how they will use their time to ensure that instructional time is maximized and wasted time is minimized. Effective teachers develop procedures to reduce time wasted in transitions between activities and between classes. They also plan rules and procedures that manage children's behaviors for tasks such as obtaining permission to go to the bathroom, sharpening pencils, turning in assignments, moving into small groups, and working in learning centers. Experienced teachers have discovered how and when children are likely to get "off-task" and devise ways to avoid off-task behaviors.

The amount of time allocated for social studies is often limited. Therefore, social studies teachers must plan to use their time wisely. Plan strategies for moving children in and out of groups, plan procedures for cycling children through computer games and simulations, and structure your classroom so reference materials are readily available.

3. *Academic Learning Time.* Academic learning time is the time when students are successfully working toward an educational outcome. Effective teachers plan instruction so students spend a significant portion of their class time working on tasks related to their intended outcomes.

Children also spend more time on learning activities that provide them with success. According to Brophy and Good, teachers should ask questions that are answered successfully approximately 75 percent of the time. Seat work activities should produce a success rate of at least 90 percent.

This text describes a variety of teaching strategies that will enable you to involve your children actively in social studies. These strategies contribute to students' ability to achieve success and the likelihood that they will utilize their time well.

A Positive Learning Environment. Berliner described the learning environment in terms of climate, and he cited four climate factors that contribute to children's achievement.

1. *Expectations.* Achievement scores are higher in classrooms in which teachers communicate their goals and maintain high expectations. Of course, these expectations cannot be unreasonably high or children will likely become frustrated and fail.

Children's social studies achievement is related to your expectations. If you expect high levels of achievement, youngsters are likely to match your expectations. If you expect social studies to be exciting, students will be enthusiastic. If you expect your students to use good citizenship skills, they will behave appropriately. If you expect students to analyze social studies phenomena critically, they will think critically.

2. *Appropriate Environment.* Children perform well in classrooms in which order and academic focus are present. Effective classrooms are pleasant, yet businesslike environments. Further, the climate of the entire school contributes to the classroom climate.

Environmental factors foster citizenship education. If you have a democratic environment, students are more likely to develop democratic attitudes and behaviors. If you have an autocratic environment, students are unlikely to develop democratic values and beliefs.

3. *Managing Deviancy.* This relates to the manner in which teachers respond to children's misbehavior. Classrooms should be positive environments with supportive teachers. Management and discipline strategies should be sensible and positive.

Children tend to use lower-level thought processes when working in stressful situations. A negative, intimidating discipline style creates unnecessary anxiety and may inhibit learning. It also inhibits development of democratic attitudes and behaviors.

Doyle's concepts of publicness and history are relevant to this point. All children, even well-behaved ones, view the teacher's behaviors and develop perceptions and anticipations about the way a teacher will respond to misbehavior. Well-behaved children will become anxious and less likely to involve themselves in social studies activities if they fear unfair teacher reprisals. Effective teachers exercise positive management styles.

4. *A Cooperative Learning Environment.* Positive classroom environments encourage the participation of all children. Cooperative learning contributes by involving all children, improving interpersonal relationships, helping each child become successful, and helping them become more responsible for others.

Cooperative learning skills are critical in the development of democratic citizenship. Consider how you would teach children democratic values like justice, equality, and fairness. It is unlikely that youngsters will acquire these values by listening to a lecture. Children must interact with others in cooperative settings to develop these values.

Teaching Practices. Teacher behaviors in the classroom have a profound effect on learning. Brophy and Good (1986) described seven teaching behaviors that contribute to higher levels of achievement.

1. *Structuring.* Structuring refers to the manner and order in which teachers present information to their students. Students' learning is enhanced when teachers actively present information, state the objectives, outline information to be learned, and reinforce important points. Teachers who make frequent use of examples and analogies show that they have prepared good lessons. Effective presentations include reviews during the presentation as well as at the end of the presentation.

Social studies teachers must modify this principle when using active learning strategies like inquiry, role playing, and discussions. New learning must have a conceptual focus and be related to children's levels of understanding. An alternative, child-centered structure is necessary.

2. *Redundancy.* Information should be repeated throughout a lesson sequence. Children need opportunities to reconsider information and main points as they learn. Effective teachers have a knack for relating new learning to previous learning, which helps children see relationships.

Social studies teachers can implement this principle by relating concepts to children's lives. For example, when teaching a lesson about industry in another state or country, the teacher could begin by examining examples of local industries.

3. *Clarity.* Clear presentations are naturally better than vague or confusing presentations. Effective teachers plan well and therefore have well-organized, clear presentations. Clarity is an essential ingredient in effective questioning as well. Clearly stated questions reduce ambiguity and elicit better responses from students.

Clarity is important in social studies, but a questioning attitude is also important. In a lively discussion children will ask a number of thought-provoking questions for which you may not have answers. Rather than avoid these discussions because of the clarity principle, let children know that you do not have an answer and that ambiguity is an important aspect of learning. Clarity must not be interpreted in social studies as limiting opportunities for students to investigate and question actively.

4. *Enthusiasm.* Effective teachers are enthusiastic, and their enthusiasm is contagious. They are excited about the topic, about learning, and about the students they teach. Students then become more excited and more willing to apply the effort needed to learn. Consider how much drudgery a child might experience when assigned to a classroom headed by an unenthusiastic teacher. Consider your own enthusiasm toward social studies. If you lack enthusiasm you will not develop exciting social studies lessons.

5. *Pacing.* Effective teachers pace their lessons in such a way that children do not get "lost" or inundated with information. Relatively easy information may be taught quickly, but complex ideas and skills need to be taught at a slower pace. Effective teachers also pause frequently to let students consider and reconsider ideas. Effective social studies teachers plan lessons so that youngsters have ample time to develop an understanding of the topic.

6. *Questioning.* Questioning is an integral aspect of teaching. Teachers need to question students to maintain attention, to provide opportunities to practice newly learned information, and as a means of determining whether or not students are grasping the information. This topic will be considered in greater detail in Chapter 11.

7. *Monitoring.* Teachers must actively walk around the room checking students' progress. This monitoring results in more interactions between children and the teacher and contributes to higher achievement rates. Monitoring allows teachers to spot problems and help correct those problems before youngsters master the wrong skill. The monitoring process also allows teachers to reinforce students who are performing the work appropriately.

Monitoring has also been successfully used by many teachers to minimize behavior problems. Students are less likely to misbehave when the teacher is nearby.

An excellent social studies program will provide numerous opportunities for children to work in small groups. The teacher needs to visit with the groups frequently to monitor their progress and to encourage them to consider alternative perspectives. This is an opportune time to ask thought-provoking questions that require youngsters to consider alternative solutions.

Evaluation. Effective teachers demonstrate noteworthy evaluation skills. Berliner described three factors that should be considered in the evaluation process: tests, grades, and feedback.

1. *Tests.* Test questions should relate specifically to the objectives developed in the lesson. Unfortunately, too much of what is tested in schools has not been taught.

A second problem is the manner in which tests are scored. Teachers too frequently score students' responses to test items as either correct or incorrect. They fail to analyze incorrect responses to determine students' understanding.

Teachers should analyze incorrect responses as a means of evaluating progress and understanding.

A third problem is the use of low-level recall questions. Social studies is comprised of numerous high-level concepts that cannot be evaluated using low-level questions. Map-reading skills, critical thinking skills, and cause-and-effect relationships cannot be evaluated using low-level questions.

2. *Grades.* Grades can contribute to increased achievement, but they should be used judiciously. The judicious use of grades may also contribute to the development of more positive attitudes toward social studies.

3. *Feedback.* This concept was briefly mentioned under the earlier heading, "Monitoring." As teachers monitor students during instructional settings they should provide them with feedback. Children performing a task incorrectly should be redirected. Similarly, teachers should acknowledge children's successful work.

Feedback is critical in social studies when students are learning complex skills such as constructing graphs. It is also critical when students are demonstrating inappropriate social interaction skills.

Additional Characteristics of Effective Teachers

The characteristics described in the preceding sections present a partial description of effective teaching. Most of the evidence for these characteristics emerge from studies of low-ability children participating in basic skills instruction such as math and reading. These studies utilized direct instruction techniques with children from lower socioeconomic backgrounds.

Ross and Kyle (1987) noted several important educational goals that are not nurtured by instructional practices used in these studies. Problem-solving abilities, self-esteem, creativity, attitudes toward school and teachers, independence, and curiosity are not nurtured in direct instruction settings. They concluded that teachers should be flexible. With the diversity and complexity of concepts taught in social studies, teachers cannot limit themselves to direct instruction practices.

During a speech to social studies educators, Lee Shulman (1987b) described efforts to evaluate a lesson about the *Federalist Papers*. He used a direct instruction evaluation format to analyze the lesson. Although the lesson was excellent, he stated that he could not evaluate it using direct instruction criteria. He added that many social studies and literature concepts cannot be taught using direct instruction techniques. Alternative instructional formats are necessary to teach complex social studies concepts effectively.

Shulman (1987a) described effective teachers in terms of four characteristics: reasoning, comprehension, transformation, and reflection. Effective teachers must be knowledgeable, rational, thinking human beings who can mediate between the content they teach and the children they are teaching. The four characteristics identified by Shulman, when combined with the flexibility described by Ross and Kyle, provide five additional characteristics of effective teaching. These characteristics must be considered concurrently with the research-based characteristics described earlier.

Flexibility. Teachers must possess a variety of instructional skills. They need to be able to teach lower-level skills through direct instruction techniques. They must also be able to use inductive, child-centered techniques when they want students to discover and inquire. This is particularly important for helping children learn to use the investigative procedures and critical analysis used by social scientists.

Flexible teachers have a range of behaviors that will enable them to be teacher-directed or child-centered as situations dictate. Inflexible teachers lack alternatives.

A greater variety of instructional strategies are needed in classrooms. An over-reliance on a single strategy limits learning. Research indicates that there is no "one best" approach; a variety of instructional techniques is preferable. Variety will also make social studies more exciting.

Reasoning. Teaching is a complex activity requiring extensive teacher knowledge and understanding in several categories. Teachers must know the content and skills they will teach; they must understand principles of learning and apply those principles to the needs of their students; they must know how to use and adapt instructional materials, and they must have a variety of instructional abilities that will enable them to adapt instruction for their students. To tie this knowledge together, teachers must be able to reason.

Citizenship also requires the ability to reason. Teachers who model reasoning skills in social studies are more likely to help their students learn to reason and to examine issues critically.

Comprehension. Effective teachers must understand the content they are teaching. They must know the content well enough to consider all aspects of the topic so that they can organize instruction and information appropriate for their students' knowledge and ability levels.

When teachers do not understand the content, they are unable to respond to students' questions. They cannot present the information in understandable ways. When teachers do not understand the topic they often present the information as something that must be memorized rather than understood and applied. Many social studies concepts are complex and not easily reduced to learning by memory. Reading a map, using an atlas, and understanding the primary causes of an event illustrate the complexity of social studies concepts. Teachers who understand the concepts are more likely to help children understand.

Transformation. Transformation is the process of adapting the teacher's sophisticated knowledge of a topic to a level appropriate for the students. A thorough comprehension of content is a necessary prerequisite as teachers attempt to transform the information for their students.

As effective teachers transform their knowledge to ways appropriate for their students, they create a variety of learning environments that are designed for the needs of students. Of course, teachers who lack a comprehension of the subject matter will be unable to transform information in ways that will benefit students.

Reflection. Reflection occurs after a teaching episode has been completed. Good teachers reconsider their performance, their students' performance, and the appropriateness of the instructional activities. Good teachers continuously evaluate their effectiveness through reflection as a means of improving their effectiveness. Rather than expressing relief when a particularly difficult lesson has been completed, reflective teachers analyze the lesson to identify ways to improve future lessons. Teachers who fail to reflect ultimately limit their ability to improve their professional skills.

The Personal Side

There is a personal side of effective teaching that must be mentioned. Teaching is an interpersonal activity that involves personal relationships between teachers and students.

Roueche and Baker (1986) described characteristics of excellent teachers that included a more personal dimension of the act of teaching. They described three main topics: motivation, interpersonal skills, and cognitive skills. It must also be noted that many of the characteristics of effective teaching described above are reinforced by the three categories described by Roueche and Baker.

Motivation. Excellent teachers are committed to their students as well as themselves. They are excited about education and the prospects of their students' achievement. Motivated teachers reveal interests in their students that extend beyond the classroom, and they are more readily available to students after class. They are intangibly rewarded by the successes of their students. Finally, motivated social studies teachers spark their students' interests in social studies.

Interpersonal Skills. Effective teachers develop a positive rapport with students and demonstrate respect for them. They also display empathy—they understand the many demands, fears, and frustrations their students experience. Effective teachers maintain high expectations for children, maintain a warm, businesslike classroom environment, and have a positive regard for their students. These characteristics are prerequisites to developing an atmosphere in which democratic citizenship can develop.

Cognitive Skills. Effective teachers know their students and personalize instruction based on students' needs. They utilize a variety of well-organized instructional techniques that actively involve all class members. Effective teachers also actively pursue personal improvement through reflection and innovation.

Summary of Effective Teaching Characteristics

Many aspects of effective teaching are outlined above. Characteristics of effective instruction included ideas useful in direct instruction situations. Yet there are concerns regarding the limitations of direct instruction. Direct instruction practices appear to inhibit attaining many social studies outcomes such as problem solving, higher-level thinking skills, creativity, self-esteem, independence, curiosity, and positive attitudes toward school and teachers.

Additional characteristics of effective teaching include flexibility, reasoning, comprehension, transformation, and reflection. Teaching is a complex activity occurring in complex classroom settings. Teachers must possess an impressive array of expertise if they are to function as true professionals.

SUGGESTIONS

Before describing specific suggestions, pause for a moment and consider the type of teacher you want to become within the next five years. Consider this your five-year professional development plan. To help you construct a mental picture of yourself you should think about excellent teachers you have had as models. It may also be helpful to consider the weak teachers. As you develop an image of yourself, also consider the characteristics of effective teachers described above.

Joyce and McKibbin (1982) described five types of teachers operating in our schools. The five categories included teachers at varying stages of effectiveness. They will be described below. Consider each category and identify the type of teacher you want to become.

The first category consists of teachers labeled as *omnivores*. Omnivores are incessantly striving for professional improvement. They read, attend workshops, and talk to others as they search for new and better ways to teach. Omnivores are positive, self-actualized individuals.

The second category consists of *active consumers*. They are best described as "partial omnivores." Active consumers are "less driven" but are positive and eager to improve their skills.

Passive consumers, the third category, are more dependent on their environment. They will conform to the expectations of their principals and colleagues. They will grow professionally if placed in positive environments, and they will atrophy if assigned to schools with minimal professional demands.

The fourth category is comprised of *resistant teachers*. The "resistants" have entrenched themselves and are reluctant participants in the change process. Many resistants actively oppose attempts to help them improve their professional skills.

Further, they often attempt to establish an informal power structure within the school that serves to subvert changes so they can protect the status quo.

The final group is the *withdrawn category* of teachers. It is difficult to get these teachers involved in professional improvement programs and they fail to grow. Because they do not grow professionally, they get left behind.

Becoming an effective teacher takes time, commitment, and perseverance. Constructing a realistic image of yourself as an ideal teacher is a place to begin. But do not stop with only a view; consider the competencies you need to become an effective master teacher. This section of this chapter is divided into three subtopics that will help you organize your thoughts and efforts regarding your professional improvement. Specific suggestions are included in the three sections.

Professional Development Plan

Success does not occur by accident. If you are to become an effective teacher you must work hard. A long-term professional development plan will enable you to direct your hard work toward the direction you deem important.

The first step is to identify your philosophy of education and your views of the learning process. Ask yourself, What should education achieve? and, How should I structure learning activities in my classroom to achieve these outcomes? Chapter 1 outlined several contemporary philosophies and learning theories.

You must understand what you believe and you must know what you expect your students to accomplish. Failure to do this will tie you and your students too closely to the curriculum guide and the textbook. You will be unable to adapt instruction to meet the needs of your students, and you may cease to make critical decisions regarding their needs. You may be like a fully rigged sailboat without a course to sail. You and your students will meander with little direction.

It helps students when teachers share ideas about lesson plans and classroom situations.
Photograph by Laimute E. Druskis.

As you identify your philosophical and psychological beliefs about education, you should strive to identify long-term goals that are consistent with your beliefs. You must also determine what you hope to accomplish each year and how the yearly goals will contribute to your long-term goals.

Once you have identified your philosophy of education, stated your beliefs regarding the way children learn, and have identified your long-term and yearly goals, place those statements in a conspicuous place. Refer to them frequently. As you periodically refer to these statements you should ask yourself how well you are accomplishing them, whether or not they are still valid, and whether or not they need to be modified.

Student teaching and the first year of teaching are conforming experiences. The challenges, frustrations, and complexities of classroom teaching often modify teachers' goals and expectations. Further, other teachers and administrators indirectly support conformity. Work to avoid the adoption of questionable practices.

Your professional development plan should include attending workshops, enrolling in graduate classes, and participating in professional organizations. As you strive to improve you are also encouraged to read teacher's magazines and share ideas with other staff members.

The National Council for the Social Studies (NCSS) is an organization devoted to improving social studies education. You should join NCSS or your state affiliate. Read their publications and attend their conferences. Through your membership and participation you will be exposed to a wealth of new ideas.

A professional development plan will enable you to develop a greater variety of instructional strategies; it will help you to consider new demands and innovations; it will provide you with opportunities to reexamine your views of teaching. Finally, it will enable you to grow as a professional.

Instructional Planning

A long-term professional development plan is critical to becoming an effective, master teacher. However, short-term instructional planning is critical to the immediate success of your students as well as your own mental health. Instructional planning includes daily, weekly, and unit planning. It includes all the plans that teachers make as they prepare specific lessons and activities for their students.

Perhaps the most critical aspect of your immediate success lies in the area of classroom management (discipline). Before you meet with your students for the first time you should give considerable thought to your expectations for their behavior in your classroom. Effective classroom managers spend the first few weeks of school socializing children into the classroom. They establish a few essential, workable rules, communicate the rules and the reason for the rules to students, and spend time helping them follow the rules during the first few weeks.

Good teachers plan each day's lessons. They also look ahead to see where lessons lead. One disadvantage of being a student teacher and first-year teacher is that you will not have a clear idea of the direction the curriculum is guiding you and your students. Nevertheless, take time to look ahead as you plan for each day.

Daily planning is an important aspect of effective teaching. You must plan so that lessons are designed for your students. If you are using a textbook, plan ways to adapt the text to meet your students' needs. You must also consider the effectiveness of prior lessons as you plan. You may discover that students have not mastered the skills necessary for the next lesson and you must therefore reteach an objective. You may also discover that the students were uninterested and thus you will need to plan a more motivating activity.

Early in your first year as a teacher you may find the demands on your time to be too great to allow time to plan creative social studies lessons. Follow the curriculum or textbook rather closely at first. About the time you get your classroom well organized and begin feeling comfortable, your students will begin expressing concerns about social studies. This is the time to begin developing creative adaptations to the social studies program. It is the time to utilize alternative activities that actively involve your students.

Take time to develop and teach an exciting social studies unit and then return to the standard curriculum or textbook for a while. Then, while utilizing the text, begin planning another unit. Throughout your first year you will continue developing a few units interspersed with the more traditional lessons. By the end of your first year you will have actively engaged students in several exciting social studies units that you developed expressly for them. During your second year of teaching you can use the units developed during the first year and develop a few more units. By the time you have taught for several years you will have developed a creative, child-centered set of social studies units that maintain your students' enthusiasm as well as your own.

Few professions are more demanding than teaching. Teaching in elementary schools is physically, emotionally, and psychologically challenging. Classrooms are complex environments. Teachers must plan well if they are to reduce the physical, emotional, and psychological demands of teaching.

Reflect

At this point you might ask yourself to consider the next thirty years of your professional career. There are some teachers who can boast that they have had thirty years of different experiences. Sadly, there are other teachers who may have had one year's experience thirty times. Do you envision yourself modifying, adapting, and improving the range of your expertise or do you envision yourself as a person finding an easy way to teach and then repeating the process throughout your professional career?

Planning lesson plans and dealing with classroom problems require reflective thought.
Photograph by Irene Springer.

Effective teachers consistently examine the effects of their behaviors on their students. They use this information to identify strengths as well as areas requiring greater attention. Many education programs require student teachers to maintain diaries during their student-teaching experience. The diary is an attempt to encourage student teachers to reflect on their performance. You might consider keeping a diary as you begin your professional career. The diary will help you develop the habit of reflecting on your performance.

Reflecting on your behavior and the effects of your behavior will enable you to improve. It is rather amazing that hard-working, reflective teachers have fewer discipline problems and more successful students.

Reflection should occur on both a daily and long-term basis. Each day you should reexamine the teaching and learning that took place in your classroom. This analysis will enable you to plan appropriate lessons for the next day. Reflection should also occur at a higher level on a regular basis. Each week you should consider your successes and failures. Take time to evaluate your efforts relative to the long-term goals you have identified. When you discover that your teaching skills need improvement in a certain area, you will have already diagnosed the difficulty and will be ready to consider options for improving your skills.

SUMMARY

It seems pointless for people to prepare for teaching if they do not intend to commit themselves to becoming effective teachers. Nevertheless, some do. This chapter described aspects of effective teaching that have emerged from observations of effective teachers as well as the professional judgments of noted educators. Suggestions have been provided to help you become an effective first-year teacher and to guide you as you strive to become an effective master teacher.

Table 3–1 outlines effective teaching characteristics. You should informally rate yourself on each item and identify priorities for your improvement. Refer to this list and your self-rating frequently as you strive to improve your teaching competencies. Also remember that you can be effective and not excel in each area.

Every child should have an effective teacher and every teacher should experience the pride of being effective.

SUGGESTED ACTIVITIES

1. Develop a description of the type of teacher you would like to become within five years. Examine characteristics described in the chapter and Table 3–1. Identify areas you feel are your strengths. Also identify areas you feel you will need to develop. Now make a plan outlining the items you will need to strengthen during the upcoming year.

2. To develop a better understanding of the importance of setting goals, identify a personal goal you can accomplish during the present semester. The goal may relate to weight loss, exercise, nutrition, worship, or any other behavior you would like to change. Then list at least three specific things you can do to achieve your goal. Check your progress on a weekly basis. As you work toward your goal you should realize the value of setting goals.

3. Observe an elementary-school teacher and record examples of effective teaching characteristics.

4. Interview several teachers and children. Ask them to identify characteristics of effective teachers. How do their lists compare with the characteristics presented in this chapter?

5. Read an article in an educational journal about improving the effectiveness of teachers.

Teachers benefit from cooperative planning.

chapter 4

Planning Lessons and Units

Well-planned programs are effective programs.

(Van Cleaf, 1979)

AS YOU READ...

- support the statement, "Well-planned programs are effective programs."
- describe the elements of a well-planned lesson
- identify the strengths and weaknesses of the four lesson plan models
- develop a rationale for using the unit approach

INTRODUCTION

Planning is one of the most important aspects of effective teaching. Teachers can be enthusiastic, supportive, intelligent individuals, but they will be unable to teach well without an appropriate "game plan." A sports analogy may help illustrate the importance of planning. Many teams have exceptionally talented athletes, yet they may do poorly in game situations. The most obvious reason for poor performance is poor coaching. The coach may have an inadequate scouting report of the opponent and therefore may not have prepared the team adequately. The coach may have failed to help athletes develop and practice basic skills. Or, the coach may have been unable to mold the talented athletes into a cohesive team. On a long-term basis, the coach may have been unable to attract athletes for critical positions on the team.

Effective teachers are similar to coaches in many ways. They develop good scouting reports regarding the challenges their students will present. The skill and ability levels of children are considered prior to instruction. Teachers also consider the children's interests as they develop motivating lessons. Like good coaches, good teachers also have an understanding of their goals. Good coaches know how good athletes should perform; good teachers know what children will be able to do as a result of instruction. Good coaches mold a group of athletes into a team, and good teachers help their students function well as a group.

This chapter describes the importance of planning, components of the planning process, four lesson plan formats, and unit planning. You need an effective, well conceived plan before teaching a lesson. Failure to plan well ultimately results in poor teaching, frustrated or confused students, and wasted time. Further, children are most likely to misbehave when the teacher has failed to plan appropriate lessons.

THE IMPORTANCE OF PLANNING

An advertisement for an automobile oil filter shows a mechanic warning, "You can pay me now...or pay me later." By installing a new oil filter on a regular basis, drivers can avoid expensive engine repairs when their cars get older. The cost of preventive maintenance is relatively minor in comparison to major mechanical repairs. There is a lesson in the oil filter commercial for teachers. Planning is preventive maintenance that allows you to operate and maintain a well-run classroom.

Well-planned programs are effective programs. Studies of preschool and primary-grade programs demonstrate that the degree of planning and organization is a critical factor in the success of the programs. The philosophy upon which each program is premised is much less of a factor. Behavioristic programs effectively achieved academic goals when well-planned and organized. Similarly, cognitive developmental and Montessori programs effectively achieved academic and social goals when well planned and organized. Programs were ineffective

There is still a lot of work to do after the children go home.

Photograph by Ken Karp.

when poorly organized. Elementary classrooms must be well organized and teachers must plan well if children are to achieve educational goals.

A tremendous amount of activity occurs in elementary classrooms, and effective teachers plan ways to manage instruction and children within their classrooms. They plan procedures, classroom rules, activity sequences, seating arrangements, grouping arrangements, materials, lesson pace, and instructional strategies to achieve their goals.

Parker (1984) used the term "mental scripts" to describe one function of planning. Teachers' plans serve as mental scripts guiding them through lessons. Well-planned mental scripts enable teachers to present appropriate instruction and allow them to respond to unanticipated events. Students may raise unexpected questions, a visitor may enter the classroom, or several students may decide to visit with one another during the lesson. A well-planned lesson ensures that the teacher understands the topic well and may readily deviate from the lesson to react to unanticipated events. A well-planned lesson then allows the teacher to return to the lesson with minimal discontinuity.

The characteristics of effective teaching described in the previous chapter are based on effective planning. Planning is the time when teachers reflect on the objectives for instruction and the needs of the children. While simultaneously considering these two variables, teachers consider the most appropriate instructional strategies for the lesson. Of course, effective teachers have a variety of strategies from which to choose.

As teachers plan lessons they examine the content to determine how well they understand the content and how they will transform the content for their students. If teachers do not understand the information, several options are available. They may decide to delay teaching the topic until they can develop a better understanding; they may invite a resource person to present the information; or they may use the inquiry strategy. An inquiry activity will allow the children and the teacher to investigate the topic.

Many social studies lessons lack continuity from one lesson to the next. Textbooks often do not provide continuity, and the scheduling of social studies, often for short periods of time on alternating days, contributes to lesson discontinuity. Teachers can overcome these limitations by assuming more responsibility for planning their social studies lessons. Teachers must consider available resources and the schedule as they plan lessons that relate to one another.

Planning is critical to the success of a substitute teacher as well as the regular classroom teacher. Substitutes should not be considered as baby-sitters. A substitute can help your students learn only if you have planned well. Failure to plan well for a substitute is unethical. Teachers who do not plan well enough for a substitute are wasting their students' instructional time, allowing opportunities for youngsters to misbehave and wasting taxpayers' money.

Murphy's Law applies also to planning. The principal inevitably decides to visit classrooms on those days when teachers have not had time to plan their lesson adequately. Further, children elect to misbehave more readily on these same days, even while the principal may be visiting.

Plan well and you will do well. Planning is critical to your success and to your mental health.

ELEMENTS OF EFFECTIVE PLANNING

Most school districts have curriculum guides for teachers. Teachers should look to the curriculum for guidance and then plan lessons that are appropriate for the needs and interests of their students. Teachers must also consider their own strengths and interests as they plan lessons. As you gain experience you will discover that some topics in the curriculum are more important than others. You will also learn that you may need to spend considerable time on some topics and omit or provide minimal instruction for others.

The elements of effective planning are described in the following sections. You should integrate these elements into your planning process as you develop lessons for your students.

Outcomes (Goals and Objectives)

Planning for instruction is somewhat like planning an itinerary for a trip. You need a destination, a means of travel, and a predetermined route. Lessons are trips from one level of knowledge to another and require a destination, means of travel, and a route. The outcomes of a lesson are the intended results, and they are stated as goals and objectives.

Goals are general statements. Your goals should be based on the development of a conceptual understanding of the topic. Goals are statements of the larger picture and are reached after several related objectives have been achieved. As you plan you may identify the same goal for several lessons and you may periodically return to the same goal throughout the year.

Objectives are usually statements of specific outcomes for each lesson. They are short-term learning statements that provide a specific focus for a lesson. The rationale for using objectives is that they provide a destination for each lesson. With a specific destination in mind, teachers are better able to organize lessons that will achieve their objectives.

Educational literature has referred to several types of objectives that have minor differences for the classroom teacher. Some educators use the term *instructional objective* to describe the specific instructional intent of a lesson. Others use the term *behavioral objective* because they believe that all instruction should be validated by observable changes in students' behavior. The differences are minimal and a matter of personal preference.

Several methods have been proposed for writing objectives. Some are quite cumbersome, requiring considerable time to write them well. Hunter (1982) proposed a succinct method of writing objectives. According to Hunter, each objective should specify the content children will learn and the behavior they will demonstrate as they learn the content. Some sample objectives are:

1. Children will locate cities using map coordinates. (The content children will learn in the lesson is the use of coordinates, the behavior is locating cities.)
2. Children will name three community helpers. (The content for the lesson will be community helpers; the behavior will be to name examples of community helpers.)
3. Children will share materials while working on a group assignment. (The teacher in this situation will talk to children about the need to share while working together in small groups,;the teacher will then observe children to determine whether or not they are sharing.)

Try developing sample objectives for the following concepts. Remember to include content and behavior statements.

rivers	California gold rush
service jobs	importance of the Nile River
equality	using an encyclopedia

A student teacher was once observed attempting to teach seven objectives in a thirty-five-minute-period. Obviously, none of the objectives were taught well. Rather than attempt to teach too many objectives, identify your specific objective and then develop a lesson that enables students to learn the objective well. One objective per lesson is recommended. However, at times you may be able to teach two related objectives during the same lesson.

The length of a lesson is related to the length of time it will take children to master the objective. Some objectives can be learned quickly; other objectives may require several days. Difficult objectives will require several lessons related to different aspects of the objective.

Content

Lessons are designed to help children learn something new. Teachers must decide what they want children to learn and then make content decisions about the kind of information needed for the objective. This type of decision requires teachers to consider information from the perspective of the children. Some information may be appropriate, other information inappropriate and therefore omitted.

Most educators agree that new learning must be related to children's existing knowledge. Piaget described this concept using the terms *adaptation, accommodation,* and *assimilation.* Learning is a process of adapting one's present thinking to a new, more sophisticated level. Teachers present information related to children's existing knowledge level, and they encourage children to extend their knowledge to a more complex level (accommodation). Teachers then provide practice activities that enable children to strengthen (assimilate) the newly accommodated idea. The content you select should support this progression.

Materials

Materials are essentially resources and include textbooks, films, library books, computer programs, museums, manipulative materials, maps, photographs, pictures, and people. As you plan your lessons you must consider the types of materials available and the appropriateness of the materials.

Frymier (1977) stated that materials should be selected according to the needs of the learner. For example, children with little motivation for schoolwork react best to highly motivating materials; they do not react well to curriculum materials that are not motivating. Conversely, highly motivated children are likely to re-

Children enjoy working with a variety of manipulative materials.
Photograph by Ken Karp.

spond well to material regardless of its motivational value. However, we often use low motivational materials for the entire classroom and reserve the creative, motivating materials and activities for our more capable and gifted students.

Most explanations of elementary children's learning styles indicate that children learn best through active involvement with manipulative materials. While many teachers accept this premise, few children have opportunities to participate actively in lessons. Most classroom activities are passive; they require children to read a textbook, listen to the teacher, and complete workbook or worksheet assignments. For example, most children are expected to learn to read maps by studying maps illustrated in their textbooks. This is a passive way to teach map reading. An active alternative would be to require students to construct maps of their neighborhood and then describe the characteristics of their maps. Consider the importance of active child involvement and select materials that will actively involve your students.

Social studies should teach children about their world. Select materials and resources from the children's familiar environment. Utilize community resources such as speakers, residents of nursing homes, museums, business leaders, and parents to enliven social studies. Community service groups like the American Heart Association, American Red Cross, and 4-H provide useful resources for teachers. Additional resources include:

Family members	Chamber of Commerce	Historical sites
Regilious groups	Veterans groups	Clubs
Picture files	City directories	Retired teachers
	Antique dealers	

Newspapers are also excellent resources. There is a national program called Newspapers in Education that helps teachers utilize newspapers as resource materials. A St. Louis company, PRIDE, sells copies of newspapers published on a number of historically significant dates (*Dred Scott* decision, Lincoln's assassination, Japanese attack on Pearl Harbor, etc.). For more information call your local news editor or write: PRIDE, 1310 Ann Ave., St. Louis, MO 63104.

Strategies and Activities

Activities are the behaviors performed by children; strategies are behaviors performed by teachers. Activities may require active or passive child involvement. Constructing a salt map is an example of active involvement; listening to a lecture is an example of a passive activity.

Teaching strategies include lecturing, questioning, discussing, and assigning work to children. Other teaching strategies include inquiry, concept attainment, cooperative learning, simulations, and role playing. The chapters in Part III of this text describe a variety of teaching strategies appropriate for elementary social studies.

As you plan lessons you will need to select a variety of strategies and activities for each aspect of the lesson. In most lessons you will introduce the lesson first. After introducing the lesson you will teach the objective to your students. After teaching the objective you will usually provide opportunities for students to practice the newly learned objective. A variety of strategies and activities should be used for each portion of the lesson.

Closure

When you finish a lesson it is advisable to provide a brief means of reconsidering the important points. Closure occurs at the end of a lesson and offers teacher and students an opportunity to reconsider the lesson's objective. Closure may consist of asking students to identify important characteristics, main points, primary causes, representative examples, or definitions of terms related to the lesson.

When parents ask their children, "What did you learn in school today?" most children respond, "Nothing!" One teacher developed a closure technique to correct this phenomenon. She asked students, "When your parents ask what you learned in social studies today, what will you tell them?"

Extension Activities

One reality of classrooms is that some children finish their work before others. Effective teachers provide extension activities for children completing work before the end of the class period. Extension activities should be related to the lesson's objective and should require relatively little teacher supervision. Crossword puzzles, word-searches, posters, mobiles, and puzzling problems are possible extension activities.

All activities should be motivating and actively involve children. Your extension activities should not be creative rewards for your more capable children. If you find that your extension activities are more enjoyable than the activities within the main portion of your lesson you should consider improving the quality of the required activities.

Evaluation

Evaluation is an integral aspect of teaching. Pretests are often given prior to planning a lesson. Pretest information is then used in the lesson planning process. Effective teachers evaluate children during instruction to determine whether or not they are learning. Teachers evaluate children's work at the end of lessons to determine whether or not they need to reteach the objective before proceeding to the next objective. Finally, effective teachers evaluate children at the end of a series of lessons to determine how well they learned the topic.

LESSON PLANNING MODELS

Planning is an important aspect of effective teaching and requires more consideration than the type of information that can be included in the little boxes of teachers' customary lesson plan books. Experienced teachers do a considerable amount of thinking about lessons and do much of the planning mentally. This may work well for experienced teachers, but it does not work well for student teachers and beginning teachers.

This section of the chapter describes four planning models. As you consider each model determine your preferences and the types of models used in school districts in your area.

The lesson plan formats described in the following section include a sample lesson plan illustrating each format. The sample lesson plans have similar objectives and as many similar activities as possible. As you examine the four lesson plan formats note similarities and differences. While some appear more complex than others, you should observe that there are many more similarities than differences.

A Traditional Planning Model

The traditional model has many variations; but generally requires teachers to first identify an objective. Once teachers have identified an objective they select strategies and activities that will enable students to achieve the objective. Finally, teachers plan a means of evaluating children's learning. A lesson plan following this format is illustrated in Table 4–1.

This type of lesson plan format is relatively easy to use and provides a framework for thorough planning. This model can be quite effective when teachers take the time to develop thorough lessons.

Table 4–1 Sample Traditional Lesson Plan

Grade level:	First grade
Topic:	Neighborhoods
Objective:	Children will name three important objects in the school's neighborhood.
Materials:	"Make Way for Ducklings," drawing paper
Activities:	

1. Ask children to state examples of people, buildings, and businesses in their neighborhood.
2. Read "Make Way for Ducklings."
   Remind children to listen for things in the story that are in their neighborhood.
3. Discuss the story. (*Note:* Many traditional lessons end here.)
4. Tell children to draw a picture of their neighborhood.

Evaluation:	Examine children's pictures to determine if objective has been met.

The basic components of the traditional format are included in all lesson plan models. They have been adapted and embellished in the following models.

Hunter Model

Hunter (1982) developed a model of effective teaching based on her observations of effective teachers. Her instructional model also represents her views about the importance of mastery learning. In mastery learning an objective is identified, instructional activities are presented, and students are evaluated to assess mastery of the objective.

Hunter elaborated on these points and proposed a multiple-step model. Her model includes preinstructional decisions, instructional decisions, and post-instructional decisions.

Preinstructional planning requires teachers to specify an objective, analyze the tasks involved in learning the objective, and sequence the tasks. As teachers analyze and sequence the tasks they also consider the capabilities of their students.

After identifying an objective and the tasks, teachers must plan strategies and activities to teach the objective. The first aspect of the instructional act is the anticipatory set, or introduction. The anticipatory set may include telling students the objective of the lesson, establishing a purpose for the lesson, and relating the lesson to previous learning.

After planning an anticipatory set, teachers must plan ways to teach the information. Input and modeling are the processes that teachers use to relate the objective to students. Input may be described as "telling," and modeling may be described as "showing." Hunter encouraged teachers to use a variety of input and modeling techniques.

Checking understanding and *guided practice* are the next aspects of Hunter's model. Checking understanding requires teachers to ask questions frequently during the lesson to determine whether or not students are learning. In addition to questions, teachers are encouraged to monitor children's work. At the end of a lesson teachers should either formally or informally evaluate the work to determine how well students learned the objective. You must plan ways to check your students' understanding.

Once teachers have provided input/modeling activities and have checked for understanding, students need opportunities to practice the new information. The practice immediately following input and modeling is called *guided practice*. It must relate directly to the material presented during the input and modeling portion of the lesson. This will help reinforce the objective and ensure that children are successful. Success is an important variable contributing to high achievement levels.

Guided practice must be closely monitored by teachers. As teachers monitor children during guided practice they provide reinforcement for children performing correctly. For children performing incorrectly, teachers redirect children's efforts so they will perform the practice activity correctly. *Reteaching* is the term used to describe the process teachers use as they redirect children performing tasks incorrectly.

Independent practice is the next aspect of a Hunter lesson plan. Independent practice allows students to perform additional practice with considerably less teacher supervision. It also provides teachers with opportunities to extend the lesson's objective.

A sample lesson plan based on Hunter's model is illustrated in Table 4–2.

Table 4–2 Sample Hunter Lesson Design

Concept:	Neighborhood—place or region near (area surrounding) where you live or where you go to school.
Generalization:	Neighborhood can supply our needs for health, safety, and happiness.
Objective:	Students will group things in neighborhoods in the categories of contributing to 1) being healthy, 2) being safe, and 3) being happy.
Materials:	Drawing paper, crayons, book *Make Way for Ducklings*.
Sponge Activity: (if needed)	"While we're getting ready, think of what the word 'neighborhood' means."
Anticipatory Set:	"The neighborhood of something is the area, region, or places nearby." (Teacher does not get definition from students because of the chance of introducing errors at beginning learning.) "For example, in the neighborhood of our school, there are streets with crosswalks and stop lights, stores where we can buy things, houses where families live, and parks where we can play." "Think of what things are in the neighborhood of your house and what you do there." List student answers on board, i.e.

> store—buy things
> street—drive
> sidewalks— skateboard
> houses—sleep, eat, watch TV, etc.

Modeling *Check for* *Understanding* *Guided Practice:*	"Things in our neighborhoods help us to *be healthy* (list categories on board) such as stores to buy food, to *be safe*, such as crosswalks, and to be *be happy*, such as parks or friends. Let's categorize the things you listed in your neighborhood under these headings. Some may go in more than one category." Students categorize their list.
Objective:	"Today we're going to read a story about some ducks who are looking for a neighborhood to raise their family so they would be healthy, safe, and happy. As you read, we'll look for things that would cause them to choose or not choose a neighborhood."
Input *Checking for* *Understanding* *Guided Practice:*	Teacher or students read *Make Way for Ducklings* stopping to list elements in each category. Teacher will decide whether to read the whole story for enjoyment and then recall neighborhood elements or whether to stop in initial reading. Teacher will prompt with questions, if necessary, "Why didn't Mrs. Mallard want to stay there?" (fox, turtles, bicycles) "How would we categorize these things?" (safety) Continue through story.
Guided Practice:	"If you were going to draw something you would like in your neighborhood that would help you be healthy, what would you draw?" (Get several answers.) If you were going to draw something that Mrs. Mallard would like to keep her family healthy, what would you draw?" (Get several answers.) Repeat for "be safe" and "be happy."
Model *Check for* *Understanding* *Guided Practice:*	"Each of you will have three pieces of paper folded in half. On one you will write 'Be Happy,' on another 'Be Safe,' and on the third 'Be Healthy.' (Show model.) In one half you will draw what you would like in your neighborhood. In the other half you will draw what Mrs. Mallard would like. Think of what you might draw for 'Be Happy.' (Get two or three answers.) You see, your pictures will be different because it is what *you* think! How about 'Be Safe,' 'Be Healthy'? When you finish, we'll have fun looking at each other's pictures because they'll be different."
Independent *Practice* *Assessment:*	Students draw their pictures and decide which one they want to show. Students' pictures are displayed by students or on bulletin board and assessed for correctness of category.

Source: Hunter, M. (1982). *Mastery learning.* El Segundo, CA: TIP Publications. Reprinted with permission of Dr. Madeline Hunter and TIP Publications.

The effectiveness of mastery learning models has been analyzed rather extensively. Bloom (1984) reported that children with average ability levels were performing in the 84th percentile range when taught using mastery learning techniques in large group settings. He also stated that when mastery learning instruction occurred in a tutorial situation, achievement levels of "average learners" reached the 98th percentile level.

While the Hunter model is a variation of mastery learning, studies of classrooms utilizing the Hunter model indicate that it is not a panacea for correcting problems in education. Recent studies indicate that the Hunter model has had no impact on raising children's academic achievement. While many school districts have adopted the model as a means of improving education, academic benefits have not been realized.

Teach-Practice-Apply

Cooper, Warncke, Ramstad, and Shipman (1979) proposed a teach-practice-apply model (TPA) for teaching reading in elementary schools. The TPA model is designed to provide children with instruction, practice, and opportunities to apply the information in different contexts. The TPA model has been integrated into the Scott, Foresman elementary reading series and has been expanded to include social studies (Reinhartz & Van Cleaf, 1986).

The *teach* portion of the TPA model requires teachers to plan activities that will help children learn information and skills related to the lesson's objective. The teach portion incorporates aspects of Hunter's anticipatory set and input/modeling. Teachers should plan ways to introduce a lesson and ways to help children develop an understanding of the objective. Teaching activities and strategies can be child-centered or teacher-directed, depending on the nature of the objective and the preferences of the teacher.

The *practice* portion of the TPA model is also similar to the guided practice portion of the Hunter model. Skills and information that have been taught must be practiced if children are to develop a sense of accomplishment. Teachers are encouraged to monitor children as they work and provide assistance for those students experiencing difficulties. Practice activities should relate directly to the skills and information developed in the teach portion of the lesson.

Opportunities for children to apply new skills and information is minimal in many learning settings. Gifted children are usually the only ones who can participate in creative activities; they often are the first to finish their work and therefore get to do enrichment activities. However, all children need to participate in activities that will allow them to apply newly learned information and skills. By providing *apply* activities as part of each lesson, children use the information in different contexts and thereby extend their learning.

The teach-practice-apply model assumes that teachers will identify goals and objectives for their lessons. It also assumes that teachers will evaluate children at the conclusion of a lesson or unit to determine the extent to which students learned the objectives.

Descriptors of each component of the TPA model are shown in Figure 4–1. The sample TPA lesson plan (see Table 4–3) illustrates each component. As you examine the lesson, consider similarities between the Hunter lesson plan and the TPA lesson plan.

This model fosters child-centered and inductive teaching more readily than does Hunter's model. Unlike the Hunter model, the TPA model is not hampered by the limitations of mastery learning and direct instruction perspectives. TPA lessons generally contain a greater assortment of child-centered strategies and activities.

Figure 4–1 The Overlapping Nature of the Teach-Practice-Apply Model

Source: Reinhartz, J., & Van Cleaf, D.W. (1986). *Teach-practice-apply: The TPA instructional model, K-8,* p. 24. Washington, D.C: National Education Association. Reprinted with permission of the National Education Association.

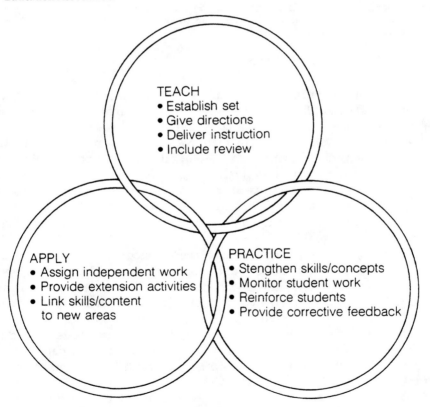

Table 4–3 Sample TPA Lesson Plan

Grade level:	First grade
Topic:	Neighborhoods
Objective:	Children will name three important objects in the school's neighborhood.
Materials:	"Make Way for Ducklings," drawing paper
Teach:	

1. Introduce lesson by asking children to name items present in their neighborhood.
2. Introduce and read "Make Way for Ducklings." Remind children to listen for examples of items found presently in neighborhoods.
3. Discuss story and items present in the neighborhood.

Practice:	Children will draw a picture of the neighborhood described in the story.
Apply:	Children will draw a picture of their neighborhood as it appears today and as it might appear in fifty years (a "now and then" picture).
Evaluation:	Examine children's pictures to determine if the objective has been met.

Source: Reinhartz, J., & Van Cleaf, D.W. (1986). *Teach-practice-apply: The TPA instructional model, K-8.* Washington, D.C.: National Education Association. Adapted with permission of the National Education Association.

A Cognitively Oriented Curriculum

A number of kindergarten programs are returning to a *cognitively oriented developmental curriculum.* A cognitively oriented curriculum is based on principles of cognitive development consistent with Piaget's theory of learning. It is in many ways similar to the Montessori program because children are actively involved in learning. In the cognitively oriented curriculum, children learn through active involvement with numerous manipulative materials. It differs from the Montessori program because children are not limited to using materials in a prescribed way. Rather, teachers are free to provide an infinite range of materials that will increase the probability of children reaching desired goals.

In a cognitively oriented setting the classroom is divided into learning centers. Centers are usually developed for the following: house area, block area, art area, quiet area, music/movement area, sand and water area, and animal/plant area. However, these centers may take on more formal names and coincide with subjects taught in the elementary school. The math area would include blocks, a computer, and classification materials. The language arts center would include reading materials, listening materials, a typewriter, and writing paper. The science area would include plants, animals, magnets, hand lenses, and other items of interest to children.

The social studies center could include maps, globes, clothing for dramatic play, and blocks. Records and books with audio cassettes could also be placed in the social studies center. Children would also be encouraged to work together to develop cooperation and interpersonal skills.

The teachers' responsibilities are demanding and challenging. Teachers in these settings determine appropriate goals for each center and then assure that appropriate activities and manipulative materials are placed in each center. Teachers interact with children while children are working in centers. As they interact with children they ask thought-provoking questions that encourage students to look at the activity from different perspectives.

The planning process for a cognitively oriented curriculum would include identifying topics for centers. The next step would be to identify goals for each center. After identifying goals, children's needs and interests are considered. With the goals and needs of the children in mind, teachers begin collecting and producing materials for each center. Do not panic at the prospect of doing this each day. Once centers have been developed, teachers usually leave the centers in place for several weeks. This enables all children to cycle through the centers. Rather than completely redevelop a center, most teachers modify centers by removing one activity and replacing it with a new one. This may be done on a biweekly basis.

Cognitively oriented curriculums include opportunities for teachers to work with small and large groups of children. Therefore, they must plan small and large group activities.

Table 4–4 illustrates a planning form useful for centers. Table 4–5 illustrates a planning form useful for small and large group activities.

The cognitively oriented curriculum has impressive empirical support. Studies comparing cognitively oriented curriculum programs with teacher-directed programs indicate that both are highly successful means of teaching academic content. However, children participating in cognitively oriented programs tend to have better social and interpersonal skills.

Table 4–4 Learning Center Planning Form

CENTER AREA:			Possible
Goals:	Activities:	Materials:	Questions
1.			
2.			
3.			

Comments to make to children during planning period to introduce the center/activities:

Comments made to children to encourage them to represent their work:

Table 4–5 Small/Large Group Planning Form

Topic:

Goal:

Activity:

Possible questions to ask children:

1.

2.

3.

Opportunity for children to represent the activity:

While few school districts have cognitively oriented curricula, the number of kindergartens using cognitively oriented curricula is increasing. If you intend to teach kindergarten you may be able to arrange your room in centers and utilize a cognitively oriented curriculum. If you teach primary grades you may be able to utilize centers part of each day and capitalize on the benefits of this instructional approach.

Many of the problems encountered in education today could be remedied if more time were set aside for cognitively oriented activities. You should include cognitively oriented activities in your classrooms.

Summary of Models

Each model has potential for improving the quality of education in our elementary schools. You must take the time necessary for thorough planning while simultaneously considering the needs of your students. Several models are more detailed than others and may be more useful for your initial success. As you become more comfortable with the planning process you will begin to consider many of the steps mentally and use a more simplified planning process.

The four models have many similarities. Please reexamine each of the models and note their similarities. You should discover that a variety of terms are used to describe the same idea.

UNIT PLANS

Units are a collection of lessons related to a single topic. They are an excellent means of organizing social studies instruction. Units may include topics such as the American Revolution, manners, a state's natural resources, transportation, community helpers, presidential elections, needs and wants, shelter, historical events, holidays, and other countries. This section of the chapter describes how to develop a unit.

The use of units extends beyond social studies. Once you know how to develop units for social studies topics you can easily use the process to develop units in health, science, language arts, reading, art, and music.

The development of units is appropriate for several important reasons. First, traditional textbooks have several limitations that unit plans can overcome. Textbooks are often difficult to read and they usually do not include presentations of the controversial issues that make social studies interesting. Most textbooks are organized in a manner that permits little time for studying a topic in any depth. Also, constant reliance on the textbook, or any approach, leads to boredom and a reduced interest in social studies.

Unit plans are a means by which teachers can develop lessons that relate more directly to children's needs and interests. Unit plans enable teachers to select a topic from the curriculum, collect a variety of instructional materials and instructional resources related to the topic, and design a series of lessons that are personalized for their students. Portions of the textbook may be included in the unit and then other resources may be added to explore the topic in greater depth.

Teachers who plan units have opportunities to design lessons that actively involve their students in the learning process. As teachers plan their own learning activities they rekindle many of the creative, exciting activities learned during workshops and their college preparation.

While the use of teaching units is widely advocated by professional educators, the realities of classroom life serve to inhibit widespread development of units. Teachers often lack the time and school districts fail to provide monetary support. Also, teachers tend to be quite comfortable relying on their textbooks.

The need for a long-term professional development plan was described in an earlier chapter. As part of your long-term improvement plan, you should consider developing a few units each year and intersperse these units with the use of the textbook. Each year you should continue developing new units and modifying units developed in previous years.

Components of Unit Plans

Because units are a collection of lessons related to one topic, the components of effective lessons apply to the development of units. A sample unit is illustrated in Appendix 4–1. Please refer to the sample unit as you consider the suggestions in the following section that apply to the additional components you need to consider.

First, a unit should have the lessons sequenced in some logical order. The order may proceed from simple to complex, past to present, concrete to abstract, or from easy to difficult. In some units the lesson sequence may be arbitrary.

Second, each unit should have an introductory lesson. The introductory lesson motivates the children and provides them with an overview of the unit. Inductive lessons often work well because they involve children in identifying a concept or solving a problem. Teachers may also present challenging problem statements and indicate that the problems will be answered during the unit.

Units should have a culminating lesson. The culminating lesson provides an opportunity for closure—it puts the finishing touches on the unit and formally ends the unit. Units about different countries often culminate with festivals or food-tasting lessons. Children have an opportunity to savor some of that particular country's culinary traditions. Some teachers require children to prepare projects during the unit and then have the social studies equivalent of a science fair as a culminating activity. Children share their projects with classmates.

Evaluation is an important aspect of instruction and should be included during the unit and at the end of the unit. Evaluation will be discussed in detail in Chapter 6, but at this point it must be mentioned that evaluation may be a formal paper-and-pencil test or it may be based on other criteria. Evaluation criteria may relate to the projects prepared by children, amount of interest displayed by children, and children's oral responses to teacher questions.

In the event you are asked to help prepare a unit for other teachers you may consider adding an introductory statement to your unit. The introductory statement should include a brief summary of the lessons in the unit and a rationale describing the reasons for teaching the unit.

Steps in Developing a Unit

Several steps are involved in developing a unit. While the steps are presented in a specific sequence in this text, you may adapt the sequence for your own planning style.

Step 1. Begin by identifying a topic for the unit and objectives related to the topic. Examine your curriculum guide or your textbook for upcoming topics that may be appropriate for a unit plan. Do this several weeks before you intend to teach the topic so you will have ample time to plan. The objectives you consider at this point are tentative. You will identify specific objectives later.

Step 2. With the identification of a topic and possible objectives, brainstorm possible activities, content, materials, and resources. Pause, reflect, and let the ideas flow. Record your ideas for later use.

Step 3. After an initial brainstorming session, begin examining available materials and resources that may be used in your unit. As you consider the materials and resources you will think of additional items for your brainstorming list.

You might talk to other teachers and your librarian to get their input. They often have excellent ideas.

Students are another resource. Take a few moments to ask them what they think about the topic and what subtopics they would like to explore. They may also identify useful community resources. Add their ideas to your brainstorming list.

Step 4. Review the list of ideas, activities, materials, and resources. Begin organizing your list by eliminating unnecessary items. Then reorganize your list into possible concepts and subtopics. By classifying related ideas together you will form the basis for the lessons within your unit.

Table 4–6 outlines a planning form useful when you reach steps four and five. This form will help you arrange your objectives, materials, and activities in an organized manner prior to preparing detailed lesson plans. This form will serve as a rough blueprint for your unit.

Step 5. Select key concepts, objectives, and learning activities for the lessons. Each lesson should have a goal (conceptual focus) that supports the unit topic. An objective is also needed for each lesson. Materials and activities must support the goal and the objective.

Table 4–6 Draft Planning Form

UNIT TOPIC: Concepts/Objectives	Content	Materials	Activities	Notes
Concept 1				
Objective				
Objective				
etc.				
Concept 2				
Objective				
Objective				
etc.				
Concept 3				
Objective				
Objective				
etc.				

Source: Van Cleaf, D.W. (1986). *Teaching elementary social studies: Supplemental materials.* Unpublished manuscript, Washburn University, Topeka. Reprinted and adapted with permission of the author.

Step 6. Develop individual lesson plans. The choice of a lesson plan format is yours; four were described earlier in the chapter.

Step 7. Teach the unit. As you teach individual lessons, retain a sense of flexibility. You may want to modify and extend lessons as you teach your unit. One exciting characteristic of a unit is that it is your own creation. You have the flexibility to modify the unit and lessons as circumstances change.

Step 8. Reflect on the effectiveness of the lessons and make notes for future changes. You will have invested considerable time developing your unit and will want to use it again.

Unit planning is an effective way to organize social studies instruction. You make decisions regarding the content, materials, and activities for your students. Units require considerable time to prepare, but the benefits are well worth the effort. If you pace yourself and develop a few units each year you will be able to manage your professional responsibilities while creating a greater number of units.

SUMMARY

Well-planned programs are effective programs. By conscientious attention to the planning process you will ensure that you are an effective teacher and that your students are engaged in exciting, purposeful learning.

Four lesson plan models were described. Each has strengths and weaknesses. Consider your style and preferences as you select a planning model appropriate for your use.

Finally, unit planning was described. Developing units will enable you to exercise your professional decision-making skills as you adapt the curriculum in creative ways for your students. The process is time-consuming, but the benefits are well worth it.

SUGGESTED ACTIVITIES

1. Examine a curriculum guide from a school district in your area. Does the curriculum guide include thorough lessons and units?
2. Examine a lesson outline in the teacher's edition of a social studies textbook. Evaluate the effectiveness of the lesson plan. Does the textbook suggest a lesson format that includes a variety of teaching, practice, and application activities?
3. Select a social studies concept and develop a lesson plan using one of the lesson plan formats described in this chapter.
4. Compare the four lesson plan formats by completing Table 4–7.

Table 4–7 Comparison of Four Planning Models

STEPS	TRADITIONAL	HUNTER	TPA	COGNITIVE
1.			Objective	Goal
2.			Teach	Furnish centers
3.			Practice	Plan, work, represent
4.			Apply	Observe children
5.				Refurbish centers
6.				
7.				
8.				

Note: Closure, extension activities, and evaluation procedures should be added to the first three models.

5. Select a social studies topic and develop a social studies unit consisting of at least four lesson plans. Lessons should be designed to teach different concepts related to the topic.

APPENDIX 4–1 Sample Social Studies Unit

The following unit was developed by Theresa Pufahl while she was enrolled in a social studies methods course. Her unit illustrates the components of a unit plan as well as a number of teaching strategies described later in this text.*

TOPIC: Transportation

GRADE LEVEL: First

RATIONALE/INTRODUCTION: Transportation is an integral aspect of children's lives. The ability to satisfy their needs and wants depends on transportation. This unit introduces children to a number of concepts related to transportation. By building on what children already know, this unit will help children develop a better understanding of transportation.

Lesson 1
(One or two days)

GOAL: Children will consider the many modes of transportation

CONCEPTS: Transportation, vehicles, bar graph

BEHAVIORAL OBJECTIVE: Children will list 10 different kinds of transportation

MATERIALS: Positive and negative examples of transportation, transportation flash cards, graph paper, crayons, manilla folders, maps, globe

INTRODUCTION: State, "Today we are going to play a guessing game."

TEACH: (A concept attainment activity—see Chapter 10)

1. Provide the following instructions:

    - I will give you a clue.
    - I will show you some pictures to help think of the answer.
    - Do not say the answer until I ask for it.

2. The clue is—"These are things that people use."
3. Show children the following pictures one at a time, alternating between positive and negative examples. State whether each is a positive or negative example.

Positive Examples	Negative Examples
(1) car	**(1)** Tide detergent
(2) airplane	**(2)** hair curlers
(3) bus	**(3)** furniture
(4) truck	**(4)** toothpaste
(5) bicycle	**(5)** food
(6) motorcycle	**(6)** cat
(7) train	**(7)** teddy bear
(8) roller skates	**(8)** flowers

Source: Theresa Pufahl, student. Reprinted with her permission.

4. Ask children to name other examples of the concept.
5. Ask children to name the concept (transportation).
6. Ask children how each of the examples relates to the concept. For example:

   • Why is a bicycle a form of transportation?
   • Why is a box of Tide not an example?

7. Have children develop a definition of transportation.

PRACTICE: Place transportation flash cards face down. One at a time, have each child pick a card and give the rest of the children clues as to what it is. Other children guess the form of transportation being described.

APPLY: Brainstorm other forms of transportation. List ideas on the chalkboard and have children make a chart of the different kinds that they can think of. Classify them by types (land, air, water or personal use, business use).

In groups of two, assign children destinations. They must determine what forms of transportation could be used to travel to each destination. Possible destinations:

Go to the KWIK Shop to get a candy bar.

Go to Chicago to see a Cubs game.

Travel to California to go to Disneyland.

Travel to Hawaii to see a volcano.

Go to the North Pole to see Santa.

CLOSURE: Have children reexamine their charts and describe the concept of transportation.

EXTENSION ACTIVITIES:

1. Children may draw pictures of various forms of transportation on a manilla folder. Use the folder to store children's work.
2. Take children on a walk around the neighborhood and record the types of transportation they see. Use the data collected to make a bar graph.

EVALUATION: This lesson will be a success if children are able to brainstorm some unusual types of transportation. They must also be able to list at least 10 types of transportation.

Lesson 2
(Two days)

GOAL: Children will recognize and understand traffic signs.

CONCEPTS: Traffic signs and symbols, vehicles, transportation, pedestrian.

BEHAVIORAL OBJECTIVE: Children will match six traffic signs to their meanings.

MATERIALS: Traffic sign flash cards, traffic dominoes, construction paper, yarn, hangers, crayons, hole punch, scissors

INTRODUCTION: Yesterday we talked about different kinds of transportation. Today we will talk about the traffic signs that vehicles must obey.

TEACH: (Guided Discussion—see Chapter 10)

1. Discuss traffic signs as follows:

   • Ask children to provide examples and nonexamples of traffic signs. (*Example:* stop sign; nonexample—restroom sign.)
   • List examples and nonexamples on the board.
   • Ask children what the examples have in common.
   • Ask children what the nonexamples have in common.
   • Ask questions such as the following to allow children to assign an attribute value to the examples:

       (1) Which of these signs do you think is the most important and why?
       (2) Do you think it is more important to stop at a railroad crossing or at a stop sign and why?
       (3) Why do we need to have special signs for handicapped people?
       (4) Would there ever be a time when it would be okay to ignore a red light? If so, when? If not, why?
       (5) Does the importance of the traffic sign depend of whether you are driving or walking?

2. Ask children to develop a definition for traffic signs.
3. Show children the traffic sign flash cards and review the meaning of each sign.

PRACTICE: Play the following matching game:
     Place the traffic sign flash cards face down on the floor. Children pick up a card and tell what sign it is and what it means. If the child is correct, the child keeps the card.

APPLY: Have children draw five different traffic signs and make a mobile by hanging each of the signs on a hanger.

CLOSURE: Have children tell about the traffic signs on their mobiles. Conclude that traffic signs are very important so that drivers and pedestrians can travel safely.

EXTENSION ACTIVITIES:

1. Have children make a display from cardboard with two pockets, one for traffic signs for drivers and one for traffic signs for walkers. Children then make signs and put in appropriate pocket.
2. Play the traffic sign domino game.

EVALUATION: Children will be successful if they can correctly explain the meanings of the six most common traffic signs.

Lesson 3
(Two days)

GOAL: Children will learn the importance of having and obeying traffic rules.

CONCEPTS: Traffic signs, traffic rules, symbols, maps, transportation, vehicles.

BEHAVIORAL OBJECTIVE: Children will demonstrate an understanding of traffic on their neighborhood maps.

MATERIALS: Poster board; toy vehicles; tape.

INTRODUCTION: Today we will discuss the rules that traffic signs represent.

TEACH: Review the meaning of the traffic signs used in the last lesson.

Ask, "Where else do we have rules besides in transportation?" Allow children to give examples to include: home, school, church, games, sports.

Ask, "Why do we need rules at school or in church?" "Why do we need rules on a baseball team?" "Why do we need traffic signs?"

PRACTICE: Present the following moral dilemma (see Chapter 13 for description of the moral dilemma procedure):

Imagine that you are at home playing outside with your dog, Freddy. Suddenly Freddy runs out into the street and is hit by a car. Freddy is hurt and needs to get to the veterinarian right away.

You put Freddy in the car and race off to the vet's office. You're really worried about Freddy and you don't want him to die.

As you drive Freddy to the vet's office, should you ignore the speed limit and drive fast to get to the vet as quickly as possible?

Have children justify their answers by asking *why* they would or would not drive fast.

Finally, *ask* a series of probing questions:

(1)   What might happen if you drive too fast?

(2)   What might happen if you drive at the speed limit?

(3)   Is it more important to save your dog or to be more careful so that you don't put yourself and others in danger? What makes your choice more important?

(4)   Would getting a ticket for speeding be worth saving your dog? Why?

(5)   Which would be more dangerous, driving fast or running through a stoplight? Why?

(6)   Would there ever be a time when it would be okay to break traffic rules? When and why?

APPLY: Have small groups of children develop imaginary neighborhood maps on large sheets of paper. They should include streets, buildings, parks, railroad tracks, etc. Children should determine the locations of traffic signs and place the signs on their maps. Children can then justify their placements at each location. They may also use toy cars and drive imaginary trips.

CLOSURE: Ask children to answer this question, "Why do we need traffic signs and rules?"

EXTENSION ACTIVITIES:

1.   In groups of two have children do a creative writing activity, "What if we had no traffic rules?" Nonreaders may dictate a language experience story.

2.   Children may make a poster encouraging others to obey a traffic sign (such as a speed limit in a school zone).

EVALUATION: This lesson will be a success if children demonstrate an understanding of traffic rules while they construct their neighborhood maps.

Lesson 4
(Two or three days)

GOAL: Children will consider transportation forms of the past and possibilities for the future.

CONCEPTS: Past, future, transportation, vehicles, pioneer life, covered wagon, Oregon Trail, survival, necessities.

BEHAVIORAL OBJECTIVE: Children will list 10 items that people traveling on the Oregon Trail in a covered wagon would need to survive.

MATERIALS: Shoe boxes, tape, construction paper, paper fasteners, cardboard, glue, scissors, crayons, styrofoam, toothpicks, *When Pioneers Pushed West to Oregon* by Elizabeth Rider Montgomery.

INTRODUCTION: Today we are going to learn about a form of transportation that people used a long time ago—the covered wagon.

TEACH: Say, "A very long time ago people traveled in covered wagons. We call these people pioneers."

Briefly provide the following information and show pictures from Montgomery's book.

Many people decided to move west to a new place where: not many people lived, the government would give them free land, the weather was good for farming, the soil was rich, there were trees to build homes and fences, fishing and hunting were good.

The only way to get there was by covered wagon (show picture of covered wagon—front cover of Montgomery's book).

There were no roads, only a trail to follow (show picture of Oregon Trail map, pp. 14, 15 of Montgomery book).

The trip was very slow and long. The wagons could only go two miles an hour and 15 miles per day. Compare to a car today—65 miles an hour and 650 miles or more per day. The trip took six months to complete. There were no lights, no running water, no stoves, and no stores.

The wagons had to cross rivers on rafts (show picture on p. 58).

Sometimes the weather was terrible (show picture on p. 50).

Ask, if you and your family were moving a long way, how would you travel and what would you pack?

Say, "If you listen carefully as I read you will find out how one family prepared to travel along the Oregon Trail in a covered wagon."

Read and paraphrase excerpts from *When Pioneers Pushed West to Oregon.*

PRACTICE: Assign the following inquiry question: "If you were going to travel across the country in a covered wagon, what would you pack?"

Have children work in groups. Provide pictures showing pioneer life. Give them time to look over the pictures, discuss information from the reading, and generate some ideas.

Have children contribute their ideas to a list on the chalkboard (guide children toward necessities for survival).

APPLY:

1. Children will make a covered wagon out of a shoe box.

    - Cover shoe box with brown construction paper.
    - Draw spokes and/or color two sets of wagon wheels.
    - Attach wagon wheels to box with paper fasteners.
    - Glue cover onto box.

2. Have children draw pictures of items that they would need to pack for a pioneer trip using the list they made during the practice portion of the lesson. Then children can pack their things into their covered wagons.

CLOSURE: Have children tell the group one thing that they learned about pioneer travel. Ask them to describe similarities and differences between travel today and in the past.

EXTENSION ACTIVITIES:

1. Provide pictures and information about other historic forms of transportation. Have children make a time line out of a piece of styrofoam. Place a toothpick with a picture of the form in its place along the time line (ships, 1450; railroad, 1825; airplane, 1903; model T, 1908).

2. Make a drawing of a form of transportation of the future. Share drawings with the rest of the class.

EVALUATION: Did children include basic necessities in their covered wagons?

It is good for different types of children to be together. They learn much from each other.

Photograph by C. E. Pefley.

chapter 5

Personalizing Instruction

"Effective teaching involves, first, understanding the individual, then arranging those variable factors in the environment that help a person learn."

(Frymier, 1977, p. 17)[*]

AS YOU READ...

- describe how the following factors affect education: cultural values, learning style, cognitive stages, psychosocial stages, temperament, parenting style, and gender
- consider categories and suggestions for personalizing instruction

[*]*Source:* Frymier, J. (1977). *Annehurst curriculum classification system.* West Lafayette, IN: Kappa Delta Pi. Reprinted by permission of Kappa Delta Pi, an International Honor Society in Education.

INTRODUCTION

To the average person, uncut diamonds have little aesthetic appeal. However, to an experienced diamond cutter each stone is viewed as a potentially valuable gem. The diamond cutter carefully examines each stone, studying its unique characteristics before transforming the stone into a valuable jewel.

Excellent teachers are like diamond cutters. They see each child as having potential and unique characteristics. Effective teachers attempt to make valuable transformations for each of their students. Like the diamond cutter, teachers study their students, plan appropriate strategies for helping them reach their potential, and then use appropriate strategies and activities.

David Elkind (1981b) criticized society and our schools for hurrying children. At one point he compared education in many of our schools to factories. He stated that we have an assembly line form of education in which children are viewed as raw materials on a conveyor belt. Each child receives the same instruction at the same pace. Unlike the diamond cutter and the caring, effective teacher, many adults treat children as if they are identical to all other children. Individual needs and differences are frequently not addressed. Lacking the careful scrutiny of the master diamond cutter, many of our children are subjected to inappropriate instructional techniques.

You will encounter children with a variety of differences. Avoid labeling children because of their differences.

Photograph courtesy of the United Nations.

Children are different. They are individuals with different strengths, needs, personalities, backgrounds, and potentials. Effective teachers recognize these differences and develop lessons based on their students' differences. This is an admittedly challenging task.

Teachers are responsible for managing large groups of children. The demands inherent in managing groups of children often affect teachers' abilities to respond to the personal needs of their students. Teachers frequently develop well-organized procedures for assuring that the classroom is an orderly environment for learning. They frequently rely on large group instruction and teacher-directed techniques to maintain orderly classrooms. Reading, workbook, and ditto sheet activities are often used to teach and manage large-group instruction. However, the use of such activities may not maximize children's learning. With an emphasis on developing well-disciplined classrooms, the needs of individual youngsters may be overlooked.

This chapter presents several dimensions related to individual differences. The chapter then proposes ways to modify instruction in order to meet the individual needs of children.

By describing categories of differences there is a risk of nurturing existing stereotypes. The following discussion is an attempt to describe how children differ, not provide labels or stereotypes for children. Children exhibit multiple characteristics from a variety of dimensions. They cannot and should not be assigned a specific label.

DIMENSIONS OF INDIVIDUAL DIFFERENCES

This section of the chapter presents four categories of differences affecting children and their education. Cultural, intellectual, social-emotional, and gender differences are described. This section also describes the culture of our schools. The term *perspectives* rather than *differences* is used in the following sections to avoid connoting an idea that children who may have notable differences are in any way inferior to other children.

Cultural Perspectives

Culture is a difficult concept to define. It is an expansive concept encompassing aspects affecting everything we do. Culture includes language, lifestyles, social patterns, artistic endeavors, and religious practices. Race, gender, ethnic background, and socioeconomic status embody additional aspects of culture. Culture includes what we believe—a system of values and ideas that affect the way we socialize children, the way we learn and adapt to the environment, and how we view our future.

Kluckhohn (1950) presented a conceptual format for examining cultural values (see Table 5–1). She stated that all cultures and subcultures encounter five human problems. Cultures may be understood by examining how they respond to each of these problems. The five categories and their responses provide teachers with a model for analyzing the personal and cultural perspectives of their students. Social studies teachers may also utilize these categories as a means of helping children compare cultures.

Human Nature. The first problem all cultures encounter is assessing human nature. People may be classified as essentially good, essentially evil, or a combination of good and evil. People who view children as basically evil treat children differently from those who view children as essentially good.

Table 5–1 Kluckhohn's Five Categories of Cultural Values

VALUE CATEGORY AND POSSIBLE RESPONSES	NOTES
Human Nature 1. Evil 2. Good 3. Mixture of good and evil	How cultures view the innate "goodness" of humans.
Humans and Nature 1. Subjugation to nature 2. Harmony 3. Controlling nature	A description of values that cultures have toward the degree of control regarding interactions with the physical world.
Time 1. Past 2. Present 3. Future	Values about time affect behavior and motivation.
Meaning of Activities 1. Being 2. Being-in-becoming 3. Doing	This category provides insight into the way energy is expended. The purpose of activity is also important.
Significant Relationships 1. Lineal 2. Individual 3. Collateral	Describes power and control relationships as well as decision making.

Source: Reprinted from *Social Forces* (Vol. 28, No. 4, May 1950). "Dominant and Substitute Profiles of Cultural Orientations: Their Significance for Analysis of Social Stratification" by Florence Kluckhohn. Copyright © The University of North Carolina Press. Reprinted with permission of *Social Forces* and The University of North Carolina Press.

As a teacher you will encounter children, parents, and other educators who hold differing views on the theme of human nature. Consider your views as you interact with others and as you design learning experiences for your students. The views you hold will affect the way you prepare children for their roles as citizens. If you view children as evil you will exert a type of control that will inhibit the development of skills needed for democratic citizenship.

Humans and Nature.   The second problem all cultures encounter is the type of relationship humans have with nature. The three responses include mastery over nature, harmony with nature, and subjugation to nature. Western societies have adopted the view that people can control nature. We alter the course of rivers, produce hybrids, and develop vaccines to cure illnesses.

Some cultures and subcultures see people as pawns of nature, unable to alter or shape the events affecting their lives. Other cultures espouse a view that people should learn to live harmoniously with their surroundings.

In all likelihood you will encounter an abundance of children whose families value the control of nature. You will also encounter a few children whose families have a more harmonious value.

Time.   The third problem is time. Again, three possible views of time exist. Some cultures are future oriented, some are present oriented, others are oriented toward the past. Western industrialized cultures are future oriented. We do things today in order to build a better tomorrow. We have both immediate and long-term goals.

Traditional China and Japan have had a past orientation. Ancestors are held in high esteem and their traditions exert an influence on their present decisions.

A present orientation tends to exist in undeveloped rural areas of many third world countries. This orientation is also prevalent among people from lower socioeconomic levels. They work for present gratification, they have no significant ties to the past, and no long-range plans for the future. The long-term benefits of education are not valued.

Activity.   The fourth problem is the meaning of activities. The three types of cultural responses include a focus on *doing,* a focus on *being,* or a focus on *being-in-becoming.* Most Americans must "do" something—even to relax. We often measure time and success by how much we have done. Our classrooms keep children busy and provide little time for reflective, analytical thought.

A being orientation may be described as doing what is necessary for survival.

A being-in-becoming orientation may be viewed as an emergence from being to doing. As traditional cultures become influenced by the technological world they tend to move in the direction of the technological world. However, people with a being-in-becoming orientation are caught between the new opportunities and the lack of support from their former culture.

Relationships with Others.   The final cultural problem is relationships with others. Three responses describe the manner in which cultures react to this problem: a lineal orientation, an individual orientation, and a collateral (group) orientation.

The military, with its chain of command, has a lineal orientation. Most young children, through the later elementary grades, also reflect a lineal orientation.

Democratic, capitalistic societies have an individualistic orientation. People work to get ahead, to make a name for themselves, and to out-do others.

Communistic societies have a collateral orientation. Middle school and junior high school children also exhibit a collateral orientation. They are group oriented and make group decisions.

Successful citizens in our society learn how to adapt to a variety of orientations. However, our schools tend to reinforce lineal and individual orientations.

Values affect not only the way people behave but also their aspirations. As a teacher you will encounter children from a variety of settings who hold alternative value orientations. A belief that all children should hold similar aspirations and conform to the value structure of the school and teacher is arrogant and untenable in our democratic society. Teachers and schools must adapt instruction to meet the needs of children with differing value orientations, not expect children to fully embrace and conform to their values. You can help your children achieve their potential without forcing them to abandon their cultural values.

Intellectual Perspectives

Children in your classroom will represent a variety of intellectual differences. Intellectual differences may be described in terms of learning style and the quality of the thought processes. This section describes characteristics of learning style and qualitative differences in thinking. As you read this section of the chapter, take time to consider *your* intellectual style. You might also consider the intellectual characteristics of a close acquaintance.

Learning Style Differences. Learning style has received much attention in recent years. We know that people think differently—they have different styles. There are two important effects of learning style in social studies classrooms. First, teachers tend to view children who have learning styles similar to their styles more favorably. Second, most classrooms rely on one style, thus neglecting the needs of children with other styles.

Kolb (1976) described four types of learning style categories based on differences in the perceiving and processing dimensions of thinking. Kolb identified these as convergers, divergers, assimilators, and accommodators. Characteristics of the four learning styles are illustrated in Figure 5–1.

Engineers, technicians, computer scientists, and accountants exhibit converger traits. Divergers often specialize in the arts, humanities, and social work. Many teachers demonstrate diverger traits. Assimilators enjoy working with theoretical models, reasoning inductively, and integrating information. Assimilators tend to

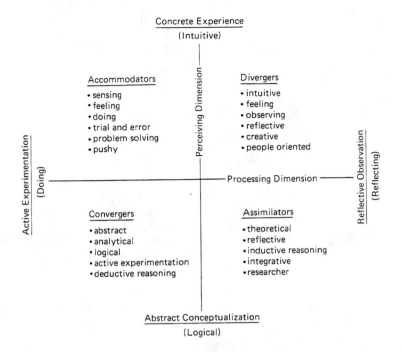

Concrete Experience
(Intuitive)

Accommodators
• sensing
• feeling
• doing
• trial and error
• problem solving
• pushy

Divergers
• intuitive
• feeling
• observing
• reflective
• creative
• people oriented

Perceiving Dimension

Active Experimentation
(Doing)

Reflective Observation
(Reflecting)

Processing Dimension

Convergers
• abstract
• analytical
• logical
• active experimentation
• deductive reasoning

Assimilators
• theoretical
• reflective
• inductive reasoning
• integrative
• researcher

Abstract Conceptualization
(Logical)

Figure 5-1 Characteristics of Kolb's Learning Styles

Source: Van Cleaf, D.W., & Schkade, L.L. (1987). Student teacher learning styles: Another dimension of reform. *Teacher Education and Practice,* 4, pp. 25–34. Reprinted with permission of *Teacher Education and Practice.*

Source: Kolb, D.A. (1976). *Learning style inventory. Technical manual.* Boston: McBer. Adapted with permission of McBer and Company.

be theoretical scientists, researchers, and planners. Accommodators tend to prefer technical and practical occupations such as marketing and sales.

Educators are now considering another aspect of learning style—the relationships between learning and cerebral hemispheric specialization. Left-brain children have different learning needs from those of right-brain children. In addition to left- and right-brain descriptions of learning style, the importance of the limbic system is also being explored. The limbic system controls emotions, long-term memory, and the spiritual aspects of cognition. Figure 5–2 illustrates right- and left-brain as well as cerebral and limbic characteristics.

The school curriculum, which has a left-brain emphasis, appears to hinder the learning of many children. Children include an abundance of both right- and left-brain learners. Further, each teacher likely favors either a left- or right-brain preference. The teacher's task is to select activities and strategies that will meet the different needs of children.

Emotions play an important role in the decision-making process. Many important decisions, including voting preferences, are based on emotional rather

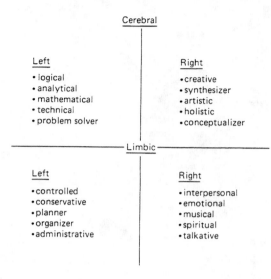

Figure 5–2 Characteristics of Cerebral and Limbic Thought

Source: Van Cleaf, D.W., & Schkade, L.L. (1989). Brain hemisphere preferences of student teachers with selected academic majors. *Teacher Education and Practice, 5,* 39–44. Reprinted with permission of *Teacher Education and Practice.*

than rational thought. You can help your children become better critical thinkers by helping them discover how emotions affect the decision-making process.

Intellectual Differences.   Piaget described differences in the development of intelligence that have been classified into four stages of cognitive development. Of the four stages, two are most prevalent in elementary schools and are described in this section.

Preschool and primary-grade children tend to be in Piaget's preoperational stage. They are intuitive learners embarked on the process of developing logical thought. Preoperational children attend to the salient, most notable characteristic of an event. They derive conclusions from this type of one-dimensional reasoning. For example, a person with gray hair is a grandparent, a person with long hair is female, an American cannot share membership in another group (such as being an American and a Baptist). Preoperational children are beginning to develop a stable classification structure and are learning to arrange items in serial order (first to last, smallest to largest, worst to best, past to present). Socially they are beginning to emerge from egocentric thinking in which they assume everyone thinks and sees the world from their perspective.

During the primary grades and well into the intermediate grades, children are developing concrete operational skills, which represent Piaget's next level of cognitive functioning. They begin to think in terms of classes (or sets) and they can arrange items and events in an orderly series. They are less intuitive and can solve concrete problems more logically. They have difficulty with syllogistic reasoning, solving abstract problems, and thinking hypothetically, which are abilities characteristic of Piaget's formal operational stage.

Some children begin to make a gradual transition to formal operational thinking in the upper elementary years. While children may begin to make this transition, they are not formal operational thinkers and should therefore be taught as concrete operational thinkers.

Children's understanding of social studies concepts are limited by their cognitive abilities. The ability to reason, understand cause-and-effect relationships, and sequence events in chronological order exemplify these limitations.

Social-Emotional Development

Children in your classroom will have a variety of cultural orientations and an array of intellectual abilities. They will also have many different social and emotional characteristics. This section of the chapter describes three factors affecting your students' social and emotional characteristics: psychosocial stages, temperamental predispositions, and the effects of parenting styles.

Psychosocial Differences. Erikson (1963) described the development of emotionally healthy individuals as they progressed through a series of challenges resulting from personal, social, and cultural confrontations. The manner in which these confrontations are resolved affects a person's psychological and emotional development. The first four of Erikson's eight stages affect the elementary child and therefore are appropriate for a brief consideration.

Erikson's first stage, *trust versus mistrust,* occurs during infancy. Infants need to develop a sense that the environment is relatively predictable and supportive. The second stage is *autonomy versus shame or doubt.* In this stage children must learn to control objects, people, and events in their world. They test and challenge adults as well as siblings. Of course, they must also learn that there are limits to their autonomous exercises.

The preschool years are a time of wonder and exploration for young children. During the third stage, *initiative versus guilt,* children need opportunities to exercise initiative by exploring their world, testing their abilities, and satisfying their insatiable curiosity. The numerous questions young children ask is one example of their initiative.

Young children enter both school and the fourth stage, *industry versus inferiority,* at about the same time. In modern Western society, children must learn to read, write, quantify their world, and interact with diverse groups in socially acceptable ways. Essentially, children in the industry stage must develop a belief that they are learning the skills of society and will therefore be able ultimately to participate successfully as adults.

Children who have not resolved the first three stages prior to entering school pose special challenges for teachers. For some children, teachers will need to nurture a sense of trust. Other children may need opportunities and encouragement to develop autonomy within the classroom setting. Other children may need opportunities and encouragement to exercise initiative. You need to be aware of their needs and modify instruction and expectations to help them resolve social-emotional needs while learning essential skills.

Temperamental Differences. Children appear to be born with temperamental differences that affect both their socialization and their behavior in school. Thomas and Chess (1977) identified three types of temperament. Some children are relatively easy to raise and are referred to as *Easy Children.* They adapt well to new situations and generally have positive dispositions. There are, of course, youngsters who are difficult to work with. They react intensely to new ideas and changes in the environment; they are also moody and somewhat negative. These youngsters are called *Difficult Children.* The third group is relatively passive. Children in this category respond slowly to change. In the classroom they often have difficulty beginning and finishing work. These children have been called *Slow-to-Warm-Up Children.*

None of these groups are more or less intelligent than others, but they do have different predispositions for responding to learning and change. While Easy Children pose no special challenges, they may be overlooked because of demands made by the other children. Difficult Children are manageable, but you need to be firm, consistent, and persistent with them. Choose your "battles" carefully with Difficult Children so you are not reacting to everything they do. These youngsters are the ones who need to expel excess energy and should not be denied recess.

Slow-to-Warm-Up Children are not lazy, although it would be tempting to dismiss them as lazy. They work slowly, may become confused if tasks appear overwhelming, and often have difficulty initiating tasks. These children are capable of doing the work, but they need to have assignments modified. Break up tasks and assignments into smaller, more manageable parts. Slow-to-Warm-Up Children also need more encouragement than do Easy Children. Provide praise and feedback for these youngsters as they complete portions of their work rather than waiting for them to complete the entire task.

Parenting Style Differences. Parent styles also have an impact on the children you will teach. Baumrind (1967, 1971) studied a group of preschool children and found that they could be classified into three categories. Children in two of the groups had difficulty interacting with other children and appeared to be less content than children in the third group. Baumrind also questioned the children's parents and discovered a relationship between parent styles and children's behaviors. Baumrind discovered three parent styles corresponding to the three types of children. More recent studies have confirmed Baumrind's findings.

Permissive parents lack a belief that they can exercise control over their children. They have rules, but impose the rules inconsistently and fail to control negative behaviors. While many permissive parents love their children, they fail to provide the guidelines and control necessary for the development of psychological security. Their children have weak role models and therefore get mixed signals regarding appropriate and inappropriate behaviors. Thus, the children lack self-control and are not as content as children associated with authoritative parents.

Authoritarian parents tend to exercise control that is too rigid. They often expect children to do things they are not developmentally capable of performing. Standards are established, but frequently are beyond the capabilities of the children. Authoritarian parents often do not express a warm, loving acceptance of their children. Rather, they tend to remain distant and do not openly express affection. These parents also tend to use negative forms of punishment to control their children. The children have difficulty "measuring up" to their parents' expectations and do not receive adequate emotional support. They are anxious and often have ineffective social skills.

Authoritative parents exercise control and have expectations that are appropriate for the developmental levels and abilities of their children. These parents also tell children the reasons for rules and expectations and allow the children to seek justification for parental decisions. Children's independence is also nurtured by authoritative parents. Finally, authoritative parents have a warm, loving relationship with their children.

Children raised in authoritative settings generally are well adjusted, have good social skills, and exercise initiative. These children behave in responsible ways in classrooms and other social settings. Children raised and educated in this type of atmosphere are more likely to demonstrate positive citizenship behaviors.

You need to have appropriate expectations and you should express a warm, loving regard for your students. However, you must also exercise appropriate control. Good teachers, like good parents, should be authoritative.

In an ideal classroom you would expect to see children working independently, attempting difficult problems with little frustration, and contributing to the smooth functioning of the classroom. Few classrooms are ideal because many children do not have the personal and emotional characteristics necessary to function this way. Erikson's theory, temperamental differences, and parenting style affect the behaviors of children. You must provide a classroom atmosphere that supports children's emotional needs if you hope to help them achieve academically.

Gender Differences

Many commonly held beliefs about differences between the behaviors and abilities of boys and girls are not consistently supported by research. Many of the past research results reporting significant differences were flawed. In summarizing the primary differences between boys and girls, Gage and Berliner (1988) stated that boys tend to be more aggressive than girls. They also reported that girls tend to perform better on tasks of verbal ability whereas boys perform better in the areas of mathematics and spatial ability. This does not imply that all boys are more aggressive and better in math than girls. Nor does this mean that all girls have better verbal skills than do boys. These are group comparisons, but individuals within one group often perform better than many individuals within the opposite group.

Many of the perceived differences between boys and girls result from cultural expectations. We often expect children of one sex to behave in one way, children of the opposite sex to behave in yet another way. Thus, children's behaviors may be the result of the way adults socialize them rather than inherent biological differences.

You should examine your values regarding gender-appropriate behavior. Do you expect boys to be independent problem solvers in your classroom? Do you expect girls to be passive and more dependent on you for help? In classrooms led by teachers who held similar expectations for boys and girls, behavior and achievement scores for the two sexes were similar.

Boys can develop sophisticated verbal skills, and girls can develop sophisticated spatial and mathematical abilities. The extra aggression demonstrated by boys can be channeled, and girls can be encouraged to become more independent and assertive. Boys and girls can think critically and develop altruistic attitudes. Boys and girls are equally capable of developing leadership skills. The increase in the number of women elected and appointed to leadership positions illustrates the point. The teacher is the key, however. Your children will achieve in direct proportion to your expectations.

Summary: The Culture of the School

Schools have been criticized for not adapting to the individual needs of their students. Instruction in many social studies classes consists of students reading from a textbook and completing workbook pages or ditto sheets. Most of the instruction occurs in teacher-directed, large-group settings. While children enrolled in our classrooms represent a variety of cultural backgrounds, cognitive abilities, and social-emotional characteristics, there is little instructional variety. Children are expected to conform to the prevailing values and instructional format.

The cultural categories proposed by Kluckhohn can be used to describe the culture of many schools. Schools appear to be middle-class institutions supporting middle-class values. Our schools tend to view children as a mixture of good and evil, with slightly more emphasis placed on the evil end of the continuum. Our schools promote a cultural value of humans over nature. We keep children busy throughout the day "doing things." Little time is provided for reflection, daydreaming, or play. Our schools are oriented toward individual development rather than group efforts.

Children arrive at school with a variety of intellectual differences. They have different learning styles and function at varying levels of cognitive development. The school has a left-brain curriculum that may not be appropriate for right-brain learners. Teachers have a predominate teaching style that often conflicts with children's cultural values and needs.

Temperamental differences and the effects of parenting styles must also be considered. Schools often expect all students to behave as if they had easy temperaments and came from authoritative homes. Schools often expect all students to be able to sit and concentrate for similar lengths of time. They expect students to be polite and responsive to our requests. Some students readily adapt to our expectations, but others cannot.

Our classrooms are occupied by both boys and girls. While we have many culturally based expectations for them, we must realize that we are educating children for roles as democratic citizens. Women are assuming a greater number of leadership roles and men are assuming more nurturing roles. We cannot inhibit our children's future because of expectations based on inappropriate culturally ascribed gender differences.

PERSONALIZING INSTRUCTION: PRINCIPLES AND STRATEGIES

The first part of this chapter described factors affecting individual children. This part suggests ideas you may use to develop instruction appropriate for the personal needs of your students.

The concept of personalizing instruction means that you examine the nature of your students and the nature of the content you teach. You must then bring the two together. You may use individualized learning, small-group learning, and whole-group learning to personalize instruction.

It is rewarding for a teacher to help individual children and see them progress.
Photograph by Laimute E. Druskis.

As teachers make decisions regarding the relationship between content and students, they make decisions about the objectives they select and the degree of mastery students will be expected to demonstrate. Time, reteaching provisions, room arrangement, selection and adaptation of materials, and the types of instructional activities are additional factors involved in decisions to personalize instruction. The following suggestions are classified under these factors.

Content Decisions

While you are responsible for teaching goals and objectives outlined by your curriculum, you have a responsibility to adapt the curriculum to meet the needs of your students. If you do not have that flexibility you and your students will experience difficulties.

One method of personalizing content decisions is to determine the minimum degree of mastery you expect all your students to attain. This will enable you to ensure that your slower students master essential objectives. Of course, many of them will be capable of achieving well beyond the minimum level. You should plan additional activities that will extend learning beyond the minimum level for your more capable students.

The use of extension activities is another method of personalizing content decisions. Some youngsters work more quickly than others, and some have a better understanding of a concept than do others. Children who finish early or who express an interest to pursue a topic in greater depth may have their personal needs satisfied through extension activities. Of course, extension activities should be creative, challenging, and require little teacher supervision. They should not be additional drill-and-practice problems. Sample extension activities include constructing crossword puzzles, illustrating data on graphs, or solving perplexing problems.

Content decisions should also include considerations of children's experiential backgrounds. While teacher's guides and curriculum guides often recommend teaching specific content to students, they cannot address your own students' specific needs. The suggestions in these guides should be modified so they are appropriate for your classroom.

For example, a curriculum guide might specify an objective, learning to use coordinates to locate places on a map, and suggest using a map of the United States. You could adapt the lesson by substituting a map of your neighborhood or city. The children will learn how to use coordinates, but they will be using a map of a more familiar environment. Many curricula include an objective related to satisfying needs and wants. To develop this objective the guide might suggest using a textbook passage illustrating a distant setting using a white middle-class scene. You could adapt the content and include illustrations of people representing ethnic variations consistent with the ethnic composition of your community. Once you recognize that most objectives and concepts can be taught utilizing a variety of topics and materials you will be more capable of personalizing instruction.

Workbooks and ditto sheets are used extensively in many classrooms. While they have their limitations, they may be modified in various ways and used more effectively. First, you may skip inappropriate pages. Second, you may delete inappropriate questions or problems. Third, do not use workbook and ditto sheet assignments as busy work. Students most in need of additional assistance will get the least benefit from busy work. Fourth, rewrite important pages and include your own questions. They should be open-ended, thought-provoking questions.

Time

Time is a variable that affects learning. The more time you provide for learning, the more students will learn. However, there are limitations that affect personalizing instruction. As you examine objectives in the curriculum you must decide how long you will allocate for each objective. Some objectives may be inappropriate for your students and may be skipped. For example, most social studies text series include concepts of latitude and longitude as early as third grade. These terms are inappropriate for most elementary school students and should be avoided.

Other objectives may be relatively unimportant and should receive minimal time. Younger children often spend time learning about appropriate dress for winter activities. This is a topic with which children in northern regions are familiar and should therefore receive minimal emphasis.

You will also identify important objectives. Allocate more time to these objectives.

Time and a child's working speed interact and can create difficulties for teachers. Slow-to-Warm-Up Children are capable learners, but they work slowly. Some children are perfectionists and spend too much time attending to unnecessary details. For children who need more time to complete tasks you might consider modifying the task. Rather than requiring them to do every item, you may reduce the number of items they are required to complete. They will be more likely to complete the limited number of tasks and feel successful for the work they have completed. If they are inundated with too much work they will complete less, become frustrated, and may create discipline problems. You can improve the rate at which they work, but this is a long-term process requiring continuous efforts and must be premised on success.

Time is a variable that contributes to achievement discrepancies between fast and slow learners. We often move more capable children quickly through the curriculum. We expose them to more content and skills than slower learners. Slower learners are paced slowly through the curriculum, usually more slowly than they are capable of proceeding. Consequently, they fall further behind other children. Consider your expectations of children and then examine how you pace their learning.

Reteaching

Some children will learn the material the first time it is presented. Others will require reteaching. The reasons for this are varied. Children must relate the topic to their past experiences—they must make connections between the information you teach and their own knowledge. Some materials may use inappropriate cultural references; some information may not relate to a child's prior experiences. At times there may be inconsistencies between the teaching style and the child's learning style.

As you plan instruction consider alternative ways to teach the information. Then, if several children do not understand the information, you can reteach the information using one of the alternatives. Care should be taken so you don't teach the information in the same manner it was taught the first time. You may subject children to a "double dose" of the same failure.

Reteaching usually occurs while other children are engaged in practice or application activities. As children are working you should monitor their work and provide reteaching opportunities for those experiencing difficulties. You may also reteach an objective when the other students have left the classroom (after school or during recess).

Grouping

Grouping children in a variety of ways and for a variety of reasons is a way to personalize instruction. At times children's personal needs may be met by grouping together youngsters with similar abilities. In other instances it may be feasible to group children according to their interests. For example, a unit of study about family roles may require groups of first-grade children to explore roles as a group project. Children could be assigned to groups according to their interest in one of the roles.

Cooperative learning strategies provide another aspect to grouping. In cooperative learning situations children are assigned to small groups and expected to help one another learn. Cooperative learning will be described in later chapters.

Room Arrangement

Room arrangement has an effect on learning. If you want to implement individualized learning you should arrange the room so children have access to the materials while being able to work independently. The use of learning centers and research centers will require a room arrangement that allows children to receive large-group instruction as well as freedom to move from assigned seats to areas of the classroom containing the centers. Extensive use of grouping strategies requires a classroom arrangement in which children sit facing one another. Desks can be turned toward each other, tables may be used, and work areas in the room may be designated for group activities. If you prefer to teach children as a large group using teacher-directed methods you will want to arrange your room with children sitting in rows facing the area from which you will teach.

Curriculum Materials

Curriculum materials and instructional activities (the next topic) often overlap. Therefore, as you read these two sections you should consider how these two topics support one another.

One method of personalizing instruction for children who have difficulty reading curriculum materials is to rewrite the material. You can retain the basic content while modifying the vocabulary and readability of the passage. This is a time-consuming process, however, and you could enlist the support of a parent volunteer or teacher aide.

If rewriting the text is not feasible you could modify the passages in an existing text. You might eliminate unnecessary words and sentences, thus reducing the amount of material children are required to read. Simply marking through unnecessary sentences may be all that is necessary.

An alternative to editing and rewriting reading materials is to record the text information on an audio cassette. Poorer readers could listen to the cassette as they read along in the text. Again, because of constraints on your time you might consider enlisting the help of an aide, a volunteer, or one of your more capable readers.

Curriculum materials should reflect the cultural values of your children. As you consider curriculum materials, examine the values, customs, and lifestyles portrayed. Children from different cultures extract different information when exposed to the same materials. Your children will learn more readily if they can relate their social studies materials to their personal experiences.

Curriculum materials should also represent the values, customs, and lifestyles of cultures *not* reflected in your children's backgrounds. Children need opportunities to learn about similarities and differences between their own culture and other cultures. A primary emphasis of multicultural education programs is to help children develop an understanding and appreciation of other cultures. Curriculum materials should be selected to support this aim.

Curriculum materials should address the personal characteristics of your children. For example, Frymier (1977) helped classify curriculum materials based on social, emotional, intellectual, and motivational characteristics of children. Matching curriculum materials with the characteristics of your students will increase their interest in the subject and will maximize achievement.

The computer is a relatively new instructional material. Computers may be used for drill and practice, programming, word processing, games, simulations, and data base construction. Computers can be exciting if the programs are exciting, or they can be as boring as the worksheet. Computers can help you personalize instruction if you select appropriate programs for your students. They can also be highly effective devices if you allow youngsters to work together at the computer.

Games and simulations are effective and exciting learning materials. They actively involve children and enable them to practice and master information in a motivating manner. Instruction is personalized through games and simulations because of their motivational value and the feedback that is provided.

Instructional Strategies and Activities

Teachers and students engage in a variety of activities in the teaching-learning process. Teacher strategies include talking, demonstrating, questioning, monitoring and reteaching, modeling, and assigning work. Children's activities include listening, completing worksheets, manipulating materials, playing games, reading, and making projects. Variety is indeed the spice of life and is essential for personalizing instruction. The following activities will help you personalize instruction. Many of these ideas are developed in greater detail in other chapters of this text.

Active Involvement. Perhaps the best way to personalize instruction is to involve your children actively in the use of manipulative materials. Manipulatives may include blocks, salt dough maps, games, and clothes used for dramatic play. Manipulative activities include constructing graphs, maps, and time lines as well as learning reference skills by participating in inquiry activities. Learning is a process of making intellectual connections between what students know and what you want them to learn. Manipulating materials encourages students to make these connections in personally meaningful ways.

Manipulative activities should have an educational purpose. If children are interacting with materials for no apparent educational purpose you may be wasting valuable instructional time. As children interact with manipulative materials you should monitor their activities and ask them to describe their work. Encourage your students to explain their work and how they think the activity relates to your objective. Thought-provoking questions and suggestions encourage youngsters to make the necessary connections between their activities and your educational purposes.

Products. Requiring children to make a product related to their activities is also a developmentally appropriate method of personalizing instruction. The Ypsilanti Perry Preschool Project's cognitively oriented curriculum (Hohmann, Banet, & Weikart, 1979) requires children to represent (illustrate) what they have learned. Children may tell others what they have learned, but they are encouraged to make concrete products illustrating what they have learned. Children may create maps, cartoons, posters, songs, or language-experience stories as they represent their knowledge.

Representing learning requires youngsters to reconsider the information and apply it in a different way. This allows teachers to evaluate each child's level of understanding. This also incorporates creativity into the learning process because children are encouraged to represent their thinking in a variety of creative, personally meaningful ways. Responding to questions at the end of a social studies reading passage requires children to represent their learning, but is overused and therefore relatively ineffective. Creative alternatives are needed.

Individualizing. Individualizing instruction is another way to personalize teaching. Teachers can plan lessons for individual children as a means of responding to specific needs. There are a variety of continuous progress materials on the market that enable children to proceed through a set of objectives at their own pace. Programmed learning materials and many computer-assisted instructional programs allow youngsters to proceed at their own pace.

Programmed learning materials and individualized instruction strategies appear to be more appropriate in subjects such as math and reading. Objectives and skills in these subjects are sequenced according to difficulty, thus allowing children to move from levels of lesser complexity to levels of greater complexity. Social studies is a subject that does not readily lend itself to individualized work. Many of the goals and objectives of social studies are based on topics rather than sequenced according to complexity. Further, social studies goals and objectives attempt to help children develop social-interaction skills. These skills are seldom nurtured through individualized work.

Grouping Students. Grouping strategies, although described earlier, warrant a brief inclusion in this section. Children can support one another's learning when assigned to groups.

Independent Study. Independent study projects are another means of personalizing instruction. Children may select an aspect of a social studies topic being taught and conduct an in-depth study of the topic. This investigation can be managed by developing a contract with children. The contract should specify the topic of the children's independent study project, questions they intend to investigate, possible resources, and projects that will enable them to illustrate (represent) their findings. The teacher then guides children through the process. Children become experts on an aspect of the topic and can generalize that expertise to other aspects of the topic. Independent study projects are also more effective when two or three youngsters work together.

Independent study projects should not be limited to older and more capable children. Primary-grade children and low-achieving children can also benefit from independent study activities.

Questioning. Questioning techniques are yet another method of personalizing instruction. Questions may be low-level, recall questions requiring children to reconsider important factual data. Higher-level questions should also be asked. Higher-level questions are open-ended and require children to consider the application of information to their own lives. Effective questioning strategies are described in Chapter 11.

Learning Centers. Learning centers are used effectively by many teachers to personalize instruction. The teacher develops a series of learning centers and then cycles children through the centers. Each center may have required activities as well as a selection of alternative activities. As children work in the centers they choose activities most appealing to their interests and needs. (See Figure 5–3.)

Tutors. Tutors are valuable assets and have been used effectively to meet the needs of many children. Gifted and talented children might work with a tutor who acts as a mentor. The mentor helps these children explore possibilities in the areas of their strengths and interests. Parent volunteers have been used to provide help for children needing basic skills assistance. Volunteers can often provide children with the individual help and personal attention a busy teacher cannot provide.

Peers may also be used as tutors and older children can tutor younger children. The tutor and the children receiving the help benefit from the tutoring arrangement.

Variety. A theme that runs throughout this text is variety. A variety of instructional strategies will enable you to maintain children's interest while providing alternatives appropriate for their various learning styles. Role playing, inquiry, demonstrations, films, discussions, simulations, games, and the use of moral dilemmas are alternative strategies that add variety to instruction and facilitate personalized instruction.

Figure 5–3 An example of a learning center. Learning centers are a means of personalizing instruction.

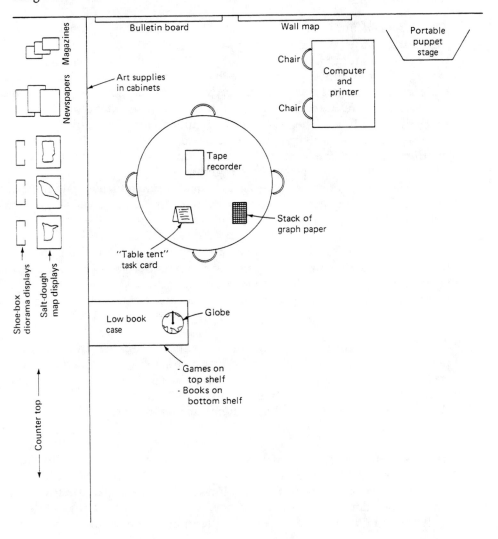

SUMMARY

Individual rights, freedoms, and responsibilities are important values in our society. We defend an individual's right to speak freely, worship freely, select an occupation freely, and associate freely. A major goal of the socialization process is to help children embrace the importance of individual freedoms and individual differences in a democratic society. We can only do this by recognizing and celebrating individual differences in our young.

This chapter described factors contributing to individual differences in children. Cultural, intellectual, social-emotional, and gender differences were described. Each one of these topics contributes to the challenges of teaching. The teacher's role is to develop instruction that makes learning appropriate for students. This can be done by recognizing differences in your students and personalizing instruction for them.

Personalizing instruction is not an easy task. It will be difficult to personalize instruction effectively as you begin your professional career. However, you can gradually improve your ability to personalize instruction and thus improve your effectiveness. To do this, consider the needs of your students and reflect on the effects of your instruction. Gradually try new ideas and judge the effects of your new ideas. Nine separate suggestions were listed in this chapter to help you make your teaching more meaningful for the personal needs of your students. The suggestions presented in the following chapters will also help you.

SUGGESTED ACTIVITIES

1. Observe an elementary-age child in a variety of settings. Then develop a summary of the child's characteristics utilizing the topics presented in this chapter.

2. Compare the description of the child you studied with a summary of a different child prepared by one of your classmates. Identify differences in the educational needs of the two children.

3. Administer conservation and formal operations tasks to children to determine how they reason (such tasks are described in many educational psychology texts).

4. Observe and sketch the room arrangement of several elementary classrooms. Note the arrangements of the desks and the existence of learning-center activities on bulletin boards, tables, and countertops. To what extent do teachers arrange their rooms to personalize instruction?

Children enjoy displaying their work. Everyone likes to be praised and encouraged for their talents.

Photograph by Laima Druskis.

chapter 6

The Evaluation Process

But is my child trying hard?

(Parent)

AS YOU READ...

- describe the limitations of current evaluation practices
- describe the major purposes for evaluating children
- define key evaluation terms
- diagram the evaluation cycle
- describe alternative formal and informal ways to evaluate children

INTRODUCTION

One of the observations that emerge from parent–teacher conferences is the response received from parents when they learn that their child is not achieving well. Invariably their immediate response is: "But is my child trying hard?" Although the child's academic development is an important aspect of education, the child's personal development and social development are also important.

As you begin working in an elementary school setting you will discover a tremendous emphasis is placed on evaluating children. Sadly, most of the formal evaluation occurring in elementary schools focuses on the acquisition of knowledge, not personal or social aspects of learning related to democratic citizenship. To make matters seemingly worse, the types of knowledge tested are considered low-level, recall information.

Sometimes it helps if the parent and the teacher can talk to a student at the same time.
Photograph by Vista/Floridal Caravella.

The questions posed by parents when informed that their children are not performing well academically indicate that parents are concerned about other types of learning. Parents and teachers know that children must be educated to do more than recall information from memory. Children must be educated to work hard, persevere, get along with others, and utilize knowledge in practical and beneficial ways.

If these kinds of abilities are important, their importance is not reflected in the types of evaluations frequently used in our schools. Studies of the types of questions contained in teaching materials and the types of questions asked by teachers indicate an overwhelming reliance on lower-level questions.

There is cause for optimism. Recently an increased emphasis has been placed on developing children's critical-thinking abilities. If critical-thinking abilities are developed, new forms of evaluation will need to be utilized in classrooms to assess children's progress. Several states are now mandating changes in the way students are taught and evaluated. For example, Illinois and Michigan are among the first states to develop tests that assess higher-level knowledge. These states require teachers to include evaluations of students' higher-level thought processes.

The benefits of asking higher-level questions have research support. When teachers ask higher-level questions, students' achievement improves significantly.

Evaluation is a necessary aspect of effective teaching. Evaluation has many beneficial outcomes. Yet current evaluation practices in the elementary schools have serious limitations. This chapter describes the purposes of evaluation, the vocabulary of evaluation, the evaluation cycle, limitations of evaluation, and a variety of formal and informal suggestions for evaluating social studies.

This chapter serves as an introduction to the evaluation process. It is not designed to make you an expert on testing and evaluation. Such an expertise develops with experience as well as participation in additional education classes and workshops.

THE PURPOSES OF EVALUATION

Evaluation has many useful purposes. School districts evaluate the effectiveness of their programs and their teachers. At the classroom level, teachers use testing and evaluation techniques for a variety of reasons.

To Plan and Evaluate Classroom Instruction

The measurement and evaluation process is a cycle rather than an endpoint in the instructional process. Effective teachers are constantly assessing their students. The model, presented in Figure 6–1, illustrates the cyclical nature of the process.

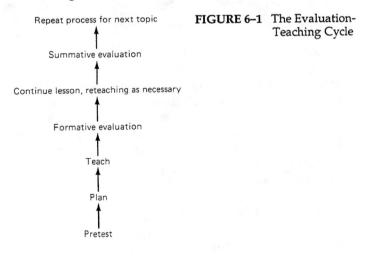

Repeat process for next topic

↑

Summative evaluation

↑

Continue lesson, reteaching as necessary

↑

Formative evaluation

↑

Teach

↑

Plan

↑

Pretest

FIGURE 6–1 The Evaluation-Teaching Cycle

Effective teachers evaluate students prior to teaching as an aspect of the planning process. The pretest may indicate what parts of the topic may need to be presented more carefully, aspects of the topic children are more interested in, and children who know the material well enough to "test out" of the lesson. Based on pretest information, teachers can personalize teaching and make lessons more relevant for their children.

Effective teachers measure and evaluate, usually informally, during the lesson. This is called *formative evaluation*. Teachers ask questions, solicit students' comments, and assign sample practice problems to determine if students understand the lesson. This information is used to make decisions to continue with the lesson or to reteach portions of the lesson.

Effective teachers evaluate students at the end of a lesson, a process called *summative evaluation*. Teachers evaluate at this point to determine how well the goals and objectives have been mastered.

Teachers measure and evaluate students periodically, such as at the end of a chapter or a unit. End-of-chapter and end-of-unit evaluations are done to gain insights into how well students remember the important information and skills taught in a series of lessons.

Effective teachers measure and evaluate their charges before, during, and after instruction. They evaluate as a means of planning and evaluating instruction.

To Diagnose

Evaluation serves a diagnostic function. Teachers may use diagnostic tools to evaluate a student having difficulties. Formal diagnostic testing is not prevalent in social studies; most diagnostic tests are limited to reading, language arts, and mathematics. However, results of reading and mathematics diagnostic tests can provide useful information for social studies teachers. For example, if you discover that your students have weak reading skills you will need to modify the way you use text materials.

To Differentiate Instruction

Evaluation information obtained from diagnostic tests is often used to identify the types of instructional strategies students may need. Evaluation information is also used to make pacing decisions. You may decide to spend more time on a certain part of the lesson. You may decide that some students may need additional practice while others will need extension activities. Evaluation information provides knowledge that will enable you to modify and personalize instruction for every member of the class.

To Select and Place Children

Many elementary schools group children by ability levels. In many classrooms children are grouped into a high group, an average group, or a low group.

Although many schools group children in reading, language arts, and math, they often do not group children by ability in social studies and science. Many educators believe that children need opportunities to work with children of differing ability levels and social backgrounds. They argue that a mixed, heterogeneous grouping policy is appropriate in social studies and science.

To Inform Parents

Parents are partners in the educational process. Parents have a right and a need to know how their children are performing in school.

To Reinforce Children

Children need feedback about the results of their efforts. They need feedback from the teacher to inform them that they are doing well. They also need to know when they are not doing well and what they can do to improve. New teachers are frequently surprised when they tell children that they are doing well and children respond, "Really! I wasn't sure."

To Reinforce the Teacher

Teachers need to know how well they are doing. Evaluation will provide you with feedback about the success of your efforts. If you have done well you are reinforced for your work. If your students do not do well, you have information that will enable you to improve.

School districts and teachers evaluate students for a variety of reasons. Effective evaluation will enable you to improve your teaching, adapt instruction to meet the needs of your students, assess the effectiveness of new strategies and activities, and communicate students' progress to students and their parents.

THE VOCABULARY OF EVALUATION

Before considering additional evaluation topics it may be helpful to define several terms related to the evaluation process. The terms are listed under two categories: measurement and evaluation. *Measurement* is essentially a means of collecting information about students' progress. *Evaluation* refers to the types of professional judgments teachers make based on the information they obtain through the measurement process. This section does not present an exhaustive list of terms, only a minimum number essential for your initial teaching success.

Measurement

To measure is to count. We measure temperature, height, and weight. We also measure children's abilities and achievement.

Measurement in education often requires the use of tests and numbers. A test is a measurement device used in schools to produce scores. Teachers collect scores from a variety of measurement devices to make evaluations (judgments) about children.

Test. A test is a formally prepared device used to measure students' abilities, achievement, or interests. Most tests require paper-and-pencil responses.

Many formally prepared tests are used by teachers. Some of these tests are developed to coincide with chapters or sections of a textbook series. *Norm referenced* and *criterion referenced* tests are other examples of formally prepared tests.

Pretest. A pretest is conducted prior to planning or delivering instruction. Pretests are used to determine a student's needs, knowledge levels, or interests.

Posttest. This is a test given after a lesson or unit has been completed. Teachers usually use posttests to measure mastery of a lesson's objectives.

Mean. This is another word for the term *average.*

Scores. A score is usually a numerical representation of a student's work. *Raw scores* indicate the number of items the student responded to correctly. *Percentiles* are ratios based on a 100-point scale.

Dispersion. Dispersion is a term used to describe the range of scores. Simply reporting a mean score may be misleading. Scores must be examined to determine the range of the scores used to produce the mean. For example, a first-year teacher had several situations in which children's report card grades were in the above-average range. They consistently received high grades for projects and tests but seldom completed the written daily assignments. An analysis of the dispersion among the children's grades indicated certain strengths and weaknesses.

Test Bias. This is a term used to describe the possible negative effects that occur when a test favors one group over another. Many tests have been criticized because they tend to be biased in favor of white middle-class children. Minority children may have difficulty on certain tests because of the wording of questions or the examples used in the questions.

Teachers must be careful when constructing tests to ensure that tests are not biased against poor readers or differences related to gender, learning style, or culture.

Evaluation

Evaluation is the process of considering information for the purpose of making a judgment. The report card grade exemplifies one type of evaluation. Teachers use a variety of formal and informal procedures to collect information so they can assign report card grades. Formal devices, such as teacher-made and professionally prepared tests, are one source of information. Informal procedures include the use of observational records and number of assignments completed.

Formative Evaluation. Formative evaluation occurs during the instructional process. Teachers observe children, ask questions, and assign practice problems to assess understanding.

Summative Evaluation. Summative evaluation usually occurs at the end of a chapter or at the end of a unit.

Grades. Letter grades are judgments based on analysis of a student's work. They may be used to indicate the quality of a single assignment or to report progress for an entire reporting period. They are quite subjective because the teacher makes personal decisions regarding what to teach, what to test, and the minimum scores for each grade.

Many other terms are used in test and measurement literature. The terms described in this section will enable you to proceed with the remainder of the chapter.

LIMITATIONS OF EVALUATION

It was recently reported that standardized achievement test results in each of the states were in the above-average range. It would appear that there are no states in the below-average range, prompting some to ask, "How can everyone be above average?"

There is excessive emphasis placed on testing children on a regular basis, and there are several problems with current testing practices. This section of the chapter describes several major difficulties with testing and evaluation.

Low-Level Questions

As mentioned earlier, most tests administered by classroom teachers are considered low-level, recall-type tests. Here teachers require children to learn recall information as a means of demonstrating acceptable achievement. Teachers, as a rule, do not administer tests requiring children to apply information or use analytical abilities. As a result, children quickly discover one aspect of the school's hidden curriculum—if you intend to earn good grades, study the facts.

Weak Correlations (Relationships)

Standardized achievement tests frequently do not test many of the goals and objectives stressed in a school district's curriculum. Gage and Berliner (1988) reported findings based on comparisons of objectives taught in three fourth-grade math texts and objectives tested by five standardized achievement tests. They indicated that the relationship between the number of objectives taught and the number of objectives tested ranged from 47 percent to 71 percent. Thus, in many situations fewer than half of the items on a standardized achievement test were presented in the textbook.

The same phenomenon is found at the classroom level. Classroom teachers frequently use tests that do not adequately test the information and skills emphasized during instruction—even when the tests are prepared by textbook publishers.

Misuse of Test Scores

Test scores are frequently used incorrectly. For example, SAT scores have been incorrectly used as measures of a school district's ability to prepare children for college and as a mark of the quality of the district's programs. The SAT is a measure of aptitude rather than academic achievement. Aptitude includes many nonschool and home variables.

Standardized group achievement tests (Iowa Test of Basic Skills; Stanford Achievement Test; Metropolitan Achievement Test; California Achievement Test) are often used to assign children to groups. However, these achievement tests are not appropriate for evaluating individual children. They use randomly selected items that often do not match the objectives of the curriculum. They are group tests and are not designed to test for mastery.

Tests are a way to assess children's learning. Don't forget to use alternative methods to assess and evaluate children.

Photograph by Ken Karp.

Schools frequently use these scores to report progress to parents and to place children into ability groups. The use of standardized group achievement tests for these purposes is in effect using questionable and limited information for making educational decisions. It is similar to a physician using a thermometer as the primary means of diagnosing and treating individual patients.

Time-Consuming

Grading can have a positive effect on children's achievement and their attitudes toward school. However, an excessive amount of time is spent testing children.

Because of school district concerns over accountability, many students are required to take standardized achievement tests each year. Further, many states are now requiring students to take state-mandated competency tests at certain grade levels to demonstrate mastery of essential skills (minimum competencies). Students lose several days of instructional time taking these tests.

In addition to time spent taking achievement and competency tests, many teachers set aside time to teach the objectives contained on the tests so students will perform better. Teaching test-taking skills is also usurping instructional time. Allocating instructional time to teach test-taking skills to elementary children is a questionable practice.

Quantifying Individuals

Educators and the public tend to place too much importance on test results. Although numerical scores tend to have an aura of immutable authority, they are at best a point at which we can begin to develop a better understanding of children. Test scores are not conclusions.

Some Outcomes Cannot Be Measured

The human potential is infinite; tests are limited. There are many human behaviors that cannot be measured with the evaluation instruments currently available. For example, the abilities to share, cooperate, contribute to group efforts, act as a model citizen, or solve many complex social problems are difficult to measure by using tests.

Limitations in the Primary Grades

For primary-grade students, a test is often a challenge that extends beyond their ability to express what they know. For example, test scores are negatively affected by youngsters' inability to follow directions. Rather than provide an accurate indication of what children have learned, tests may provide low scores because of the difficulty children have in following directions.

Kindergarten and primary-grade teachers are being urged to resist using standardized achievement tests. Experienced teachers understand the difficulties young children experience during the primary grades.

Labeling Children

Tests can provide useful information about children. But tests cannot describe the complexities of children. Some children perform well on tests; others, equally as intelligent, do not perform well on tests. When educators do not understand the limitations of testing and the uses of test scores, they may inadvertently label children. A child may be labeled as gifted, slow, or average. Once labeled many children are placed in groups that maintain the expectations for the label. Children placed in slow groups move at a slow pace and have little chance of catching up to children in higher, faster-moving groups.

Teachers may subconsciously label children based on test scores. If a teacher sees a high test score, the expectations will likely rise and the teacher will challenge the children. Unfortunately, the inverse is also true.

Use for Professional Evaluation

An increasing number of school districts are basing teacher and principal evaluations on students' test scores. Many of the tests used in schools were designed to judge the effectiveness of curriculum and mastery of objectives, not to evaluate professional staff.

Several dangers exist in this practice. First, additional instructional time may be spent helping students study for the test. The second major danger is that subjects normally receiving nominal emphasis on standardized achievement tests, such as the fine arts and social studies, will receive less emphasis in the school day. A third problem relates to affective development. Most formally prepared tests do not measure affective development. *Affect* relates to attitudes and beliefs, which are difficult to measure. Democratic values and beliefs, affective in nature, may therefore receive less emphasis. A danger exists in that we may educate youngsters who can perform well on tests but who cannot function effectively in a democratic society.

Bredekamp and Shepard (1989) used the term "high stakes testing" to describe the misuses evident with current testing practices. We are using tests for promotion, retention, teacher evaluations, and resource allocation purposes. Testing and measurement procedures have severe limitations, and the misuse of these instruments can have negative effects on a child's education. If you begin to realize that there are problems with current evaluation practices you will be better able to use measurement practices wisely and judiciously in your classroom.

SUGGESTIONS FOR MEASURING ACHIEVEMENT

An elementary social studies program should include three areas of study: knowledge of content, skills, and democratic values and beliefs. These areas differ widely in the ways they are taught and the ways in which progress is evaluated. Content and skills may be evaluated using low-level and high-level techniques. Democratic values and beliefs are more readily inferred by observing children's interactions and examining affective aspects of learning. Clearly, several different measurement and evaluation practices are necessary in a comprehensive social studies program.

This section of the chapter provides suggestions for you as you attempt to measure and evaluate improvements in your students' academic achievement. As with most educational practices, some of the evaluation ideas presented in this chapter are appropriate in some situations and not in others. You must determine the purpose of your lesson and then select the most appropriate means of measuring and evaluating your students.

Using and Modifying Prepared Tests

Textbook series have a set of tests that accompany them. They usually consist of questions at the end of a chapter and separate spirit master or black line master pages that can be reproduced on a copying machine.

Do not take the time as a beginning teacher to develop your own written multiple choice, true-false, or fill-in-the-blank tests. Your time can be better spent planning exciting, creative lessons and designing other means of evaluating students' learning. But you can develop adequate tests by rewriting some of the test items accompanying your text. Examine the test materials accompanying your textbook and modify the questions on those tests. Delete unimportant questions, modify other questions, and add questions that reflect your instructional emphasis.

The types of questions you add should include higher-level questions. For example, you might ask your students to compare an historical event presented in the unit you just completed with a similar event from an earlier unit. Or you may ask students to evaluate the probable effects if an event had been altered.

Teacher-Made Tests

Constructing written tests can be exciting and useful. However, good test construction is a difficult process (and may be delayed until you have been teaching for a while). The following suggestions will enable you to construct your own tests. These suggestions may also be used to evaluate formally prepared tests.

First, a good test is designed to evaluate the goals and objectives that were actually taught. Select important goals and objectives that were adequately presented during instruction as the basis of your test questions. Many educators rightfully suggest that your test questions emerge from your objectives.

The second suggestion is to develop clearly worded questions. A typical elementary classroom exhibits a wide range of reading abilities. Your poor readers may be unable to respond to your questions if they cannot read well enough. The wording of test items has a second problem. Students may misinterpret the meaning of your questions if the questions are poorly constructed or if the wording is biased against their language abilities. Children may respond differently from how you anticipated. You will quickly discover misunderstandings as you grade their responses.

The third suggestion is to include a variety of low- and high-level questions. Children need opportunities to respond to higher-level thought-provoking questions as well as low-level recall questions. Higher-level questions may require children to compare and contrast two or more events, relate a topic of study to a current event, or predict how the future may be affected by the event. Finally, you might ask children affective questions about their attitudes toward aspects of the topic.

The fourth suggestion is to consider alternative methods of measuring and evaluating students. You might allow them to write test questions and then construct a test utilizing (after editing) their questions.

The final suggestion is to inform students what is important enough to be tested. Children do not always have a clear understanding of a topic, even after it has been taught well. They may be struggling to make sense out of the information and be unable to determine what is important. Providing information that will help them prepare for the test will enable them to prepare more thoroughly. It also serves as an additional teaching strategy because it emphasizes the important aspects of the topic.

AFFECTIVE AND SUBJECTIVE SUGGESTIONS

While teachers must evaluate children's academic achievement, or the *product* aspect of teaching, they must also evaluate the *process* involved in teaching and learning. Process measures are usually more informal and are usually used to determine how children learn, how well they enjoy topics, and how well they interact with other children. This type of evaluation is more subjective, requiring teachers to utilize their professional judgment.

Attitudinal Surveys

Attitudes are important in the learning process. Although it is important to teach content and skills, it is also important to help children develop positive attitudes about themselves, others, and the topics they are studying. It does little good to teach problem-solving skills if students later use those abilities to commit crimes. Similarly, it does little good to teach about other cultures if students simultaneously develop prejudices against members of those ethnic groups.

Attitudinal surveys usually take the form of teacher-made measurement devices. A Likert scale is one means of allowing children to indicate their attitudes. The Likert technique uses a series of statements pertaining to the topic being evaluated. Each statement is followed by a scale on which children indicate their response to the statements. Likert scales usually have a three-, five-, or seven-point range. The points are placed along a continuum. Children then read each statement and indicate their attitudes about each statement on the Likert scale.

Many primary-grade youngsters may have difficulty reading the statements. For children who cannot read well, teachers may use happy faces, neutral faces, and sad faces. The teacher can read each statement and allow the children to circle or draw the appropriate type of face. Figure 6–2 illustrates attitudinal questions using Likert scales.

Figure 6–2 Sample Attitudinal Survey

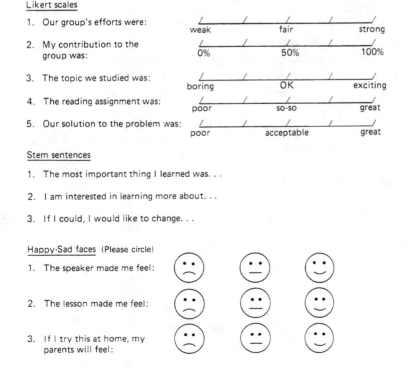

Likert scales

1. Our group's efforts were: weak   fair   strong

2. My contribution to the group was: 0%   50%   100%

3. The topic we studied was: boring   OK   exciting

4. The reading assignment was: poor   so-so   great

5. Our solution to the problem was: poor   acceptable   great

Stem sentences

1. The most important thing I learned was. . .

2. I am interested in learning more about. . .

3. If I could, I would like to change. . .

Happy-Sad faces (Please circle)

1. The speaker made me feel:

2. The lesson made me feel:

3. If I try this at home, my parents will feel:

Stem Sentences

Stem sentences can be used to assess children's attitudes. You may ask them to respond, either verbally or in writing, to questions such as:

> My favorite part of the lesson was...
> My behavior is likely to change in the following ways...
> I was surprised to learn...
> I didn't realize cities...
> My view of the people we studied has changed in the following ways...
> (Several additional examples are included in Figure 6–2.)

Stem sentences are useful and adaptable to a variety of measurement and evaluation purposes. The topic will be presented more thoroughly in a latter section of the chapter.

Observation Checklists

Proponents of cognitively oriented programs suggest that teachers spend a considerable amount of time observing how their students interact with activities and with other students. These observations then become the basis for planning future lessons and evaluating students' progress.

As you embark on your career you need to begin observing your students. To help you guide your observations, checklists are helpful. To make your own checklist simply determine the types of behaviors you are interested in observing and list those behaviors on a sheet of paper. Then place each child's name on one of the lines of the checklist and begin making notations on a regular basis (see Figure 6–3).

My first checklist was designed to assess my students' ability to cooperate with one another. I placed the form on a clipboard and began observing youngsters as they worked on group projects and while they played at recess. I gained useful insights into the needs and behaviors of children and discovered areas of good and poor social development. I also quickly began refining the behaviors I had originally listed on my checklist.

It is difficult to evaluate democratic values and beliefs. However, the use of checklists can provide information on the extent to which children behave in ways compatible with a democratic society. Behaviors associated with democratic values and beliefs are listed below and may be used to develop your own checklist.

Characteristics Indicative of Democratic Values

tolerant	altruistic	fair
cooperative	respects others	empathic
nonprejudiced	respects property	rational
concern for others	respects diversity	shares
dependable	respects justice	open
egalitarian	participation	self-control

Child	Behaviors							Comments
	Sharing	Cooperating	Contributing to group	Taking turns	Patient	Accepts criticism	Working independently	
John								
Mary								
Suzy								
Fred								
Matt								

Observations may be recorded using tic marks to denote behaviors, or a code
may be used to record positive behaviors (+) and negative behaviors (−).
You might note dates and circumstances regarding negative behaviors in the
comment section. This may be useful for referrals or parent-teacher
conferences.

Figure 6–3 Sample Behavioral Checklist

Source: Van Cleaf, D.W. (1986). *Teaching elementary social studies: Supplemental materials.* Unpublished manuscript, Washburn University, Topeka. Adapted and reprinted with permission of the author.

Projects

Elementary social studies should actively involve children in a variety of projects. Children might make dioramas depicting an historical settlement, construct collages of needs versus wants, make flowcharts diagramming the processing of natural resources into finished products, or draw posters advocating fire safety in

Children should be encouraged to create many interesting projects.
Photograph by David W. Van Cleaf.

the home. As children participate in the construction and completion of these projects they are involved in representing information, obtaining additional information, analyzing information, and applying the information.

Projects are excellent teaching activities and excellent devices for evaluating children's learning. Evaluation of children's projects should occur at two levels. First, you should monitor children as they are working on their projects—formative evaluation. Listen to their comments, consider the implications of their questions, ask them questions about the work they are performing, and determine the reasoning behind their decisions. This information provides insight to youngsters' understanding of the topic as well as their interest in the topic.

The second opportunity to evaluate projects occurs when children have completed the projects—summative evaluation. Finished projects should be evaluated to determine the extent to which children display an understanding of the topic you have taught. You might want to develop an evaluation checklist to guide your assessment of children's projects.

Whether you use a checklist or simply assign a grade, you should determine your criteria for the evaluation. Criteria should include knowledge and understanding of the topic as reflected by the project. Your evaluation may also reflect children's cooperation and contributions to group efforts. Creativity may be a third criteria.

Avoid evaluating the "neatness" of children's projects. Some children are meticulous workers but do not understand what they have done. Other children may have an excellent grasp of the topic and have a creative project, yet because of their style, the project may be somewhat messy.

Portfolios

Many professionals develop portfolios, which include samples of their work. Artists, architects, and clothing designers maintain professional portfolios.

Children can develop portfolios of their work. A child's portfolio could simply consist of a folder containing examples of his or her work. It may also include photographs of projects too awkward to fit in the folder. Finally, a child's portfolio might include self-written comments about feelings, attitudes toward topics, and things the child wants the teacher to know that may not emerge from the evaluation process.

Portfolios are excellent devices for parent–teacher conferences. By arranging the information chronologically you can trace the child's progress during the reporting period as well as throughout the entire school year. Portfolios also enable you to evaluate and illustrate the quality of children's work as an alternative to assigning grades. By maintaining a portfolio of key examples you can quickly and easily evaluate and share children's progress with parents.

Journals/Diaries

As students participate in a series of lessons about a topic they may be asked to take time each day to record entries in a journal or diary. They can be encouraged to restate the important points learned during the lesson as well as what they enjoyed or did not enjoy. Review entries periodically to assess children's attitudes toward the subject and the kinds of information they consider important.

Journal entries will provide you with a wealth of information and insights into the minds of your students. The use of journals is also an opportunity to integrate social studies and writing.

Think Aloud

Jones, Palincsar, Ogle, and Carr (1987) suggested assessing children's thinking by encouraging them to think aloud as they work. By listening to children's comments as they work you can gain insights into their thought processes, the aspects of the topic they consider important, and the relationships they see. If some of your students are shy, the authors suggest having them tutor other students. By listening to the lessons they present to others you can gain insights into their thinking.

Language-Experience Stories

Language-experience stories are used most frequently in the primary grades as a means of helping children learn to read. A child or group of children dictate a story about a topic and an adult writes the story on the chalkboard or a piece of paper. If the story is written on a piece of paper it is usually typed later so the students can read it more easily.

Language-experience stories can also be used as an evaluation device in social studies. After studying a topic, children can dictate a story or the answers to a series of questions. You should write the information dictated by the children and then provide time for them to reread the stories and make pertinent changes. You can evaluate the story to determine how well your students learned the information.

Volunteers, such as parents and older children, can assist you as you evaluate individual students in this manner. Individual responses can be dictated to the volunteer, evaluated by you, and then placed in the child's folder.

Sentence Strips

If you are working with nonreaders you may adapt the language-experience technique and use sentence strips. Sentence strips are long, single-line portions of primary writing paper. As children complete an activity or a learning center they dictate a sentence describing the work they completed. The adult writes (using manuscript writing style) the child's statement and reads the statement back to the child.

Each sentence strip becomes a record of the child's activity and can be placed in the child's folder. You may also send the sentence strips home each day as a report of what the children did in school.

Not only are sentence strips excellent evaluation devices but they also foster beginning reading skills. Like the language-experience stories, the sentence strips contain the child's statements and are more easily reread by the child.

I was pleasantly surprised by parents' reports that the highlight of many school days was when the children read their daily collection of sentence strips to parents. I also discovered that most of the refrigerators were covered with sentence strips.

Semantic Maps

Semantic maps are diagrams illustrating the relationships among terms, concepts, and major ideas taught in a lesson. At the completion of a lesson or unit, you may provide children with a list of terms, concepts, and major ideas and then allow them to develop a diagram illustrating the relationships. Figure 6–4 illustrates a variation of a semantic map developed by Steve Henry.

As you evaluate children's semantic maps you should realize that there may be a variety of possible relationships. A sense of flexibility is needed when evaluating these maps.

To extend the usefulness of semantic maps, you might ask children to explain their maps and their reasoning. You might also encourage youngsters to add related terms and ideas not included in the original list. This is a variation of a word association activity and should help you gain interesting insights into children's reasoning processes.

Find examples of the concept, natural resources, in the following list and complete the semantic map. Add two examples of your own.

People	Soil	Coal	Oil	Forests
Deer	Cows	Aluminum Cans	Rivers	Cars
Fish	Flag	T.V.	Police Officer	Buildings

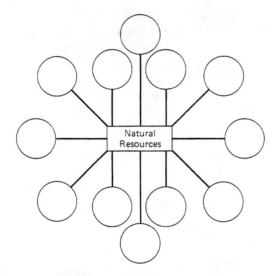

Figure 6–4 A Semantic Map

Source: Adapted from a semantic map ("Ancient Greece") that was submitted as a course requirement by Steve Henry, Northern Hills Junior High School. Reprinted and adapted with permission from Steve Henry.

Classroom Meetings

Glasser (1969) encouraged teachers to involve children actively through the use of three types of classroom meetings: educational-diagnostic, social–problem-solving, and open-ended. Educational-diagnostic classroom meetings are designed as an evaluation tool.

Educational-diagnostic classroom meetings may be used as a pretest to help identify areas of interest and the level of children's knowledge prior to developing a lesson or unit. The teacher might identify the topic of an upcoming unit and ask for children's thoughts. Appropriate questions include: What do you know about the topic? Have you ever visited a place related to the topic? Does anyone in your family or neighborhood know something about the topic? What specific aspects are you interested in exploring?

Educational-diagnostic classroom meetings are also an effective means of evaluating children at the conclusion of instruction. You may ask them to tell you what they learned, what they felt was most important (and why), how this parallels with their own lives, how their attitudes changed, and important lessons for their future.

Educational-diagnostic classroom meetings do not readily lend themselve to assigning formal grades. However, they do allow you to obtain importan information about children's levels of understanding and attitudes that paper and-pencil tests do not provide.

The second type of classroom meeting is a social–problem-solving classroom meeting. When personal or social issues arise in the classroom, children should discuss the problem. As they discuss the problem they should be encouraged to devise appropriate solutions. This type of classroom meeting provides insights into the ways youngsters perceive problems and how they attempt to resolve them.

Many educators recommend involving children in the process of establishing classroom rules and discipline guidelines. Social–problem-solving classroom meetings are an excellent means of involving children in discovering the need for rules, the benefits of rules, and the importance of participating in the governance process. While children are actively participating in the classroom meeting they are engaged in an important aspect of the democratic process.

Glasser's third type of classroom meeting is the open-ended meeting. Open-ended meetings should be structured to allow children to discuss thought-provoking problems, issues related to their lives, or current events. Open-ended meetings provide teachers with opportunities to evaluate children's thoughts, concerns, and attitudes about events affecting their lives.

Sociograms

A sociogram is a technique sociologists and educators have used to map interaction patterns among individuals within a group. A sociogram requires people to identify others with whom they prefer to associate. I asked my students to list four children with whom they would like to sit while traveling on a field trip.

The results present insights into children's feelings about others and must be used carefully. I used the information to help develop seating charts so that every child was sitting next to a child with whom there was compatibility and when assigning children to small groups.

Discussion Risk

The discussion risk activity (Jacko, 1981) requires children to discuss possible responses to a series of thought-provoking questions. After discussing possible responses they select an answer to the questions and risk a number of points on the strength of each response. This activity is a motivating alternative to traditional testing practices.

The procedure begins by the teacher identifying a series of open-ended, thought-provoking questions. The number of questions should be limited to three, four, or five questions because of the time involved in the discussion phase of the activity.

During the class period the teacher presents the first question to the class and encourages members to discuss views and information pertinent to the question.

Several minutes should be allocated for the discussion of each question. When the discussion of the first question has ceased, each child should record an answer for the question and then determine how many of the points allocated for each question they care to risk. Figure 6–5 illustrates an example of a worksheet for recording answers and risking point values.

When each question has been discussed and children have determined responses and number of points risked, the teacher may lead a follow-up discussion and inform the youngsters of the correct responses. Children may score their own papers and compute their scores.

While the points children earn have a high motivational value, they may not be appropriate for entry in the grade book. If you intend to record a grade for children's performance, you should base the grade on the number of questions youngsters answer correctly rather than the total points scored. Some children are risk-takers, whereas others are more conservative. By recording total points you may be grading personality styles rather than academic performance.

Topic: Shelter   Grade Level: Primary

Child's Name _____

Questions	Answer	Points Risked	Points Awarded
All living things need shelter.	_____	_____	_____
There is one best type of shelter for people.	_____	_____	_____
Different types of materials are used to build shelters for people.	_____	_____	_____
A home and a house are the same thing.	_____	_____	_____
Total points			_____

Figure 6–5 A "Risky" Activity

Source: Van Cleaf, D.W. (1986). *Teaching elementary social studies: Supplemental materials.* Unpublished manuscript, Washburn University, Topeka. Adapted and reprinted with permission of the author.

The types of questions, amount of time provided for the discussions, and the scoring procedure should be adapted to reflect the content taught and the ability levels of your students. Point values for younger children may be limited to three or five, depending on their mathematical abilities. Fifth- and sixth-grade children might actually be able to score in the negative range, thus reinforcing their use of negative integers.

Stem Sentences

Stem sentences were briefly described earlier as an alternative means of assessing children's attitudes. They may also be used to evaluate other types of learning. Stem sentences consist of an unfinished statement requiring students to add their comments to complete the statement. Responses may be short enough to complete the sentence or they may consist of several paragraphs.

Responses to the stem sentence should provide insights into student attitudes toward the topic. Stem sentences also provide students with a somewhat unstructured way to respond to content questions. Rather than being limited by the design of traditional true-false, multiple-choice, and essay tests, students have more freedom to respond to a series of stem sentences. Examples of stem sentences related to primary-grade and intermediate-grade lessons are contained in Figure 6–6.

Figure 6–6 Sample Stem Sentences

Primary Grades (needs and wants)

1. My home is a need because…
2. Jeans are a need, a fur coat is not, because…
3. The most important needs are…
4. Life without enough food would be…
5. If everybody had all they wanted…
6. We can help others by…

Intermediate Grades (energy)

1. As an energy source, coal is…
2. Nuclear energy is…
3. Without energy, we would…
4. In 50 years, our energy will be…
5. The relationships between energy and our behavior…
6. To conserve energy…

SUMMARY

Measurement and evaluation are critical components of effective teaching. Lesson planning must be based on information about students' needs and interests. Failure to assess students prior to planning lessons usually results in teaching lessons that do not adequately address your students' needs. Pre-assessment information is a must for effective teaching.

Effective teachers also evaluate students while engaged in the teaching process. Formative evaluation provides information about children's progress during instruction. When teachers discover that children are frustrated, confused, or uncertain about an objective being taught, effective teachers use alternative ways to reteach the information before moving to more complicated material. Reteaching should also be provided before administering a final evaluation.

Failure to assess children during the instructional process may contribute to the development of negative attitudes toward the topic. Children are more likely to develop positive attitudes when they understand the topic. Formative evaluation and reteaching are important aspects of maintaining positive attitudes.

The summative aspect of the measurement and evaluation process continues to be important. Teachers must determine how well their students have learned. However, you are encouraged to go beyond traditional tests to make summative judgments.

This chapter described a number of evaluation suggestions. As you attempt to assess your students' progress you are encouraged to utilize a variety of these techniques.

Chapter 2 described the scope of a social studies program. A comprehensive social studies program should include goals and objectives related to social studies knowledge, skills, and democratic values and beliefs. Traditional measurement and evaluation practices do not enable teachers to adequately measure children's progress in each of these three areas. Traditional practices may inhibit effective social studies instruction because goals and objectives that are not tested are generally not taught.

The suggestions appearing in this chapter include alternatives that will allow you to go beyond the limitations of traditional evaluation practices. You will be more capable of teaching a comprehensive social studies program that includes knowledge, skills, and democratic values and beliefs.

SUGGESTED ACTIVITIES

1. Examine a blank report card used by a school district in your area. In what way is it an evaluation device? How well does it report information to parents? What type of information does it report?

2. Examine questions appearing at the end of a chapter in a social studies textbook. You might also locate an end-of-chapter test in a teacher's guide of the workbook or black line master. Are the questions related to the major concepts in the chapter? Are the questions primarily low-level questions?

3. Using the end-of-chapter test from the above activity, design an alternative means of evaluating children. Use the suggestions provided in this chapter.

Knowledge can help children understand the rest of the world.

Photograph by Rona Beame, Photo Researchers, Inc.

chapter 7

Methods for Teaching Map Skills

Whatever direction I'm headed is north!

(*An acquaintance*)

AS YOU READ...

- describe the weaknesses with current methods of teaching map skills
- determine the importance of allowing children to construct their own maps
- list and explain five map skills
- describe two exciting ways to teach each map skill

INTRODUCTION

The quote on page 141 suggests that at least one of my acquaintances has had difficulty learning to read and use maps. However, the problem is widespread. For example, I participated in a map-reading activity with approximately 200 Army infantry officers at Fort Benning, Georgia. Most of the officers were college graduates and had finished at least two years of ROTC instruction. As part of their training they had completed coursework in map reading. In addition to map reading in ROTC, these infantry officers had completed twelve years of elementary and secondary school education. Yet a significantly large number of these men could not satisfactorily complete a map course. They had to return on another day for additional help. Many teachers also experience difficulties using map-reading skills.

If you consider the introductory quote along with the difficulties experienced by young Army officers and teachers, you should readily infer that problems exist regarding the quality of map-reading skill instruction. But map-reading skill development does not need to be a difficult task. Anyone can learn to read maps if the person receives appropriate instruction. Teaching children to read maps in the elementary grades should be a relatively easy and exciting instructional event.

Two problems appear to affect and limit the way children learn to read maps. The first problem is related to our definition of maps. Simply stated, we tend to have a formal, sophisticated view of maps—maps aren't real unless they are formally prepared by cartographers. This view limits the way we teach mapping skills because we are limited to beautifully and accurately prepared products made by others. Once you limit yourself to the use of maps made by others, you move away from teaching children from a concrete basis. In this case, once you rely on maps made by others, you no longer use the children's immediate environment as their instructional basis for map reading.

Second, map-reading instruction is often poor because of the curriculum materials we use. Children frequently are introduced to map-reading skills by looking at maps made by others. These maps represent distant and unfamiliar environments. This is a result of selecting nationally developed curriculum materials. It is too expensive for a national publisher of curriculum materials to develop concrete map materials related to a child's environment in Fort Smith, Arkansas, while also being concretely related to a child's environment in Spokane, Washington. Rather than develop materials appropriate for each child's city or neighborhood, publishers use maps that are of distant, abstract places. This violates the learning principle that suggests new skills must be learned through familiar and concrete means rather than abstract means.

Curriculum materials often reflect another weakness. Too frequently the skills and activities developed through curriculum materials are not appropriate for the developmental levels of the students. Concepts such as scale, latitude, longitude, projections, and computing scale-to-miles ratios are not appropriate for

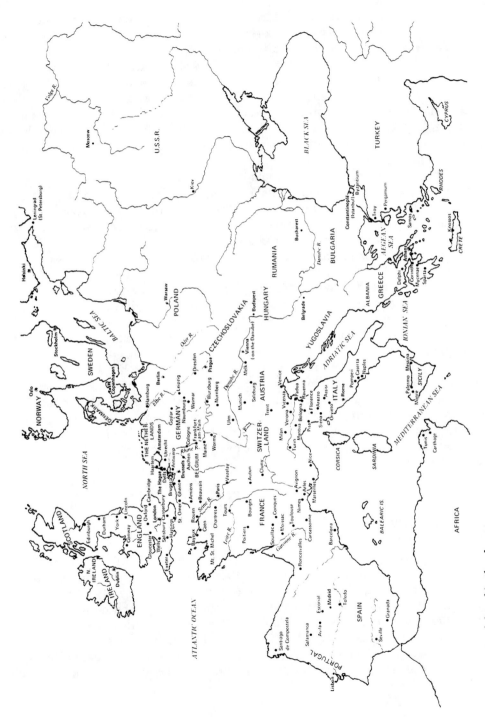

A map is a useful tool in the classroom.

a vast majority of elementary children. However, these concepts and skills are present in most elementary textbook series.

To help correct the difficulties experienced with map-reading instruction raised by the first problem, a new and less formal definition of maps should be accepted. While maps are symbolic representations of space, they need not be limited to formally prepared maps. An informal and more appropriate definition of maps is that they are illustrations and pictures of an area. With this view of maps in mind, teachers have more freedom to help children learn map-reading skills. Teachers will be able to use methods and materials that are more developmentally appropriate for their students.

Once an informal view of maps is accepted we can address the second problem—the curriculum materials. Because map-reading instruction can be viewed as helping children understand "pictures" of different areas, youngsters can be encouraged to develop pictures of their immediate world. Teacher-made maps of the children's world can also be developed. We can move away from, or at least delay, the use of formally prepared maps of unfamiliar areas.

This will make map-reading instruction concrete because children work with maps related to their concrete, immediate environment. By providing children with opportunities to develop and read maps of familiar environments, they will eventually develop the abstract skills necessary to read formally prepared maps that appear in textbooks, encyclopedias, and atlases.

Using concrete materials to teach map-reading skills has several benefits. First, as students participate in the activities you will develop a better understanding of their abilities and needs. This will enable you to identify additional ideas and activities appropriate for your students. Second, students will have opportunities to develop a concrete understanding of many geography concepts. For example, as youngsters work with maps of their familiar environment they will learn how people have adapted to the environment.

MAP SKILLS AND ACTIVITIES

The NCSS Task Force (1989) presented a list of six map skills appropriate for elementary education. They are: (1) orient a map and note directions, (2) locate places on a map and globe, (3) use scale to compute distance, (4) interpret map symbols and visualize what they mean, (5) compare maps and make inferences, and (6) express relative location. Table 7–1 lists the six skills and the degree of emphasis recommended by the NCSS for each skill. In this text, skills two and six are combined because they both relate to location. The resulting skill categories are explained in the following sections. Appropriate activities for teaching each skill are also presented.

Table 7–1 NCSS Elementary Map Skills

SKILL	LEVEL OF INSTRUCTIONAL EMPHASIS[*]	
	Grades K-3	Grades 4-6
Orient a map and note directions	Minimum or none	Intense
Locate places on map and globe	Minimum or none	Major
Use scale and compute distances	Minimum or none	Some
Interpret maps and symbols and visualize what they mean	Minimum or none	Some
Compare maps and make inferences	Minimum or none	Some
Express relative location	Minimum or none	Minimum or none

[*]NCSS levels of emphasis are, in ascending order of emphasis: minimum or none, some, major, intense.

Source: NCSS Task Force on Scope and Sequence (October 1989). In search of a scope and sequence for social studies. *Social Education, 53,* p. 386. Adapted and reprinted with permission of the National Council for the Social Studies.

Before explaining each skill, it is necessary to reiterate the importance of concrete experiences. Elementary-grade children are somewhere within the preoperational and concrete operational stages of development; they are concrete learners. The best way to teach map skills to them is through the use of concrete activities.

The most useful concrete mapping activity is to require children to construct their own maps. The maps they construct should be of areas with which they are familiar. As children construct maps of familiar environments they get a double dose of concrete learning. First, they are actively involved in the map-making process. They are manipulating symbols while considering relationships between objects and locations. They are making decisions regarding the way they intend to represent their area. Second, map-construction activities are concrete because the children are representing areas with which they are familiar. This familiarity allows students to focus on the process of mapping and the skills involved in map reading. It helps avoid the frustrations that occur when children are required to work with abstract information and unfamiliar places.

Many of the map activities described in this chapter are based on the notion that children should construct their own maps. Even junior high and high school students should have opportunities to construct maps of familiar areas before attempting more complex map activities. However, not all of the activities in this chapter require students to construct maps. Some of the activities require the use of maps of familiar environments made by other people. Teacher-made classroom and playground maps, neighborhood maps, city maps, state maps, and even maps of the country and other parts of the world may be used when children have the ability and are familiar with the area represented.

Map Symbols

By the time children enter school they have developed the ability to use concrete symbols. Maps of course use many symbols to represent items in the environment, but most map symbols are relatively abstract. For example, brown represents elevation; black and red lines symbolize roads; yellow patches of color may represent a large city; a star may represent a capital city. While children can use symbols, the map symbols they use must be concretely related to their levels of understanding.

Children's Maps. Perhaps the best way to help children develop an understanding of the use of map symbols is to begin by having them construct their own maps of familiar environments. Children can make maps of their classrooms, their bedrooms, or the playground. As they construct their maps, you need to visit with them and ask them to explain what they are doing. You should ask questions such as, "What does this stand for? Why did you decide to use that kind of a figure? What else might you use to illustrate that? Why did people place that object in that particular location?" These questions will encourage children to state the relationships between their symbols and the objects they represent.

Constructing Legends. The next step is to have children develop a legend, or key, that will help others "read" their maps. You can show children examples of legends on formally prepared maps and then have them develop legends for their maps.

Valentine Maps. Snyder (1987) described a mapping activity for Valentine's Day. Children are given paper and asked to draw an outline of a large heart on the paper. This outline becomes the outline of a new land, "Heartland." Children add lakes, rivers, oceans, cities, topographic features, and points of interest. These imaginative places can be given valentine names such as Cupidville, Romance River, and Serenade Sea. A legend should be added when the maps have been completed.

Highway Maps. Mary Ada May, a third grade teacher, kept state road maps in her room. When she had extra time she would distribute the road maps and ask her students to locate items illustrated in the legend. She would identify an item in the legend and her students would locate places on the map where similar symbols were located.

Symbo. Hatcher (1983) proposed a variation of bingo as a means of helping primary-grade children recognize map symbols. Her game, Symbo, is played like bingo. The letters S-Y-M-B-O are the letters across the top of the game. Map symbols are drawn on the children's cards to replace the numbers that normally exist on bingo cards. As the teacher calls out letters and symbols, the children cover appropriate symbols on their playing cards.

Children's Literature. Children's literature can provide opportunities to help students develop the ability to use map symbols as well as other map skills. As you read stories to children, whether they be in the form of picture books or books with few pictures, you can have the children develop a map for the stories. *Call It Courage, The Pushcart War,* Dr. Seuss books, and other books lend themselves to mapping activities. As children listen to a story they must decide what items to include on their maps, where to place the items, and how to symbolize the items.

Cuisenaire Rod Maps. This activity was designed to help children develop an understanding of the relationship between three-dimensional objects and the two-dimensional symbols that appear on most maps. Small groups of children should be given outline maps of the streets intersecting near the entrance of the school. The children should also be given Cuisenaire rods. Children then construct maps of buildings in the neighborhood using the Cuisenaire rods.

Children must arrange the rods in various ways to represent the different sizes of the buildings. Some of the buildings may be single-story structures and only one rod tall. Other buildings can be taller and represented by stacking rods on top of one another.

When children complete their neighborhood maps they should trace around the base of each building and remove the blocks (see Figure 7–1). The result is a map of the neighborhood that has been transformed from a three-dimensional map using blocks to a two-dimensional map using lines. Take time to discuss the relationships between the "block buildings" and the two-dimensional outlines of the buildings. You may then look at maps in social studies texts and compare maps in the texts to the children's maps (Van Cleaf, 1985).

Bird's Eye View. Another way to help children understand that maps represent objects from an overhead view is to have them place an assortment of objects on their desks. They should draw the objects as they appear from an overhead position. A legend can be added to their "desk maps."

Topographic Maps. Elevation and landforms are illustrated on maps through the use of symbols. This topic is included as a separate subsection because the symbols used to represent topography are more abstract and therefore more difficult for children to understand. You should not expect most elementary-age children to master an understanding of topographic

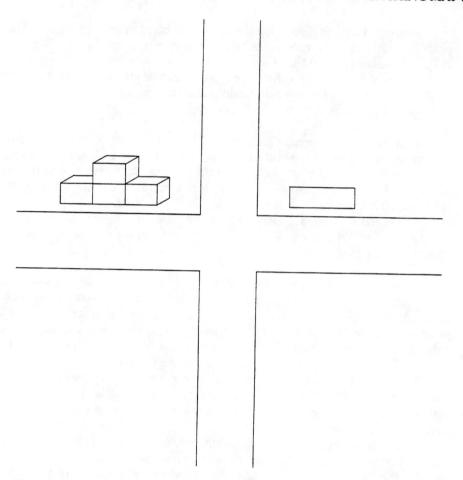

Figure 7–1 Cuisenaire Rod Map

Source: Van Cleaf, D.W. (1986). *Teaching elementary social studies: Supplemental materials.* Un-published manuscript, Washburn University, Topeka. Adapted and reprinted with permission of the author.

maps, but you can introduce them to the concept and help them develop an initial understanding.

Topographic maps use symbols such as colors and contour lines to repre-sent elevation and relief. Colors and contour lines are abstract because they do not appear on the earth. Children cannot see them. Further, there is little concrete relationship between the symbols used to represent elevation and the items they represent.

Before sharing topographic map activities, the differences between elevation and relief should be stated. According to Muir and Frazee (1986) *elevation* repre-sents the vertical height of an area, generally above sea level. *Relief* is used to describe landforms and differences between landforms. These concepts are illustrated by comparing the Great Plains and the Adirondack Mountains. They have similar elevations but quite different reliefs. One is a rather flat landform whereas the other is mountainous.

A fifth-grade teacher designed an activity to help children understand contour lines. A clay hill was made and placed in an empty container. With the children assisting and observing, water was added to the container until it reached a depth of one centimeter. A child was then directed to draw a line around the hill at the water line. When this first line was drawn more water was added until the depth of the water reached two centimeters. Another line was then drawn around the hill at the new water level. This process continued until the hill was completely submerged. The hill was then removed from the water and children were directed to look at the hill and the lines around the hill from an overhead position. They were then asked to sketch what they observed as they looked at the hill and the contour lines.

This activity should be followed by showing children topographic maps containing contour lines that are similar to the hill you develop for the activity. Such maps may be obtained from a local National Guard or military reserve unit, from a local soil conservation office, or from your community or county surveyor's office.

Orient a Map and Note Directions

This skill category is a combination of two subskills—orienting a map and using direction terms. *Orienting* a map refers to placing a map in such a way that north on the map is aligned with the geographic direction for north. It is not, as the introductory quote indicated, altering the geographic direction of north when a person happens to change direction.

A second aspect of orienting maps is equally important. Teachers usually teach map skills by using maps hanging vertically on the wall or illustrated vertically on an overhead projector. Children are asked to follow along using copies placed horizontally on their desks. This requires children to transpose the vertical and horizontal maps and often creates difficulties.

The use of directions is somewhat more complicated. It will take more time for children to develop a useful understanding of directional terms. The ability to use directions is related to the child's developmental level. Preschool and primary-grade youngsters are egocentric. They have difficulty seeing things from the perspective of other people. The ability to understand and express directions related to map-reading skills will be limited by children's ability to decenter and view the world from perspectives other than their own.

Kindergarten and primary-grade teachers quickly discover these difficulties as they attempt to teach direction terms to their charges. One of the more humorous examples occurs when teachers play Simon Says. If the teacher states, "Simon says raise your right hand," and the teacher raises his or her right hand, the children will inevitably mirror the teacher and raise their left hands.

Direction terms are difficult to learn, particularly when you consider the basis of direction terms. Some terms, such as *north, south, east,* and *west,* are based on the earth and are external to children. Other terms are related specifically to the children. *Left* and *right* are abstract terms based on the child's own body. When one child wants to give directions to another using terms such as left and right the child must be able to decenter and give directions from the other child's perspective. A third direction term is relative to the child and the child's current task. *Over, above, near, closer,* and *under* are examples of terms relative to the child's immediate activity. As the child's position changes, or as the relative location of the objects change, the terminology used to express the locations and relationships must change.

Pattison (1966) reported that the child's ability to use direction terms emerges in a developmental progression. First, an understanding of environmentally based terms such as *over, near,* and *up* develops. Then an understanding of personal terms such as *left* and *right* develops. Finally, understanding of global terms such as *north* and *south* develops.

A 1941 study by Lord reported that in classrooms where children faced north the children had a better sense of direction than in classrooms where they faced in other directions. Perhaps there is a message here for architects as well as teachers. We may improve map-reading achievement by building schools in which all classrooms face north.

Orienting maps and noting directions are important map skills. The following suggestions will help you develop concrete, exciting ways to help your students acquire these skills.

Label the Classroom. Several activities can be used to help children develop a knowledge of direction terms. Simon Says has already been mentioned as an exciting way to help children learn direction terms. Labeling the classroom with the cardinal directions (north, south, east, west) as well as intermediate directions (northeast, southeast, southwest, northwest) will also help children learn direction terms. The labels provide youngsters with concrete reference points regarding the directions. They are useful when playing Simon Says or when working with other map activities.

Orienting Maps. Helping children orient their maps is a relatively easy process. First, label the classroom walls with the appropriate cardinal directions (north, south, east, west). Then instruct children to align their maps so that north on their maps is pointed toward north in their classroom. If your classroom faces in a direction other than north have your children turn their desks or tables so they are seated facing north when using maps.

Compass Rose. As children participate in map activities they may be asked to add a compass rose, a circle containing the cardinal directions, to their maps. Although younger students may not completely understand the task, repeated use will help them gain familiarity with the concept and nurture their understanding.

Small-Group Work. Critical to developing an understanding of direction terms is the ability to communicate with others and consider another person's perspective. An informal yet effective way to do this is by requiring children to complete map activities in small groups. Groups of two are preferable because two students are easily kept on task. As children work with one another they talk about the activity. As they talk they communicate and clarify their ideas. This interaction provides feedback that encourages children to decenter and consider the other person's perspective.

Grid Pictures. The use of grid pictures is another activity that will enable children to use direction terms. Grid pictures require children to use grid lines and directions to construct pictures. A grid picture is illustrated in Figure 7–2 and requires children to plot a series of points and construct a picture by connecting the points. As with the game Battleship, children are using grid lines and directions while participating in a motivating activity.

Grid pictures are relatively easy to develop. Once you have developed a few you can ask children to develop additional grid picture activities in their extra time.

Figure 7–2 Grid Picture

Source: Van Cleaf, D.W. (1986). *Teaching elementary social studies: Supplemental materials.* Unpublished manuscript, Washburn University, Topeka. Adapted and reprinted with permission of the author.

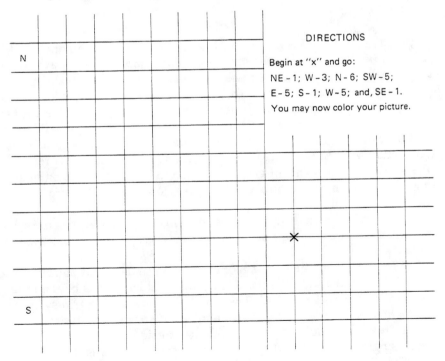

DIRECTIONS

Begin at "x" and go:
NE - 1; W - 3; N - 6; SW - 5;
E - 5; S - 1; W - 5; and, SE - 1.
You may now color your picture.

You might keep old coloring books in the classroom. These coloring books should have large, relatively simple pictures that are appropriate for use as templates for grid pictures.

Figure 7–2 illustrates this activity using directions (NE-1). However, the activity could be modified to require children to use coordinates to plot the points. The directions for this variation might read, "Begin at B-4. Continue plotting the following points: D-6; E-7; F-9; etc."

Mapping Routes. Children enjoy looking at maps of the school and the surrounding neighborhoods. Provide city maps for students and allow them to locate the school and their homes. Then have the children trace a route from the school to their homes. (It may be helpful to laminate your maps.) Children can then develop a set of directions that would enable other children to reach their homes from the school and from other places.

The ability to understand and use direction terms is closely related to the location skills outlined by the NCSS Task Force. The next section outlines several map-construction activities that are equally appropriate for developing the direction skills described in this section. As you read the next section, consider the relationships between direction skills and location skills. Also consider the overlapping usefulness of activities for teaching both skills.

Locate Places

Maps can be considered as visual records of the locations of important places. Most maps are used to locate places such as a street, a town, a vacation spot, or a travel route. Because maps are usually used to locate places, children must develop this ability.

Direction terms are often used by people to help others locate places. For example, "Smith Street is just south of Ryan Street." "Tenth Street is next to 9th Street." "Take the freeway south, turn left at the second bridge, and go one street past the railroad tracks." Using direction terms such as these is helpful in many daily situations but often are cumbersome and readily misinterpreted. Cartographers have used systems of grid lines to aid in locating places on maps. The use of grid lines is a more precise way to express location and therefore an important social studies skill.

City and state maps often use a coordinate system such as the system used in the game Battleship. One set of coordinates is expressed by letters. The second set of coordinates is expressed by numbers.

While most elementary-age children can understand simple coordinates, the ability to use and understand longitude and latitude is beyond the grasp of these youngsters (Muir, 1985). The longitude and latitude grid system is a four-quadrant system whereas the use of letters and numbers as described above uses a more readily understood single-quadrant grid system. The relationship between single-quadrant and four-quadrant grid systems is illustrated in Figure 7–3. The difficulty in using a four-quadrant grid system can be related to the

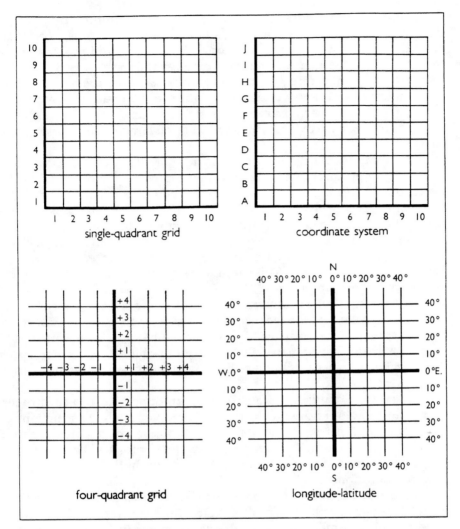

Figure 7-3 Single- and Four-Quadrant Grids

Source: Muir, S.P. & Frazee, B.M. (1986). A developmental perspective. *Social Education, 50,* 199–203.
Reprinted with permission of the National Council for the Social Studies.

difficulty many individuals experience plotting positive and negative points along
a grid system with x and y axes.

Perhaps the best way to help children develop a workable understanding
of location terms as they relate to map reading is by encouraging them to
construct their own maps of familiar places. As with other map activities,
children should be allowed to construct maps while working in small groups,
preferably groups of two. Of course, as they work together they should be
allowed to talk to one another. As they talk you will overhear them using

direction terms to express the location for objects on their maps. They will be telling one another to place "this object next to that one," or "that chair should be a little more to the left," or "I think we should put that in B-4." As they construct their maps and as they engage in the construction process they are using map directions to locate places. They are also experiencing the necessity to decenter and express locations in such a way that people with different perspectives can understand them.

The following activities will help you teach location skills to your students.

Block Maps. Blocks are present in most kindergarten and preschool classrooms. Blocks are an excellent means of developing map skills, including expressing locations. With blocks the children can build airports, cities, garages, stores, and neighborhoods—which are rudimentary maps. As children make these "block maps" they are representing aspects of their environment and developing initial map-reading skills. Children can readily manipulate and move their blocks around to represent objects in the environment. Blocks can be stacked, stood on end, and placed next to one another. This provides not only flexibility but also numerous opportunities for manipulation.

Because children are working in groups they are using direction and location terms to communicate the placement of blocks and other objects. While they are not receiving direct instruction from the teacher they are nevertheless developing sound and lasting map skills. Your responsibility is to provide opportunities for children to use blocks in such a way that they are representing aspects of their environment.

Your role extends beyond providing an opportunity to construct maps. You should talk to children while they are involved in the construction activity. Ask them questions about the placement of objects and the items their blocks represent. Ask them to describe their completed projects. This integrates language and map-reading skills and helps foster the notion that maps are a form of communication.

Blocks may be borrowed from the kindergarten teacher in the building if you do not have any in your room. Milk cartons, Cuisenaire rods, and even Monopoly houses and hotels may be used as alternative materials for block map construction—even for sixth-grade children.

Picture Maps. Students can also construct maps using pictures. The pictures can be cut out of magazines, newspapers, or books. A kindergarten teacher had children sketch outlines of houses on large sheets of paper. The youngsters subdivided their houses into rooms and then began cutting pictures of appliances and furniture from magazines so they could furnish their houses.

This activity also served as a classification activity. As the children selected pictures they had to categorize them by rooms.

Magazine pictures cannot always be found to help children represent items in their environments. Sometimes they must draw their own pictures. Children can be encouraged to think of their favorite park and then construct a map of that park. If magazine pictures are not readily available, children can draw their own pictures, color them, cut them out, and arrange them on a sheet of poster board. Finally, children can draw additional items to complete the maps of their favorite parks.

In each of these situations the youngsters made conscious decisions regarding the location of objects included on their maps. They were also asked to share their maps with others, thus reinforcing locations and relationships of objects on their maps.

Mapping Origins of Toys. Messick and Chapin (1989) described an activity conducted with kindergarten children. As children brought toys for their show-and-tell sessions the teacher would place dots on the globe to indicate the country in which the toys were made. As a result, children became more familiar with the names and locations of other countries.

Classroom Maps (with coordinates). Single-quadrant grid maps can be used to help children develop location skills. Perhaps the best way to begin is with a teacher-constructed map of the classroom that has grid lines. You can begin the activity by asking students to point to the locations of different places depicted on their individual copies of the map. They should point out items such as their desks, the teacher's desk, one item in front of the teacher's desk, something to their left and right, an item located in the southern part of the room, etc.

After children have had an opportunity to use the classroom map and locate items using terms such as *left, right, north,* and *south,* you can introduce the map's grid lines. You should avoid frustrating the children with a lecture about grid lines. Teach the skill inductively by asking them to point to the object located at a given coordinate. "Point to the object located at D-11." Give children a few moments to think this through and discover an appropriate response. Children should be encouraged to help their neighbors who are having difficulty. You can monitor their progress and provide assistance for youngsters experiencing difficulty. You should then continue asking them to locate additional items as you call out coordinates.

When children appear to have a good understanding of the use of coordinates to locate objects, you can name objects on the map and ask them to name the correct coordinates. Again, you should allow children to help one another and you should provide needed assistance.

The use of an inductive teaching technique is recommended because: (1) children often learn things better when given an opportunity to discover and "figure things out" for themselves and (2) we sometimes confuse children when we introduce new skills and strange-sounding vocabulary terms before we provide opportunities for them to perform a new skill. In this situation the term *coordinate* could frustrate and confuse children to the extent that they consider the task to be much more difficult than it really is.

After children become comfortable using the coordinates to locate items on the classroom maps, you can tell them the vocabulary term. You might say something like, "By the way, map makers call these grid lines and they call these letters and numbers *coordinates*." The children will have mastered the skill in a pleasurable and nonconfusing way. They will then readily learn the correct terms. The next time the skill is used you can use the correct terms to remind children of their definitions.

The third-grade teacher who used highway maps during brief periods of extra time also used the maps to locate places using coordinates. She would ask, "What city is located at C-5?" or "What are the coordinates for the state capital?" She also had her children use coordinates to locate different map symbols, thereby allowing children to strengthen location and symbol skills simultaneously.

Treasure Maps. Treasure maps are an exciting idea that will help children use the information contained on maps. Treasure maps have a hidden or buried treasure and a set of directions designed to lead the treasure hunter to the treasure. Children can be given maps of the classroom, school, or playground and directions leading them to a predetermined hiding place on the map. Children also enjoy developing treasure maps that they can then share with their peers.

Hurricane Map. As mentioned earlier, latitude and longitude are not appropriate for most elementary-age children. Latitude and longitude require the use of a four-quadrant grid system that is not introduced to children in math until pre-algebra or algebra. With this admonition stated, you may informally introduce children to latitude and longitude. The activity requires youngsters to plot the daily movement of the eye of a hurricane. You can give students a copy of a map of the Gulf of Mexico or the Atlantic Ocean that contains lines of latitude and longitude. (Since you are using a map of a limited area, you will avoid the confusion of four-quadrant systems. You will be using a portion of one quadrant.)

You should spend a little time each day plotting the new location of the center of the storm. This data may be obtained from the National Weather Service, local TV or radio weather forecasters, or the Weather Channel. Rather than begin the activity by defining the terms *latitude* and *longitude*, simply tell the children to plot a point for the set of coordinates. You can show them how to do this by displaying a copy of the map on the overhead projector and then plotting the point. You can then help individual youngsters having difficulty or ask the others to help one another. After plotting the center of the hurricane for several days you can talk about possible locations where the storm will cross land and the types of warnings and preparations needed for residents of those areas.

This activity is recommended only if you pursue it inductively. You will frustrate children if you try to teach latitude and longitude formally. This activity will introduce children to the terms longitude and latitude in a useful way because they are using the data to make predictions. They are not completing the activity to master a skill they are not ready to master.

The hurricane activity is also a useful means of considering the far-reaching effects of hurricanes. For example, in 1988 hurricane Gilbert was responsible for numerous deaths and considerable destruction of property, yet drought-stricken farmers in the Midwest received needed rain from the hurricane.

Columbus's Voyage. Andrews (1988) suggested charting the voyage of Columbus. Obtain a copy of Robert H. Funson's *The Log of Christopher Columbus* so that your students can plot the daily progress of Columbus's voyage to the New World.

Orienteering. Orienteering is a sport that requires the use of map-reading skills as individuals navigate a course from start to finish. While Olympic participants use maps and compasses to navigate a course in the fastest possible time, orienteering is an activity that is easily modified for use by elementary-school children. It will require youngsters to use maps to navigate a map course designed by their teacher. A third-grade teacher designed an orienteering activity for his children. They were provided with a map of the playground (see Figure 7–4) and allowed to navigate the course in groups of two while being supervised by a parent volunteer. While each pair of children took turns navigating the course, the remainder of the children were involved in classroom activities.

As the children moved from the starting point they were directed to proceed from one point to the next in numerical progression. As they reached each point they were to look for an index card containing the number for that point as well as a letter designated on the card. The letter located at each point was then entered on the corresponding blank of the map so that a message appeared when children had successfully reached all of the points. In this instance the message was, "Mapping fun."

This relatively simple orienteering activity may be adapted to more difficult levels by providing children with maps that direct them from one point to the next using cardinal directions and distances (Point 1: E-50m; Point 2: S-25m; etc.). A more advanced variation could require children to use a compass and distances to move from one point to the next (that is, point 1: 90 degrees–45m; point 2: 375 degrees–70m; etc.). Materials that contain excellent additional suggestions are readily available from the Boy Scouts and Girl Scouts.

Balloon Globes. Children can divide inflated balloons into hemispheres to develop a conceptual understanding of hemispheres. Papier-mâché globes can also be constructed and divided into hemispheres. The continents can then be added.

Using Scale to Compute Distances

While the NCSS Task Force listed this as a single skill area, it actually represents two separate skills; scale and distance. *Scale* describes the size of an area

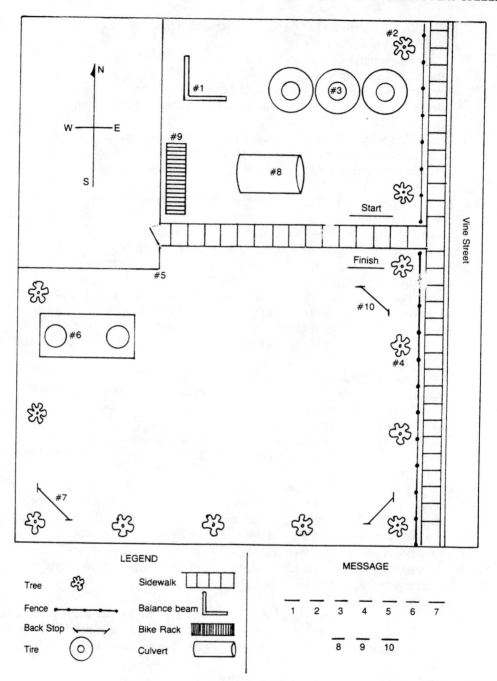

Figure 7–4 An Orienteering Map

Source: Van Cleaf, D.W. (1981). Strengthening map skills through orienteering. *Social Education, 45,* 462–463. Reprinted with permission of the National Council for the Social Studies.

illustrated on a map. *Distance* refers to the amount of space between objects and places on a map. Both skills are relatively abstract and mastery of either is not a practical expectation for most children in elementary school. Muir (1985) stated that the ability to compute distances on maps requires youngsters to use third- and fourth-grade mathematical skills, but cautions that few children will understand these skills in map applications until the fifth or sixth grades. While young children can understand the notion that large objects may be represented by smaller symbols, distance computations and comparisons of maps with different scales require an understanding of ratio. Ratio is a concept introduced in the upper elementary grades.

The following ideas will enable you to introduce the skills related to scale and distance in ways that are appropriate for children in the elementary grades. The activities are designed to introduce the skills to children; they are not designed to develop mastery. The children can enjoy the activities, gain a better understanding of maps, and develop a foundation for later mastery.

Fairy Tale Maps. Fairy tale maps are an exciting way to introduce the idea of scale and distance in an inductive manner. I used an adaptation of Ellis' (1986) fairy tale map idea during a summer enrichment program with a group of children ranging from second through sixth grade. I gave each child a piece of one inch graph paper and began telling them about several observations I made while flying over an area of the Midwest. I told children to make a map of my observations and help me decide who lived in the area. (*Note:* The area of the Midwest I was referring to was settled under the auspices of the Northwest Ordinance. Accordingly, the area was surveyed and ultimately subdivided into square-mile sections of land. Local counties were responsible for rural roads and usually built roads in east-west and north-south directions intersecting every mile. The result is that the countryside looks like graph paper.)

I began by telling the students that as we flew over an area I noticed a house one mile south and one mile east of the northwest corner of an area. Children were to draw a house and barn in the appropriate square of the graph paper. I also told them that I noticed initials on the roof of the barn, LRR. I told them that as I continued my flight over the area I noticed a hill nestled in some woods. The hill was approximately one and one-half miles east and one mile south of the house. Again, I noticed initials on the hill above what looked like an entrance to a den. The initials were WH. The children were instructed to draw the objects in the appropriate location on their graph paper maps. I continued describing my observations by telling the youngsters that I noticed a cottage and a shack surrounded by stacks of firewood. Initials were also on these dwellings. After the children added this last information to their maps I told them that I had discovered more information regarding other items such as railroad tracks, streams, bridges, and paths on my return flight. The maps were then put away until the next day when I could share additional information.

We continued the next day adding more information to the maps using terms such as *north, southwest, one mile east,* and so on. I finally told the children that I had actually flown over the area where Little Red Riding Hood lived. The initials represented the homes of the story's characters. Of course the younger children seemed to believe me. The older ones expressed disbelief that anyone would make such a claim, yet they quickly suggested making maps of other fairy tales.

This was an inductive teaching activity. Children were using direction, distance, and scale concepts without formal instruction. They determined their distances from one object to the next, followed and used direction terms, and worked with a scale in which one inch represented one mile. I extended the scale aspect one step further by having the students develop a similar map on one-half-inch graph paper. Thus they were required to change the scale. The concept of distance was introduced after the maps were completed by having the children develop legends for their maps and construct distance scales (that is, one inch equals one mile).

Walk a Square Mile. This idea was shared by Dorcas Cavett. She took her students on a field trip, and had them walk a square mile. Can you think of a more concrete way to develop an understanding of square mile, distance, and scale? By looking at a map of an area containing a square mile, walking the square mile, and then looking at the map when the trip is completed is a sure way to get children to develop a healthy understanding.

A Million Millimeters. Another suggestion that may help children develop an understanding of scale and distance is to walk a million millimeters. A group of third-grade children measured pieces of rope ten meters long (10,000 mm). They went outside and began stepping off the lengths of the ropes until they had traveled one million millimeters. They then went back to the classroom and looked at maps of the area and determined the number of city blocks represented by one million millimeters.

Bulletin Board Maps. A bulletin board may also be used to help children develop an understanding of scale and distance. At the beginning of the year a map of the classroom should be constructed within the confines of the bulletin board. A week later the classroom map should be replaced by a map of the school, also constructed within the confines of the bulletin board. A week later a map of the neighborhood should be constructed within the bulletin board space. This procedure can continue by constructing maps of the city, the state, the country, and finally the world in the same area. Each time the map is changed you can point out the changes in the area represented by the same amount of bulletin board space. You may even challenge students to find different size maps of the city, state, country, or other geographical areas.

Compare Maps and Make Inferences

As the old adage states, a picture is worth a thousand words. Maps are pictures and represent a sizable amount of information. Children should be able to look at maps and obtain information. They should also be able to use maps to discover relationships between information on several maps. For example, topographic and population maps can be used to help students discover the relationships between landform and population density. Similarly, children can see the relationships between rainfall and land use by comparing rainfall maps and land-use maps. The real challenge for teachers is to educate students so that they can use maps as valuable resources.

As with several previous map skills, a sophisticated ability to compare maps and use them to make inferences may not emerge until late in the elementary years. Nevertheless, elementary-age children can participate in map activities that will introduce them to different types of maps and encourage them to use maps to solve problems.

Hypothetical Maps. Ryan (1980) suggested using hypothetical maps to solve problems. Children are provided with a map of an area and asked to use the information to solve a problem. For example, the map illustrated in Figure 7–5 was presented to a group of second- and third-grade children. The children's task was to identify a location for a new elementary school. When youngsters had identified possible locations, the teacher led a discussion. The children were asked to identify their locations, the reasons for their selections, and reasons for not selecting other sites. Of course there was no right or wrong answer; therefore, children were free to explore optional locations.

Amusement Park Maps. A group of students in a social studies methods class had children examine maps of Six Flags Over Texas, an amusement park, and then develop maps of an "ideal" amusement park of the future. Amusement park maps require children to consider several problems as they prepare a park of the future. They must consider current likes and dislikes as well as possible changes. They may also be required to consider possible geographic locations and themes for their parks.

Current Events Maps. Children may also examine maps related to topics in current events discussions. Often there are geographic considerations related to current events. Using maps in conjunction with a discussion of the difficulty the Soviet Union was having in its war in Afghanistan illustrated that the difficulty was due in large part to the problems that traditional military forces confront in fighting in a mountainous region. The importance of the Persian Gulf may be demonstrated by showing children natural resource maps, import/export maps, and maps illustrating the religious composition of countries in the Gulf area.

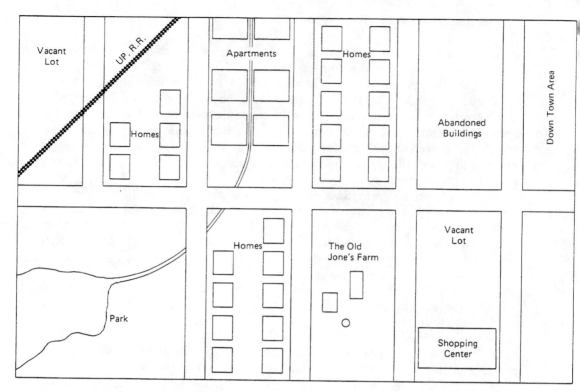

Figure 7–5 Hypothetical Map

Source: Ryan, F.L. (1980). *The social studies sourcebook: Ideas for teaching in the elementary and middle school*, p. 41. Copyright © 1980 by Allyn and Bacon. Adapted and reprinted with permission of Allyn and Bacon.

Recreational Maps. I recall a barber who was more of a bass fisherman than a barber. He fished in a watershed area in the Midwest in which a number of lakes were constructed by the Army Corps of Engineers. The barber had collected a variety of maps produced for each lake in the watershed area. He had aerial photographs of the land made before the projects had been started, he had aerial photographs of the lakes during the construction phase, and he had topographic maps of the lakes before and after construction. Before he would go out to fish he would examine his maps and identify the most appropriate fishing spots under the existing water and weather conditions.

Topographic and aerial photographs of similar areas could be provided for children who would be asked to locate a variety of recreational areas. Excellent fishing spots, hunting spots, or possible locations for campgrounds are recreational areas children can locate using topographic and aerial maps.

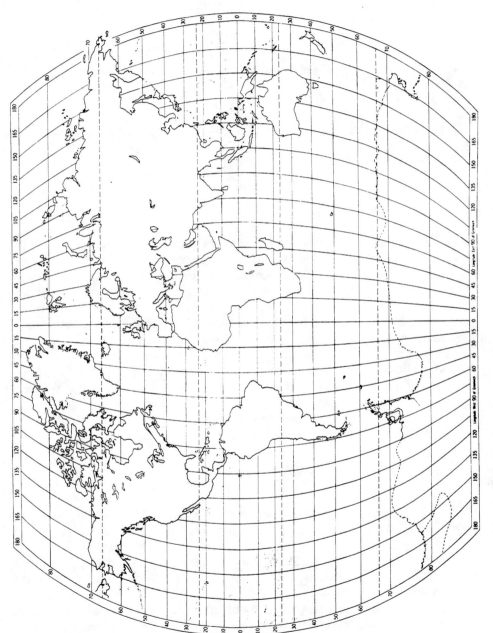

A projection map of the world. Projection maps contain distortions.

Mystery Island. Zevin (1969) described an activity in which children were presented with a series of maps containing information about a mystery island. Children were required to consider the information contained on each of the maps and identify a suitable location for a major population center. This activity is described more completely in Chapter 9.

Historical Maps. Compare historical and current maps to identify changes and reasons for changes. For example, compare a map of the original thirteen colonies and a current map of the area. Ask children to determine why the westward boundaries were limited.

Land-Use Maps. Determine how people have adapted to geographical features by examining land-use maps. How do rivers, airports, and lakes affect people's use of areas?

CAUTIONS

Decisions regarding what to teach and how to teach are as important as deciding what should not be taught. Unfortunately, many educators and publishers are not knowledgeable about the needs and limitations of elementary-school children. For example, children can learn to construct and read maps of familiar environments well before they can understand abstract maps of distant places. Single-quadrant grid systems are appropriate, but latitude and longitude systems are too abstract for young children. The concept of map projections appears in several elementary social studies textbook series. However, the concept is not appropriate before seventh grade.

Many basal reading series include map-reading activities in their workbooks and black line masters. These activities are paper-and-pencil activities and generally not appropriate for elementary-age children. Exercise care when selecting and using these materials so that you do not have your students participate in inappropriate activities simply because they are "in the book."

SUMMARY

Map-reading activities should be exciting and concrete. Children can learn to read maps with relative ease if instruction is geared to their developmental levels. Six map-reading skills have been identified for the elementary grades by the NCSS Task Force (1989). Two of the skills were combined and described together in this chapter. Concrete, motivating activities designed to help you teach these skills were also presented.

Children must become actively involved in map-making and map-reading activities. Remember, people who can make maps can also read maps.

SUGGESTED ACTIVITIES

1. Observe an elementary-age child construct a map of something in the environment. Encourage the child to describe the process as the map is being constructed.

2. Review the mapping lessons in several elementary social studies textbooks. Compare the percent of maps related to the children's familiar environment to the percent of maps of distant environments.

3. Locate the following types of maps in your state's section of an atlas: natural resources, population, vegetation, topographic, industrial use, agriculture, and rainfall. Identify as many relationships among the maps as possible. For example, what are the relationships between topography and population?

Elementary students are capable of learning to read many types of graphs.

Photograph by Vivienne, Photo Researchers, Inc.

chapter 8

Methods
for Teaching
Graphing Skills

A picture is worth a thousand words.

Chinese proverb

AS YOU READ...

- describe a developmentally appropriate sequence for teaching graphing skills
- describe activities that may be used to teach graphing skills at each graphing stage
- describe how the relationships between the variables *time* and *quantity* affect the type of graphs produced
- list the steps involved in constructing four types of graphs

INTRODUCTION

Graphs are pictorial representations of quantities. Many graphs illustrate relationships between two or more quantities, such as a bar graph comparison of the populations of several states in a region of the country. Other graphs illustrate changes that occur in the value of one item over a period of time. Changes in one state's population over a number of years would be illustrated using a line graph.

Graphs are important tools for social scientists because they succinctly display large amounts of information and complex relationships. Graph skills are also important for children. The ability to use graphs will help them obtain and interpret information. Youngsters can extract a vast amount of information from graphs, even if they have limited reading skills. Graphing also provides them with alternative means of representing their own data and findings.

The NCSS Task Force (1989) included the ability to interpret graphs as one of the essential skills for elementary social studies programs. But the development of graphing skills is not limited to social studies. Math, science, and reading programs share responsibility for graph-skill instruction.

Although these content areas share responsibility with social studies for graph-skill instruction, most elementary methods textbooks provide little guidance for prospective teachers. This chapter has been included in the text because an adequate description of techniques for teaching graphing skills is missing in most elementary methods textbooks.

Elementary-grade students are capable of learning to read and interpret many types of graphs. This chapter will assist you in teaching graph skills to your students. The chapter includes a description of a developmentally appropriate stage progression for teaching graph skills, a description of four types of graphs, and the steps involved in constructing the graphs. Suggestions on how to teach children to construct and read a variety of graphs are also included here.

There is an underlying philosophy present in this chapter. Your students will easily learn to read graphs if they have numerous opportunities to construct graphs. As with map reading, children will learn the principles involved in reading and interpreting graphs from the experiences they have constructing graphs. Further, initial graphing instruction is most beneficial when the activities are related to your students' immediate experiences.

DEVELOPMENTAL STAGES

The Nuffield Foundation (1967) described a progression of five stages related to the development of graphing skills. The progression begins at a concrete level and gradually leads children to pictorial and abstract graphs. Each of the stages is described below. Because these five stages do not describe more difficult graphing skills appropriate for instruction in the upper elementary grades, this section also includes a description of several additional ideas.

Stage 1

Stage 1 activities involve children in the development of rudimentary graphs that are limited to comparisons of two quantities. Rudimentary graphs are produced when children use concrete materials and pictures to illustrate and compare quantities. For example, primary-grade students could each be given a block to represent themselves. The children could then place their blocks in columns according to the sex of each child. The result would be two columns of blocks representing the total number of boys and girls in the group.

Young children can make block graphs.

Photograph by David W. Van Cleaf.

If your students are having difficulty using objects to represent items, you could have them form a people graph. To form a people graph, children line up in columns according to the given topic. For example, boys could line up in one column and girls in another. The result is a graph illustrating the number of boys and the number of girls in the class.

This activity gets the children actively involved in the construction of a graph. People graphs also help illustrate the importance of maintaining a one-to-one correspondence between children in each column. As children participate in the graphs they must line up next to one another and avoid bunching up.

Children should have opportunities to compare the two quantities represented by their graphs. They should be encouraged to use terms such as *greater than, less than,* and *more than* to describe the quantities. This is essential because children not only need to construct graphs, but they also need to develop the ability to examine the data contained in their graphs.

Several additional ideas may prove useful as you help your students develop concrete graphs appropriate for this stage.

1. Children could line up and make people graphs of the number of children wearing tennis shoes versus the number not wearing tennis shoes; the number of children who walk to and from school versus the number who do not walk to and from school; or the number of children whose favorite food is pizza versus the number whose favorite food may be tacos.
2. Children could graph the number of students eating hot and cold lunches each day.
3. Children could use beads to represent data and string the beads to illustrate their comparisons. The bead graphs are fun to construct and are concrete. If cereal, such as Fruit Loops, is used the graphs can also be very tasty.
4. Monopoly houses and hotels could be used to graph the number of children living in houses and those in apartments.
5. Children can be given two types of wrapped candy and make a graph of their favorite type of candy.

The use of concrete objects is important for teaching graph skills to young children. Concrete objects enable children to understand the relationships between the objects and the items they represent. They also can be easily manipulated and arranged to maintain a one-to-one correspondence.

Stage 2

In Stage 2 the number of quantities illustrated in children's graphs is extended. Stage 2 graphs also assume a more permanent form.

Children can construct graphs of the months in which they were born. The teacher provides a sheet of paper on which the months of the year have been written across the paper. Each child is given a colorful sticker and instructed to write his or her name on it. Each child then places his or her sticker in the column corresponding to the month of birth. When this is completed the class has a graph illustrating the number of children born in each month.

After constructing the graph, children should have an opportunity to compare the quantities in the columns. They may be asked to indicate which month has the most birthdays, the least, the months with similar numbers of birthdays, or months in which no birthdays are represented.

In this stage children may begin using pictures that they draw to represent objects on their graphs. For example, children could draw pictures of themselves and glue their pictures in the columns representing the months in which they were born.

The graphs produced during this stage should retain a one-to-one correspondence. That is, one picture must represent one item represented on the graph, and equal spacing of items in each column must be maintained.

The ideas and activities described for Stage 1 graphs may be extended for use during Stage 2. This is easily accomplished by identifying and collecting data for additional categories of the same topic. For example, their candy graphs could include additional types of candy. Children could also be given a package of M & M's and construct a graph of the different colors. They can then draw pictures or use some other means of representing items on their graphs.

Stage 3

Stage 3 represents a transition from pictures to the use of more abstract representations, such as paper squares. Thus, children make a transition from concrete objects and picture graphs to bar graphs.

The students could begin by drawing pictures of an item such as their pets and placing those pictures in appropriate columns on paper. They should then use squares of colored paper to represent their pets and affix the squares to appropriate columns on another graph prepared by the teacher. Blue squares could represent dogs, green squares could represent cats, and yellow squares could represent fish.

Some social studies methods students used this activity quite successfully with kindergarten and first-grade children. Youngsters were given index cards and instructed to draw a picture of their favorite pets. When the pictures were completed the methods students asked them to tape their pictures in appropriate columns on the chalkboard. After the quantities were compared and discussed the students gave the children paper squares (approximately 3" × 3"). Children were then asked to place their squares in appropriate columns representing their favorite pets. The index-card graph and the paper-square graph were then compared. An example of a similar activity is illustrated in Figure 8–1.

Additional suggestions for developing Stage 3 graphing skills include:

1. Drawing faces on index cards and coloring the hair to represent the child's hair color. The children may then tape the cards in the appropriate categories and compare the data. This activity should be followed by providing children with blank paper squares and requiring them to color the paper squares the color of their hair. The squares should then be affixed in columns for the appropriate categories.

2. This same procedure could be used with the topic *favorite food*. Children first draw pictures and construct a classroom graph of their favorite foods. They can then use paper squares to construct a similar graph.

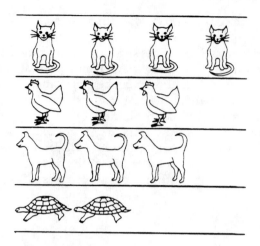

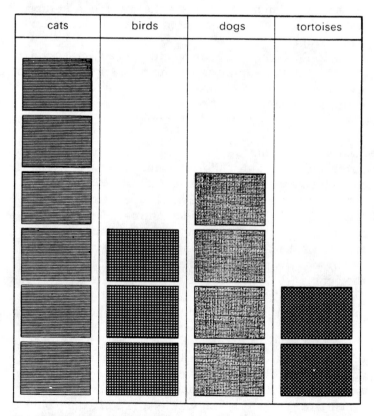

Figure 8–1 Picture and Paper Square Graphs

Source: Nuffield Foundation (1967). *Pictorial representation,* pp. 14–15. New York: John Wiley. Reprinted with permission of the Nuffield Foundation.

Stage 4

A transition from using pictures and paper squares to the use of graph paper occurs in Stage 4. Students learn to use abstract columns on graph paper to illustrate data. Using the data related to children's favorite pets, your students could be given graph paper, designate a column for each type of pet, and then color one square in each column for each pet. They should add a vertical axis parallel to the columns illustrating the number of pets in each category. This axis should be numbered to create a number line. The number line makes the graph easier to read and introduces the students to skills developed in the next stage.

A transitional activity may be needed if children are experiencing difficulties constructing graphs by coloring the squares on the graph paper. You may find it helpful to place blocks on the graph paper and then allow your students to trace around the column formed by the blocks. Cuisenaire rods work well with metric-ruled graph paper and Uniflex cubes work well with one-inch graph paper. When the blocks are removed the children can color the squares and form columns.

Additional Stage 4 activities may include ideas already described in previous stages as well as the following topics: favorite TV shows, favorite football teams, types of family cars, modes of traveling to and from school, occupational preferences, natural resources, rainfall, election results, vacation spots, etc.

Stage 5

In this stage children begin making bar graphs. This type of graph is considered abstract because children must use bars to represent data.

Squared graph paper should be used initially as it provides children with concrete reference points that assist the construction of the bars on their graphs. Children can color a square on the graph paper to represent each item in the categories being graphed. As the squares are being colored they become the bars on the graph. After constructing bar graphs using graph paper, children can proceed to constructing bar graphs on unlined paper.

Graphs produced in this stage should have axes, which are the horizontal and vertical number lines. The vertical number line provides the means by which students establish the lengths of the bars representing each quantity. Your students should also construct a horizontal axis on which they can arrange the categories of their data.

Most graphs use the horizontal axis for the categories they intend to compare. If children were comparing the number of pets owned by their classmates they would write the types of pets along the horizontal axis. Researchers usually place the independent variable, which is the item they identify for comparison, along the horizontal axis. The vertical axis is used as a number line representing the quantities of the variables being compared. Researchers place the dependent variable along the vertical axis.

Additional Developmental Considerations

These five stages progressed from concrete graphing activities to pictorial graphing activities and ended with relatively abstract graphing activities. These are important steps and necessary for the development of graphing skills.

Additional aspects of graphing must be considered when children have achieved competence with Stage 5 bar graphs. To this point the vertical axes have been numbered using multiples of one. That is, children count by ones. However, there are times when number lines cannot be numbered sequentially counting by multiples of one. Thus it may be necessary to count by multiples of two, five, or ten. For example, if children were graphing the daily temperature during a hot spell, the paper on which they were constructing their graphs would probably be too short to number from one through 115. In such a situation children could develop a number line counting by multiples of five.

A second concept relates to a picture on a picture graph representing more than one item. At times one picture may be used to represent a number of items. Population graphs may use one figure to represent thousands of people. Similarly, a picture of one barrel of oil may represent a million barrels of oil. Children in the upper elementary grades are exposed to such graphs in their social studies textbooks and need opportunities to construct similar graphs.

The stages described above proceed from the construction of concrete to pictorial and finally to abstract graphs. Consider the abilities of your students as you develop your graphing lessons. Your students may become frustrated if you present activities beyond their levels of understanding. They will become bored if your lessons are too easy. Finally, graphing requires children to follow a series of steps. Provide ample time as you lead your students through each step. If you rush, your students may become confused by the steps rather than the conceptual nature of the graphing process.

CONSTRUCTING FOUR TYPES OF GRAPHS

Elementary school children will be exposed to four types of graphs: picture graphs, bar graphs, line graphs, and circle graphs. As you recall, graphs are used to compare quantities, but there is another critical attribute that has not been mentioned. Time is also an attribute that must be considered when graphing data. The idea that graphs represent a quantity element and a time element is important in selecting the type of graph you want to construct.

Picture graphs are used to represent comparisons of different quantities at a given time. The comparison of the number of boys and girls in a class is a comparison of two quantities at the specific time the comparison is made. The next day the data may change—a new student may be admitted or several others may be absent—and the data on the graph are no longer accurate.

Bar graphs also illustrate comparisons between two or more quantities at a given time. If your class constructed a bar graph comparing the number and types of pets owned by the students it would be accurate for that time only. The acquisition of new pets, pets getting lost, or the arrival of a new child in the classroom would change the data represented by the graph.

Circle graphs are relatively easy to read, but not to construct. Circle graphs show percentage comparisons of several quantities at a given time. A circle graph may illustrate how children spend their day. However, the percentages may change from day to day and the graphs become inaccurate.

Each of these three graphs is used to compare several quantities at a specific time. Line graphs, however, are designed to compare changes in a quantity over a period of time. For example, graphing daily temperature changes would be done on a line graph. Similarly, daily or weekly fluctuations in the price of a stock or the price of gold would be represented on a line graph.

This section describes the steps required to construct each of these four types of graphs. You may require your students to follow each of the steps or you may modify lessons as necessary for your graphing activities.

Picture Graphs

Although picture graphs may not be as accurate as other types of graphs, they are visually appealing and relatively easy to construct, read, and interpret. Remember, picture graphs usually represent a comparison of several quantities at a given time period. The following steps are recommended. (See sample picture graph.)

1. *Collect the data.* Children should be encouraged to gather the data they will use for their graphs. They may simply look around the room and count the number of boys and girls or they may count the number of class members with light and dark hair. Allowing students to collect the data will make the activity more meaningful and more concrete.

2. *Construct a table.* A table will enable the children to organize their information in a way that will be easier to use as they begin constructing their graphs. If children were graphing the types of pets owned by class members the teacher could construct the following table on the chalkboard and add the appropriate types of pets and corresponding number for each.

Type of Pet	Number of Each
Dog	
Cat	
Bird	
Fish	
Snake	
etc.	

A child's picture graph.

3. *Construct the graph.*

   a. *Draw the vertical and horizontal axes.* Children will probably need guidance the first few times they draw axes. You might help them initially by providing paper that includes the axes.

   b. *Select a unit of measure.* Usually you will have one picture represent one item. Older children may elect to have one picture represent a greater number of items. For example, they could have one silver coin represent one thousand ounces of silver production.

   c. *Draw the pictures on the graph.* If you are using pictures drawn by children and then affixed to a classroom graph, you would have them affix their pictures to the appropriate place on the graph.

   d. *Label the axes.* In this step the students provide written names for each axis. If the class is involved in graphing the number of pets, students might label one axis "types of pets" and label the other "number of pets." This process can be omitted, but it does help others read and interpret their graphs.

   e. *Title the graph.* Graphs are somewhat like stories. A title will enable others to determine the main idea before they examine the contents. The title for a graph about the children's pets might be, "Our Pets."

Bar Graphs

There are essentially two types of bar graphs. There are bar graphs that have spaces between adjacent bars, and histographs that do not have spaces between adjacent bars. The term *bar graph* is used in this text to describe both variations.

Bar graphs are the most widely used type of graph. They are somewhat more accurate than picture graphs, but they are also more abstract. Like picture graphs, bar graphs illustrate comparisons between quantities at a given time period. The following steps should be followed as you lead your students through the process of constructing bar graphs. The steps are similar to the steps described for constructing picture graphs; therefore this section provides a limited number of comments.

1. *Collect the data.*

2. *Construct a table.*

3. *Construct the graph.*

   a. *Draw the axes.* Again, children may need help as this may present difficulty.

   b. *Select a unit of measure.* When constructing bar graphs a unit of measure will be used to construct the number line, usually the vertical axis. Unless otherwise appropriate, the unit of measure should be one.

   c. *Identify the positions for each category.* If you are graphing the types and numbers of pets owned by children in your classroom you would decide where to place each type of pet along one of the axes (usually the horizontal axis).

   d. *Plot the quantities in the appropriate column and shade in or draw the bar.*

   e. *Label the axes.*

   f. *Title the graph.*

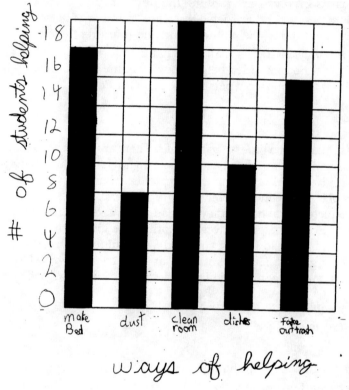

The Working Class

Joshua Schoenhofer

A child's bar graph.

Because most schools are used as voting places during elections, children could conduct exit polls. They could interview voters as they leave the voting booths and ask them to indicate for whom they voted. After surveying the voters, children could graph their data onto bar graphs. The data could be used to predict the outcome of the election.

Line Graphs

Line graphs are usually the most accurate type of graphs. They are particularly useful for illustrating changes in the value of one quantity over a period of time. The focus therefore is on changes in one quantity rather than comparison of several quantities. However, as children's competence in constructing line graphs improves they can create line graphs that illustrate changes in several quantities during the same time period. The following steps are recommended for the construction of line graphs.

1. *Collect data.* An example about graphing daily temperature changes will be used to illustrate the process. If you use this example, you might allow children to collect the data. Each day a child may call the time and temperature phone number or read an outside thermometer at a predetermined time. The first day begins by developing a table, drawing axes, titling each axis, developing a number line along the vertical axis, and plotting the first temperature reading. Each day new temperatures can be added to the graphs.

2. *Construct a table.* Develop a table similar to the one below.

Day	Mon	Tue	Wed	Thur	Fri	Sat	etc.
Temp	57	60	54	58	62	?	

3. *Construct the graph.*
   a. *Draw axes.*
   b. *Select units of measure.* Days will appear along the horizontal axis and degrees along the vertical axis (you might use multiples of 2). If graph paper is used, children should number the lines on the graph paper rather than the spaces. The use of lines will make it easier for them to locate points and their graphs will be more accurate. Similarly, the days of the week should be represented along lines rather than spaces.
   c. *Plot the points.* In this case children will make dots for the daily temperature. The dots should be relatively small pencil marks. Since they have numbered the lines of the graph paper it will be easier to locate the appropriate points. You may notice that many of the children draw light lines from the horizontal axis and the vertical axis as a means of determining where the two intersect. This is a typical practice and is acceptable.
   d. *Connect the points.* Children may use rulers to connect each point or they may sketch the lines.
   e. *Label the axes.*
   f. *Title the graph.*

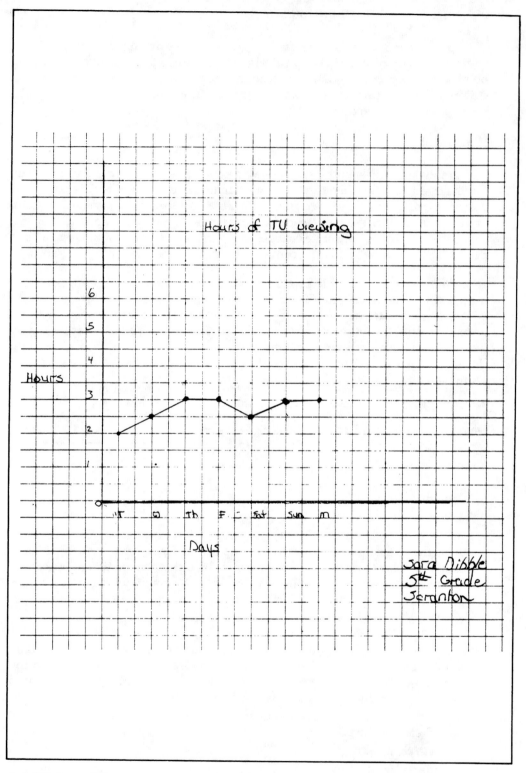

A child's line graph.

Line graphs, such as graphs of the temperature changes, may be used to illustrate two additional concepts. Line graphs are useful for predicting future changes in the data. As your students add data to their temperature graphs each day they can predict what the temperature will be the following day. They must examine their graphs and use the data on their graphs to make their predictions. This is called *extrapolation*.

Because school is not in session on Saturdays and Sundays, students will not have data for those two days. While some children may want to mark their weekend temperatures at zero because no data are available, this is not appropriate. Children can use existing graph data to infer what the temperature may have been on dates for which data are missing. Children should examine data for the days before and after the missing data and infer what the temperature might have been. This is referred to as *interpolation*. Extrapolation and interpolation are excellent ways to encourage children to use the data on their graphs to make predictions.

One of the most useful and exciting line-graphing activities my students participated in was graphing the local university's weekly football scores. Each member of my third-grade class received a piece of graph paper with the axes drawn on the graph paper. I had also written the following along the horizontal axis: Week One, Week Two, Week Three. I did not include additional weeks as I intended to allow children to add these later in the season.

After the first game we briefly talked about the game and the best way to illustrate our team's score on the graph. The children quickly discovered the need to develop a number scale along the vertical axis. After they added numbers to the vertical axis they plotted the team's points for the first game. The children asked if we were going to record the other team's score, and we decided to include the opponent's score. Our team's score was plotted using a dot and the opponent's score was plotted using an x.

The graphs were then put away until Friday, when students were asked to examine their graphs and predict the score of the next game. I recorded their predictions. On Monday, after the weekend game, the predictions were checked and the actual scores were recorded on their graphs.

This cycle—predictions on Fridays and graphing on Mondays—continued through the football season. In addition to developing line-graph skills in an exciting way, the children became remarkably accurate with their predictions. As a matter of fact, several began bringing information sheets quoting the weekly point spread.

Many communities have recycling centers. Children can graph the weekly prices for items such as aluminum cans and newsprint. They can then predict (extrapolate) the amount of change that will occur before the next price quote is published.

Most states have enacted mandatory seatbelt laws. An interesting graphing activity was conducted as one state's seatbelt law was phased in. Children observed the number of people wearing seatbelts prior to implementation of the law and then at one-week intervals after the law became effective. Of course, care was exercised to keep as many variables as possible constant. Although the seatbelt laws may now be in effect in your area, new laws may present similar opportunities to collect and graph data.

Older children could collect daily temperature information and the amount of electricity used by their community. They could then develop a line graph for each set of data and compare relationships between temperature and electrical use.

Children could select a type of fruit, vegetable, or other commodity and record weekly changes in the price charged by a local grocery store. After several readings have been recorded they can interview the grocer to determine reasons for the fluctuations in price.

Another suggestion relates to the number of children eating school lunches. Each day the students should record the number of classmates eating the school's lunch and note the menu for the day. They can then graph daily changes in the lunch count and identify favorite and least-liked foods.

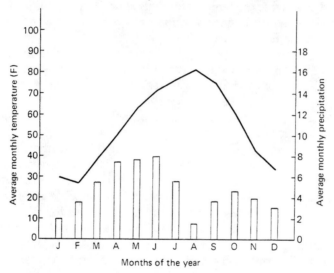

Sample climograph.

Climographs are another variation. A climograph uses a combination of a line graph (to illustrate monthly average temperatures) and a bar graph (to illustrate average monthly precipitation). Children may construct a climograph for their community and make comparisons with climographs of other communities. (See example of climograph above.)

Circle Graphs

Like picture graphs and bar graphs, circle graphs illustrate a number of quantities at a given time. Circle graphs are relatively easy to read but quite difficult for most young children to construct. Children should first understand the concept of degrees and that a circle consists of 360 degrees. They must also understand how to compute percent, fractions, and ratios because they will need to determine the portion of the data that falls within each part of the circle. They will need to be able to convert the percent or proportion of the data to the total area of the circle to represent the data effectively. Finally, students will need to count the number of degrees along the circumference of the circle and draw radii for each area. This is a rather difficult task for most elementary-school children.

The steps required to construct circle graphs are listed for your information, but caution is advised.

1. Collect information to be graphed.
2. Convert data to percentages.
3. Convert percentages to degrees (one percent is equal to 3.6 degrees).
4. Draw a circle and one radius for a starting point.
5. Use a protractor to mark the degrees for each portion of the data and draw a radius for each.
6. Label the sections.
7. Title the graph.

Simple circle graphs can be constructed before children are capable of using the mathematical skills outlined above. They can collect data and approximate the area within the circle for each portion of the data. For example, students could make a rudimentary circle graph illustrating the proportion of boys and girls in the class. Similar circle graphs could illustrate the proportion of children by hair color, favorite pets, or how they spend the time during a typical school day. Remember, because the children cannot make accurate demarcations on their circle graphs they should be allowed to make "rough" approximations.

You can also help young children construct circle graphs by drawing circles for them and providing them with fractional pieces (like pie slices) that will fit within the circles. You are advised to use relatively simple fractional parts with denominators of 2, 4, and 8. The children can then select precut portions representing their data and place the pieces in the circles. You might use round paper plates rather than drawing circles on sheets of paper.

Construction Cautions

Children are going to make mistakes as they construct their graphs. These mistakes are normal and indicate the uniqueness of children's thought processes. Several of the more common errors are mentioned in this section.

The first caution relates to maintaining a one-to-one correspondence. If children make a people graph comparing boys and girls, the boys and girls should line up next to one another rather than bunch up. Similarly, if children are making picture graphs they should arrange their pictures so that pictures in the different columns are spaced in the same way.

A second caution relates specifically to picture graphs and bar graphs. Pictures should be similar in size. It may be useful to have children draw pictures on index cards as a means of maintaining similar-sized pictures. If paper squares are used to represent data the squares should be the same size. If children are

A child's circle graph.

constructing bar graphs care should be taken so that the width of the bars are similar. Failure to attend to these points may mislead children when they interpret the data on their graphs.

A third caution relates to numbering the axes. Children often construct their number lines using the data collected rather than using a consistent numerical scale. For example, children might have constructed their vertical axis for the temperature line graph using the temperatures contained in the table (see Figure 8–2) rather than establishing a number line.

A fourth caution is similar to the third but usually occurs as children construct the horizontal axis. They must maintain an equivalent distance between each item on the axis. Youngsters often fail to note this requirement and may have two lines separating Monday from Tuesday and Tuesday from Wednesday, but then use three lines to separate Wednesday from Thursday.

Figure 8–2 Incorrect number line

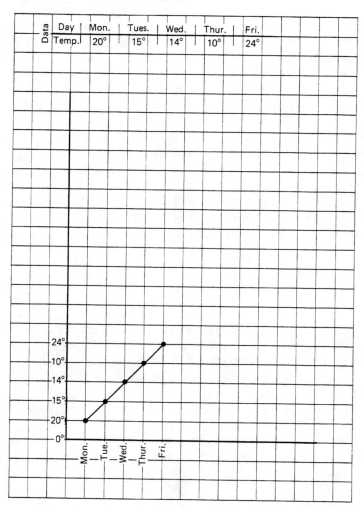

Data	Day	Mon.	Tues.	Wed.	Thur.	Fri.
	Temp.	20°	15°	14°	10°	24°

Fifth, children often number or label the spaces rather than the lines when constructing line graphs. This makes it difficult to plot points accurately. This practice is usually developed when children are constructing bar graphs because the bar graphs use the spaces.

A final caution relates to the youngsters who mark zero when they have no data for a point. This was mentioned during the description of line graphs when many of my students marked zero for temperatures on Saturdays and Sundays. Children also like to start their graphs by drawing their lines from zero. Thus, if they were graphing daily temperatures starting with data for Monday they would connect a line from zero indicating that the temperature on Sunday was zero.

GETTING THE MOST FROM GRAPHS

Several suggestions will enable you to help your students derive the most benefit from graphing activities. As your students begin graphing activities they should participate in a period of planning with you. You can describe the activity and solicit input from the children, who may be asked to identify possible kinds of data to collect as well as ways to collect the data. After suitable plans have been considered, they should participate in the actual graphing activity. Finally, children should be allowed to reflect on the work they have completed. This is an important step and one that is frequently overlooked. Discussions of the graphs and the work that students have completed should occur at this point.

However, discussions are not usually sufficient because of the amount of talking involved. The Nuffield Foundation suggested the use of "White Papers." White Papers are short written comments about the graph and the graphing activity.

Motivation is an important consideration in any learning experience. You can ensure that motivation is high and that children will learn from the activity if they work with familiar topics and collect information relevant to their interests.

SUMMARY

Graphs are symbolic representations of quantities. They may be used to compare several quantities at a given time. Picture graphs, bar graphs, and circle graphs are generally the most appropriate graphs for illustrating these types of data. Graphs may also be used to compare changes in one variable over a period of time. Line graphs are usually the best type of graph for this purpose.

Stages involved in the development of graphing skills were described in this chapter as were recommended activities. The stages proceeded along a developmental continuum moving from the use of concrete representations of data, to pictorial representations of data, and finally to abstract representations of data.

You are encouraged to provide children with numerous concrete and pictorial experiences prior to the use of abstract forms of representation.

Social mathematics is a new concept emerging in social studies education (Hartoonian, 1989). As children study social phenomena they are required to use mathematical abilities to express relationships. Graphing is one primary means of introducing youngsters to social mathematics.

This chapter is built on the belief that children who can construct graphs can also read graphs. The chapter described the steps necessary to help children learn to construct their own graphs.

Graphing can be an exciting learning experience if presented and developed in appropriate ways. The information in this chapter, when combined with your creative ideas, will enable you to teach graphing skills with a high degree of professionalism.

SUGGESTED ACTIVITIES

1. Develop a graphing lesson for primary-grade children. Begin with a people graph and then have students construct a picture graph.

2. Count the number and types of cars parked in your neighborhood. Construct a bar graph illustrating the number of each type of car. You may classify cars by manufacturer or by the country of origin.

3. Record changes in a quantity over a period of time. Daily temperature, the time of sunset, the growth of a plant, the prime interest rate, the number of miles driven, or changes in the price of a stock or a commodity can be used for this activity. Construct a line graph.

4. Brainstorm possible topics you might use as you help children learn to construct picture, bar, and line graphs.

Children should be actively involved in the process of learning. Using a library's card catalog is one way.

Photograph by Ken Karp.

chapter 9

Teaching Content Through Inquiry

What's inquiry? I don't know, but I'll try to find out.

(Jake, grade 3)

AS YOU READ...

- describe how inquiry supports the product and the process aspects of teaching
- list and describe the four steps in the inquiry process
- develop a rationale supporting inquiry instruction. Support your rationale with examples of inquiry activities described in this chapter

INTRODUCTION

Educators often view learning from two perspectives—as either a product or a process. In a *product-oriented* classroom the emphasis is on the information that students will learn. Names, dates, facts, descriptions of events and their causes illustrate the type of material taught in a product-oriented classroom.

The emphasis in a *process-oriented* classroom is somewhat different. Process-oriented classrooms focus on the processes of learning. *Investigation, discovery, analyzing values, problem solving,* and *inquiry* are terms illustrating the teaching emphasis in process-oriented classrooms. Such classrooms focus on *how* information is acquired rather than an emphasis on *what* is learned, which is characteristic of product-oriented classrooms.

The teacher's and children's roles differ depending on whether they are in a product- or a process-oriented setting. Product-oriented classrooms are teacher-directed. The teacher is in charge and controls the information that is presented. Textbooks are used in traditional ways in most product-oriented classrooms because of the content they contain. Children are relatively passive in this type of environment.

The teaching-learning emphasis in a process-oriented classroom is more child-centered. Children become actively involved in the processes of learning. They are required to think critically and solve problems. The shift in emphasis moves from the mastery of extensive information to an emphasis on considering important information appropriate to solve problems, make decisions, and identify relationships.

Process-oriented teachers remain in control of their classrooms, but the type of leadership exercised is different. Process-oriented teachers *guide* children more frequently than they *tell* children. They are facilitators of learning in that they orchestrate lessons and guide their students through lessons. Children discover and consider appropriate content, but within the context of using the information.

Inquiry is one of the strategies used in process-oriented classrooms. Inquiry is a child-centered instructional strategy that encourages children to investigate problems and discover information. The process is similar to the procedures used by social scientists investigating problems and discovering information.

Research findings reported by Muir (1979) indicate that elementary-grade children perform better on tasks requiring higher-level thinking when involved in inquiry activities. Improved cognitive processing and the development of content knowledge are important functions of a sound social studies program, and improvements in both result from inquiry activities.

This chapter describes the inquiry process and sample activities.

INQUIRY STEPS

The inquiry process is a variation of the scientific method. While the scientific method and the inquiry method are generally described as five-step processes, teachers may combine or expand the steps to suit the purpose of any given inquiry activity. Table 9–1 enumerates the steps in both the scientific method and a modified inquiry format appropriate for elementary-age children.

The essential difference between the two models is the manner in which the steps have been modified. When working with young children the number of steps in the inquiry process should be modified so that the hypothesizing step is included within the problem statement. Because of the nature of elementary children and the flexibility needed to pursue a variety of topics using the inquiry process, the four-step inquiry model shown in Table 9–1 is recommended. The four steps are (1) problem identification, (2) data collection, (3) data analysis, and (4) conclusion.

Table 9–1 Comparisons of Scientific and Inquiry Models

SCIENTIFIC METHOD	PROPOSED INQUIRY
1. Definition of problem	1. Identify problem (and hypotheses or questions)
2. Statement of hypotheses	2. Collect data
3. Deductive reasoning (implications of hypotheses)	3. Analyze data
4. Collection and analysis of data	4. Draw conclusions
5. Confirming or rejecting hypotheses	

The four-step inquiry model is described in the following paragraphs. As you read about the four steps you might consider how you utilize the inquiry process as you make major decisions in your personal life. You should also consider how you will use inquiry with your students.

Step 1: The Problem Statement

Without a problem there is nothing to investigate. Therefore, the inquiry process should begin with a problem requiring resolution. A third-grade teacher, tired of her students' constant complaints about the poor quality of the school's hot lunches, presented them with the following inquiry problem: "Are the school's hot lunches as bad as you claim?"

Inquiry is not limited to solving problems. Children can use inquiry to learn more about a specific topic. For example, my fifth-grade students were required to select topics related to the Revolutionary War period. I had listed a number of topics on the board. Topics included lifestyles, war technology, political and military leaders, issues leading to the war, transportation, trade, and major battles. Students were then required to select a topic and to identify four questions they would like to answer regarding the topic. They then began collecting information that would help them answer the questions.

Many advocates of inquiry recommend that researchers generate hypotheses related to their inquiry problem. An hypothesis is a statement of what you expect to find. However, not all social science research problems are amenable to hypothesizing. Social scientists will often identify research questions rather than use hypotheses. The researchers are not certain what they will find and the use of questions gives them more flexibility as they pursue their investigations. Your students may use either hypotheses or research questions in their inquiry activities.

In the "hot lunch" inquiry activity the children identified hypotheses explaining why the lunches were bad. Sample hypotheses included: the cooks don't know how to cook, the food is bad, the person who makes the menu doesn't know what kids like. In the American Revolution inquiry activity the children identified research questions. A group of children investigating the lifestyles structured their investigations to answer the following questions: What were the houses like? How were the homes furnished? What kinds of hardships did people encounter? What kinds of clothes did people wear?

While scientists and social scientists suggest that the hypothesis/question process be a separate step, elementary-age children should include this as part of the problem step. By combining the problem with the hypotheses/questions you will help students clarify the focus of the problem. The hypotheses/questions provide clarification of the problem and a clear direction for the students' investigations.

Step 2: Collect Data

Data must come from resources, and it is at this point that inquiry goes beyond the limitations of traditional classroom practices. Children's social studies reports usually consist of information copied directly from an encyclopedia or textbook. Children transcribe considerable information, but they learn little about the topic.

Children will need information as they pursue the answers to their problems. Scientists and social scientists alike spend an extensive amount of time collecting their data—some spend years collecting data. Social scientists do not limit their resources to entries in textbooks and encyclopedias. Although children do not have years to collect data for their inquiry activities, they should be provided sufficient time to consult a variety of resources for their investigations.

Inquiry is more exciting and more appropriate when children are encouraged to collect data from a variety of resources. Resources come in many forms. Print resources include the social studies text, encyclopedias, library books, and other reference materials. Print resources can also include travel brochures from travel agencies, sale materials from manufacturers, newspapers, diaries, journals, magazine articles, and historical documents.

In addition to print resources, there are "people" resources. Students investigating topics related to the American Revolution called high school and college history teachers for information. People are marvelous resources. Experts can provide factual data and interesting accounts. Individuals who have lived through a period of our past can provide exciting anecdotes that make the event come to life. Political leaders can also be called on to provide information for inquiring children. Most people are excited to share their knowledge when asked by others, especially interested youngsters.

Data may be obtained from other forms of media such as films, audio cassettes, videotapes and TV. The entire class need not view the material. Only those children who need the information for their particular investigation should be required to view the material.

Data may also be obtained from personal observations. Students examining the need for a speed zone near their school could enlist the help of a police officer with a radar gun. They could observe and record the speed of vehicles passing their school. Primary-grade children investigating the relationships between weather and dress could record weather conditions and the types of clothing people wear in different conditions. When sufficient data are collected the children can begin examining and analyzing their information.

Step 3: Analyze Data

As children are collecting data they need to examine its relevance to their investigation. Some materials and information can be eliminated while others retained for closer scrutiny. It is during this phase that children learn much of the content related to their topic. The data are examined in terms of the children's research problem and are therefore more useful and meaningful.

As data are analyzed, children are actually manipulating and mastering the information. They must ask whether or not the information applies, how it applies, and how it can be used to resolve their problem. As they examine the data in this way they are developing a thorough understanding of the content.

Step 4: Draw Conclusions

The inquiry process directs the children toward the resolution of their problem. The conclusion is the point at which they combine the relevant information obtained from their resources into a coherent response. Their responses should pertain to the initial problem and research questions/hypotheses.

Conclusions may consist of written reports or they may take the form of projects such as those seen at science fairs. Elementary-school children should have numerous opportunities to develop projects that illustrate their inquiry activities. The development of projects requires that students identify the most relevant information while avoiding the pitfalls of having them copy information for a written report. Projects may consist of charts, posters, video displays, skits, and dioramas. Table 9–2 contains a list of ideas.

Table 9–2 Inquiry Projects

Poster	Graph	Model
Chart	Flowchart	Radio ad
T.V. ad	Newspaper ad	Skit
Puppet play	Mobile	Poem
Collage	Map	Game
Diorama	Teaching lesson	News article
Brochure	Scrapbook	Coloring book
Crossword puzzle	Word search	Picture
Travel guide	Want ad	Parade float
How-to booklet	Book jacket	Language-experience story
Study cube	Cartoon	Mural
Concept map		

Source: Van Cleaf, D.W. (1984). Guiding student inquiry. *The Social Studies, 75* (3), pp. 109–111. Adapted and reprinted with permission of the Helen Dwight Reid Educational Foundation. Published by Heldref Publications, 4000 Albemarle St., N.W., Washington, D.C. Copyright © 1984.

After projects have been completed you may require a final written report. Using the information contained in their projects as their data base, students can write a paper describing what they learned. Since they will not have access to their texts or encyclopedias, their papers will not be transcriptions of textbook or encyclopedia entries. Thus they will need to think about the information they have used in developing their projects. They will also need to think about how they want to share that information in a written paper.

EXAMPLES OF INQUIRY ACTIVITIES

Although the steps outlined above form the basis for a complete inquiry activity, inquiry activities need not use each of the steps. This section presents examples of inquiry activities. Several of the activities require youngsters to utilize each of the inquiry steps while others require them to participate in several of the inquiry steps. A matrix illustrating how the inquiry lessons described in this section relate to (and deviate from) the four inquiry steps will then be presented.

Mystery Island

The Mystery Island activity (Zevin, 1969) requires children to consider geographical information contained on a series of maps to solve a problem. The activity is begun as children are given the first of four maps and instructed to solve a problem—Where is the best location for "the biggest city" on the island? Children are encouraged to generate numerous hypotheses (or predictions) based on the information contained within the first map. Children must also utilize the knowledge they have from prior lessons and previous experiences. After they consider the information from the first map, students are given the second map and asked to verify or change their initial hypotheses. This process is repeated as the third and then fourth maps are given to the youngsters.

Zevin suggested that this activity be conducted with children working in small groups. The small-group atmosphere encourages them to generate additional ideas regarding possible solutions to the problem.

The activity is concluded with a discussion of the locations that the students selected for the city. They are also encouraged to substantiate their solutions with reasons emerging from the data on the maps and the personal knowledge they bring to the learning activity. They can discuss the strengths and weaknesses of other possible locations, thereby testing alternative solutions.

Variations. Students in social studies methods courses have used this idea in many different ways. One variation was used as sixth-grade children were introduced to a unit on Japan. The youngsters were given an outline map of Japan's main island and told to identify locations for the island's four largest cities. Naturally they were not told that the island represented Japan until the discussion portion of the activity. As in the Zevin activity, several maps were presented. Finally, the methods students told the children that the island was part of Japan, the country they would be studying during the next few weeks.

A real map of Japan was then shown to the children, who compared their own selections for the four populous areas with the actual locations of Japan's four largest cities. The discussion included topics such as the relationship among geography, conditions necessary for human survival, and human comfort needs.

Another variation was illustrated by a fourth-grade class learning about early California settlement. The fourth grade children were given a map of California that included major waterways. They were told to identify strategic locations for forts and missions. The external boundaries of the state were modified into an amoeba shape so the children wouldn't know it was a map of California until the follow-up discussion. Three additional maps were presented to the children. Finally, children compared their maps with actual maps of early California exploration and settlement.

Figure 9–1 illustrates Janet Smiley's adaptation of the Mystery Island map activity. She introduced fourth-grade children to a unit on Hawaii using the Mystery Island procedure. (See Figure 9–1.)

As a final variation, children could be required to examine photographs and street maps of cities representing a variety of geographical regions. As they examine the maps they should identify the ways that people have adapted to the environment. For example, lot lines and streets in the Midwest are usually in square or slightly

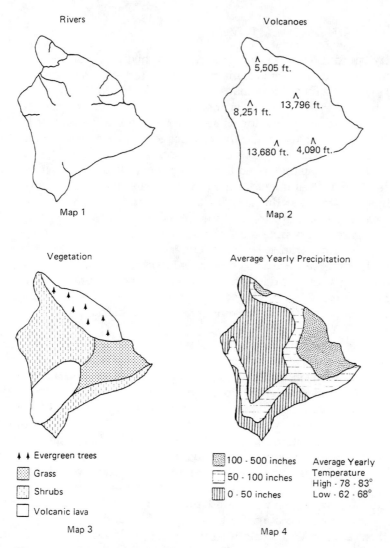

Figure 9–1 Mystery Island Map Activity

Source: A student's adaptation illustrating Jack Zevin's Mystery Island Map Activity. Zevin, J. (May 1969). *Mystery Island: A Lesson in Inquiry. Today's Education, 58,* (#5), pp. 42–43. Reprinted with permission of the student, Janet Smiley, who adapted the maps, and the National Education Association.

rectangular shapes. However, lot lines along major waterfronts are often narrow and deep. Children could be asked to suggest reasons for these differences.

Other geographic features have led to other types of human adaptation and can be investigated by comparing maps of different living areas. For example, children can examine pictures of farms in a grain-producing area and compare them to farms in cotton-producing or tobacco-producing regions. They should consult agricultural and land-use maps to help them discover the reasons for the differences.

Newspaper Birthday

An inquiry activity described by Martin and Van Cleaf (1983) required elementary-school children to research events occurring on the day they were born. The class was discussing history and the teacher wanted to help children get a better appreciation for historians and their tasks. After a brief discussion of history and ways to locate information from the past, children were taken to a nearby library and required to locate and read newspapers printed on the day of their birth. They were to identify major international, national, state, local, and sports events. They were also required to examine advertisements and compare past and current prices of items (see Figure 9–2).

Figure 9–2 Birthday News

Source: Martin, R.J., & Van Cleaf, D.W. (1983). Language arts students improve writing skills. *Catalyst for Change*, 12(2), p. 17. Adapted and reprinted with permission from Catalyst for Change, East Texas State University.

Name: _____

Birth date: _____

City: _____

State: _____

1. Go to the local library or newspaper publisher and read a paper printed on the day you were born. Then complete the following:
    a. Front page headlines were:
    b. Major national news events:
    c. Major state news events:
    d. Interesting sports news:
    e. Interesting local news:
2. Interview your parents to obtain the following information:
    a. occupation at that time:
    b. age:
    c. their likes and dislikes (have they changed since then?):
    d. favorite activities (have they changed?):
    e. an interesting fact about that day:
3. List seven items advertised in the newspaper on your birthdate and compare the cost of those items to the price today

Item	Cost Then	Cost Now
1.		
2.		
3.		
4.		
5.		
6.		
7.		

Children were also required to utilize oral history techniques. They interviewed parents or another adult and asked them to recall human-interest events occurring on the date of their (the children's) birth.

Many Hallmark gift shops offer a similar service. For a modest price the shops will provide information on events occurring on the day a person was born.

Variations. We tend to study history starting with the past and working toward the future. One teacher attempted to start with the present and work backward to the past. After children examined the newspapers published on the day they were born, they studied newspapers published on the day one of their parents was born. International, national, state, and local events were compared. Also, lifestyle differences were examined through advertisements in both papers. Children then went back generation by generation, making similar comparisons. Concepts such as transportation, housing, clothing, entertainment, and current events were considered for each generation. They also discussed the meaning of the concepts *generation* and *change*.

Newspapers and magazines can be used in another way as a basis for inquiry activities. For example, provide children with newspaper ads representing a different region of the country or a different season of the year. Children should examine the ads and describe the lifestyles of the people as well as geographic characteristics (climate, landforms, region).

Big Burgers

Field trips are exciting learning experiences for youngsters. A second-grade teacher integrated an inquiry assignment with a visit to a McDonald's restaurant. While on the field trip, children were required to identify the ingredients in a Big Mac hamburger. They were also asked to identify the types of jobs required to prepare the ingredients as well as the final product. When children returned to the classroom they were required to look through various product and natural resource maps and identify possible geographical areas from which ingredients were produced or grown. Figure 9–3 illustrates the worksheet children were given prior to the field trip.

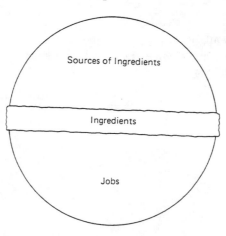

Figure 9–3 Big Burgers

Source: Van Cleaf, D.W. (1986). *Teaching elementary social studies: Supplemental materials.* Unpublished manuscript, Washburn University, Topeka. Adapted and reprinted with permission of the author.

This activity required children to consider information from a variety of sources. They observed processes during the field trip, interviewed the tour guide, and examined product maps. This activity did not require them to resolve a problem or to arrive at a conclusion; thus, the students did not utilize the complete inquiry process. Their emphasis was on the data-collection and data-analysis steps.

Variations. Similar activities could be done with other businesses that provide a finished product to the consumer. Pizza is an appropriate product because of its popularity with children and the relative ease of visiting pizzerias. Sixth-grade students not only completed an activity similar to the Big Burger activity (using the ingredients of a pizza) but they also used the information for consumer math problems. They used different-sized pizzas to learn how to compute the area of a circle and then analyzed the cost per square inch for small, medium, and large pizzas.

A student teacher developed another variation. She presented second-grade students with a product map of their state. Children first discussed the types of fast-food restaurants and then the types of food served in such establishments. Students were then required to examine the natural resource maps and to develop a fast-food restaurant that served fast-food products made from their state's natural resources. Menus, logos, and advertisements were included as activities in the lesson.

The Big Burger activity could be extended in yet another direction. Children could study the environmental and economic impact of certain businesses. How many people do the businesses employ? How much energy do they use? How much do they rely on natural resources. McDonald's, for example, uses amazingly large amounts of natural resources for its supply of paper-packaging products as well as its food ingredients. Children can investigate the effects and influences businesses have on a community while strengthening their inquiry skills.

The Battle of the Alamo

Armstrong and Savage (1974) outlined an inquiry lesson about the Battle at Lexington. They collected various historical accounts of the battle and raised the age-old question: Who fired the first shot? They presented three textbook accounts, several newspaper accounts, a diary entry, and statements made by British and colonial soldiers. Each account differed, and students were required to compare the accounts so as to develop their own conclusions.

The Armstrong and Savage idea was adapted by a teacher in Mansfield, Texas. Marianna Ellis developed a variation for the Battle of the Alamo. Ellis examined information from a variety of resources. She paraphrased the information and developed scripts that were then tape-recorded for the lesson. After introducing children to the lesson and stating the problem, her fourth-grade students listened to the taped accounts of the battle. As they listened, they made notes about the pertinent information for later use. Her students were then required to analyze the data and to develop their own plausible accounts of the battle. The scripts and the note-taking sheet developed by Ellis are in Appendix 9–1.

Variations. This type of activity can be used with any historical event for which a variety of primary and secondary sources are available. A fourth-grade teacher collected and tape-recorded information about Quantrill's raid on Lawrence, Kansas, during the Civil War. The children listened to the accounts and then developed their own account.

Mini-Investigations

Van Cleaf (1984) proposed a modified research format appropriate for elementary-age children. The activity begins with a planning phase. The planning format illustrated in Figure 9–4 will enable you and your students to develop workable investigations.

The teacher begins the planning phase by identifying a general topic for study. Children then get into groups of two or three and identify several specific questions they would like to answer regarding the topic. They then identify possible resources they can consult for information related to each question. Resources should include people, media, print materials, and personal observations. Groups of students then determine ways to illustrate the answers to their research questions. These illustrations are referred to as *projects.* A partial list of

Figure 9–4 Mini Investigation Planning Form

Source: Van Cleaf, D.W. (1984). Guiding student inquiry. *The Social Studies, 75*(3), pp. 109–111. Adapted and reprinted with permission of Helen Dwight Reid Educational Foundation. Published by Heldref Publications, 4000 Albemarle St., N.W., Washington, D.C. 20016. Copyright © 1984.

Names of Group Members: _____ ; _____ ; _____
I. Our topic is: _____
II. Our plan is:.

Research Questions	Resources	Projects
1.		
2.		
3.		
4.		
5.		

motivating projects is listed in Table 9–2. The teacher should work closely with the students during the planning phase by suggesting possible research questions, additional resources, and interesting projects.

The planning phase is followed by the work phase. This is the time during which students collect and examine resources. As the resources are examined, students should be reminded to disregard information not related to their research questions and focus only on needed data. During this phase the students also construct the projects that will illustrate answers to their questions. This is an important process because youngsters must make decisions regarding what information to use, the need for additional information, and how to best illustrate their findings. Because they are working in small groups they are discussing the information and committing much of it to memory. This helps them develop a better understanding of the topic. The teacher's role during this phase is to ask and answer questions about the work in progress. The teacher also provides assistance for students when they encounter difficulties.

Each group may be required to develop a *fact file*. As they consult resources to answer their research questions they should be required to make a list of interesting facts. This fact file may then be used at the conclusion of the mini-investigation project as a data source for written reports. This is somewhat similar to using note cards for report writing. It introduces children to a process they will find useful throughout their education.

Mini-investigations usually require at least a week to complete. A two-week period is preferable for more in-depth investigations. During the initial class period, teacher and students should discuss the topic and work through the planning phase. The next several class periods should be devoted to research and project development. Students may need to go to the library for materials, preview films and other audio-visual materials, call on people and community resources, and analyze their information.

During the work sessions children begin to construct their projects. This is a worthwhile activity and time must be provided. The teacher should continue to monitor and provide assistance.

The mini-investigation activity may be concluded with the presentation of the projects at a social science fair, similar to a traditional science fair. Parents and other children in the school can be invited to preview the work and visit with the project designers.

Variations.   The mini-investigation activity is appropriate for children at any grade level. Kindergarten and primary-grade children should investigate only one, or perhaps two questions. The resources they use will need to be audiovisual oriented and people oriented rather than relying too much on reading materials.

Children finishing early, regardless of age, may be required to research an additional question. Children experiencing difficulty can be given more time to work on one or two questions and have some research questions deleted from their planning forms. Finally, children who have gotten excited about a specific area may be allowed to skip one or more of their research questions and pursue the area of special interest in greater depth. This flexibility will allow you to be much more responsive to the needs and interests of individual youngsters while remaining confident that learning is taking place.

The mini-investigation format can also be used for individual students who have expressed a special interest in a topic. In a sense it provides a way to help structure independent study for gifted youngsters. For example, after reading a story about Hellen Keller, a child became excited about blind people and how they meet their needs. She and her teacher outlined a mini-investigation plan and she was given time during school to work on her plan. One of the resources included visiting a teacher in a program designed to help people losing their sight prepare for their future. The child visited the teacher and toured the facility in which the program was housed. (This visit was scheduled during a school day. The principal approved the visit and the girl's mother took her to visit the facility for the day.)

Oral History

Oral history is a means of obtaining information about historical events by interviewing people living at the time of the event. Children should interview people who participated in the event as well as those who lived at the time but did not participate directly. For example, oral-history projects related to a war should include interviews with members of the military who participated in actual battles. Interviews with civilians who remained home are also suggested. Descendants of individuals may also be used. Oftentimes families relate interesting information about earlier events from one generation to the next, and these accounts can be quite informative.

One purpose of the oral history process is to obtain a variety of views and information about an event. People's views, memories, and feelings provide a richness not available through most printed sources and thus help make the event "come alive."

While studying the hardships of life on the Great Plains, a fifth-grade teacher invited a woman to speak to the students about a blizzard that occurred during the woman's childhood. The visitor shared a number of human-interest stories about the effects of the blizzard, the losses that resulted from the storm, and the activities she and her family participated in while snowbound. Her description of the event included anecdotes about life at that time that the children considered quite interesting. There were no refrigerators, snowplows, or snow blowers. The family didn't even have indoor plumbing, which precipitated several interesting questions.

I invited a lifelong Topeka, Kansas, resident to my methods class to provide insights about the city's development from the perspective of a black community member. We learned how black people were attracted to the city by opportunities to work for the railroad, how they developed their own local communities, such as Mud Town and Tennessee Town, within the city, and how early housing patterns influenced today's housing patterns. We also learned about segregation in Topeka leading up to the landmark 1954 Supreme Court case, *Brown* vs. *Topeka Board of Education.*

The Foxfire project is an example of a remarkably successful oral-history project. The inception of the Foxfire project began in 1966 when Eliot Wigginton modified the requirements for his high school students. They were not motivated by traditional instructional practices. Rather than continue with traditional practices, Wigginton decided to require his pupils to interview area residents and make written records of their folklore, customs, and crafts.

Oral history is an inquiry activity because students are required to interview people to gain information and insights regarding a specific event or era in history. It may also be used to explore changes in society. For example, changes in transportation, shelter, education, medicine, views toward women and views toward minorities are topics appropriate for oral-history projects.

The steps in oral-history projects should include the following. Identification of the topic occurs first. Students then identify possible people to interview. These may be relatives, neighbors, residents of nursing homes, or members of service groups.

Because the interview is the basic method used in oral-history projects, students must plan and outline their interviews. They must consider the main points they want to explore and then develop appropriate questions. Artifacts are important and students should ask if they can look at any artifacts as part of the interview. Once information has been obtained, students must identify some means of reporting their findings. The projects listed in Table 9–2 offer useful ways to report findings for oral-history projects.

Oral history has several limitations worth noting. First, the information is usually derived from the memory of the person interviewed and therefore may contain many inaccuracies. Time changes the way people view things. What they consider important now may differ from the importance placed on the event or portions of the event when it occurred. People may also view the event differently now because they may fail to remember pertinent information. Second, individuals are biased and the bias may affect the information presented. An individual who was against America's intervention in Viet Nam may present a different perspective from an individual who favored our intervention. Third, misinterpretation may occur. The person being interviewed may misinterpret the questions and the students may misinterpret the responses. A fourth limitation is time. Interviews take time.

ANALYSIS OF INQUIRY EXAMPLES

As stated earlier in the chapter, inquiry activities may include only portions of the inquiry steps and still remain beneficial for children. The following discussion describes the degree to which the examples of inquiry activities presented in this chapter address the four inquiry steps. Table 9–3 illustrates the relationship in a more concise manner.

The Mystery Island activity in Table 9–3 is a modified inquiry activity. It engages children in a problem and consideration of alternative hypotheses. Data collection is not a factor because the data are contained on the maps, which are presented by the teacher. Children do analyze data as information relates to the problem, and they are expected to develop a conclusion.

Table 9–3 Analysis of Inquiry Activities

INQUIRY STEPS	MYSTERY ISLAND	BATTLE OF THE ALAMO	BIRTHDAY NEWS
Problem (questions/ hypotheses)	E	E	
Data Collection	Provided by teacher	Provided by teacher	E
Data Analysis	E	E	E
Conclusion	E	E	

INQUIRY STEPS	BIG BURGERS	MINI-INVESTIGATION	ORAL HISTORY
Problem (questions/ hypotheses)		E	E
Data Collection	E	E	E
Data Analysis	E	E	E
Conclusion		E	E

E, Emphasized.

Source: Van Cleaf, D.W. (1986). *Teaching elementary social studies: Supplemental materials.* Unpublished manuscript, Washburn University, Topeka. Adapted and reprinted with permission of the author.

The activity related to the Battle of the Alamo (Table 9–3) has a similar emphasis regarding the inquiry steps. The data are presented by the teacher; therefore the students do not identify possible resources nor are they required to collect data.

The Birthday News activity can also be characterized as a modified inquiry activity. The emphasis is on data collection and data analysis. Although this is not a complete inquiry activity, children are enthusiastically engaged in two aspects of inquiry—data collection and data analysis.

The Big Burgers activity has no significant problem to resolve. The activity requires children to focus on two inquiry processes—data collection and data analysis.

The Mini-Investigation and the Oral History activities shown in Table 9–3 are examples of complete inquiry activities. Each step, from problem identification to developing a conclusion, is included and is critical to the success of the activity.

SUMMARY

This chapter presented the inquiry method as a four-step process. The four-steps were described and examples of inquiry activities appropriate for elementary students were outlined.

Inquiry teaching can be exciting for both students and teacher because it is an alternative to the usual routine. However, the inquiry method can lose its effectiveness and motivational value if it is used too frequently or if it is misused.

In 1909 Fling reported that the teaching of history was in a deplorable state because history teachers did not know how to conduct investigations. Similar criticisms are voiced today. Too many teachers are spending too much time lecturing to students. Then as now, teachers either do not know how to investigate or do not provide students with opportunities to investigate. Rather than investigate (that is, clarify issues, seek answers to questions or research problems) children in typical classrooms are usually presented the information as a finished product that must be committed to memory—at least until they take the test. This chapter described the inquiry process and provided exciting inquiry activities. You should embrace inquiry as a viable teaching strategy and utilize inquiry teaching on a regular basis.

SUGGESTED ACTIVITIES

1. Interview a teacher and ask the teacher to describe difficulties with inquiry teaching.
2. Outline a mini-investigation regarding a major purchase or the resolution of a problem of personal interest to you. Specify the problem, research questions, resources you might use, and ways to illustrate your findings.

3. Go to the library and examine a newspaper published on the day you were born. Compare the types of events reported then with the types of events reported today. Also compare the cost of items. You might then examine a newspaper published on the day one of your parents was born. Make similar comparisons.

4. Select a social studies textbook for an elementary grade. Quickly review the contents of a chapter. Then develop an inquiry activity to teach the same concepts.

APPENDIX 9–1   What Really Happened at the Alamo?

Directions: As you listen to the recorded voices (children may read the dialogue) please write down the information on the recording form (see Appendix 9–1 Table).

APPENDIX 9–1 TABLE   Information Recording Form

	Number of Mexican Troops	Skill of Mexican Troops	Number of Texans	Skill of Texans	Time of Day	Length of Seige	How Many Mexicans Killed	How Many Texans Killed	Who Committed Atrocities
Louis Moses Rose									
Travis' Servant Boy Joe									
Santa Anna									
Andrea Candalaria									

Source: Ellis, M. (1985). *What really happened at the Alamo?* Unpublished manuscript, Mansfield, TX. Reprinted with permission from Marianna Ellis, a former student.

VOICE 1:   Andrea Candalaria (hotel proprietor; good friend of Sam Houston)

I had received a letter from Gen. Sam Houston asking me to nurse and care for Col. Jim Bowie, who was dying of tuberculosis. I left my hotel and went to the Alamo.

On the 22nd of February, Santa Anna, with an army of more than 3,000 men, demanded surrender of the Alamo. Col. Travis answered with a cannon shot, and so the siege of the Alamo began.

Santa Anna received Mexico's top combat soldiers daily. Only thirty-two brave replacements came into the Alamo on March 1st. Because supplies and ammunition were low, the guns were only fired occasionally.

After Col. Bonham returned with the fatal news, we all knew that we were doomed. Not one of us was in favor of surrendering. There were just 180 men inside the Alamo. Col. Travis was the first man to die. He was shot through the head while standing by his cannon on the southeast side, near the place now occupied by the Menger Hotel. The Mexican infantry charged across the plaza many times.

Col. Crockett and a dozen good men stood, guns in hand, behind the front door. I sat by Col. Bowie's bedside. The only protection Col. Bowie had was his knife and a pair of pistols that Col. Crockett had loaded for him the night before. The Mexicans poured everything they had into the attack. Suddenly a sheet of flame lit up the Alamo. Col. Crockett fought to the bitter end. The Mexicans charged him with their bayonets. After his bullets ran out, Col. Crockett began clubbing the enemy to death with his rifle, Betsy. Finally the Mexicans overpowered him with their bayonets.

They murdered Col. Bowie before my very eyes. As I saw the Mexican soldiers swarm into the room, I threw myself across Col. Bowie. A bayonet pierced the flesh on my chin. Col. Bowie killed at least twenty enemy soldiers before he died.

All was silent now. The massacre had ended. One hundred eighty of the bravest men in the world had fallen and not one had asked for mercy. I walked out of the cell, and when I stepped on the floor of the Alamo, the blood ran into my shoes. It was over.

VOICE 2: Santa Anna (President of Mexico and Commander in Chief of the Mexican Army)

I had just been overwhelmingly elected President of Mexico. I would show the people that I intended to rule the country with an iron hand. I would not be intimidated by this stupid band of rebels from Texas. I was determined to make an example of them. They may have defeated my brother-in-law, Gen. Cos, at San Antonio, but they had never faced the likes of the great Santa Anna. The Texans would be no match for us. I was leading 5,000 soldiers, the cream of the Mexican army. My generals were trained like no others. I knew the Texans were divided in command, and most of them had seen no fighting. Besides, what was a handful of puffed-up volunteers against the great Santa Anna? I was prepared to sacrifice my whole army to put down this rebellion.

On the evening of March 5th, I ordered my men to stop firing. The red flag was raised, and the bugler played *deguello*, the death march. I would show no mercy to those inside. I divided my army into four columns, and we surrounded the Alamo on every side. At 4:00 A.M. on March 6th, I gave the signal to attack. The first columns to attack carried crowbars, axes, and ladders to climb the walls.

During the first assault, the commander of the north column was trampled to death when he fell from his horse. My men killed many more of each other than the Texans did. On the third assault, I watched as my men stormed the Alamo through a break in the north wall.

I had no choice other than kill them all. My honor and that of all Mexico was at stake. I had to show Sam Houston and the people of Texas that Santa Anna would rule supreme.

After the battle was over, I rode inside the walls of the Alamo. I found their commander, Col. Travis, lying across his cannon; Col. Bowie was in his bed covered with dead Mexican soldiers; James Bonham lay by his cannon near the southeast wall. I finally found Col. Crockett at the entrance of the cemetery buried under a pile of my best soldiers.

I gave orders for the rebels' bodies (there were at least 500) to be taken and piled outside the mission grounds. I had logs sandwiched between the layers of bodies. I then gave orders for the bodies to be burned. For miles around the burial fire could be seen by the people of Texas. They would learn to fear the great Santa Anna.

VOICE 3: Louis Moses Rose (allegedly the only man to flee the Alamo before the battle)

I entered the Alamo with my friend and commander, Col. Jim Bowie. Col. Bowie and I had fought together before. We all knew that Santa Anna was coming, but we didn't expect him to arrive so soon. Since Gen. Cos had been run out of Texas back in December, our army didn't bother to drill or even to call roll. We were seldom paid. Santa Anna was bringing the best soldiers that Mexico had to offer.

On February 23rd Santa Anna arrived with 5,000 soldiers and many cannon. The Alamo was bombarded day and night. Col. Travis had sent Jim Bonham to bring Gen. Fannin and his men. He sent men out twice with urgent pleas for help. On March 3rd, Jim Bonham rode back in alone. He was the last man to enter the Alamo.

Suddenly the cannon fire stopped. All was silent. Then we all heard the infamous bugle call, *deguello*, signifying no quarter. We knew that Santa Anna didn't intend for any of us to live.

Col. Travis called us into the courtyard. He told us the hopelessness of our situation. He said that surrender was unthinkable and escape was almost impossible. The colonel said that he had chosen to stay and die for the cause of liberty. He said that each must choose for himself to stay and die or to leave. He took his sword and drew a line in the dirt. I remember the colonel's exact words: "I now want every man who is determined to stay here and die with me to come across this line. We must sell our lives as dearly as possible."

Tapley Holland was the first man to cross the line. Unable to rise, Jim Bowie called for four men to lift his cot over. One by one they crossed the line. I was the only left on the other side.

I was fifty-one years old; I had fought with Napoleon in Russia; I had come to Texas to live not to die. I can still hear Davey Crockett say: "You may as well die with us, old fellow, for you cannot escape."

But I had to try. I grabbed up my clothes and leaped onto the wall. I gasped at the scene before me; the ground below was strewn with dead bodies. I turned and took one last look at my doomed comrades and then jumped. I landed in a pool of Mexican blood. I headed for the San Antonio River. After I reached the river, I stopped to rest. It must have been early morning, before daylight, when I heard cannon fire. I knew the siege was over, and the final attack had begun. I would never see those men again.

When I arrived at the home of the W.P. Zuber family a few days later, they thought I was a ghost. I assured them that I was not. Mrs. Zuber said that my name had appeared in *The Register* as being among the dead at the Alamo. I told them the story of my escape. Mrs. Zuber had me repeat it over and over so that she could remember it. It was her son who first told my story to the public thirty-seven years after the Battle of the Alamo. My name appears on the walls of the Alamo as a J.M. Rose, one of the brave who died for the liberty of Texas.

VOICE 4:   Col. Travis's slave boy

I came with Col. Travis from Alabama. Col. Travis was a kind man and probably the bravest man I ever knew. I will miss him now that he is gone.

When Col. Travis heard that Santa Anna was just across the river, he ordered everyone to take refuge inside the old mission building. Col. Travis said that help was coming any minute. We had too many good men to be scared of old Santa Anna. Col. Crockett said to me, "Don't worry, little fella, me and 'Old Betsy' won't let them Mexicans do you harm."

Col. Travis sent his lifelong friend, Mr. Bonham, for help. We knew he would bring the rest of the Texas army any day now. Santa Anna had surrounded us, and we could see Mexicans from every side.

I have never seen such fancy dressed soldiers in my whole life. Nobody ever told me fighting men wore clothes like that. They had on red coats and the brightest blue pants I ever did see. They had big black hats on their heads. They all had swords and holster pistols. They looked like they were going to Sunday school instead of fighting Texans. We just laughed and laughed while we watched them parade around in those fancy clothes.

Then one day Col. Bonham rode back in, and the gates of the Alamo closed behind him. He came up to Col. Travis's room where I was polishing the colonel's sword. Col. Bonham said no help was coming, and that he had come back to fight with us. Col. Travis turned white as a ghost and didn't say a word. He just sat down at his desk and started to write. Col. Travis sent four more letters out that very night.

Col. Travis called everybody together and told us that no help was coming. I never heard nobody talk the way my Col. Travis did that day. When he finished talking, nobody wanted to give up. I was crying. I knew I'd never leave Mr. Travis.

Nearly everybody was asleep when the Mexicans started firing their guns and running like wild folks at the walls. It was still dark outside. I stood up just in time to see Col. Travis slump down over his cannon. I ran as fast as I could, but when I got to him, he was already dead. He had been shot in the head. I was plenty scared. I ran as hard as I could over to the chapel. I knew a good hiding place. When I got to the door, I saw soldiers swarm through a break in the wall. Everybody was screaming. There were so many of them our men didn't have time to reload their guns. The Texans were swinging their guns back and forth trying to beat off the Mexicans. I just knew the world was ending.

Just me and the two ladies was left. All the others was dead. I just knew old Santa Anna was going to kill me too, but he acted like he didn't even see me. I'm never going inside those walls again as long as I live.

Source: Ellis, M. (1985). *What really happened at the Alamo?* Unpublished manuscript, Mansfield, TX. Reprinted with permission from Marianna Ellis, a former student.

Children must have many opportunities to organize, sort, and classify information.

Photograph by Rona Beame, Photo Researchers, Inc.

chapter 10

Concept-Attainment Teaching Strategies

Good teachers give a lot of good examples and bad teachers don't.

(Heather, grade 5)

AS YOU READ...

- define the terms *concepts* and *generalizations*
- list and explain the elements of a concept
- develop a rationale supporting the use of concepts as a basis for teaching social studies
- describe the two attributes of concept teaching and describe the differences between deductive and inductive teaching
- describe ways to teach concepts deductively and inductively

INTRODUCTION

Without the ability to organize, store, process, and retrieve information in an efficien way, our mental capabilities would be like a powerful computer without an operatin; program. Concepts are the means by which people organize informatin in thei minds. Concepts are therefore an essential aspect of the mind's operating program.

Concepts have been described as mental organizations and as categories o thought. Concepts include categories of objects, events, people, ideas, and sym bols. Similar to groups or sets of items, each concept is comprised of members witl similar characteristics. Examples of object concepts include bicycles, maps, graphs pencils, and flags. Examples of event concepts include holidays, celebrations censorship, and elections. There are also people concepts such as presidents children, adults, prisoners, ranchers, and teachers. Idea concepts include democ racy, freedom, justice, honesty, and creativity.

Symbols are concepts too. Social studies symbols include map symbols weather symbols, cultural symbols, and religious symbols.

Each concept has characteristics, called *attributes*, that allow people to group similar items into the concept. For example, the concept *tundra* includes land areas that share the following attributes. The land areas are cold, located in the far north or high elevations of mountains, and support small grasses, plants, and moss Trees do not grow in tundra areas.

Suburb is another social studies concept. The attributes of suburbs in clude proximity to an urban area, types of dwellings, and the primary types of economic activities.

The mind, like computers, organizes and stores information.

Photograph courtesy of BASF Systems Corp.

ELEMENTS OF CONCEPTS

According to Joyce and Weil (1986), concepts have four elements. A brief description of these elements will enable you to understand the nature of concepts better. The description of the elements will also help you learn how to teach concepts more effectively.

Each concept has a *name*, which is the first element of a concept. Because humans use communication to express their ideas, they label (name) their ideas with words. When a teacher mentions the word *friend*, students can mentally visualize their concept of friend. The names for concepts often become vocabulary terms for social studies lessons.

Many social studies concepts are complex and not readily expressed by a simple definition or a concrete definition. Rule of law and electoral college are examples of complex concepts. They are difficult to define, and children's definitions will vary according to their understanding of the concept.

Each concept has examples of items included within the concept; therefore *examples* are the second element of a concept. For a child, items exemplifying the concept *friend* might include names of friends, behaviors such as being nice, and activities such as doing things together. These would be positive examples.

Many concepts are developed by considering items and attributes that are nonexamples. Unfriendly people, enemies, and being mean may emerge as nonexamples of the concept friend. While the nonexamples are not part of the concept, they do help clarify and define the concept.

Each concept also has *attributes*, the third element of a concept. Attributes are essentially characteristics contained within the examples. Each of the child's friends (which are examples) may behave in certain ways. They share, cooperate, help one another, and enjoy doing things together.

The common attributes are the essential characteristics used to classify an example within the concept. Using the friendship example, there may be many children in the classroom who share several of the characteristics of a particular child's concept of friend. However, many of the children may not be classified as a friend of a particular child because a certain attribute may be missing. A child might attend school with other children who share, cooperate, and help others, but who do not play with the child outside of school. Thus the classmates would not be classified as friends.

The fourth element of a concept is *attribute value*. Most attributes have a range of acceptability. A friend might need to be very sharing and highly cooperative whereas an acquaintance may not need to meet such high standards. These differences occur because of the relative importance of the values the child places on the attributes of friendship.

Table 10–1 illustrates the four elements of a concept. It also illustrates the elements as they relate to the concept of freedom. You might develop a similar illustration for the following social studies concepts: family, responsibility, natural resources, Midwest, manufacturing, or suffrage.

As people organize their world mentally, they form and use concepts. Concepts make learning easier and enhance our ability to use information. An understanding of the elements of concepts will enable you to implement a variety of exciting teaching suggestions described later in the chapter.

Table 10–1 Illustrating Elements for the Concept Freedom

ELEMENT	DESCRIPTION	EXAMPLE (FREEDOM)
1. Name and definition	A word to label the concept	Freedom
	A statement describing the concept	Freedom is the ability to make choices
2. Examples and nonexamples	Items exemplifying the concept	American flag, eagle, Statue of Liberty
	Items contrasting the concept	Jail, concentration camp, Nazi flag
3.. Attributes	Characteristics that the examples share	Lack of constraints, free movement, free choice
4. Attribute values	Degree or range of each attribute's acceptability	/_____/_____/ no freedom some freedom complete freedom /_____/_____/ can't speak one's mind some limits can say anything

Note: The definition is often developed after the other elements of the concept have been considered.

Source: Joyce, B., & Weil, M. (1986). *Models of teaching*, p. 30. Englewood Cliffs, NJ: Prentice Hall. Adapted and reprinted with permission of Prentice Hall, Inc.

BENEFITS OF CONCEPT TEACHING

Using concepts as the basis for teaching social studies has many benefits. This section of the chapter describes many of the benefits derived from using concepts as an instructional focus.

Increased Achievement

Concept-based instruction has been shown to have a positive effect on children's achievement. McKinney, Larkins, Ford, and Davis (1983) compared concept-teaching strategies to a number of other strategies, including methods used in most textbook series. They concluded that teaching concepts by utilizing definitions, examples, and analyses of examples was superior to traditional forms of teaching.

Facilitates Communication

Concept learning is beneficial because it enhances our abilities to interact with one another. As individuals attempt to communicate with others they reach into their minds and search for the ideas they wish to share. This is the deep-structure of language. They must transform their deep structure ideas into surface-structure language. Surface-structure language includes verbal and nonverbal communication that is readily perceived by the listener. The listener receives the verbal and nonverbal communication and then searches his or her deep structure for a conceptual understanding.

Concepts are a major aspect of deep structure. If one of the individuals in the conversation does not have a conceptual understanding of the topic, communication does not occur. If a person's mind is filled with facts rather than a mechanism for organizing facts into concepts, communication becomes more cumbersome. The listener must spend more energy attempting to reconstruct the speaker's meaning. Social studies teachers may encounter this phenomenon. If children have learned a series of facts, but have not had an opportunity to determine relationships between the facts, children will have difficulty understanding the teacher's comments.

Concepts can be discussed in various settings.

Photograph by Ken Karp.

Personalizing Instruction

Teachers can teach a concept in a variety of ways, using a variety of facts and examples. They can personalize instruction by adapting the facts, examples, and experiences so they are appropriate for their students. Units about early settlers, such as the Pilgrims, often require children to learn information related to the era, but with no reference to children's present lifestyles. By including references to the children's lives, the teacher can personalize the lessons. The children will learn more, feel more successful, and become more motivated toward social studies.

More Complex Understanding

Piaget described learning as a process of integration and substitution. From a perspective of teaching concepts this means that as children develop, their existing concepts become more complex (integration) and new concepts emerge from existing concepts (substitution).

The spiral curriculum described in Chapter 2 is based on this assumption. As children participate in a conceptually oriented spiral curriculum, simple concepts are taught in the lower grades. The same concepts are taught and retaught at more sophisticated levels as students proceed through the grade levels. Information is added to existing concepts to make them more complex. As concepts become more complex, they are employed to develop new concepts and to form generalizations.

The concept *money* illustrates this process. Young children learn about the value of money. Older children learn about the uses of money relative to capital, goods, and services. High school and college students learn about exchange rates and devaluation.

Problem Solving and Reasoning

Another benefit of concept-based instruction is improved problem solving and reasoning. Mature problem solving requires individuals to consider sets of data to resolve a problem. If individuals have well-developed conceptual structures they can use concepts related to the problem to make decisions, even when specific data are not available.

A well-developed conceptual structure will enable individuals to generalize from specific instances to general applications. The inverse is also valid. As children's conceptual abilities improve they can examine general situations and extract specific bits of data. Inductive and deductive forms of thinking are enhanced.

The election process exemplifies this principle. Individuals must consider competing candidates and platforms for each office. To do this they obtain information about the candidates, and they make inferences about each candidate's suitability. A well-developed conceptual understanding of the issues and the challenges of the office enables the electorate to make reasoned decisions.

BEYOND CONCEPTS: GENERALIZATIONS

Concepts emerge from facts, content, and experiences. Concepts themselves become more complex and abstract as children integrate new information into their conceptual structures and as they substitute new conceptual views for prior concepts. At some point concepts interact or are applied to different situations. When this occurs concepts become generalizations.

Generalizations may be described in two ways. First, generalizations are relationships between two or more concepts. For example, a relationship between the concepts *population* and *landform* (for example, few people populate mountain regions) is a generalization. The relationship between age and intelligence is another example (older people tend to be more intelligent than younger people). The relationship between conservative political views and political party affiliation is another example.

Generalizations may also be described as statements about a concept. Marzano and Arredondo (1986) stated that a generalization is a statement that is followed by a series of supporting statements. They provide the following example (p. 50).*

Generalization:	"At times life gets difficult."
Example relationships:	"Finances become a problem."
	"A period of poor health may develop."
	"Family problems can crop up."
	"Work may become dull and boring."

In the above generalization the emphasis is not on the concepts (life and difficulty). Rather, it is on the relationship between life and difficulty expressed in the statement. The supporting statements express the relationships, clarify the generalization, and elaborate on the generalization.

Like concepts, generalizations may be either concrete or abstract. The generalizations "Fruit is nutritious" and "Good people share" are relatively concrete. Other generalizations may be highly abstract. "The value of the dollar is related to the trade deficit" and "Scarcity of goods increases costs" are examples of abstract generalizations.

Children must develop a solid understanding of concepts before they can be expected to generalize beyond the concepts. Excellent social studies teachers must therefore help organize instruction so concepts are emphasized. Teachers must then help children apply the concepts to new areas and in combination with other concepts.

STRATEGIES FOR TEACHING CONCEPTS

Concepts may be taught deductively or inductively. There are two attributes that are included in both approaches. The two attributes are "definition" and "examples." The order in which the two attributes are presented differentiates the two approaches. If the definition is presented first, and followed by examples, the strategy is *deductive*. Conversely, if the examples are presented first, and then followed by the definition, the strategy is *inductive*.

Of course, excellent teachers do not stop with the presentation of a definition and several examples. They provide a variety of follow-up activities to help students develop a better understanding of the concept. They provide opportunities for students to practice the concept and apply the concept to new areas or higher levels of application.

This section of the chapter describes a variety of concept-attainment teaching strategies that are variations of the basic deductive and inductive approaches.

Deductive Strategies

Four *deductive* teaching strategies are described here. The first two are familiar; the second two are relatively new and potentially quite useful.

Textbook Approach. The approach most frequently used in textbooks is deductive. Most textbook lessons begin with a list of vocabulary words contained within the reading passage. Teachers define and discuss the vocabulary terms before students read the passage. Students then read the passage for additional information about the terms.

Reading the text is usually followed by a review or practice activity. After children finish reading the passage, teachers often require them to answer a series of questions about the passage. The follow-up activities are designed to strengthen children's understanding of the concepts.

Research studies indicate that the use of textbooks to teach concepts in this manner produces marginal achievement results.

Lecture. At times elementary teachers present information through brief lectures. The traditional lecture is usually a deductive approach. Whether giving a formal or informal lecture, teachers provide information about the topic and then embellish their points with examples.

Gagné Strategy. Gagné (1965) proposed a modification of the deductive approach as a means of teaching concepts. According to his strategy teachers should present three examples of items exemplifying a concept and three items that do not exemplify the concept. For example, if a teacher is teaching the concept *peninsula,* the teacher would:

1. Show a picture of a peninsula and state, "This is a peninsula."
2. Show a picture of an isthmus and state, "This is an isthmus."
3. Show a second example of a peninsula and state, "This is a peninsula."
4. Show a picture of an island and state, "This is an island."
5. Show a third picture of a peninsula and state, "This is a peninsula."
6. Show a picture of a chain of islands, like the Florida Keys, and state, "This is a chain of islands."

After presenting the three examples and nonexamples, additional examples and nonexamples should be presented. The children should then be required to classify the additional items as either examples or nonexamples. By correctly classifying the additional examples, children demonstrate an understanding of the concept. The teacher can then infer that the students understand the concept.

According to the Gagné model, the teacher is not required to provide a definition as part of the concept-attainment process. He believed that students would learn the concept and the name of the concept by observing the examples and listening to the teacher's labels.

Gagné's model has been classified as a deductive strategy because the teacher provides the labels as the examples are presented. If a teacher allowed the students to develop a definition at the conclusion of the activity it would be classified as an inductive activity.

Merrill-Tennyson Strategy. Merrill and Tennyson (1977) developed a deductive strategy for teaching concepts that is more thorough than the Gagné strategy. There are four steps in this strategy. The teacher first provides a *definition* of the concept. The definition includes the critical attributes of the concept. The second step, *expository presentation,* requires the teacher to present a series of examples and nonexamples. The examples are paired so that an example is given first and then followed by a nonexample. The presentation of example and nonexample pairs continues until several have been presented. Merrill and Tennyson recommend that the examples and nonexamples be arranged from simple to difficult. Children should be shown the easier examples first.

As the examples and nonexamples are presented, the teacher should identify the critical attributes related to the concept. This ensures that students identify the specific characteristics of the examples that place them within the parameters of the concept. For example, if teaching the concept *peninsula* the teacher would want children to learn that a peninsula is like a finger extending into a body of water. As each example is shown the teacher would tell children to observe the relationship between the land and the water. The steps in the process are listed below.

1. Definition: A peninsula is a portion of land that extends into a body of water. It is almost surrounded by water.
2. Show a picture of Italy and state, "This is an example of a peninsula. Notice how it is almost completely surrounded by water."
3. Show a picture of Australia and state, "This is not a peninsula. Notice how it is completely surrounded by water."
4. Show a picture of Florida and state, "This is a peninsula. Notice how it is almost completely surrounded by water."
5. Show a picture of Ohio and state, "This is not a peninsula. Notice its relationship to water."
6. Show a picture of Korea and state, "This is a peninsula. Notice how the water almost surrounds the entire land area."
7. Show a picture of Cuba and state, "This is not a peninsula. Notice how it is surrounded by water."

The third step in the Merrill-Tennyson strategy is called *inquisitory practice*. During this step the teacher provides additional examples and nonexamples and asks children to classify them as either examples or nonexamples. This enables the teacher to determine if students understand the concept and it provides students with additional examples of the concept, thus strengthening their knowledge of the concept.

The fourth and final step in the strategy is a *test*. Children are provided another set of examples and nonexamples and required to correctly classify them into the appropriate categories.

The Merrill and Tennyson format is thorough and has produced positive achievement gains when used in classrooms. It is effective because the teacher provides a definition, presents appropriate examples and nonexamples, and identifies the attributes. The format provides opportunities for students to consider and classify additional examples.

Inductive Strategies

Deductive strategies begin with a definition. The definition is followed by a series of examples and nonexamples. The examples and nonexamples are a means of illustrating the concept and its attributes. An *inductive* approach begins with a presentation of examples and nonexamples. Children are asked to develop a definition after the examples and nonexamples have been presented.

Deductive strategies tend to be teacher-directed. The definitions and the examples are provided by the teacher while children listen and observe. Inductive strategies, on the other hand, are more child-centered. While the teacher selects the concept and examples, the teacher usually requires children to provide examples as well. Further, teachers usually require children to develop definitions at the conclusion of the activity.

This section describes four inductive concept-attainment teaching strategies.

Taba Strategy. Taba (1967) proposed a concept-formation teaching strategy as a means of helping youngsters improve their levels of cognitive processing. Her concept-formation strategy has been found to be an excellent means for helping students learn concepts and classify examples.

The Taba strategy requires teachers to ask a series of questions that elicit five types of responses from students. The first set of questions requires children to provide a list of examples. Second, the teacher asks children to identify a possible basis for placing their examples into subgroups. The third set of questions requires children to identify common attributes of their examples. After they have identified common attributes for subgrouping the examples, children are asked to name or label the subcategories. Finally, children are asked to classify the items generated during the first step into the appropriate subgroups. Table 10–2 illustrates the Taba concept formation process. Try developing a lesson for two concepts, goods and services, by examining how people earn money.

Table 10–2 Concept Formation

OVERT ACTIVITY	COVERT MENTAL OPERATIONS	ELICITING QUESTIONS
1. Enumeration and listing.	Differentiation.	What did you see? hear? note?
2. Grouping.	Identifying common properties, abstracting.	What belongs together? On what criterion?
3. Labeling, categorizing.	Determining the hierarchical order of items. Super- and sub-ordination.	What would you call these groups? What belongs under what?

Source: Taba, H. (1967). *Teacher's handbook for elementary social studies*, p. 92. Palo Alto, CA: Addison-Wesley. Copyright © 1967, Addison-Wesley Publishing Company, Menlo Park, CA. Reprinted with permission of Addison-Wesley.

The Taba model is inductive because children are expected to provide examples, analyze attributes, and classify examples into groups. The children can then defend the reasons for their groups and state a definition and description of each group.

Concept-Attainment Strategy. Joyce and Weil (1986) proposed a concept-attainment strategy that is an exciting alternative to Taba's strategy. The Joyce and Weil format is easily implemented. The concept-attainment steps in this section describe a variation proposed by Reinhartz and Van Cleaf (1986).

This teaching approach begins as a guessing game. The teacher provides a clue about a concept and tells children to consider each example and nonexample to try to guess the concept.

The teacher must present a clue that is appropriate for the concept and the children's level of understanding. The development of an appropriate clue tends to create a degree of unnecessary frustration as teachers attempt to implement this strategy. This frustration quickly disappears as they gain experience and confidence. To avoid the difficulties of developing a clue, Joyce and Weil suggest that you merely tell children that the examples have something in common. Children should be reminded not to state the concept until the teacher asks for the solution.

After presenting the clue the teacher presents a series of examples and nonexamples. Similar to the Merrill and Tennyson strategy, the examples and nonexamples are paired and ordered in a sequence emerging from easy to difficult. The best examples and nonexamples should be presented first. The number of examples and nonexamples you present will depend on the concept and the availability of examples, but five sets of example/nonexample pairs are suggested as a minimum.

The examples you present may be words, pictures, or models of objects. When working with younger children you should use pictures or objects. Pictures may be cut out of magazines or selected from library books. Pictures and objects are preferable because children can visually identify the attributes.

After presenting the pairs of examples and nonexamples, ask children to provide additional examples and nonexamples. This step enables teachers to determine which of the children have discovered the concept. It also enables youngsters who may not yet be certain of the concept to consider additional examples provided by their peers.

At this point the children should be asked to name the concept and develop a definition of the concept. This is an inductive strategy and the children's definitions may be a little cumbersome. However, since the students will have constructed their own definitions, learning is reinforced. Of course, teachers should encourage students to modify their definitions if they are inaccurate or incomplete.

The fifth step in this concept-attainment strategy is to conduct a class discussion in which children are asked to indicate how each example and nonexample relates to the concept. This encourages children to reconsider the attributes of the concept and provides an opportunity to strengthen their knowledge of the concept.

This step also requires children to consider attribute values, one of the elements of concepts. For example, in a concept-attainment lesson about basic needs, children were shown a picture of a pair of jeans as an example of a basic clothing need. A picture of an expensive fur coat was presented as a nonexample. During the follow-up discussion children had to explain the differences between two types of clothing. They were asked, "Why was one classified as a basic need and the other was not classified as a basic need?" The discussion was lively and enabled children to identify the attribute values that may place examples into different categories. In this case the children decided that there was a concept of clothes as basic needs, and another concept, luxury, that includes expensive clothes.

Table 10–3 illustrates a concept-attainment lesson following the steps outlined above. The example is a primary-grade lesson for the concept *needs*.

Joyce and Weil encouraged teachers to take time to discuss the children's thought process. That is, the children should be encouraged to reconsider the thinking strategies they used as they considered each example and nonexample. As a final step, teachers should ask the following types of questions:

1. What did the first example make you think of?
2. Did the first nonexample change your thinking?
3. How did your thinking change when you saw the second example?
4. Continue this process for each of the examples and nonexamples.

Table 10–3 Sample Concept-Attainment Activity

Concept: Needs

Present Clue: I am thinking of something about basic survival

Present Examples (Picture of items):

	Examples	Nonexamples
	House	Airplane
	Cereal	Coffee
	Shirt	Mink coat
	Water	Soft drink
	Igloo	Mansion
	Shoes	Office building
	Cooked chicken	Dishwasher

Ask children for additional examples and nonexamples.

Ask children to name the concept.

Ask children to develop a definition of the concept.

Discuss the relationship between the examples and the concept.

1. Why is house a positive example?

   How might other cultures satisfy this need?

2. Why is an airplane a nonexample?

3. Why is cereal an example? What other examples might have been presented?

4. Continue with remaining examples and nonexamples.

Source: Reinhartz, J., & Van Cleaf, D.W. (1986). *Teach-practice-apply: The TPA instructional model, k-8*, p. 30. Washington, DC: National Education Association. Adapted and reprinted with permission of the National Education Association.

Helping children reconstruct their thought processes appears to help them refine their problem-solving skills. As youngsters become more conscious of their thinking they begin to discover how their thinking strategies vary in different situations. This procedure also exposes children to the thinking and problem-solving strategies used by other children. In one sense, this is a means of fostering *metacognition*. Metacognition relates to a person's conscious awareness of how he or she solves various problems and completes various learning tasks.

After you and your students have used this concept-attainment strategy several times you can require them to develop concept-attainment activities. Give children a concept and have them collect appropriate examples and nonexamples. They can also develop an appropriate clue. This actively involves children in an exciting activity. Further, children become more knowledgeable about a concept because they must select the examples and nonexamples.

Guided Discussion. The third inductive concept-attainment teaching strategy is a guided-discussion strategy described by Reinhartz and Van Cleaf (1986). The guided- discussion strategy is constructed on the four elements of concepts (cited earlier in the chapter): name, examples and nonexamples, attributes, and attribute value. A fifth element, a definition of the concept, has been added.

The teacher's task in preparing a guided discussion is to identify an appropriate concept for this type of teaching activity. Children should have some degree of knowledge about the concept. Their knowledge could be about the concept at a basic level, or their knowledge could be about related concepts and experiences. If the children have little knowledge about the concept they will be unable to respond to questions and a discussion would be inappropriate.

With an appropriate concept for the discussion the teacher guides children through the following steps. First, *state the concept.* A statement such as, "Today we will discuss the concept, *cities*" initiates the lesson. The teacher then proceeds to the second step, *eliciting examples and nonexamples from the children.* The teacher can ask a pair of questions: "What are examples of cities?" and "What are examples of places people live that are not cities?" Or, the teacher may use declarative statements, "Name several examples of cities" and "Name several examples of places people live that are not cities." Children's responses should be listed on the chalkboard for later comparisons.

Each concept has *attributes,* the third element of a concept. The next set of questions requires children to examine the list of examples and nonexamples and to identify attributes of the concept. The teacher might instruct students to look at each list and then describe items that are attributes of cities. The teacher might state, "Now look at the examples of cities; what do these cities have in common? Now look at the list of nonexamples; in what ways are they different from cities?" At this point the attributes identified by the children may be listed on the chalkboard.

The next element of a concept is *attribute value.* Most attributes have a value range. For example, if one of the attributes of cities identified by the children was a large population, the attribute value would range from fairly large to extremely large. Rock Springs, Wyoming, may be placed at the small end of the range; Madison, Wisconsin, might be placed midway along the range; and New York City would be placed at the high end of the population value range. If the presence of large buildings was one of the attributes identified by children, the attribute range would be a continuum ranging from relatively few large buildings to an impressive number of large buildings.

The attribute value portion of the guided discussion provides teachers and children with opportunities to engage in higher-level thinking skills. Questions such as "At what point does a suburb or town become a city?" require children to consider the range of attribute values and to arrive at a subjective determination. Another type of question also requires youngsters to reconsider the concept at a higher intellectual level. For example, "In what ways is life better in a city than in a town or suburb?" and conversely, "In what ways is life better in suburbs and towns?" require children to ponder higher-level responses. Similar thought-provoking questions motivate children and encourage higher-level thinking.

The final step in the guided discussion strategy is to ask the children for a *definition* of the concept. After considering the elements of a city, children should be able to define the concept *city*, describe key attributes, and identify attribute values of the concept.

The guided-discussion strategy is effective because it encourages students to become actively involved. It is also effective because it encourages them to consider higher levels of thinking about the concept. The consideration of attribute values also helps children to develop a more comprehensive understanding of the concept.

Concept-Pattern Strategy. Marzano and Arredondo (1986) proposed an alternative way of helping children learn concepts. They suggested a process of helping children recognize concept patterns that is well suited to textbook reading assignments, lecture presentations, or audiovisual presentations. They accept the standard definitions of concepts, but rather than encourage children to classify examples and nonexamples, they suggest that children identify supporting examples.

The strategy begins with the identification of a concept. For example, if children were studying forest regions, a study of the concept *logging* would be included. As children read a passage or watch a film about logging they would be required to identify attributes of logging by listing supporting statements. Their efforts might look like this:[*]

Concept:	Logging
Support:	1. Logging occurs in forest regions
	2. Logging is dangerous
	3. People cut down trees
	4. Trees are taken to a sawmill
	5. The sawmill cuts the trees into lumber
	6. The lumber is used to build houses

[*]*Source:* Marzano, R.J., & Arredondo, D.E. (1986). *Tactics for thinking.* Alexandria, VA: Association for Supervision and Curriculum Development. Adapted and reprinted with permission of the Association for Supervision and Curriculum Development (ASCD) and Robert Marzano. Copyright © 1986 by ASCD. All rights reserved.

Marzano and Arredondo developed this strategy as a means of helping children develop alternative thinking strategies. As children are assigned work they should determine the type of thinking pattern necessary to complete the assignment. Other patterns include generalization patterns (described in a following section), sequence patterns, process and cause patterns, and similarity and dissimilarity patterns. Marzano and Arredondo's book, *Tactics for Thinking,* is an excellent resource.

Teaching Generalizations

Generalizations are relationships between two or more concepts. They are also statements about concepts requiring support and clarification of statements. A more detailed description of generalizations was provided earlier in the chapter.

The Taba model, the concept-attainment model, the guided-discussion model, and the concept-pattern model described in the preceding sections contribute to the development of generalizations. Through each of the four strategies, children are required to compare attributes of examples and non-examples. As children compare the attributes, they begin to discover that concepts are not rigid. Rather, concepts are often fluid and overlapping. As children discover this they begin to discover relationships between and among concepts, which then enables them to make generalizations about the concepts. This section of the chapter describes two methods of teaching generalizations.

Taba Generalization Strategy. Taba (1967) proposed a second strategy designed to help children learn to generalize. She called this strategy, "Interpreting, Inferring, and Generalizing." Teachers are required to lead children through a three-step process. Children must first consider data and determine appropriate and inappropriate information. The teacher encourages children to state what they found or what they know about the topic. Taba suggested asking, "What did you notice? see? find?" (p. 101) as a means of helping children provide the necessary information.

The second step of the procedure requires children to relate points to one another. Children need to identify relationships. Taba suggested that teachers ask questions requiring youngsters to consider and explain why something happened. The sample question she listed to illustrate this type of question was, "Why did so-and-so happen?" (p. 101).

The last step is to encourage children to consider implications of the information and make inferences from the information. This encourages children to generalize beyond the information and concepts. Taba suggested asking the following questions in this step: "What does this mean? What picture does it create in your mind? What would you conclude?" (p. 101).

The example in Table 10–4 illustrates the format that is followed when using the Taba strategy.

Table 10–4 Interpretation of Data

OVERT ACTIVITY	COVERT MENTAL OPERATIONS	ELICITING QUESTIONS
1. Identifying points.	Differentiating.	What did you notice? see? find?
2. Explaining items of identified information.	Relating points to each other. Determining cause and effect relationships.	Why did so-and-so happen?
3. Making inferences.	Going beyond what is given. Finding implications, extrapolating.	What does this mean? What picture does it create in your mind? What would you conclude?

Source: Taba, H. (1967). *Teacher's handbook for elementary social studies,* p. 101. Palo Alto, CA: Addison- Wesley. Copyright © 1967 Addison-Wesley Publishing Company, Menlo Park, CA. Reprinted with permission of Addison-Wesley.

Generalization Patterns. Marzano and Arredondo (1986) described a generalization pattern that is somewhat similar to their concept pattern described in the preceding section. Marzano and Arredondo described generalizations as statements about concepts and relationships between concepts. The generalization pattern consists of a generalization statement about two or more concepts. The generalization statement is followed by a series of supporting statements. The following social studies example illustrates a generalization pattern about the concepts *wheat* and *natural resources:*

Generalization statement:	Wheat is an important natural resource.
Support statements:	Wheat produces income for farmers.
	Wheat is an ingredient in many foods.
	We sell wheat to other countries to feed them.
	Farm-implement dealers depend on wheat farmers for income.
	If a drought destroys a wheat crop, many farms and businesses suffer.

As children read passages or obtain information from other resources, they can be required to consider generalizations and identify supporting statements from their studies.

Source: Marzano, R.J., & Arredondo, D.E. (1986). *Tactics for thinking.* Alexandria, VA: Association for Supervision and Curriculum Development. Adapted and reprinted with permission of the Association for Supervision and Curriculum Development (ASCD) and Robert Marzano. Copyright © 1986 by ASCD. All rights reserved.

SUMMARY

Concepts are mental categories of thought. They are groupings or sets of items with similar characteristics. Concepts may be sets of objects, events, people, ideas, or symbols.

Concepts are the cornerstone of an excellent social studies program. The subject matter, skills, and democratic values and beliefs that comprise the scope of the social studies curriculum can be taught more effectively by organizing instruction around key concepts. Rather than inundating children with an endless number of facts, a focus on concepts will more readily help them understand social studies. Further, they will be more likely to retain the information taught during social studies instruction.

Concepts can be taught either deductively or inductively. Whether teaching deductively or inductively, two critical attributes are involved in teaching concepts—a definition and examples of items within the concept (examples may be positive or negative). If you teach deductively you will provide the definition first and then present appropriate examples. Deductive teaching is primarily a teacher-directed approach. To teach a concept inductively you would present a series of examples and then encourage children to develop a definition. Inductive teaching is more child-centered. This chapter described several deductive and inductive strategies for teaching concepts.

Concepts emerge from facts, content, and experiences. As concepts become more complex and begin to overlap with other concepts they become generalizations. This chapter described generalizations and several strategies for teaching generalizations.

Schools are being criticized for teaching the basics poorly. Yet we will not improve education significantly by continuing to focus on low-level basic knowledge. A conceptual focus is one means of raising achievement. By organizing facts and skills around key social studies concepts, students will learn, understand, and retain the information they are taught. Further, they will be able to understand complex relationships and therefore become better problem solvers.

SUGGESTED ACTIVITIES

1. Select a concept from an elementary social studies textbook. Identify and list at least five positive and five negative examples. Outline the steps you would follow if you were going to teach the concept deductively and inductively.

2. Select several concepts presented in an elementary social studies textbook. Read the section of the textbook in which each concept is developed. How well do the textbook entries develop the concepts? Are there sufficient examples?

3. Select a concept with which you think children would have some degree of familiarity. Use that concept to outline lessons exemplifying the suggestions described in this chapter.

Reading and then asking questions is one way for children to learn.

Photograph by Laima Druskis.

chapter 11

Effective Questioning and Discussion Strategies

Sometimes the teacher asks too many questions.

(student, grade 1)

AS YOU READ...

- describe the major difficulties with current questioning practices
- describe primary benefits of using effective questions and discussions
- define the term *taxonomy* and describe how a taxonomy can help you improve your questioning skills
- identify key suggestions for improving questioning skills
- describe alternative discussion strategies

INTRODUCTION

The Greek philosopher and teacher Socrates taught his students by asking them questions. He helped them expand their knowledge inductively, drawing upon their current knowledge as a basis for developing more sophisticated ways of thinking. He would skillfully ask a series of questions designed to lead his students from considerations of their current levels of knowledge to new levels of understanding. This method of teaching is called the Socratic method and is advocated as an excellent method for helping children actively construct a more sophisticated understanding of their world.

This chapter will help you develop your ability to ask a variety of questions and actively engage children in class discussions. The two topics, questioning and discussions, are contained in the same chapter because good questioning skills are prerequisites to conducting effective discussions. Also, good discussions extend the effectiveness of questioning techniques.

Teaching is one of the oldest professions.

Photograph courtesy of The Library of Congress.

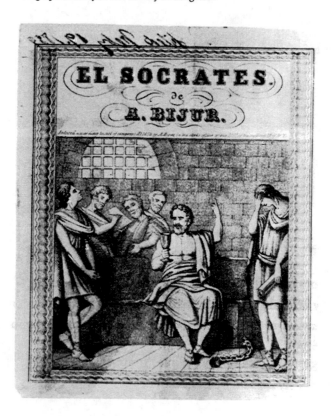

Questions are statements made by teachers to elicit responses from children. Discussions are dialogues among individuals. In classrooms, dialogues can be between children and teacher, or they can be interactions among children. During discussion activities, questions are usually asked to initiate, direct, and maintain the interaction. Questions serve as prompts to stimulate interaction and to keep the discussion focused.

Excellent questioning skills are necessary for learning as well as conducting effective and lively discussions. Questions stimulate interaction, they keep the dialogue on track, and they guide students as teachers attempt to develop the educational purpose of lessons.

Poorly conceived questions can mislead students, create confusion, and elicit incorrect responses. Poorly conceived questions and poor timing can inhibit lively discussions. An inappropriate balance of low-level questions can result in a focus on facts without a conceptual understanding. Effective questions enhance discussions. Both lead to improved teaching, increased motivation, and higher achievement.

This chapter includes five major topics. The first section describes the primary purposes of questioning and discussions. The second section explores the relationships between questioning and classification structures called *taxonomies*. The third section considers current research findings related to the use of classroom questioning practices. The fourth section presents suggestions and guidelines for improving your questioning skills. The fifth section describes classroom discussion strategies and offers suggestions for improving classroom discussions.

PURPOSES

Utilizing questions and discussions as teaching strategies has many beneficial outcomes. This section of the chapter describes seven major reasons for using questions and discussions in classrooms. The benefits associated with each reason are included.

Evaluation

Chapter 6 described the processes and purposes of evaluation. Teachers evaluate children for a variety of reasons before, during, and after instruction. Questions are a critical aspect of each stage of evaluation. Questions during the pretest stage provide teachers with information that will enable them to personalize instruction for their students. During instruction, questions can determine whether or not students understand the lesson and whether there is a need to reteach confusing portions of a lesson. Questions are asked at the end of an instructional sequence to provide teachers with feedback regarding the effectiveness of the instructional strategies used, how well children learned, and information regarding the need to modify future lessons. Because many social studies concepts are complex, such as states' rights and separation of powers, teachers must continuously evaluate children's learning.

Drill and Practice

Children must have opportunities to master information once it has been taught. For example, children need many opportunities to practice the names of states in a region of the country, the names of individuals participating in an historical event, the functions of each branch of government, or the use of map coordinates.

Questions are a means of providing such practice. During a lesson on natural resources, the teacher might ask children to name natural resources found in the school, community, and state. Or, after reading a section of the text, the teacher may ask children a series of questions as a means of reviewing and practicing the important information presented in the reading passage.

As teachers ask drill-and-practice questions they are providing students with opportunities to develop a sense of mastery of the important information. The questions also indicate to children what information is important.

Academic Achievement

The skillful use of questions is a strategy by which teachers move children from an existing level of understanding to a higher level. Teachers begin by asking questions to help children clarify their existing levels of knowledge and understanding. These initial questions encourage children to identify key experiences from their lives that relate to the point being developed. This information is then used as a foundation that helps children move to a more sophisticated level of understanding.

For example, an elementary-grade teacher was teaching a unit on the principle *rule of law*. In an introductory lesson the teacher asked students to describe the rules that they were expected to obey in the classroom, lunchroom, at home, and while shopping in a store. Children were then asked to describe the rules that governed their parents' behaviors. Next, children were asked to identify who was responsible for making the rules governing their behaviors and their parents' behaviors. After establishing a knowledge base emerging from the children's experiences, the teacher was ready to extend students' thinking to a new level. At this level children were asked if rules could ever be changed, under what circumstances, and by whom.

Although this type of learning is more time-consuming than lecturing, several important benefits accrue. First, this is a strategy that requires children to think and process information. Therefore, they are utilizing a combination of lower-level and higher-level thinking skills. Second, this type of approach can be highly motivating because children have opportunities to describe familiar information. Very few wrong answers are provided, thus contributing to the motivational value of this method. Third, children are skillfully moved to a more sophisticated level of understanding because the new level of knowledge is based on their previous knowledge.

Critical Thinking

Questioning and discussion activities, when done correctly, include a variety of lower-level and higher-level questions. Lower-level questions help establish the factual foundation, whereas higher-level questions require children to use critical thinking skills as they analyze, evaluate, and apply the information.

In the late 1970s and early 1980s there were a number of mandates to return to the basics (reading, writing, and arithmetic). However, it quickly became apparent that young people must also learn to think critically. The need to develop students' critical thinking skills is nurtured through the use of a well-designed set of questions. A sample question might be: "How would your community be different if located in a different geographical region, if it were an island, if major transportation routes were changed?"

Involve Children

Questions are an excellent means for involving children in the learning process. Engaging children in questioning and discussion activities can be motivating for children. They appear to enjoy opportunities to share information and ideas with others.

Exciting questioning and discussion lessons contain several thought-provoking and novel questions. An example is, "What would your life be like if the French had not sold the Louisiana Territory?" These questions increase the motivational quality of the lesson because children are provided opportunities to consider open-ended questions for which there are exciting possibilities. Because children find these questions motivating they become more involved in the activity.

Interpersonal Skills

Interpersonal skills are a critical aspect of social studies. Involving children in class discussions nurtures the development of cooperation and other interpersonal skills. As children communicate with one another they begin to see the other's point of view. They also must practice cooperation and positive interpersonal skills by listening to each other, taking turns speaking, and learning to disagree tactfully. As children participate in discussions these skills are reinforced.

Teacher and children seated in a small discussion group.

Photograph by Ken Karp.

Affective Development

Much of the information and skills taught in elementary social studies classrooms tends to be factual. Little time is afforded to children's attitudes, feelings and beliefs—the affective side of social studies. Questioning and discussion activities enable the teacher to ask students how they feel about topics studied in their lessons. Students may also consider how an event affects the quality of their lives and how the quality of their lives might have changed if alternative decisions had been made. Questioning is an excellent means of helping students integrate affective and knowledge aspects of social studies.

This section described the major reasons behind question and discussion strategies. The next section examines the levels of classroom questions by relating questions to classification structures called taxonomies.

TYPES AND TAXONOMIES

The terms *low-level* and *high-level* questions are used as a general means of classifying and analyzing teachers' questions and the cognitive demands placed on children. Teachers' questions have been classified in more specific ways, often paralleling classification structures called taxonomies. This section of the chapter describes two *taxonomies* and concludes with a useful model for developing your questioning skills.

Benjamin Bloom and his colleagues (1956) developed a taxonomy classifying educational objectives. Bloom's taxonomy describes a hierarchy of educational objectives in the cognitive and skill domains. Many educators have proposed developing questions that reflect the various categories identified in Bloom's taxonomy. Research findings supporting this practice are mixed. Nevertheless, the practice continues and appears to be a means of encouraging teachers to analyze and expand their questioning skills.

Bloom's Taxonomy

Bloom's taxonomy identifies six categories of objectives related to the content and skill domains of educational objectives. This classification structure began with low-level, fact-oriented objectives and progressed to higher-level objectives requiring more complex mental processing. The six levels of objectives are, in ascending order, knowledge, comprehension, application, analysis, synthesis, and evaluation.

At the *knowledge* level, learning consists primarily of being able to recall factual information. The second level, *comprehension*, relates to the child's ability to understand the information and explain it in some concrete, simple way. *Application* requires children to use the information they learned in other familiar situations. *Analysis* moves to a higher cognitive functioning and is the process of identifying and describing part-whole relationships. *Synthesis*, the fifth level, requires children to examine separate ideas or parts of something and combine them in a new way. The final level is *evaluation*, which requires children to make judgments about topics they study.

Frustrated with the complexities of Bloom's taxonomy and the difficulty teachers experience as they attempt to differentiate among the six categories, alternative taxonomies have been proposed. Barrett's taxonomy is described next and is followed by a model useful for social studies.

Barrett's Taxonomy

Thomas Barrett proposed a three-category taxonomy related to reading comprehension. His taxonomy included literal comprehension, inferential comprehension, and evaluative comprehension. *Literal comprehension* is based on factual recall of information presented in a passage. *Inferential comprehension* requires children to make inferences from information presented when the text does not explicitly provide the answer. Children are expected to go beyond the information presented in a passage as they examine sequences, make comparisons, identify cause-effect relationships, and predict outcomes. *Evaluative comprehension* requires children to make judgments about topics presented in the text. Questions related to validity, appropriateness, worth, and fact versus opinion exemplify evaluative thought. Barrett also included the category *appreciation* as an aspect of evaluative comprehension. Appreciation involves personal and emotional responses to the reading passage. Imagery and the ability to understand the story's characters are other aspects of appreciation (Smith & Barrett, 1979).

A Useful Synthesis

Orlich and his colleagues (1985) offered a convenient way to classify questions. They recommended convergent, divergent, and evaluative questions as three essential categories. These categories are a creative, useful synthesis of many educational taxonomies.

Convergent questions are lower-level, recall questions that reflect the knowledge and comprehension levels of Bloom's taxonomy. Convergent questions are also indicative of the literal category described by Barrett.

Convergent questions are used by teachers to help students focus on the correct answers. They require children to recall information from prior instruction, reading passages, or personal experience. As such, they enable teachers to help children practice and strengthen their knowledge of essential subject matter.

Many of the purposes of questions described earlier in the chapter are addressed through the use of convergent questions. Drill and practice are an essential part of mastering important information that is a prerequisite to later learning. The Socratic method of instruction requires teachers to base new learning on prior knowledge, and convergent questions are necessary to help children recall pertinent information. Although you might think that critical thinking would exclude the use of convergent questions, critical thinking requires children to consider factual data as a basis for proceeding to higher level processes.

Convergent questions are necessary. Facts are important, both for mastery and for higher-level thinking. However, too many convergent questions are used in classrooms. A more appropriate balance between convergent and divergent questions must be achieved.

Divergent questions do not focus on facts, nor do they focus on the "right" answers. Students are encouraged to explore possibilities, alternatives, creative options, and a variety of responses. This term incorporates the higher levels of Bloom's taxonomy and Barrett's inference category.

Divergent questions support several of the purposes of questioning outlined earlier in the chapter. Divergent questions are important for critical thinking because they encourage children to consider alternative ideas. The motivational aspect of questioning is also supported by divergent questions. Children enjoy thinking about possibilities, particularly when they are encouraged to provide novel responses. The Socratic method also relies on the use of divergent questions. With a factual basis established through the use of convergent questions, learners proceed to more advanced levels of knowledge. This is nurtured through the use of divergent questions. The affective aspects of questioning are also reinforced with divergent questions. As children consider possibilities they often include their attitudes, feelings, and beliefs about the topic.

Sample convergent and divergent questions are listed in Table 11–1.

Evaluative questions are an extension of divergent questions. Evaluative questions, like Barrett's and Bloom's highest levels, require children to make judgments about their responses and support their judgments with thoughtful reasons.

Table 11–1 Primary- and Intermediate-Grade Sample Questions

Topic: Responsibility

Grade Level: Primary

Convergent Questions

1. What are examples of responsibility?
2. What responsibilities do you have?
3. What responsibilities do parents have?
4. What responsibilities did the character in the story fail to exercise?

Divergent Questions

1. How do your responsibilities change as you get older?
2. What would school be like if no one acted responsibly?
3. What would our city and country be like if no one acted responsibly?
4. How can people be encouraged to act more responsibly?

Evaluative Questions

1. Why do we need to act responsibly?
2. Do prisons help people act responsibly?
3. What are the most important responsibilities for children? For adults? Why?
4. What advice do you have for parents, teachers, and community leaders?

Topic: Declaration of Independence

Grade Level: Intermediate

Convergent Questions

1. What is the Declaration of Independence?
2. When was it written?
3. What war resulted from signing the Declaration of Independence?
4. What issues led to the Declaration of Independence?

Divergent Questions

1. What would have happened if the Declaration of Independence had not been signed?
2. How could the colonies and England have settled their differences without war?
3. What effects has the Declaration of Independence had on our lives today?

Evaluative Questions

1. Were the colonists' complaints against England justified?
2. Defend the colonists' decision to sign the Declaration of Independence?
3. Why are the freedoms outlined in the Declaration of Independence important?
4. What must be done to preserve our freedom?
5. Why are some people not treated as equally as others?

Source: Orlich, D.C., Harder, R.J., Callahan, R.C., Kravas, C.H., Kauchak, D.P., Pendergrass, R.A., & Keogh, A.J. (1985). *Teaching strategies* (2nd ed.). Lexington, MA: Heath. Adapted and reprinted with permission of D.C. Heath and Company.

Evaluative questions are essentially "why" questions. Children may propose a variety of possibilities when asked divergent questions. Evaluative questions provide opportunities for children to consider and substantiate the appropriateness of divergent responses. Examples of evaluative questions are also included in Table 11–1.

Responses to evaluative questions may be factual, or they may be highly subjective. When children are asked to judge or substantiate their responses they should include factual and experiential support, but they should also express their intuitive and affective reasons. If children were professionals, we might refer to the intuitive and affective reasons as professional judgment.

Evaluative questions support several of the purposes of questioning. Evaluative questions are necessary for critical thinking. Children must learn to substantiate ideas if they are to become disciplined critical thinkers. Each level of government considers a diversity of controversial issues. Effective citizens must be able to understand and analyze these issues. They must learn that as they attempt to solve problems they must consider facts, examine possibilities, and then evaluate the potential usefulness of alternative solutions. If attempting to convince others, children must go through the evaluative process. The affective purpose of questioning is also addressed through evaluative questioning. Children must be able to substantiate answers with factual support as well as their attitudes toward the topics.

This portion of the chapter described several ways of classifying questions. It then described a synthesized taxonomy of questions that should enable you to utilize a variety of questions in your classroom as you strive to develop a workable balance between low-level and high-level thinking. Perhaps a good way to summarize the types of questions emerging from this classification structure is the following. Convergent questions focus on absolutes, divergent questions focus on possibilities, evaluative questions require children to consider probabilities.

RESEARCH ON QUESTIONING

In recent years the field of educational research has accumulated a collection of well-designed studies. Many of these studies provide insights into effective questioning practices. As a backdrop to describing suggestions for developing effective questioning skills, several of the key results of these research studies are reported in this section.

Gall (1970) reported that a majority of teachers' questions were lower-level questions. Approximately 80 percent of the questions teachers ask are low level; the remaining 20 percent are higher-level ones requiring more sophisticated levels of cognitive processing.

Redfield and Rousseau (1981) analyzed a number of studies and concluded that an increased use of higher-level questions leads to higher achievement. They found that teachers could raise the achievement levels of children achieving at the

Timing is an important factor when questioning students.

Photograph courtesy of Seiko.

50th percentile to the 77th percentile by increasing the percentage of questions requiring higher cognitive thought.

Wixson (1983) concurred with these findings. Wixson explained that the level of a teacher's questions has a direct effect on the level of the students' cognitive processing.

Giaconia (1987) reported that the cognitive level of teachers' questions was a critical factor in eliciting higher-level responses from students. If teachers want their students to produce higher-level responses, they should ask higher-level questions.

Several research studies support using convergent and divergent questions. Low-level, convergent questions are often a useful and necessary means of helping children master content and skills. But many social studies goals specify improving children's abilities to think and solve problems. High-level, divergent questions are useful for this purpose. A balanced mixture of convergent, divergent, and evaluative questions appears appropriate.

IMPROVING CLASSROOM QUESTIONS

This section of the chapter offers a variety of practical suggestions. The suggestions are organized into four categories: planning, learning environment, teaching practices, and evaluation.

Planning Considerations

Well-planned educational programs are effective programs. When teachers consider the goals and objectives for their lessons and then plan appropriate activities, children learn. This phenomenon also holds true for questioning. The following suggestions will help ensure that your questioning lessons are well planned and effective.

Purpose. The types of questions you ask will differ depending on the purposes of your lesson. For example, if you need to provide opportunities for your students to master certain information, you should plan to ask low-level, drill-and-practice questions. However, if you intend to help them evaluate the feasibility of a certain decision, a series of low-level and high-level questions should be planned. Low-level questions will enable children to consider their existing knowledge about the topic. This serves as the basis for the higher-level questions. Higher-level questions will encourage children to consider divergent possibilities as well as evaluative analyses of possible solutions. These higher-level questions move children beyond the confines of the data.

In many aspects of life, form follows function. The form of your questions will be dictated by the function (purpose) of your lessons. The primary purpose for asking questions was described earlier in the chapter and will dictate the types of questions you should plan.

Placement. After determining the purpose and types of questions, determine where to place your questions within the sequence of the lesson. Questions designed to motivate students and encourage them to pay attention to main points should occur early in the lesson. Drill-and-practice questions should occur after information has been taught. Higher-level questions may occur after a knowledge foundation has been developed or when considering divergent, creative possibilities. Evaluative questions should occur at the end of the questioning sequence. Specific placement depends on your purpose and the level of children's understanding.

Time. As you plan questioning sessions you should consider the length of time you intend to devote to the questioning portion of the lesson. Discussions with primary-grade children should be relatively brief. Between fifteen and twenty minutes is appropriate for intermediate-grade children.

Prepare Your Questions. During the planning phase you should make a list of the questions you intend to ask. Effective questions must be prepared in advance and used as a script to direct the flow of the lesson. While you are encouraged to ask spontaneous questions during the lesson, failure to prepare questions in advance generally reduces your effectiveness. It is difficult to construct effective questions while you are in the midst of a lesson.

As you prepare your questions, please consider the following suggestions. They will help you prepare clearly worded questions and increase the probability that students will learn from the experience.

1. *Clarity.* Children have difficulty responding to poorly worded questions. Children's incorrect responses are often the result of a poorly worded question

rather than a lack of knowledge. They may not understand the question or the question may provoke several avenues of thought. Consider some of the exam questions you have been asked while in college. The poorly worded ones create confusion. They do not allow you to exemplify your knowledge of the topic.

Poorly worded and poorly conceptualized questions are readily observed. A poorly worded question is almost inevitably followed with a paraphrased question. It is as if the teacher recognizes how poor the first question was and quickly restates the question using different words. This creates difficulties for children who are still attempting to understand the first question.

Once you know the purpose of your questioning you can develop clearly, crisply worded questions. Generally, shorter questions are better because there are fewer clauses for children to consider. If you want children to consider several points, ask several questions, one question for each point you want them to consider. Then you may ask a question requiring children to tie each of the points together.

2. *Avoid asking yes/no questions.* Questions requiring either a yes or no response usually require low-level thinking. Several yes or no questions may be appropriate; however, too many may limit discussion and higher-level thinking.

The question "Is socialism bad?" illustrates a poor question. Children need opportunities to consider the strengths and weaknesses of socialism. A better question would be, "What are the strengths and weaknesses of socialism?"

3. *Ensure that children have an appropriate knowledge base.* Few activities fail more quickly than asking questions when students do not know the answers. Children will avoid responding because they do not want to fail.

Responses to open-ended, divergent questions will be inhibited if children do not have an adequate knowledge of the topic. If you wanted to ask children how their lives would be different if their basic needs were satisfied by living in a different environment, they would need to have an understanding of basic needs and how their needs are met through their immediate environment. Unless students have a certain basic level of knowledge about a topic, asking divergent and evaluative questions is pointless.

4. *Difficulty.* As you plan your questions you should develop a range of questions that will enable children to respond successfully. Also plan some questions that are more difficult and require children to think.

5. *Balance lower- and higher-level questions.* By planning a mix of lower-level and higher-level questions you can help children practice essential information and then consider the usefulness of the information. Both lower-level thinking and higher-level thinking are nurtured.

Learning Environment

Effective teachers establish positive learning environments, and positive learning environments are necessary for effective questioning sessions. The following suggestions will enable you to establish an environment conducive to effective questioning.

Personal Philosophy. Your attitudes toward children and convergent, divergent, and evaluative thinking will have an impact on the types of questions you will ask and the types of responses you will accept from children. Do you feel comfortable with convergent responses? Do you enjoy divergent responses? Are you able to allow students to provide evaluative responses to issues studied in class? To what extent are you a teacher-directed or a child-centered teacher? The trend in social studies is to consider children as active participants in the learning process.

Model Acceptance. Effective teachers have a way of making each student feel important, and they have an accepting attitude toward their students. They respond to children's answers with dignity and respect. This may be difficult to do when children respond incorrectly, but effective teachers have found ways to maintain children's dignity.

Effective teachers accept children, but they do not accept incorrect answers as being correct. They acknowledge children's attempts, provide opportunities for children to respond to easier questions, and ask questions that elicit correct responses.

Model Uncertainty. Teachers should model a degree of uncertainty as they question their students and respond to their questions. By always responding with a correct answer you are implying that there is a correct response to every question. However, in a complex world there may be several possible solutions to a problem, or there may be no immediate solution. Children need to learn that there is a degree of uncertainty and that they may need to think about some questions for a long time before they identify an answer.

Seating Arrangement. The seating arrangement will either nurture or inhibit the interaction that emerges during questioning activities. A traditional row-by-row seating arrangement fosters interaction between the teacher and the children. When children are seated in a circle they are more likely to interact with each other.

Teaching Practices

Several suggestions are offered here that will enable you to improve the effectiveness of your questioning while you are interacting with your students during instruction. In many ways, they are extensions of the suggestions previously described.

Probe. When a child responds incorrectly, the teacher may probe by asking leading questions that will enable the child to focus on a pertinent aspect of the question and move toward the appropriate response. For example, a teacher asked the question, "What community helpers keep us healthy?" A child responded, "The firefighters." The teacher then said, "Yes, the firefighters can help us sometimes, but who are we more likely to visit when we are not feeling well?"

Redirecting. Redirecting questions to other children is an alternative to probing. If the child responds incorrectly, ask other children. In the above example, rather than lead the child toward the answer through probing, the teacher might have responded, "Yes, your answer is partially correct. Now I would like someone else to suggest another community helper responsible for our health."

Avoid Run-on Questions. If you plan your questions well you will avoid ambiguous questions. However, during instruction you may feel that one of your questions is confusing your students. Don't panic. Rather than paraphrase the question immediately, wait a few moments. If children are still confused, you might ask them to tell you what they think you are asking—ask someone to paraphrase the question. If they are still confused, then attempt to restate the question. Restating a question quickly usually produces greater confusion, so avoid run-on questions by pausing for a few moments.

Selecting Respondents. Research indicates that it may be better to call on a child before asking the question rather than asking a question and then calling on a child. This appears to reduce anxiety because the children do not have to worry about who will be called on to respond.

Wait-Time. Rowe (1974) used the term *wait-time* to describe two types of pauses teachers should use to improve the effectiveness of their questioning practices. Wait-time I is the pause that occurs between the teacher's question and calling on a child to respond. While most teachers pause for a second or less before calling on a child for a response, waiting an additional few seconds results in more accurate as well as higher-level responses. Optimum wait-time ranges from three to five seconds.

Wait-time II occurs after a child has answered the teacher's question, but before the teacher acknowledges the child's response. This wait-time allows children time to reconsider responses and to elaborate on their responses.

While wait-time I and II are effective means of promoting more elaborate and higher-level responses, wait-time may not be appropriate in every situation. In drill-and-practice situations quick responses are desirable and wait-time is disregarded.

Acknowledge Children's Responses. Providing children with information about the correctness of their responses (feedback) is related to increases in children's achievement. Therefore, teachers should provide an indication regarding the appropriateness of children's responses. Correct and incorrect responses should be acknowledged.

Evaluation

Suggestions for improving your questioning skills cannot end when you complete the lesson. Effective teachers are reflective. They reconsider their effectiveness after they have ended a lesson. Improving your questioning skills will require you to reflect on the effectiveness of your questioning periodically.

Checklist. You may develop a checklist and record the types of questions you ask your students during a lesson. A checklist could be quite simple, consisting of columns for recording convergent, divergent, and evaluative questions. As you ask a question you should use a check mark to record the type of question in the appropriate column. At the end of the lesson or a series of lessons you can evaluate your questioning skills by comparing the percent of convergent, divergent, and evaluative questions asked. A sample checklist is illustrated in Table 11–2.

Table 11–2 Informal Questions Checklist

LESSON TOPIC:		DATES (5):
Type of Question	Frequency	Total
Convergent	⊔⊔⊣ ⊔⊔⊣ ⊔⊔⊣ ⊔⊣⊤⊥	23
Divergent	⊔⊣⊤⊥ ⊔⊔	7
Evaluative	⊔⊔	2

Names of children responding (optional):

Recordings. Another means of evaluating your questioning skills would be to record several lessons. You may use either an audio or video recorder. As you review the tapes of your lessons mark the types of questions on a checklist similar to the one illustrated in Table 11–2. After marking the types of questions on the checklist, identify the names of the children who responded to your questions and the number of times each child responded. This will help you determine the types of questions you are asking and whether you are calling on all children. This technique is also an effective means to determine the percent of questions children answer correctly.

Analyze Lesson Plans. A third assessment technique requires you to analyze former lesson plans. As you reexamine prior lesson plans you can categorize questions by types and levels.

DISCUSSIONS

This chapter is designed to help you develop effective questioning and discussion skills. The major portion of the chapter has been devoted to questioning because effective questioning skills are prerequisites to conducting effective discussion lessons.

To understand the term *discussion* better, it may be helpful to compare discussions to drill-and-practice activities. Most classroom questioning activities have been described as drill and practice. They are recitation activities. Teachers ask a majority of lower-level questions that elicit factual, convergent responses from students. The usual purpose for this type of questioning is to help strengthen and reinforce the student's knowledge of a topic. The typical teacher-child interaction in this setting is unilateral. The teacher asks a question and requires the student to produce a correct response. Children respond individually and direct their responses to the teacher; they do not direct their responses to other children.

Discussions are more open-ended than traditional drill-and-practice activities. Discussions are designed to encourage children to solve problems, compare and contrast ideas, identify possibilities, and evaluate actions. While discussions include convergent questions, they rely on divergent and evaluative questions to encourage youngsters to consider higher-level, open-ended responses.

Discussions may also be described as bilateral. During discussions teachers encourage children to interact more openly with both the teacher and with one another. While the teacher maintains control over the direction of the discussion, the teacher encourages a more open form of interaction among all participants.

Types of Discussions

This section of the chapter describes useful suggestions and activities.

Open Discussions. Taba (1967) and Glasser (1969) recommended that children have opportunities to engage in open-ended discussions. Children are encouraged to freely state ideas, problems, feelings, and attitudes. For example, after studying a topic or reading an excerpt from the text, children may be asked to describe what they considered important. Open discussions are an excellent means of discussing current events. Children can discuss their feelings as well as their concerns. Thought-provoking situations can also be included in open discussions.

Comparative Discussions. Comparative discussions are a means of helping children reconsider information from a lesson by asking them to identify similarities and differences, to compare and contrast, to identify pros and cons, or to describe cause-and-effect relationships. Taba suggested using charts to help children make appropriate comparisons. For example, in a lesson about community leisure-time activities, children could help develop a chart listing leisure-time activities in their community and leisure-time activities in a different community (see Table 11–3).

This type of strategy is a discussion because children must examine information at a higher level of cognitive processing. Further, while there may be some answers that are better than others, there is a range of possible responses.

Table 11–3 Leisure-Time Activities (comparative discussion)

OUR COMMUNITY (Arlington, Texas)	COMPARISON COMMUNITY (Denver, Colorado)
Six Flags Over Texas	Skiing
Wet and Wild	Denver Broncos (football)
Boating	Mountain climbing
Texas Rangers (baseball)	Fishing
Dallas Cowboys (football)	Museums
Camping	Camping
Fishing	Hiking
Museums	Canoeing

1. The teacher first elicits information from the children for the chart.
2. The teacher then asks children to compare the two columns noting similarities and differences.
3. The teacher then asks children to identify reasons for the similarities and differences.

Source: Taba, H. (1967). *Teacher's handbook for elementary social studies.* Palo Alto, CA: Addison-Wesley. Copyright © 1967 Addison-Wesley Publishing Company, Menlo Park, CA. Adapted with permission of Addison-Wesley.

Socratic Method. This type of discussion requires the teacher to carefully structure a set of questions that move children from lower-level responses to higher-level ones. In this type of discussion the teacher attempts to develop a point. After asking questions that establish a factual basis, the teacher posits questions that encourage children to make inferences, establish rules, or develop definitions.

For example, one teacher wanted to develop the concept of change. After studying various services (dentists, TV repair, teaching) children were asked to identify the types of services their families used. They were then asked to identify services their grandparents may have used as young children. Finally, children were asked to indicate how services might change in the future.

Social Problem-Solving Discussions. Glasser (1969) encouraged teachers to involve children in solving problems affecting them in school. Glasser likened this type of activity to a teachers' meeting in which the teachers and principal consider and attempt to resolve problems within the school. In the classroom the teacher and children work together discussing classroom problems and solutions to those problems.

Problems may include theft of children's money and materials, too much noise in the classroom, failure to take turns, maintaining a clean classroom, or treating one another with respect. The problems are limitless and emerge from the children and the problems they encounter.

ReQuest. Manzo (1985) proposed a child-centered questioning activity that requires youngsters to formulate questions. After reading a passage or studying new information, children develop questions to ask the teacher. This activity reinforces their learning and nurtures critical thinking skills.

Inquest. Shoop (1987) adapted the ReQuest activity by having children assume the role of investigative reporters. While studying an event, a child is called on to assume the role of a character who participated in the event. Other class members are required to develop questions and interview the character. Again, information about the event is reinforced and children develop critical thinking skills.

Debate. Another means of involving children more actively in class discussions is through debates. After studying a social studies topic the teacher first identifies several issues related to the topic. The teacher then surveys children to determine whether they support or do not support each issue. Topics are then assigned to children for the debates. Class members can either work individually or in small groups of two or three. They should brainstorm possible points, reexamine the information they studied, ask parents and other adults for supporting information, and then organize a response.

Rather than follow a formal debate format, elementary-school students should be encouraged to present their points and ask questions about the points raised by other teams. After opposing teams have presented their ideas, the rest of the class should be encouraged to ask questions and add ideas.

Topics may include irrigating desert regions, the location of a new landfill, secrecy in government, limiting immigration, or making English the official language. This is an exciting variation to classroom discussions because children are the experts and they query one another. The teacher is removed from the interaction pattern.

Guided Discussion. The guided-discussion format described in Chapter 10 is another means of directing lively discussions about social studies concepts.

Additional Suggestion. "The principal classroom activity that characterizes thinking skills instruction is discussion" (Ruggiero, 1988, p. 98). To improve the effectiveness of classroom discussions, he offered the following suggestions.

1. Consider the topic in advance. If you are effectively to guide children during a discussion and achieve maximum impact, you must have a solid understanding of the topic. If you are somewhat uncertain, take sufficient time to study the topic before the discussion.
2. Prepare a set of main questions in advance. Teachers must develop a set of main questions during the planning process. Although you may deviate

from the line of questioning during the activity, your questions provide you with the blueprint you need to get children back to the point and keep the discussion moving.

3. Listen to children's responses. As they respond to your questions you need to "think on your feet" and analyze their replies. By listening to their responses you can determine whether they understand the lesson, whether they know the information, and whether or not they are proceeding in the direction you had planned. As you listen you may find that you have to develop follow-up questions, provide additional information for children, probe their responses, or redirect responses to other class members. Further, you might discover that the discussion is not proceeding well and you may need to end it.

4. Use discussion starters. Discussions are livelier and more children are likely to participate if the topic is interesting. Discussion starters are a means of motivating children and getting them interested in the topic. Thought-provoking questions are one type of discussion starter. An example of a discussion starter that could be used for a discussion about community governance might be, "What would happen if our city's leaders quit?"

    Interesting or thought-provoking pictures and cartoons can also be used as discussion starters. Cartoons such as "Peanuts" and "The Far Side" are humorous, yet they often utilize topics related to the personal and social aspects of children's lives. *National Geographic, Life,* and the major news magazines contain excellent pictures that may serve as discussion starters.

    Newspaper headlines also function as discussion starters. The supermarket checkout stands usually exhibit weekly publications with outlandish headlines. You might also make your own headlines and use them as discussion starters.

5. Play Devil's advocate. As elementary children are discussing a topic, they frequently explore a single perspective of the topic. If left this way, children quickly arrive at a point of agreement and fail to explore alternative aspects of the topic. You can raise alternative and often less popular views as a means of enticing children to explore the topic from several sides. By playing Devil's advocate, you increase your students' interest in the discussion. Remember, however, children want to please their teachers. Be sensitive so they do not perceive you as viewing them negatively.

SUMMARY

Questioning is an integral aspect of teaching, and teachers ask a lot of questions throughout the day. Yet typical questioning practices have limited effectiveness. The most significant limitation is the abundance of low-level, convergent questions. With a little effort you can improve your questioning skills and help your students master information. You will also develop their higher-level cognitive processes. The suggestions in this chapter will enable you to monitor and improve your questioning skills.

This chapter also included suggestions for improving classroom discussions. Discussions are a means of actively engaging children in the learning process. Effective discussions will require you to use effective questioning skills. By integrating the questioning and discussion suggestions described in this chapter you will have a means of helping children master content as well as developing their creativity and critical-thinking skills.

By working to improve your questioning and discussion abilities you will eventually be able to move children to higher levels of thinking, just as Socrates did with his students.

SUGGESTED ACTIVITIES

1. Record the types of questions your instructors ask in their classes. Classify the questions in two ways. First, classify them as either higher-level or lower-level questions. Then classify them as convergent, divergent, or evaluative.

2. Obtain an elementary social studies textbook and examine the questions listed in the text. Classify the types of questions using the categories listed in activity 1.

3. Using the same textbook, select a concept from one of the chapters and develop a number of questions for the categories listed in activity 1.

4. If you have access to children, ask them a series of questions. First, do not use wait-time, then ask similar questions using wait-time. Examine the differences in the children's responses.

5. Select a concept from an elementary social studies textbook and develop a series of questions you would use to engage children in a discussion of the concept. Use two of the discussion formats described in this chapter.

Dressing up and playing are good learning activities and are lots of fun for children.

Photograph by Laima Druskis

chapter 12

Interactive Teaching Strategies: Role Playing, Simulations, and Games

I hear and I forget.
I see and I remember.
I do and I understand.

(Chinese proverb)

AS YOU READ...

- describe the similarities and differences among role playing, simulations, and games
- identify possible ways you can use each strategy to teach social studies
- describe the strengths and weaknesses of these three teaching strategies
- develop a rationale for using computers to enhance social studies instruction

INTRODUCTION

Many of the activities described in other chapters actively involve children in the learning process. The topics presented in this chapter also actively involve children, but they are more interactive in nature. Role playing, simulations, and games are strategies requiring children to make a series of decisions and modify their actions during the experience. Children must formulate responses, make adjustments and adapt their responses as the activities unfold. In short, children must participate, think, and adapt.

Role playing is defined as a process in which children assume the roles of other people. As they engage in the role-playing activities they gain a better understanding of the roles other people play.

The *simulation* strategy engages children in learning experiences paralleling real-life situations. For example, many driver-education classes use driving simulators. The driving simulators allow the learners to encounter many of the serious challenges of driving without suffering the negative consequences of making errors in actual driving situations.

Games are another type of interactive activity. Games require children to follow a set of rules as they respond to a series of challenges. Trivial Pursuit and Battleship are examples of games that can be adapted to reinforce social studies objectives. Unlike simulations, games have little parallel with real-life situations.

The following sections describe role playing, simulations, and games. This chapter also includes a section on the use of computer simulations and games. The computer section is included because of the increased availability of software and the need to integrate computers into the elementary school.

Before describing each topic it is necessary to mention that considerable overlap exists among role playing, simulations, and games. Each strategy requires children to assume a role. Each presents children with a problem or series of problems to resolve. Each requires children to follow rules and to respond to feedback. The important differences among the three types of strategies are based on their primary focus. If the activity is primarily designed to focus on the role a person plays, it is essentially a role-playing activity. If the focus is on a real-life situation, the activity is a simulation. Games have little relation to a real-life situation. Most games are motivating ways to help children practice academic skills and content.

The differences among the three strategies may be hazy at times because of the overlap that exists. The diagram in Figure 12–1 illustrates the overlapping nature of role playing, simulations, and games. Rather than be overly concerned with correctly classifying these activities, you should use your energies to utilize them when they are the best means of helping your students achieve your objectives.

ROLE PLAYING

The emphasis of role playing is on developing an understanding of others and developing social interaction skills. Role playing requires children to assume

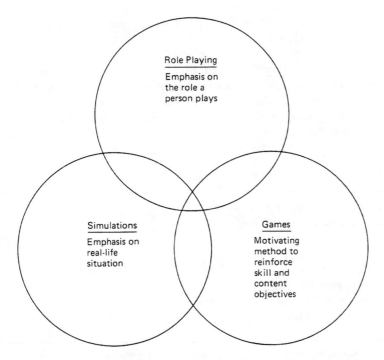

Figure 12–1 Relationships Between Role Playing, Games, and Simulations

the identity or role of another person. They might role-play a police officer at an accident scene, a legislator attempting to win support for a bill, a judge considering the severity of punishment, a president considering the veto of a bill, a parent responding to a child's request, or a child responding to temptation to use drugs. As children assume the role of another individual they can develop a sense of what it is like to be that person. They can also consider alternative responses to problems.

As children participate in role-playing activities they examine the feelings, attitudes, and perspectives of others. By engaging in role playing, children have opportunities to resolve conflicts, settle disagreements, and solve problems. Role playing also serves as a means of helping children develop alternative strategies for coping with problem situations.

An Eight-Step Process

Shaftel and Shaftel (1982) listed eight steps involved in the role-playing process. Briefly, the eight-step process includes introducing children to the role-playing situation, enacting and reenacting the situation, discussing the role-playing actions, and relating the role-playing activity to other experiences. The eight steps are listed in Table 12–1 and described in the text that follows.

In the first step, the "warm up," the teacher introduces the situation to children. The Shaftels suggest using stories, much like moral dilemmas, to motivate the children and introduce them to a role-playing situation. Sample dilemmas emerge from conflicts in history (Emancipation Proclamation, dropping the atomic bomb on Japan, or the Indian's decision to help the Pilgrims) or current events (decisions to place sixth graders in middle schools, condemning low-income housing for redevelopment, or repealing a controversial law). The teacher should take time to discuss the story with the children to help them clarify the situation and the problem presented in the story.

Table 12–1 Eight Role-Playing Steps

---

1. "Warming up" the group (problem confrontation)
2. Selecting participants for role playing
3. Setting the stage
4. Preparing the audience to be participating observers
5. Role playing (the enactment)
6. Discussion and evaluation
7. The reenactment (further role playing and discussion)
8. Sharing experience and generalizing

Source: Hendry, C., Lippitt, R., & Zander, A. (1944). Reality practice and educational method. *Psychodrama Monographs*, 9. Ambler, PA: Horsham Foundation. Reprinted with permission of the Horsham Foundation.
Source: Shaftel, Fannie, R. & Shaftel, George. (1982). *Role playing in the curriculum*, 2nd ed., pp. 48–49. Englewood Cliffs, NJ: Prentice-Hall. Reprinted with permission of Prentice-Hall.

The second step requires the teacher to select participants. The teacher should identify characters and describe the scenario. You might use volunteers rather than assigning children to the roles. Some children are shy; others may have had sensitive experiences with similar situations and are therefore too emotionally tied to the character or event.

The third step requires the actors to plan their presentations. Children should take a few minutes to outline and briefly practice their actions. They should be encouraged to focus on the flow of events rather than the specific dialogue.

In the fourth step the teacher prepares the observers. Children observing the role-playing action become intellectually involved by examining and evaluating the action. They should be told the topic of the role-playing activity and encouraged to watch for key points.

The "actors" enact the situation in the fifth step. The action is relatively brief and spontaneous. The actors should follow the planned line of action and respond to the actions of one another.

The sixth step occurs when the enactment has been completed. Here the teacher and children review the role playing. They discuss the problem portrayed, how well the actors illustrated the problem, and how well the problem was resolved. During this step the observers have an opportunity to discuss the points they observed and the actors have an opportunity to describe what they were attempting to do.

In the seventh step children make suggestions for altering and improving the role-playing event. Alternative actions and responses are considered and the actors reenact the scenario by implementing the advice and suggestions. The focus of this step is to explore alternative solutions and behaviors rather than polishing the children's acting abilities.

The final step is another discussion. Children discuss the reenactments and attempt to develop a final resolution to the initial situation. In this step the teacher must also help children relate the role-playing activity to their own lives. Children should identify situations in their own lives in which similar problems are encountered and in which similar solutions are appropriate.

The following example illustrates the steps involved in the role-playing process. Second-grade children were studying community helpers and the teacher wanted her children to learn more about the roles of police officers. The teacher began the process by "warming up" the group. She asked her students to think about contacts they have had with the police as well as the way television portrays police officers. She then told them that they would participate in a role-playing activity involving a police officer and several citizens.

The activity continued by selecting three participants. Two children were selected to act as drivers who would get into an accident. One child was selected to play a police officer.

Step three, "setting the stage," required the three participants to determine a course of action for the enactment. The police officer was to act rudely when responding to the accident. The actors were provided a few minutes to outline and practice their actions.

As the actors were preparing their skit the teacher proceeded to the fourth step with the remainder of the class. In preparing the class the teacher told the students that they would observe two drivers. A fast, impatient driver would try to pass a slower driver and cause an accident. The children were told to pay careful attention to the police officer's behavior.

In the next step the youngsters enacted the role playing scene. It was relatively brief.

A discussion and evaluation of the role-playing situation occurred in step six. Children summarized the action and were asked to suggest ways to improve the officer's behavior. They suggested that the police officer demonstrate more caring responses such as checking for injuries, reassuring the accident victims, and acting "nice."

The actors reenacted the role-playing scene, integrating the suggestions. As part of this step the children were then required to discuss the effectiveness of the changes they had proposed. They compared the behavior of the police officer in the first enactment with the "new and improved" behavior in the second enactment.

In the final step the teacher asked the students to describe their personal contacts with police officers. They considered whether the contacts were good or bad based on the behaviors of the police officers. They were then asked to describe the appropriate roles and behaviors of police officers. Children concluded that police officers should be nice and helpful most of the time. However, if they are after a criminal, they would need to be tough.

Classroom Uses

The Shaftels described nine uses for role-playing activities. First, role playing can be used to initiate a topic of study. This serves to introduce children to a new topic and is a motivating means of actively involving them in the new topic. For example, if beginning a unit on city government, children could role-play a meeting held by the mayor or city council.

Second, role playing can be used to delineate a problem requiring further investigation. If conducting an inquiry lesson on community helpers, role playing would be an excellent means for introducing this topic. The role-playing activity would help students develop an understanding of the topic they will be investigating.

Third, role playing is an effective way to help students develop empathy for others. Role playing can help youngsters develop a better appreciation for their peers, their parents, or historical events (such as slaves being sent to the Americas).

Fourth, role playing stimulates communication. Children can learn to express personal convictions and modify their behaviors to fit the dynamics of the various situations. Children are more likely to express their ideas in the relative safety of the role-playing situation.

Fifth, role playing is a means of motivating students' writing. They can be encouraged to write reactions to the role-playing situation as well as write alternative endings to the role-playing scenario.

Sixth, role playing is an effective means of helping children identify areas of weakness requiring the development of new skills. As children interact in role-playing situations they will encounter times when they do not have the skills to respond to the situation. Decision-making skills, reference skills, participation skills, and other social studies skills can serve as the basis of role-playing activities. This becomes a motivating opportunity to help children develop new skills.

The seventh use of role playing is to help students resolve social problems. As children participate in the role-playing process they should be encouraged to examine a variety of social problems. Each problem should be reexamined for the purpose of helping children develop more sophisticated and complex levels of problem-solving skills. This also contributes to their ability to accept and fulfill their social responsibilities as citizens.

The eighth use of role playing is a means of nurturing moral development. Many of the problems proposed for role-playing episodes are moral dilemmas. As children examine and resolve moral dilemmas through role playing, moral development is nurtured.

Children enjoy role playing, performing skits, or playing "dress-up." Many important social concepts are developed through these interactive activities.

Photograph by Laimute E. Druskis.

Ninth, role playing stimulates the decision-making process. As children participate in the role-playing process they encounter various problems. Children must consider the problems and pertinent information. They must then make decisions.

Benefits

A number of benefits are associated with role playing. Among the more important benefits is its motivational value. Role playing is an alternative teaching strategy that actively involves children in a way that differs from the routine of reading and responding to questions in the text. The regular use of role playing will help improve children's attitudes toward social studies.

A second benefit is that children have opportunities to resolve problems in the classroom environment. Children need opportunities to learn how to respond to problems and solve them in a variety of ways. The input from classmates will help children identify possible alternatives rather than adhering to a single, limited response.

Mastery of academic content is another benefit of role playing. Children can learn about important events in history by role-playing key historical events and decisions related to those events. They could role-play key decisions such as the colonists' decision to declare independence, President Nixon's decision to resign, the decision to break a treaty with the Indians, or the Supreme Court's decision to end school segregation. As children prepare and act out these decisions they must reconsider the events related to the decisions. Further, by role-playing key activities in government, children can develop a better understanding of the functions and branches of government.

Role playing contributes to the development of a stronger group cohesiveness in your classroom. As children work together in role-playing situations they will begin to develop a type of bond that emerges from participation in shared experiences. *Esprit de corps* develops and social studies skills are strengthened.

Role-Playing Activities

Many opportunities exist for using role playing in social studies classrooms. Seven role-playing activities are described in this section. As you examine each activity you should consider possible adaptations.

Newscast. Ryan (1980) suggested that children can role-play an anchorperson reporting a news event. The anchorperson could introduce the event and then call on reporters who are "on the scene." The news event could be a current one or an historical event.

Press Conference. We have all viewed press conferences on television. Press conferences are often held by the president, state and local government leaders, and people in business. Coaches also conduct press conferences to make newsworthy announcements.

Children can assume the role of a famous person and call a press conference. Others in the classroom can serve as members of the press corps. The child conducting the press conference should study the thoughts and actions of the person who is being portrayed. Members of the press corps should be assigned to develop questions about important issues affecting the topic being studied.

Public Interview. Simon, Howe, and Kirschenbaum (1978) proposed a variation of the press conference. Their strategy, called *Public Interview*, requires children to be interviewed by other members of the class. A child could assume the identity of a famous person and then be interviewed by classmates who are attempting to determine the famous person's attitudes and feelings about different issues.

Courtroom. Ryan suggested that children role-play courtroom scenes in which they act as lawyers arguing a case about a controversial issue. In addition to the roles of lawyers and judge, other children could act as expert witnesses and eyewitnesses. Ryan suggested role-playing a scene in which the punishment for participants in the Boston Tea Party was being argued.

Site Selection. Ryan suggested that children assume the roles of real estate agents, city planners, and business people attempting to determine and purchase a location for a new building project. They can use maps to illustrate suitable locations and discuss strengths and weaknesses as they hold hearings. Disgruntled citizens may also be included in the site-selection activity.

Many states have had several locations for the state capitol. Children could role-play a site-selection hearing regarding the location of a suitable choice for the building. The benefits of each location could be described, news reporters could ask questions about the feasibility of each site, and concerned citizens could present their views.

Local city zoning and building projects are readily useful and provide numerous opportunities for this type of role-playing situation.

Alternative History. Ryan also suggested role playing alternative resolutions for historical conflicts. He suggested role-playing alternative solutions to the Battle of Lexington as well as alternatives to taking land from the Indians.

Dialogue with Self. Simon, Howe, and Kirschenbaum described a technique that is somewhat like the cartoon scenario in which a character is confronted with temptation and hears two voices. An angel appears at one ear attempting to convince the character to resist temptation. A devil appears at the other ear and encourages the character to give in to the temptation.

In the classroom children can be confronted with a dilemma such as cheating on an assignment or dumping toxic chemicals into a nearby stream. Children develop a dialogue, both for and against the dilemma, and then prepare to present both sides of the issue. Two chairs are placed facing each other. The child first sits in one chair and presents a point. The child then moves to the other chair to make a counterpoint. The child alternates between chairs as points for and against the dilemma are presented.

As an alternative, three children could participate. One child would sit in the center chair and share the dilemma with the class. On one side of this child would be another who has the task of convincing the child to follow a certain course of action. Sitting on the other side is a third youngster who is attempting to encourage the first child to pursue an alternative course of action. The rest of the class can become involved by critiquing the arguments and by offering additional points.

Puppets

The use of puppets is an excellent variation of the role-playing procedure. Puppets are easily made out of stockings. Students can draw faces on stockings as they create puppets for their role-playing activity. My students frequently made stick puppets by drawing a form, such as a person or face, on a piece of paper. They would then cut out the picture and tape it to a ruler.

Puppets work well with children of all ages, but are particularly useful with shy children. Shy children are more likely to become involved in role-playing situations when they can use puppets. Shy children speak louder when they voice the dialogue for the role played by their puppets.

Additional Social Studies Topics

As you attempt to develop role-playing activities you may find topics related to these themes helpful.

honesty	responsibility	prejudice
cooperation	change	adaptation
friendship	human rights	altruism
historical events		historical conflicts

Role playing should not be confused with other participatory activities. Children can act out many scenes and events without engaging in role playing. For example, reenacting a posada, a festival, or a chuckwagon meal are active ways to help social studies become more meaningful and exciting, but since these activities do not require children to resolve problems or explore specific roles, they are not classified as role-playing activities.

SIMULATIONS

Simulations are activities that have real-life parallels. The airline industry uses flight simulators to train pilots prior to allowing them to fly a new type of airplane. The military uses war games to simulate aspects of battle. NASA uses numerous simulations of space flight as a means of preparing astronauts, engineers, and technicians. NASA does not want to place people or expensive vehicles in space until each system has been properly tested under simulated conditions.

Simulations are an effective and motivating way to allow children to learn things that are either too unsafe to do in real-life settings or are economically impractical. For example, a seat belt safety program allows individuals to simulate the effects of a slow-speed automobile crash. The activity is designed to let participants discover the effects of using seat belts. It would be unsafe and not economical to allow people to use real cars to demonstrate the point.

Simulations are becoming more widespread in education and do not always require expensive materials. A number of high school teachers require students to simulate parenting responsibilities by caring for inexpensive chicken eggs. Students must arrange for the care, nurturance, and safety of their eggs, just as parents must do for a newborn.

Problem-Action-Feedback Format

Educational simulations present children with a problem. The children act to develop a response to the problem and are then provided feedback about their actions. The feedback is followed by the presentation of another problem, which requires yet another response. Again, the children are presented with feedback about the effects of their responses. This format can be described as a "problem-action-feedback" format and is illustrated in Figure 12–2.

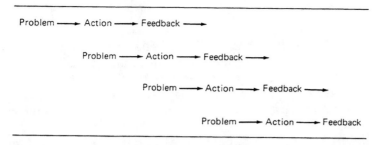

Figure 12–2 Problem-Action-Feedback Design

Source: Van Cleaf, D.W. (1986). *Teaching elementary social studies: Supplemental materials.* Unpublished manuscript, Washburn University, Topeka. Adapted and reprinted with permission of the author.

The problem-action-feedback design may be illustrated by "Lemonade Stand," a public-domain computer program designed for the Commodore 64 computer. Children are credited with ten dollars at the beginning of the simulation and must purchase raw materials such as lemon concentrate, sugar, and cups. They are also provided a weather report and are required to establish a selling price for each cup of lemonade. The computer processes the information and provides feedback for the children regarding the number of cups sold and the best selling price for the existing weather conditions. Children then have opportunities to purchase more supplies; they are presented with a new weather report, and they must set a new selling price. Again the computer provides feedback about the number of cups sold and the best selling price for the weather conditions. This process continues through a total of ten sequences. By the end of the simulation the children have discovered the need to purchase the correct amount of supplies and establish prices that are compatible with the weather conditions.

Steps

Joyce and Weil (1986) described four steps in the simulation process. First, teachers must provide an orientation for children. They must introduce them to the simulation and provide a general overview of the activity.

The second step requires teachers to train the children, who need to learn the rules of the simulation as well as procedures and goals. The roles of the participants must also be explained.

In the third step the children participate in the simulation activity. While children are participating, the teacher should monitor children's progress, make suggestions, and ask thought-provoking questions.

The final step occurs after the simulation activity has been completed. This is the debriefing step in which the teacher and children discuss the activity. During this stage the teacher also helps children discover the relationships between the simulation and its real-life applications.

Benefits

The benefits of using simulations are similar to the benefits of role playing. Simulations actively involve children and therefore have a high motivational value.

Simulations are also effective because they can introduce students to situations with real-life parallels in a relatively safe and inexpensive manner. Thus, they can experience a wide variety of experiences within the confines of the classroom.

The children also have opportunities to develop their problem-solving skills. Simulations require youngsters to consider information as they attempt to resolve a problem. Feedback is provided and a follow-up problem is presented. Children then must consider additional information as they continue the problem-solving process. This reinforces the decision-making steps and the inquiry process.

If you allow your students to work in small groups you will also nurture the development of cooperation. When children work together reacting to the various challenges, they share information, ideas, and possible responses—they must cooperate.

Examples of Simulations

Several examples are presented in this section. They do not represent an exhaustive list; rather, they serve to exemplify the simulation process. A list of computer simulations appropriate for elementary social studies appears in the final section of the chapter.

Nuts Game. Edney (1979) described a simulation activity that is relatively easy to use. The activity simulated the way people historically cooperated to conserve natural resources. Small groups of participants were provided with a bowl containing ten nuts and an ample supply of additional nuts.

The following directions were provided quickly so participants did not have an opportunity to develop a strategy. Participants were told that they would be provided a series of harvest-and-replenish periods with a goal of harvesting as many nuts as possible. The participants were also told that at the end of each harvest period they were to replenish the bowl with a number of nuts equal to the number of nuts remaining in the bowl at the end of each harvest period. Participants were not allowed to ask questions or plan a group strategy.

Participants were allowed to "harvest" nuts from the bowl. The brief harvest period was followed by a replenish period. Edney observed that most groups harvested all of the nuts during the first harvest period and were therefore unable to replenish their supply. This is the expected outcome of the first harvest period and sets the stage for the process of simulating cooperation and conservation.

Since most groups "overharvested" during the first harvest period they were given an opportunity to plan a group strategy. After strategies were developed the groups were allowed to begin the activity a second time.

After groups had developed strategies, Edney found that the groups were able to maintain a nice balance between the number of nuts harvested and the number replenished. Groups were also observed utilizing strategies that ensured that each member was able to harvest an equal number of nuts. In essence, they shared and each group member realized benefits from the strategy.

This activity parallels the "common green" phenomenon that was present in many English communities prior to the Industrial Revolution. People involved in raising livestock lived in small towns and used common greens (pastures) for grazing. If the number of livestock was too large the pasture would be over-harvested and unable to support as many head of livestock. The people had to develop strategies to regulate the number of livestock allowed to graze on the common greens.

Edney noted parallels in other aspects of conservation. Many international conflicts about fishing rights are reactions to the lack of limits on harvesting. This activity also parallels current efforts to regulate hunting and consumption of natural resources. Conservation is regulated to maintain nature's ability to replenish.

A variation of the nuts game has been used with elementary-school children. Each group of students were given two paper plates. One was to be used for harvesting, the other contained an ample supply of paper squares. Children were assigned to groups of five. One of the five was designated as the "replenisher."

Children were led through the following sequence:

1. Gave the directions quickly and did not allow discussion.
2. Quickly moved to the first harvest. The children had overharvested and could not continue.
3. Explained the rules more slowly and allowed groups to develop a strategy.
4. Began the harvest-replenish cycle again.
5. Continued to the fourth round and then informed groups that their plates could only accommodate twenty squares. Excess squares had to be removed.
6. Again allowed children to modify their strategies.
7. Continued the activity for three more rounds.
8. Discussed the effective and ineffective strategies.

This led to a discussion about situations in real life in which people had to cooperate to conserve resources. Several of the children mentioned hunting and fishing, some mentioned energy conservation, and a few mentioned soil conservation. Another child related the activity to the food chain and how the food chain would be disrupted if one element was removed.

Marguerite Henry's book *Misty of Chincoteague* may be integrated into a follow-up discussion. The wild horses in the story live on the island of Assateague. However, the island can only support 150 horses. Children can discuss ways to assure that the herd remains healthy.

Sherlock Holmes Marooned. Wales, Nardi, and Stager (1987) described a problem-solving simulation in which Sherlock Holmes and four members of his party were stranded on an island off the coast of England. The island was small, rocky, and deserted. Daytime temperatures were expected to be remain hot for at least a week. The forecast was for dry weather.

Their boat had been sabotaged and would soon sink. Before the boat would sink the party would have an opportunity to make one trip to the boat to salvage materials essential for survival.

The participant's first task was to identify the problems the party members faced and identify goals for their survival. At this point the simulation provided feedback to participants. After considering the feedback about the problems and goals, participants were presented with another situation.

A list of materials and equipment in the boat was provided for small groups of individuals participating in this simulation. Their second task was to individuallly rank the items in order of importance and select the eight most important items.

This problem-action-feedback format continued through a series of problems for the groups to resolve. As participants worked through the sequence they had an opportunity to engage in a structured problem-solving activity.

The complete Sherlock Holmes simulation appears in Appendix 12-1.

Manufacturing. Wheeler (1980) described a simulation conducted by Betty Gray and Susan Semchuk, two fourth-grade teachers in West Norwalk, Connecticut. The teachers have their fourth graders simulate a manufacturing enterprise, making items such as pin cushions, candles, key chains, and pencil holders.

The teachers lead the children through the process of incorporating their business by inviting attorneys to speak to the class. Bankers are invited in to tell children about obtaining capital and they have children fill out loan applications. Children then take the applications to the bank for processing. When the loans are approved the children sign promissory notes.

Children then determine the types and amounts of raw materials needed for the production of their product. They select other youngsters to function as purchasing agents. The purchasing agents compare price, negotiate for discounts, and buy the materials.

Children then begin producing their materials. As this is being done they consider advertising and marketing strategies.

Simulations are difficult and time-consuming to develop. Therefore, it is recommended that you use commercially prepared simulations early in your teaching career. After you have improved your professional competencies you may decide either to develop your own simulation or adapt commercially prepared simulations. Jo Ann Davis, a teacher in Carrollton-Farmer Branch School District, adapted the simulation *Pioneers* to simulate early settlement of Carrollton, Texas.

GAMES

Games, like role playing and simulations, are highly motivating interactive activities for children. Games are like simulations in many ways. However, while simulations help children develop skills and competencies in situations paralleling real life, games do not have real-life parallels.

Examples of games include chess, checkers, Trivial Pursuit, and Battleship. Many games are played on a board, but many computer games rely only on computer software.

Unlike simulations, games are relatively easy to construct. Many teachers have designed game boards out of oak tag. They develop a set of questions and direction cards that guide children's progress along the board. Teacher-made games are particularly attractive because they allow the teacher to design motivating activities that reinforce their objectives.

Benefits and Limitations

A group of students enrolled in an elementary education social studies methods course developed a list of benefits derived from using games in classrooms. They also identified several limitations of games as teaching devices. The benefits and limitations are listed below.

The benefits of games:

1. reduce boredom
2. actively involve children
3. encourage problem solving
4. develop cooperation skills
5. master skills and knowledge in a non-judgmental setting
6. used later in learning centers
7. a reward for good behavior
8. exciting alternative
9. addresses several learning styles

The limitations of games:

1. time-consuming (to make and play)
2. may be too competitive
3. difficult to evaluate

4. may be too repetitive
5. need for supervision/monitoring
6. classroom discipline

As you can see, the benefits and limitations of games are in many ways similar to role playing and simulations.

Using and Developing Games

Using games in the classroom is a relatively simple process. You should have the materials ready for children's use and then take a few moments to introduce them to the game. As you introduce the game you should state the objective and teach your students the rules. Also tell them how the game reinforces your educational objective.

Children should then be assigned to groups and allowed to play the game. As they play the game you should be available to answer questions. You may also offer suggestions for improving their play.

When they have completed the game you may want to have a follow-up discussion, which should review game strategies and how the game reinforces your objectives.

Developing games is a simple task. Many teachers design games that are variations of popular board games and television game shows. Pictionary and Win, Lose or Draw are popular variations of charades, and they are readily adaptable to the elementary classroom.

Jeopardy is a long-time favorite television game show of many adults. The Jeopardy format was used as a review of content taught by a fourth-grade teacher who had finished a unit on the state in which the children lived.

Children playing a game.

Photograph by David W. Van Cleaf.

Candy Land is a popular game of younger children. The game board and card format utilized by the Candy Land game could easily be adapted for a primary-grade unit on such topics as cardinal directions, natural resources, family roles, or neighborhoods. A kindergarten teacher developed a variation of Candy Land for a unit on manners. She made good-manner cards and bad-manner cards with the numbers one, two, and three on them. The good-manner cards had a plus sign in front of the number, thus directing the children to move forward. The bad-manner cards had a minus sign in front of the number. If a child drew a bad-manner card he or she had to move backwards the corresponding number of squares.

Several of my college students recently taught a fourth-grade social studies unit on pioneers. They reviewed a computer simulation, Oregon Trail, and developed a game to reinforce the concepts developed in Oregon Trail.

Children enjoy playing games. Games increase their enthusiasm for school, their ability to interact well with others, and their problem-solving abilities.

COMPUTER SOFTWARE

Computers can be important instructional aids for teachers. A number of excellent computer simulations and games are available for use in social studies. This section of the chapter describes how to use computer simulations and games. It also describes potentially useful programs.

According to Roberts, Friel, and Ladenburg (1988), the use of computers in the social studies curriculum provides direct support for the three primary goals of social studies education. First, computer programs help children acquire and master social studies subject matter. As children participate in the games and simulations, they must utilize social studies information. Second, social studies skills such as thinking skills, problem-solving skills, map-reading skills, and graphing skills are reinforced in many computer programs. The third social studies goal, developing democratic values and beliefs, is also nurtured through the use of computer software packages. As children work together on the computer they learn to interact with one another in socially appropriate ways.

Benefits and Limitations

Computer programs include a variety of simulations and games. The benefits of simulations and games described in previous sections apply to computer simulations and games. However, the computer provides several additional benefits. First, the computer responds quickly, therefore providing more immediate feedback for children. Children learn from the feedback they receive, and because the feedback is more timely, learning is strengthened.

Young school children enjoy working with computers.

Photograph by Ken Karp.

A second benefit of computer simulations and games is that individual and small groups of students can participate in the activity while the remainder of the class works on another activity. This is beneficial because it provides both the teacher and students with a greater degree of flexibility. The teacher can personalize instruction rather than have all students participate in the same activity.

Computer simulations and games hold exceptional promise for improving social studies instruction. However, there are several limitations. The first limitation is that most programs are designed for junior high and high school levels. There are a small number of excellent programs for grades four through six. There is a paucity of programs for primary-grade children. While the number of programs available for elementary-grade students is limited, the number is increasing.

A second problem is that many of the programs do not adequately parallel real-life experiences. The problems children encounter are superficial and somewhat contrived. While this has an important effect on the usefulness of simulations, it also affects the games. Because the games are somewhat contrived and lack sophistication, it is difficult to help youngsters generalize to the real-life parallels or the objectives outlined in your curriculum. As more educators with backgrounds in elementary education become involved in the development of computer programs, this situation will improve.

A third problem is related to compatibility. Computer software must be designed for specific computer languages and will not run on all computers. If your school has Apple computers, IBM programs will not work. While most software developers are designing programs for all computers, this will remain an area of caution as you select and utilize software.

A final limitation is teacher frustration. If you have not been trained on how to use computers you are likely to avoid using them. There are several things you can do to overcome your reluctance to use computers. First, ask your librarian to provide a list of programs appropriate for your social studies curriculum. Look over the list and identify a program that may be useful in an upcoming social studies lesson. Get a copy of the program and "play" with it. If you do not know how to use the computer, have one of your students or another teacher show you. As you review the program consider how you might use it as a supplement to your lesson.

To help you manage your students while they are working at the computer you might utilize a parent volunteer. Have the volunteer help students begin the computer program and monitor their progress.

Computer simulations and games can be highly motivating learning experiences for children. Select your programs carefully, follow the steps outlined in the simulation and game sections of the chapter, and observe how your students enjoy the challenges.

To gain maximum benefits, encourage and allow children to play the program a number of times. Repeated playing allows them to gain a sense of mastery. Also allow them to work in small groups. This encourages cooperation, interaction, and critical thinking.

Sample Software

The following is a selected list of simulations and games appropriate for elementary-school children. As you review the list, please consider social studies topics for which the programs would be useful. Also note that most of the simulations and games are for the intermediate grades.

The simulations and games described in this list have been compiled from several sources. As you attempt to identify additional programs you should consult a school librarian for updated catalogues.

Simulations

"Cave Girl Clair," elementary grades, Addison-Wesley.
Clair is a cave girl who must tend to her survival needs (fire, food, medicine).

"Jenny of the Prairie," elementary grades, Addison-Wesley.
Separated from a wagon train, Jenny confronts a variety of obstacles as she struggles to survive.

"The Market Place" (1984), grades 3–8, Minnesota Educational Computing Corporation.
A series of four programs simulating the manufacturing and marketing process. Topics include selling apples, plants, bicycles, and lemonade.

"Oh, Deer," grades 5–8, Minnesota Educational Computing Corporation.
Children simulate managing a herd of deer threatened by the encroachment of people.

"Oregon Trail" (1985), upper elementary grades, Minnesota Educational Computing Corporation.

Children traverse the Oregon Trail making decisions faced by the original pioneers.

"Our Town Meeting: A Lesson in Civic Responsibility" (1987), grades 5–8, Tom Snyder Productions.

Children assume the roles of city planners and leaders proposing a variety of projects for their city.

"Santa Fe Trail" (1984), grades 5 and up, Educational Activities.

Children travel the Santa Fe Trail, simulating challenges faced by the early travelers.

"The Voyage of the Mimi: Ecosystems," grades 4–8, Holt, Rinehart, & Winston.

Children select animals to inhabit an island and then evaluate animal population changes.

Games

"The Great Maine-to-California Race" (1983), grades 5–12, Hayden Software.

A game in which children answer questions about states as they race across the country.

"Jenny's Journey" (1984), grades 3–6, Minnesota Educational Computing Corporation.

Children are challenged to help Jenny follow a map of her town.

"The Medalists–Black Americans" (1982), grades 5–10, Hartley Courseware.

A game about the achievements of black Americans.

"The Medalists–Continents" (1982), grades 5–10, Hartley Courseware.

A game about geographic features of the world.

"Quest for the Pole" (1988), grades 3 and up, Scholastic.

As children attempt to reach the North Pole they encounter a series of obstacles that introduce them to historical and cultural aspects of the region.

"The Ripple That Changed American History" (1987), grades 5–12, Tom Snyder Productions.

A time line game in which children practice the chronological sequence of events in United States history.

"States and Traits" (1984), grades 4 and up, DesignWare.

A U.S. geography drill-and-practice game that includes locations of states, their capitals, and landforms.

"Unlocking the Map Code," grades 4–6, Rand McNally.

An activity designed to reinforce map skills (landforms, color, symbols, directions, location, distance).

"The Voyage of the Mimi: Maps and Navigation," grades 4–8, Holt, Rinehart, & Winston.

A set of four games designed to teach mapping and navigation skills.

"Where in the World is Carmen Sandiego?"* (1986), grades 4 and up, Broderbund Software.

A game in which children attempt to locate a criminal. The search takes children to various parts of the world.

SUMMARY

This chapter described three exciting interactive strategies for teaching social studies: role playing, simulations, and games. They actively involve children and provide a welcome respite from traditional classroom activities.

The use of these strategies will require you to deviate from typical teaching approaches. Because these activities are interactive, children must have a degree of freedom within the classroom. Children need to talk with one another and move about more freely as they consider and respond to the challenges of each situation. You should expect more noise and commotion. To help you retain a sense of control and order you should plan the activities carefully and thoroughly. Anticipate children's need to talk and interact with one another, then plan procedures that will encourage this in a positive, yet controlled manner. Before you begin an interactive activity you should tell your students how you expect them to behave. You should monitor them closely to minimize off-task behavior. Because many children will have had few opportunities to engage in these types of activities in previous school settings, you might also want to begin with relatively brief activities. Then lengthen the duration of interactive activities as children develop the ability to learn this way.

To improve the educational benefits of interactive activities, children should be allowed to work cooperatively, either in pairs or in small groups. The cooperative interaction among children encourages them to consider a variety of responses. The cooperative interaction also allows them to informally "test" their ideas on one another before sharing their ideas formally with the teacher and the entire class. As children discuss their ideas informally with their peers they receive feedback about the appropriateness of their ideas. Ideas can be developed, modified, and improved more readily in the relative safety of a small-group rather than large-group setting.

*Also available: "Where in the USA is Carmen Sandiego?" (1986) and "Where in Europe is Carmen Sandiego?" (1988).

The Chinese proverb cited at the beginning of the chapter aptly describes the benefits of interactive teaching strategies. When children are allowed to participate actively, learning is enhanced. Stated another way, "I do and I understand."

SUGGESTED ACTIVITIES

1. Observe preschool children playing in the dramatic play area of their classroom. List the types of topics they are role-playing. How do you think they benefit from this type of activity?
2. Select two computer simulations. Play one alone and the other with a friend. Which means is more beneficial?
3. Describe the problem-action-feedback structure of one of the computer simulations.
4. Identify a topic in a social studies textbook and design a game that will help children learn the concept.
5. With several of your peers, work through the Sherlock Holmes simulation.

APPENDIX 12–1   Sherlock Holmes Marooned

Instruction A—Define the Situation: The Explorer

Sherlock Holmes and Dr. Watson had no way of knowing that the boat they had hired to take them to a remote island had been sabotaged by Professor Moriarty. They might have guessed when the engine coughed to a stop, but they were too busy at that point worrying about the reef dead ahead of them. Blown by the strong southwest wind, the boat all too quickly ran aground. Fortunately, there was enough water to float the dinghy and although it was a tight squeeze, the five of them were soon safely ashore, one half mile away on a sandy beach.

You can't join Holmes and the others who are sitting on the driftwood that litters the shore of the island, but you can participate in their thinking. To begin, close your eyes and visualize the situation in your mind. Do you see the rocky island, feel the hot sand, and smell the fresh sea air? Now that you have some feeling about this place, *what questions would you like to have answered* so you can understand the situation that Holmes and the others face?

Feedback A—Define the Situation

Actors:	*Who is involved?*	Who are the people with Holmes and Watson? Who else is on the island? Who knows they are pursuing Professor Moriarty in this area?
Props:	*What things are involved?*	What food, water, equipment, and material do they have? What is the weather expected to be? How big is the island? What is available: food, water, shade, wood?
Action:	*What happened?*	You already know that the boat hit the reef when the engine failed.
Scene:	*When did it happen?*	What time of day is it? What month?
	Where did it happen?	Where is this island? How far is it to help?
Cause:	*Why did it happen?*	Why exactly did the engine stop?
Consequences:	*How serious is it?*	How serious is the situation? Are these people in any danger?

Information A—Data on the Situation

Holmes, Watson, the two policemen from Scotland Yard, and the owner of the boat were stranded on a very small, rocky island off the southern coast of England. There were four men, one woman, and a thousand sea gulls. Holmes recognized the potentially serious situation they faced even before the dinghy reached the sandy shore. The weather this time of year was very hot and dry and would probably stay that way for at least a week.

"Boatman! How often is a boat likely to come near this island?"

"Unless we're very lucky it may be a week or more, Mr. Holmes."

"Do you think anyone lives here?"

"I doubt it, sir. There isn't likely to be any source of fresh water in this rocky little place."

"Is there any chance we might refloat the boat and bring it ashore?"

"No, Mr. Holmes. There's a big hole in the hull. I'm pretty sure it will be pushed off the rocks and sink when the tide comes in."

"How long will that be?"

"It's 9 o'clock now, in about 5 hours, sir."

"Could one or two of us make it back to the mainland in the dinghy?"

"It's about 10 miles, Mr. Holmes. In this heat and with that wind it would either be very dangerous or impossible."

"Sergeant, when are you expected to report back to the Yard?"

"Not until tomorrow afternoon, Mr. Holmes. We won't be missed until then."

"Boatman, what kind of supplies and equipment do you have on the boat? What could we bring ashore?"

"Why do you ask that, Holmes?" Watson said.

"Because we may be here two or more days, Watson, and if we don't prepare as best we can we may be in deep trouble."

"You can't be serious, Holmes."

"Yes, Watson, I'm deadly serious. Moriarty is not our enemy now, nature is. We must get some supplies from the boat before it sinks. We'll be lucky to get one trip in before that happens, so we'd better plan very carefully. That's why I want each of you to think about what the boatman tells us and what might be on the boat. We can't carry everything. Each of us must decide what is the most important."

"Now quickly, boatman, tell us what is on the boat that we might salvage."

"Well, Mr. Holmes, we've got that two gallon cask of water and the lunch basket you brought aboard. And there's a slicker for everyone. I've got some fishing gear and there's a box with matches, rope, and some tools in it. We have some life preservers, of course. And some blankets plus a large tarp."

"What about other food?"

"There may be a few cans of beans or something in the cabin, some salt, and a bottle of whiskey."

"Is there a mirror on board?"

"Yes, I use a small one to shave now and then. My straight razor is there, too. Oh, and there's a lantern and a can of fuel for it in the cabin. There's also a compass, my navigation maps, and a first aid kit."

While all this was going on, Holmes was busy writing. "Holmes, what are you doing?" Watson asked.

"Preparing copies of this list, Watson. I want each of you to pick the eight most important items on the list I give you."

"We don't have time for your infernal games, Holmes."

"Yes, we do, Watson. This is very important. I'll explain why later. Right now I want each of you to independently decide which of these things we should bring ashore."

Each person should independently select just the top eight items. Put the letter for your selections in the column marked "You."

APPENDIX 12–1 Rating Chart

ITEM	"You"	"Group"	"SH"
a. Water, 2 gal.			
b. Lunch .			
c. 5 slickers			
d. Fishing gear			
e. Box with matches, rope, and tools			
f. Life preservers			
g. Blankets			
h. Tarp			
i. Cans of beans			
j. Salt			
k. Whiskey			
l. Mirror			
m. Razor			
n. Lantern			
o. Fuel			
p. Compass			
q. Navigation map			
r. First aid kit			

Source: Wales, Charles E., Nardi, Anne H., & Stager, Robert A. (1988). *Sherlock Holmes Marooned,* a module from the Center for Guided Design, West Virginia University, Morgantown, WV 26506–6101. Reprinted with permission of the Center for Guided Design.

Instruction B—State the Goal: The Philosopher

"We've completed our lists, Holmes. Should we set out for the boat now?"

"Not yet, Watson. We still have a good deal of thinking to do before we set out. And the place to start is with our goal. We can't work together on this problem unless we agree on our goal."

"Isn't our first goal to explain why the engine failed?" Watson asked.

"No, Watson, we're not going to be researchers this time. I doubt that we will ever know why the engine failed. If I were a betting man I'd guess it is Moriarty's work. He knew we'd be trailing him and laid a trap for us. If we are to beat him we must deal with the consequences, we don't have time to explain them.

"One of the problems we face is actually getting the supplies we need from the boat. I suggest we ignore that problem for the moment and focus on the problems we might have in the next few days."

If you were Holmes, *what problems would you identify? What goals would you suggest?*

Feedback B—State the Goal

Given the hot, dry weather that was expected during the next few days, the group quickly identified food, water, and signaling as their prime problems. All but Watson, that is. He insisted the goal was to get home safely. The others suggested goals such as survival, to survive until rescue, and to avoid dehydration.

Instruction C.1—Generate Ideas: The Inventor

"What now, Holmes?" Dr. Watson asked.

"We must identify the problems we might have when we try to achieve our goals," Holmes replied. "Since we want to avoid dehydration, we must focus first on *what might 'cause' dehydration.* And since we want to be rescued we must also identify *what might 'prevent' us from being rescued.* What can you suggest?"

Feedback C.1—Generate Ideas

The group quickly agreed that dehydration would result if they could not obtain enough water to drink or because they lost water to the hot sun, the wind, or through physical activity. They also decided that not being seen by a passing boat would prevent their rescue.

Instruction C.2—Generate Ideas: Synthesis

"That was excellent," Holmes said.

"I agree," Watson interjected, "but why do we bother with these problems?"

"Because a problem well defined is a problem half solved," Holmes replied. "We now know the major categories we must address as we generate ideas and because of that we are likely to generate more and better ideas.

"I suggest we get to that task now," Holmes continued. "The categories are the mirror image of our problems:

Obtain Water   Limit Loss   Being Seen

Let's see how many ideas we can generate now."

Feedback C.2—Generate Ideas: Synthesis

These are the ideas generated by the group.

Obtain Water	*Limit Loss*	*Being Seen*
From the boat	Limit exercise	Fire/smoke
Collect rain	Build a shelter	Mirrors
Collect dew	Lie in wet sand	Wave
Solar still	Work at night	Post a watch
Distillation		
Rationing		

Instruction C.3—Generate Ideas: Evaluation

"Can we go to the boat now, Holmes?"

"Not yet, Watson, but soon. We have only one more thing to do. We have to select the ideas we think we should pursue. To do that we must consider what is available to us on the boat. I want you to discuss both our ideas and the list of things on the boat. Since we can't bring everything back, I want *all of you to agree on the eight most important items* that we should try to bring ashore."

"Just eight items, Holmes?"

"That's right, just eight. The dinghy is not very large and the sea is rough. Make sure those eight serve the ideas you hope to implement."

Please put the letter for each of the eight items the group selects in the column marked "Group." Do not change any of the letters in the "You" column.

Feedback C.3—Generate Ideas: Evaluation

"Now, Watson, we're ready to get what we need from the boat. I want the boatman and the police sergeant to go out in the dinghy and get at least these eight items:

1. Cask of water (a).
2. 5 slickers (c).
3. Fishing gear (d).
4. Box with matches, rope, and tools (e).
5. Tarp (h).
6. Fuel (o).
7. Lantern (n).
8. Mirror (l)."

Although Holmes' list was not the same as the group list, the two men agreed to follow his orders and left with the good wishes of everyone on the shore.

Instruction 4—Thinking About Thinking

As soon as the men returned safely with all of Holmes' items plus some from their own list, Holmes called them together. "We all thank these brave men, they may have saved our lives."

"But why didn't you send them earlier?" Watson asked.

"Elementary, my dear Watson. I knew that the first danger we faced was panic and I didn't want anyone doing something rash. That's why I played my 'infernal game' as you called it. If we had rushed out to the boat we might have lost both some lives and the supplies which we desperately need. Now that we are safe, I'd like to finish our game and explain why I picked certain items. Take out the paper where you have your individual and the group selections. Write the letter for each of my choices across from the appropriate item in the column marked 'SH'. Don't change any of the other letters. I'll explain my selections as we go."

Feedback 4—Thinking About Thinking

"Now," Holmes said, "let me explain my selections.

a. The cask of water is vital because the most significant problem we face in this heat and wind is dehydration. No other problem comes close to that one as you will see by the rest of my choices."

"But why isn't food on your list, Holmes?"

"Because eating what we have in the basket will dehydrate us, Watson. Digestion requires water and we can't afford to lose what we already have.

c. "The slickers are important because we can wear them, make a shelter with them, wave them as a signal, or collect rain or dew with them.

d. "The fishing gear gives us a backup source of water."

"Of course, Holmes. As a doctor, I should have realized that raw fish provide both fresh water and protein. We could live quite well on raw fish."

"Very good, Watson."

e. "Signaling comes next. I'm sure all of us want to be rescued, but no one knows we are on this island, so we'd better be prepared to catch the attention of anyone who goes by. That means a signal fire or smoke. We have plenty of wood here on the shore, but we need matches to start the fire. I assumed that the matches on the boat would be waterproof or protected somehow."

"That's right, Mr. Holmes," the boatman said, "they are waterproof."

"Exactly," Holmes said.

"Amazing," Watson added.

"The rope and tools should also be useful when we build a shelter. Getting out of the sun and wind are important ways to avoid dehydration," stated Holmes.

h. "The tarp is for our backup water supply. We can use it to catch rain, gather dew, or as a shelter. But if it rains we can use it to line a storage basin for our water supply over there in the rocks and then transfer it to the cask."

o. "The fuel is important because it will help us start the fire whenever we need it. We can use a slicker to keep the wood dry in case it rains."

n. "The lantern may come in handy when we work at night—so we can reduce our dehydration—and in case a boat happens to pass by after dark and we don't have time to start the fire."

l. "The mirror may prove to be a valuable signaling device during the day if the sun is out or by reflecting the light from the lantern at night. Then all we have to do is hope a ship passes by—soon."

Information 4—Scoring the Game

"Now," Holmes said, "I'd like to score the results so we can discuss them. The first step is to draw a circle around each letter in the "You" column that matches one of my answers. If you selected item a, c, d, e, h, l, n, or o, circle it. Then count the number of circles and write the total at the bottom.

"Each person is likely to have a different number," Holmes said, "so I'd like you to get an average. Add these individual numbers and divide by the number of people in the group to get that average.

"Next, circle each of the letters in the 'Group' column that matches my list and count the number of circles on one of the sheets. Everyone should have the same total here."

A.   *Thinking About the Group Work*

"The group score you just calculated is probably lower than the average individual score. That happens because a group can usually arrive at a better decision than an individual, especially if the people in the group understand how to work together to share what they know and what they think. If the group score was higher, it probably indicates that the members of the group had a difficult time agreeing on the selections."

B.   *Thinking About Subject Matter Knowledge*

"Background knowledge plays a very important role in decision making. The more you know about the key elements involved in a problem, the more successful you are likely to be at finding a workable solution. In this problem, for instance, the more you know about dehydration the more likely you are to survive. In other words, the things you study and learn, whether in school or out, can help you be a more effective problem-solver."

C.   *Thinking About the Operations*

"There is one other factor that is critical here. Your decision-making work is going to be much more effective if you know which operation to use and how to perform each operation. If you are skilled at this process, you are less likely to commit one of the classic problem-solving errors, such as generating ideas before you identify the problem to be solved and state the goal to be achieved. If you properly define both the situation and the goal you are also in a much better position to decide what other information you need to proceed intelligently."

"I'm impressed, Holmes," Watson said. "I can hardly wait until we get home so I can write the story of our latest adventure."

"Thank you, Watson. I hope that won't take too long. Meanwhile, my fellow castaways, I suggest we put on the slickers, gather just enough wood so we are ready with a fire, and prepare at least a crude shelter to protect us from the wind and sun. Then we should rest quietly in the shade until evening, when it is cool enough to do the rest of our work. While we wait we can prepare our detailed plans for a longer stay here on the island."

Source: Wales, Charles E., Nardi, Anne H., & Stager, Robert A. (1988). *Sherlock Holmes Marooned,* a module from the Center for Guided Design, West Virginia University, Morgantown, WV 26506–6101. Reprinted with permission of the Center for Guided Design.

Sometimes we must sit down for what we believe in.

Photograph by Ken Karp.

chapter 13

Character Development

For Piaget, the aim of education was intellectual and moral autonomy.
(Kamii, 1984, p. 410)*

AS YOU READ...

- why should schools help children develop character?
- define: character, morality, values, attitudes, and beliefs
- describe Piaget's concept of autonomous morality. Indicate why this type of morality is important
- describe ways you can nurture children's moral development

Source: Kamii, C. (1984). Autonomy: The aim of education envisioned by Piaget. *Phi Delta Kappan, 65,* p. 410. Reprinted with permission from Constance Kamii, professor, University of Alabama at Birmingham, Birmingham, AL.

INTRODUCTION

After a number of years in which the schools were chastised for attempting to teach values and morality, we are witnessing a mandate from the public to once again focus attention on character development. Our prisons are overcrowded, the divorce rate is high, and too many people are using illegal drugs. Further, there is a perception by the public that too many public officials and business leaders are engaged in unethical activities. Because the schools share responsibility with the family and church to help children develop into the types of adults who will make positive contributions to society, there is a mandate for the schools to emphasize character development.

Character is an easy concept to define. According to Wynne and Walberg (1985/1986), "'character' involves engaging in morally relevant conduct or words or refraining from certain conduct or words" (p. 15). Thus, a person's character is judged by the way the person acts. Morality and ethics are used synonymously with character.

While character is relatively easy to define, it is more difficult to describe. Character is a somewhat "fuzzy" concept because so many values and beliefs are involved. Yet examples of character are readily illustrated by the Boy Scout Oath, the Girl Scout Pledge, and acts of civil disobedience.

While this chapter is directed at helping you foster your students' character development, it uses the terminology most frequently used by social studies educators and social scientists. *Moral education* and *moral development* therefore replace the term *character development*. Values, beliefs, and attitudes are three additional terms used in the discussion of moral development.

How important is moral development? Schaps, Solomon, and Watson (1985/1986) surveyed parents to determine their attitudes about a variety of goals for elementary schools. Surprisingly, the highest-ranking academic goal was rated ninth out of the twenty goals. The majority of the goals ranked ahead of the academic goals were related to attitudes toward others and toward learning. Parents seem to want their children to be "good," hardworking individuals, much like the traits most people identify in their eulogies. Good grades and school achievement in basic skills are important, but attitudes about school, self, and others appear to be more important. These goals form much of the foundation of moral education.

The Association for Supervision and Curriculum Development (ASCD, 1989) affirmed the central role of moral education and democratic ideals in education. Both must become unifying themes of education. Our schools are designed to help prepare children for their future roles as adults in our society; schools cannot overlook their shared role as moral educators.

At this point pause and once again consider the eulogy you outlined in Chapter 1. Reexamine the characteristics of a "good" person and determine the degree to which your eulogy described traits related to interacting well and responsibly with others. If your list is typical, the majority of the items listed in your eulogy are directly related to the person's social behaviors rather than the person's academic achievements. The mark of a good person generally relates to how well the person manages his or her own affairs in a positive, responsible manner while contributing to the improvement of others.

Moral education is a twofold task. We must help children learn the norms, mores, and values of society. These are the social standards governing behavior. However, while helping children learn these standards, schools must help children critically analyze and actively work to resolve social problems. Social problems and conflicts often arise when our standards are inappropriate or when two equally valid standards conflict with one another. In a democratic society there are often several alternative responses to a given situation. Children must learn the socially acceptable behaviors and they must be capable of resolving situations in which conflicts occur.

Pro-abortion advocates march on Washington, D.C.

Photograph by Laima Druskis.

TERMINOLOGY

Several terms are consistently used in discussions of character and moral development. It should be noted that the terms are defined in slightly different ways, depending on the philosophical or psychological perspectives of the person using the terms. This section briefly describes the terms associated with moral development from a developmental perspective.

Morality is usually defined in terms of good or bad behavior. Individuals who act and behave well are said to be moral. If an individual's actions have a positive effect on others the person is judged as being moral. Morality is also judged in terms of intentions. If a person accidentally injures another person the moral aspects of the incident are judged less severely than if an individual intentionally attempts to hurt another person.

Values are aspects of morality and may be defined as "the standards or criteria against which individual behavior and group behavior are judged" (NCSS Task Force, 1989, p. 378). Values are based on attitudes and beliefs.

Values tend to be defined by each social, cultural or ethnic group. The democratic values listed by NCSS include justice, liberty, responsibility, rule of law, freedom, diversity, privacy, and international human rights. These values are reflected in such things as due process, equal protection, and civic participation. Democratic values differ somewhat from values in socialist, communist or imperialist societies.

Beliefs are important in any consideration of values and morality. Beliefs reflect the commitment people have to their values. For example, our society values diversity. Some people believe that children should be exposed to diverse values and lifestyles. Other people believe children should be exposed to specified values. They fear that exposure to a variety of values and lifestyles will corrupt children. This is reflected in aspects of the continuing controversy in the school's role regarding the teaching of values. Another example relates to beliefs about human rights. In our society some people believe that sex and race limit human rights (men have more rights than women, whites have more rights than blacks, the Ku Klux Klan has more rights than the NAACP). Beliefs are important because they affect the degree to which people will choose one behavior over another.

Attitudes is the final term used when describing character and moral development. Attitudes are reflections of our values and beliefs. If people value education, they will generally exhibit positive attitudes about school. If they value justice, freedom, and diversity they are likely to exhibit positive attitudes toward other people. It is difficult to change attitudes without altering one's values.

THEORETICAL PERSPECTIVES OF MORAL DEVELOPMENT

This section of the chapter briefly describes the views of Kohlberg and Piaget. Specific teaching suggestions are provided in the following section.

Kohlberg

Kohlberg's interests in moral development lie primarily in the realm of people's reasoning about justice and how moral concepts of justice develop. Kohlberg presented a series of moral dilemmas to individuals. A moral dilemma is a scenario in which several values conflict with one another. Kohlberg asked people to respond to each dilemma and then asked them to state their reasons for their decisions. He analyzed the reasons and developed a hierarchy of six stages involved in the development of moral reasoning.

According to Kohlberg, the process of moral development is based on a person's reasoning about moral issues. As individuals develop they should normally be expected to progress from lower stages to higher stages of moral reasoning. He contends that higher levels of moral reasoning are better than lower levels because individuals at higher levels are more self-disciplined and require less external control.

While his six stages should be of some interest to elementary teachers, they may not be too useful because most elementary children are functioning at stages 1 and 2. However, a brief description of Kohlberg's (1985) stages is included as a means of illustrating the direction in which teachers should help children develop. Teachers should provide children with experiences that will help them gradually move to the next higher level.

Individuals in Kohlberg's first stage of moral reasoning are governed by a punishment-obedience orientation. Children behave well to receive praise and avoid punishment. Stage 2 people behave in morally appropriate ways to satisfy personal needs. A "good boy-nice-girl" orientation in which individuals seek the approval of others is the third stage. This stage usually emerges during adolescence. A "law and order" orientation is present in the fourth stage. Stage 4 individuals work to maintain the social order and to execute one's duties.

Stages 5 and 6 are the most sophisticated levels of moral reasoning. Few adults reach these stages. A legalistic, social-contract orientation is exemplified in the fifth stage. The focus is on individual rights and rule by social agreement. Individuals at stage 6 are concerned with universal and ethical principles. Abstract principles of justice, reciprocity, equality, rights and dignity are the basis of state 6 reasoning.

Piaget's Model

Piaget (1965) described moral development as a process of moving from dependency on others for moral direction to becoming autonomous, independent moral beings. This model of moral development is more useful for elementary teachers because it is not based on discrete stages. Rather, the model describes general levels of moral thought.

Teachers need to develop an understanding of how elementary-age students reason about moral situations. Teachers also need to understand the type of adult support required for nurturing the development of sophisticated adult moral reasoning necessary for the continuation of a vibrant democratic society.

Because elementary teachers encounter a developmentally limited range of children, specific stage classifications are not useful. Piaget's model avoids the frustrations of classifying children into specific stages while at the same time providing teachers with direction for enhancing moral growth.

Piaget hypothesized that infants and toddlers are premoral. They have little control over moral behaviors and actions. Children in this age-group play independently. Even when they play in close proximity to others, they appear to be more concerned about their own actions than the actions of others.

Piaget's model then outlines the progression of moral development from the premoral child, through heteronomous morality characteristic of elementary children, and into two adult forms of morality. Piaget's two forms of adult morality are referred to as *moral realism* and *autonomous morality*. Piaget also described the existence of a transitional phase that enables children to ultimately become autonomous adults. The relationships between Piaget's stages are illustrated in Figure 13–1.

Figure 13–1 A Piagetian Model of Moral Development

Source: Van Cleaf, D.W., & Martin, R. (1982). Piaget's model of moral development. *Capstone Journal of Education, 3*(2), p. 22. Adapted and reprinted with permission from the Capstone Journal of Education.

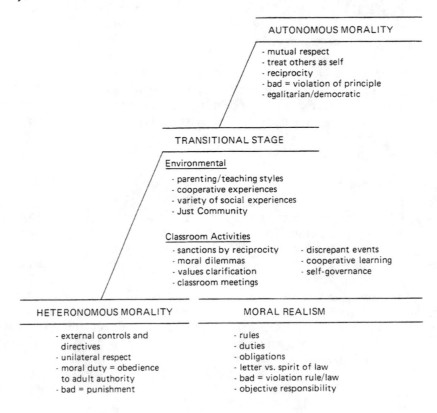

Heteronomous Morality. Heteronomous morality means that the child is controlled by others. Parents and teachers serve as the primary sources of children's external control. This form of morality is prevalent during the preschool and the elementary years. Concepts of right and wrong as well as good and bad are not internalized by these children. Right and wrong are defined by others. For example, if children are praised by an adult, they will perceive their behaviors and themselves as good. Conversely, if an authority figure punishes or scolds children, they will perceive their behaviors as bad.

Several other characteristics describe heteronomous morality. Children at this level of morality view rules in an interesting manner. Rules are treated as sacred and unchangeable. As children learn the rules for games, they cannot modify the rules because they are not capable of internalizing the intent of the rules. (Although children cannot modify rules, they readily break and ignore rules—particularly when there is little fear of getting caught.)

Another characteristic of heteronomous morality is children's perception of duty. The duty of children is to obey adult authority and conform explicitly to rules.

During the heteronomous stage, children are becoming less egocentric. They are beginning to decenter, which enables them to consider the perspectives of others. Thus, they are moving from a world in which they assume everyone thinks the same thoughts they have, to a world in which they begin to realize that they must consider the other person's perspective. This leads to the possibility of progressing to higher levels of moral development because children see the need to be more cooperative. As a result, they generally begin to view rules and adults differently.

Children who are encouraged to consider the views of others and to interact with others in cooperative ways begin making the long transition to Piaget's highest level of moral reasoning, autonomous morality. If children's attempts to become more accepting and cooperative are inhibited by over-protective or over-controlling adults, their upward progress may be arrested. These children will likely become adults who function at a level of moral realism.

Moral Realism. According to Piaget extreme constraint of children during the heteronomous stage results in a continuation of heteronomous-type reasoning into adulthood. This restrictive form of moral reasoning in adults is called moral realism. Like heteronomous morality, a person in the moral realism stage looks to rules, duties, and obligations as the means of defining moral conduct as good or bad and right or wrong. Of course rules, duties, and obligations are external standards. Good people obey rules (even bad rules) and bad people disobey the rules. To people functioning at the moral realism level Martin Luther King, Jr. would likely be considered a bad person because he broke the law.

These adults tend to follow the letter of the law. If they can't follow the letter of the law they break the law and consider themselves as having done something bad, particularly if they get caught.

Adults functioning at the level of moral realism are not too concerned with intentions; they are not likely to examine the reasons for a person's actions. Life tends to be viewed categorically as right or wrong, good or bad, and based on actions rather than intentions. These people may appear to be excellent citizens because they are likely to follow the laws and rules of society. However, they may be unable to accept diverse ideas and unable to change bad laws. They may be good neighbors, but they are not morally capable of the challenges of self-government in a democratic society. They can follow, but they cannot share in governance.

Autonomous Morality. Piaget's highest level of morality is a morality of autonomy. Individuals functioning at an autonomous level enter into and support reciprocal relationships. They use relationships to support one another rather than to further self-interests at the expense of others. People functioning at an autonomous level are more likely to follow the principles imbedded in the Golden Rule. They will treat others with respect and dignity, not because they will get a tangible reward, but because by treating others in this manner everyone will benefit.

Autonomous morality is also characterized by principled reasoning. People examine the intentions and the reasons for the rules as they make decisions regarding their own actions. If a law or rule violates a principle these individuals are likely to act according to the principle, even if they risk a fine or jail sentence. Martin Luther King, Jr., and Mohandas Gandhi broke many laws that violated principles of equality, justice, and freedom. They were arrested many times as they worked to change laws that violated moral principles.

Democratic society is built on the notion that the people make rules and laws to govern themselves. If rules or laws are bad they must be changed. A person functioning at the autonomous level is more likely to serve the needs of a democratic society. Adults functioning at the level of moral realism are more concerned with protecting the status quo and more likely to resist change (unless of course an authority figure such as president, governor, or minister encourages them to support the change).

Transitional Stage. Piaget hypothesized that a stage existed in which children engaged in activities enabling them to progress from heteronomous morality to autonomous morality. Parents and teachers must encourage children to engage in transition-enabling experiences if they want children to move toward autonomous morality. Children who do not experience transitional activities are likely to become adults who function at the stage of moral realism. Suggested activities for enhancing autonomous moral development are described in the next section of the chapter.

Piaget's explanation of moral development illustrates the differences in three types of moral reasoning. His model describes how adults should reason about moral issues and how the development of autonomous morality may be arrested if children do not have opportunities to proceed through the transitional stage.

ENCOURAGING MORAL DEVELOPMENT

Moral development is nurtured in two primary ways. First, adults can establish an environment conducive to the development of morally appropriate behavior and higher levels of moral reasoning. Second, adults can provide activities that foster moral development. This section of the chapter offers suggestions for developing an appropriate environment and specific classroom activities that nurture moral development.

As you read these sections please consider two cautions. First, moral development is a slow process. You will see limited changes in children over the length of a school year. You must be committed to the idea that one of our ultimate goals is to develop citizens who can assume the role and responsibilities of self-governance. The knowledge that these activities nurture long-term development should help you persevere.

A second caution relates to classroom discipline. Unfortunately, some of your students will have difficulty behaving appropriately when asked to participate in some of these activities. You may need to be more controlling and directive with them. They may come from environments that are characterized as extremely controlling. These children need opportunities to participate in activities nurturing responsibility and self-control, but may need extra guidance. Be patient, provide the necessary amount of guidance and control, and persevere. If elementary teachers cannot help children begin to make a successful transition to autonomous morality, children may become moral realists.

Parenting Styles/Teaching Styles

Studies indicate that certain adult characteristics relate positively to well-behaved and well-adjusted children. The primary characteristics include loving the children, having appropriately high expectations for children, explaining reasons for rules, and allowing children to explain reasons for behaving inappropriately. While the study cited in this section involved parents, the findings readily apply to the interactions between children and teachers.

Baumrind (1967, 1971) conducted a study of preschool children and the relationship between children's behaviors and parenting styles. Baumrind identified three types of children and three corresponding parenting styles (see Table 13–1). The group of well-adjusted children had *authoritative* parents. These parents were characterized as "notably firm, loving, demanding, and understanding" (1967, p. 83). They expressed support for their children and also maintained appropriately high expectations for their children.

Two other groups of children were identified in the study. Both groups were not as well adjusted as the children with authoritative parents. They tended to be more apprehensive and insecure. They were also less content, more hostile, and tended to lack self-control and self-reliance.

Table 13–1 Relationships Among Three Parenting Styles and Children's Behavior Patterns

PARENTS' CHARACTERISTICS	CHILDREN'S CHARACTERISTICS
Authoritative Parents	
Firm	Socialized
Loving	Independent
Demanding	Self-controlled
Understanding	Affiliative
Consistent	Self-reliant
Conscientious	Explorative
Secure	Self-assertive
Respected child's decisions	Realistic
Provided reasons	Competent
Clear communication	Content
Authoritarian (as compared to Authoritative)	
Less nurturant	Less content
Less involved with children	More insecure
Firm control	Apprehensive
Use power freely	Less affiliative
Provide little support	More hostile
Provide little affection	
Use of moral absolutes rather than reason	
Likely to use fright	
Permissive (as compared to Authoritative)	
Less controlling	Lack self-control
Not well organized	Lack self-reliance
Self-effacing	
Insecure about ability to influence their children	
Weak role models	
Low expectations	
Lax reinforcing of children	
Babied children	
Expressed warmth for children	

Source: Baumrind, D. (1967). Child care practices anteceding three patterns of preschool behavior. *Genetic Psychology Monographs, 75*(1) pp. 43–88. Adapted and reprinted with permission of the Helen Dwight Reid Educational Foundation. Copyright © 1967 and published by Heldref Publications, 4000 Albemarle St., N.W., Washington, D.C. 20016.

Two parenting styles were related to these children. One style was called *permissive*. These parents were described as moderately loving, but they did not provide consistent expectations and tended to doubt their ability to influence their children. The children of permissive parents were raised in environments lacking clear standards and expectations, and the children received mixed messages regarding their conduct.

The third group of parents were described as *authoritarian*. They were firm, punitive, and not affectionate. These parents demonstrated less care and love for their children while maintaining expectations well beyond children's abilities. Thus, children received little emotional support and were consistently unable to achieve at a level that would please their parents.

This study has four implications for teachers. First, effective teachers must establish a warm, emotionally supportive environment for their students. Children need to feel accepted and loved. When love and acceptance are present youngsters are more likely to adopt your standards.

Second, teachers must establish and maintain high expectations for students. These expectations must be appropriate for the cognitive, academic, and emotional characteristics of the children.

A third message is that children need opportunities to hear reasons for expectations and sanctions. The reasons help children understand the relationships between an individual's behavior and the effect it has on others. This relationship is critical to attaining higher levels of moral reasoning. Social studies should include many opportunities to help children consider the effects of people's behavior. A consideration of the positive and negative influences of people throughout history will nurture this principle.

The fourth message is that teachers must establish a set of appropriate classroom rules as well as fair, concrete consequences for breaking the rules. Children need standards by which they can measure and assess their own performance.

Cooperative Experiences

According to Piaget (1965), "Cooperation alone leads to autonomy" (p. 410). This statement indicates that only through involvement in activities that require children to interact and cooperate with others will children progress to higher levels of moral reasoning. Cooperative experiences allow children to discover and evaluate the effects their behaviors have on others.

Piaget also noted that adults cannot act as masters; they should act as collaborators arranging situations in which children engage in cooperative activities. A primary role of the adult therefore appears to be one of arranging situations in which children can work and play with other children. If you consider the prevalence of teacher-directed instruction and the amount of time children engage in individual seatwork activities you begin to wonder how today's schools are encouraging higher levels of moral reasoning.

Children will need more opportunities to work with one another if the schools are to play an effective role in enhancing autonomous morality. Whether youngsters collaborate with one another in small groups on inquiry activities or at the computer, cooperation and autonomous morality are nurtured.

Disequilibration

According to the tenets of Piaget's theory, growth occurs as children encounter challenging situations. A challenging situation is one in which a child can recognize a problem but does not have the cognitive responses necessary to resolve the problem. In moral situations, children may be confronted with the challenge of selecting an appropriate course of action, but the child's existing behaviors are not quite appropriate. The child recognizes the situation and is challenged, or disequilibrated, by the inability to resolve the situation with existing abilities. This motivates the child to begin considering alternative responses, which leads to growth.

As adults interact with children they should look for disequilibration opportunities. The adult can observe a child's behavior and raise a question about the behavior. Or, when a child offers an explanation for an action, the adult can ask the child to think of an alternative explanation.

Of course, the disequilibration process can be used too frequently and unnecessarily frustrate children. Children need to be motivated to consider alternatives, but they also need ample time to reflect on ideas and to practice alternatives before being challenged to move to the next level.

Provide a Variety of Social Experiences

Adults can enhance children's level of moral development by providing a greater variety of social stimulation. It would appear that children who are involved in a variety of social situations have opportunities to better understand the views of others and the relationships between the child's behaviors and the effects those behaviors have on others. Adults must act as collaborators. They must work with children, encouraging them to experiment with a variety of social experiences and helping them reflect on successes and frustrations within these social settings.

A Just Community Classroom

Kohlberg (1985) helped develop the Just Community program as a means of making schools and classrooms more supportive of moral development. In a Just Community setting the school and classroom become microcosms of democratic self- governance. Children and teachers work together establishing rules as well as judging misbehavior. Because the welfare of the group is emphasized, the effects that children's behaviors have on the group and group members become the primary criteria for analyzing rules and behaviors. The focus on the relationship between one's behavior and the effects on others is the essence of morality and a prime factor in promoting moral growth.

A variation of the Just Community concept has been effectively implemented in elementary schools in San Ramon, California (Schaps, Solomon, & Watson, (1985/1986). The San Ramon project is helping children increase both their prosocial behaviors and their achievement levels. The project involves youngsters in activities requiring cooperation and sharing. Activities promoting social understanding of others are also integrated into the classrooms. The children are actively involved in establishing rules, making decisions, and resolving school problems.

The Just Community concept appears to work because it actively involves children in assuming responsibility for their behavior. It also is effective because children are encouraged to assume responsibility for the welfare of others, a characteristic of good citizenship and people with character.

Natural Consequences

The rules, laws, norms, and mores of society are social-arbitrary forms of knowledge. But elementary-age children are concrete learners. The challenge for adults is to help concrete learners learn the social-arbitrary basis of morally appropriate behavior. Adults can utilize natural consequences as a means of helping children learn and internalize seemingly complex and abstract social rules.

A major step in helping children learn rules is to distinguish between punishment and natural consequences. Punishment exists when there is an arbitrary relationship between a child's behavior and the consequence imposed for the misbehavior. Kamii (1984) illustrated the abstract nature of punishment with an example about a child who does not receive dessert for telling a lie. Withholding dessert is considered punishment because there is no concrete relationship between telling a lie and dessert.

Natural consequences exist when there is a concrete relationship between a behavior and its consequence. Kamii suggests that when a child tells a lie you confront the child by stating that you have trouble believing the child. Your expression of disbelief is a concrete consequence of lying. Children will develop and internalize appropriate behaviors more quickly when the consequences are concretely related to behavior.

Punishment seems effective because it can be imposed quickly. However, because of the abstract nature of punishment, children are less likely to internalize the rule. If they do not internalize the rule they will fail to learn an important moral lesson, namely that rules are made to help people avoid being harmed. Natural consequences encourage children to internalize rules so they may gradually become more autonomous individuals.

Kamii provided several additional examples. First, if a child is misbehaving while working with others, the child should be temporarily excluded from the group. Children enjoy working with others; therefore they are motivated to adapt their behaviors so they can remain with the group. The message to children is clear and concrete: If you cannot behave while working with others you must work alone.

A second suggestion is to deprive the use of materials misused by a child. If a child misuses a computer when working on a simulation, the child should be denied the use of the computer for the remainder of the period. There is a concrete relationship between using an item for its intended purpose and losing the privilege to use that item.

Restitution is another example. If a child spills something or makes a mess he or she should clean it up. If a child breaks something he or she should either fix the object or replace it.

You can readily encourage moral development by utilizing natural consequences. The first task is to establish a workable set of classroom rules. Second, identify consequences that are concretely related to your rules. Third, explain the rules, the consequences, and the reasons for the rules. Fourth, impose the consequences consistently and judiciously. Failure to be consistent sends a message to children that they can manipulate you and the rules, which may result in nurturing a morality based on avoidance. Finally, you must have faith and patience that this approach will work. It doesn't take long, but children may be surprised by the approach and may need several opportunities to experience the consequences.

Moral Dilemmas

A moral dilemma is a scenario in which an individual is confronted with conflicting options related to a moral situation. The individual must consider conflicting options and values as he or she identifies possible responses.

As you attempt to use moral dilemmas in your classroom you should follow four steps. First present children with a dilemma. The dilemma may emerge from a literary passage, from the textbook, from a current event, or from a situation occurring during school. Topics for dilemmas may include shoplifting, cheating, human rights violations, and conflicts between the needs of society and the rights of individuals. You may need to take time during your planning process to write a one-paragraph dilemma. The dilemma should end with the character in the dilemma engaging in a controversial course of action.

The second step is to ask children to respond to the dilemma with a yes or no response. Ask, "Should the character have done that?" The children's yes or no responses are not the important aspect of the dilemma procedure. This response is merely a step that prepares them for the reasoning aspect of the procedure, the next step.

Thus, the third step is to ask children to provide reasons for their yes or no responses. This may occur during a class discussion or by assigning children to groups with one or two other children who responded to the yes or no question in the same way. Each small group should discuss possible reasons supporting their decisions and then select the most important reason. They should then report their reasons to the class.

The last step requires the teacher to act as Devil's advocate and probe children's responses. You should carefully challenge the reasons children provide as a means of encouraging them to consider alternative and higher-level responses. The sample lesson in Table 13–2 illustrates the four steps in the dilemma procedure and provides sample probing questions.

It is during steps 3 and 4 that children begin considering alternative responses and are encouraged to consider higher-level responses. As children interact with others they are disequilibrated and have opportunities to consider higher-level responses, which encourages moral development.

Table 13–2 A Moral Dilemma Activity

Step 1: Present the dilemma
Several families were traveling across the country by wagon. The Smiths' wagon broke two of its wheels. Another family, the Jones, had two additional wheels for their wagon. When asked if the Smiths could use the extra wagon wheels Mr. Jones said, "No, we have a rough trail ahead of us and need to keep our wheels in case we need them." The Jones family did offer to let the Smiths ride with them, but this would require that they leave their wagon and possessions behind.
  During the night, Mr. Smith decided to take the two wheels and leave the wagon train.

Step 2: Ask for a yes or no response.
Should Mr. Smith have taken the wheels from the Joneses?

Step 3: Ask children to support their yes or no responses. Ask, "Why?"
At this point children were asked to form into groups of three and identify the best reason for their decision.

Step 4: Ask probing questions.
The small groups reported their reasons to the entire class. As they did, the teacher asked a series of probing questions. These probing questions sparked a lively discussion.

- What if the Jones family had helped the Smiths in the past?
- Is it ever okay to steal?
- What if there was a danger of robbers attacking the wagon train or an individual wagon?
- Would it be okay if Mr. Jones had been a thief?
- What if the only doctor was in the Smith family?

Source: Joyce, B., & Weil, M. (1986). *Models of teachings,* p. 118. Englewood Cliffs, NJ: Prentice Hall. Adapted and reprinted with permission of Prentice Hall, Inc.
Source: Table 13–2 is an adaptation of a moral dilemma activity completed in class by students Susan Hansen and Ruth Gent. Adapted and reprinted with permission of Susan Hansen and Ruth Gent.

Values Clarification

Values clarification is sometimes described as an alternative means of developing values. The values clarification process is included in the discussion of moral development because it is a means of enhancing moral development.

The values clarification process has been designed to help people learn to examine and resolve situations in which competing values conflict with one another. For example, an elementary-age child may be tempted to shoplift because of peer pressure. The child is confronted with the conflicting values of stealing and peer approval. The values clarification process attempts to help children analyze situations in which conflicting values are present while also helping them develop a personal value system.

Values clarification is a seven step process that helps children develop a value system and effectively resolve value conflicts (Simon, Howe, & Kirschenbaum, 1978). The seven steps are subdivided into three categories: (1) prizing one's beliefs and behaviors, (2) choosing one's beliefs and behaviors, and (3) acting on one's beliefs. Thus, the values clarification process is designed to help children understand their values and make decisions based on their values. Further, the process encourages children to carry out their decisions and demonstrate their values in a consistent manner. Table 13–3 outlines the seven steps in the values clarification process.

Table 13–3 The Values Clarification Process

Prizing:	(1)	cherishing, being happy with the choice
	(2)	willing to affirm the choice publicly
Choosing:	(3)	freely
	(4)	from alternatives
	(5)	after thoughtful consideration of the consequences of each alternative
Acting:	(6)	doing something with the choice
	(7)	repeatedly, in some pattern of life

Note: The categories and steps in the values clarification process are being revised. Merrill Harmin's article, "Value Clarity, High Morality: Let's Go for Both," in the May 1988 issue of *Educational Leadership* describes aspects of the changes.

Source: Raths, L., Harmin, M., & Simon, S. (1966). *Values and teaching.* Columbus, OH: Chas. E. Merrill. Reprinted with permission of Merrill Harmin.

Prizing activities are designed to help children identify things that are important to them and for which they take pride. Children should be provided with opportunities to express pride in their accomplishments as well as accomplishments of family members, friends, and their country. As children experience opportunities to share the things they are proud of, they begin to see that other children have similar ideas and values. This helps reinforce many of the children's values. It also provides a forum in which children can analyze some of their values and beliefs.

A sample prizing activity presented by Simon, Howe, and Kirschenbaum requires children to respond to a series of stem sentences. Each of the stem sentences requires youngsters to identify an item for which they were proud. Children are then asked to provide responses for each stem sentence. For example:

"I am proud of/I am proud that..."

1. Any new skill you have learned within the last month or year....
2. Something you did that did not take physical courage, but which you are proud of....
3. A decision that you made which required considerable thought....
4. The completion of a task that was very laborious, but which you stuck out....
5. Some family tradition you are particularly proud of....
6. Something you refrained from doing about which you're proud.... (p. 135).

Krawetz (1984) proposed a self-esteem passport that supports the prizing process. Children can develop passports containing personal data such as name, date of birth, and address. They may also add pages describing physical, intellectual, social, and personal attributes. The passports encourage children to identify topics of personal pride.

Children should have opportunities to develop pride in their neighborhood, community, state, nation, and ethnic group. Current events discussions, holiday celebrations, and analysis of positive contributions made by others contribute to an increased sense of pride.

The second phase of the values clarification process requires children to make choices. To make choices, they must consider possible alternatives. The following rank-order questions illustrate one means of developing children's abilities to make choices from alternatives.

Which would you rather be?
_____ an only child
_____ the youngest child
_____ the oldest child

Which pet would you rather have?
_____ a cat
_____ a dog
_____ a turtle
_____ a parakeet

If you were president, which would you give the highest priority?
_____ space program
_____ poverty program
_____ defense program

(*Simon, Howe, & Kirschenbaum, 1978, p. 63*)

The third phase of the values clarification process is the action phase. It does little good to have children talk about their values and make verbal choices in the classroom if they do not act on their values and beliefs. Simon, Howe, and Kirschenbaum suggested that children have opportunities to write letters to the editor of local newspapers. As children write and mail their letters they are taking action and affirming their beliefs. The use of telegrams was presented as a variation to the letter-writing activity. Children can be encouraged to write telegrams on index cards urging a person to take a certain course of action. The telegrams can then be sent or handed to the person to whom they are addressed.

A fourth-grade class in Massachusetts became concerned about the environmental impact of plastic holders used on six-packs of soft drinks and beer. They began an active campaign in the state legislature to end the use of the plastic material. The legislature eventually enacted such a law.

The values clarification process has been used effectively in many social studies and health education programs. However, there have been criticisms of the values clarification process. The most valid criticism is related to a suggestion that children be allowed to choose freely. Teachers were initially encouraged to refrain from influencing children's choices. Many parents became upset when they learned that the schools were seemingly supporting children's decisions regarding controversial issues such as smoking marijuana or engaging in premarital sex.

Teachers can direct values clarification activities without minimizing the effectiveness of the process. Teachers should encourage children to explore as freely as possible the range of values related to an issue, but teachers also have an obligation to point out the social and legal consequences of certain decisions. If teachers ensure that children consider the legal, social, and personal ramifications for the decisions emerging from a values clarification activity, much of the criticism will diminish. Teachers will be helping youngsters consider the consequences that accompany different actions, which supports the concept of natural consequences.

Classroom Meetings

Classroom meetings have been mentioned in previous chapters. Glasser's (1969) social–problem-solving classroom meeting format contributes to moral development. This type of meeting provides children with opportunities to consider and resolve problems within the classroom and the school. During these meetings children can discuss the effectiveness of existing classroom rules and propose changes in the rules.

These discussions enhance moral development because children have opportunities to consider the relationships between rules and the children's behaviors. It also enhances the democratic value that rules are made by people and for the benefit of people. Finally, this type of classroom meeting provides students with opportunities to discover the reciprocal relationships between their behaviors and the effects their behaviors have on others.

Discrepant Events

Discussions about discrepant events are a variation of classroom meetings. Discrepant events are essentially discussions about real-life situations in which several interests conflict with one another (Baker & Van Cleaf, 1988). The events are termed discrepant because the claim of one party appears to defy children's commonsense logic. For example, an ambulance driver was recently mailed a traffic ticket for exceeding the speed limit while responding to an emergency. The teacher presented the discrepant event to the children and they discussed the reasons why the action taken did not seem "logically" appropriate. Another example emerged from a conflict in which a city's zoning code limited the type of construction in rural areas well beyond the city limits.

Discrepant events are motivating for children because the situations do not seem justifiable. Children are disequilibrated by the conflict and motivated to seek an understanding. Discrepant events relate to moral development because they help children develop a better understanding of rules, laws, and their effects on people.

Cooperative Learning

Cooperative learning is a rather general term that describes learning situations requiring children to work together. Cooperative learning is most frequently used when children are assigned a reading passage in a textbook and then required to answer questions at the end of the passage. Cooperative learning may also be used when children are involved in an inquiry activity. They can form cooperative learning groups to identify and analyze alternative solutions to a problem.

A small group of children studying together. Cooperative learning enhances academic and moral development.

Photograph by Ken Karp.

A teacher will assign students to cooperative learning groups consisting of two, three, or four members. Each member of the group is encouraged to help the other members analyze the problem and master the information.

Cooperative learning activities also contribute to aspects of moral development. As students work in their cooperative learning groups they must make decisions regarding how they will approach the learning task. They must consider the strengths and needs of their group members. Slower children work harder. The more capable children must consider the needs of the slower ones and consider ways to help them learn the information. Children must also negotiate resolutions to conflicts emerging within their groups. Essentially, they are responsible for one another and must often defer their own interests to the interests of the group.

Piaget indicated that cooperative experiences were the best means of nurturing moral development. Cooperative learning is an easy strategy to implement in classrooms and readily supports academic and moral growth.

Classroom Responsibilities

Teachers can encourage responsible behavior by assigning young students specific classroom tasks. They may be assigned duties such as feeding classroom animals, watering plants, recording the lunch count, cleaning portions of the room, and maintaining recess equipment. Children should be assigned these duties for a period of time and then have duties reassigned at the end of the period. To make this procedure a self- governance one, teachers may allow children to identify responsibilities and volunteer for specific duties.

Children become more responsible when teachers expect them to behave responsibly. Assigning specific duties provides youngsters with concrete opportunities to practice responsibility and to receive feedback for their efforts.

SUMMARY

Our children need opportunities to develop behaviors and attitudes so they can contribute to the needs of a democratic society. The schools share in this aspect of the socialization process and must therefore help students develop democratic values and beliefs. Much of this has been researched and described under the major heading of moral development.

Among the most notable conflicts each of us experiences is the conflict between self-interests and the interests of the group. A person functioning at a higher level of moral development is more likely to defer personal interests to the needs of the group. While our society values the importance of each individual, we must not forget that the strength of society is a reflection of the collective contributions of its individual members.

This chapter described two views of moral development and a number of suggestions that will enable you to foster the moral growth of your children. The need for citizens of high moral character is paramount if our nation is to remain a world leader. We cannot afford to leave character development to chance.

SUGGESTED ACTIVITIES

1. Locate and review copies of the Boy Scout Oath and the Girl Scout Pledge. Determine which of the concepts relate to character and moral development.
2. Locate a copy of one of Kohlberg's moral dilemmas in a psychology textbook. Read through the dilemma. Then develop a moral dilemma for a concept taught in elementary-school social studies.
3. Read a children's literature book. List the situations described in the book that could be used as moral dilemmas.
4. Write a letter to your local school board advocating a greater emphasis on developing autonomous morality.
5. Observe the interactions between two sets of parents and their children. One set of parents should exhibit inappropriate interactions with their child. The other set of parents should exhibit appropriate interactions with their child. You may observe in the grocery store, an athletic event, or church. Using Baumrind's parenting styles, how would you classify each set of parents?
6. Write a statement describing the manner in which you will attempt to guide children's character development.
7. Select articles from the newspaper that illustrate conflicting values. Outline possible ways to use the articles with elementary-age children.

Reading to children can enrich social studies lessons.

Photograph by David M. Grossman, Photo Researchers, Inc.

chapter 14

Reading and Social Studies

When children drop their papers in the hall, they pick up their paintings and writings and leave their worksheets on the floor.

(Joanne Marien, Ed. D., Superintendent, Haldane Central School District, Cold Spring, NY.)

AS YOU READ...

- what are the strengths and weaknesses of most social studies textbooks?
- why do you think teachers place so much emphasis on the use of textbooks?
- what is meant by *readability*? What can you do to minimize the negative influences of readability formulas?
- how can you adapt the social studies textbook?
- how can you go beyond the textbook?

Source: Quotation by Joanne Marien, Ed., D., Superintendent, Haldane Central School District, Cold Spring, NY. Quotation cited in Marzollo, J. (1988). Do worksheets work? *Parents Magazine, 63,* p. 112. Reprinted with permission of Jean Marzollo.

INTRODUCTION

One of the problems with current practices in elementary schools is that the curriculum has been neatly dissected into separate subject areas. Our schools have separate curriculums, separate textbooks, and separate materials for each subject. Further, each subject is scheduled so that it is difficult to have two subjects taught concurrently.

This was exemplified when a new state curriculum was being implemented. The new mandates made it difficult to schedule enough time to teach each subject separately. While it would have been appropriate to meet the more stringent time demands by integrating subjects like reading and social studies, many teachers and principals were reluctant to do this. They feared that the state auditors would not give the schools credit for teaching two or more subjects concurrently.

In many of today's elementary classrooms each subject tends to be taught as if it has no relationship to other subjects. Reading is taught as if learning to read is isolated from the children's social and physical world. Social studies is taught as if there is little need or opportunity to reinforce reading skills. Yet when children read they enjoy reading stories about topics taught in social studies. And when they study social studies, many reading skills can easily be taught and reinforced.

The NCSS Task Force (1989) included reading skills in its list of essential skills for social studies programs. The social studies skills related to reading include comprehension, vocabulary, and reading rate. Additional skills shared by reading and social studies include locating information, using information, using the library, and using reference materials.

The use of textbooks contributes to the separation of curriculum subjects. The poor quality of the textbooks also inhibits children's achievement.

The primary purpose of this chapter is to offer ideas that will enable you to improve the use of social studies reading materials—primarily textbook materials. As you read this chapter you will learn ways to improve your students' reading skills as well as ways to adapt materials to meet their needs.

The chapter is divided into four sections. The first section briefly describes the quality of textbooks. The second section examines the issue of readability and provides suggestions that will help you determine the difficulty levels of reading materials. The third section presents a number of suggestions that will enable you to use social studies textbooks effectively as well as to go beyond their limitations. Writing is closely related to reading and social studies and is discussed in the fourth and final section of the chapter.

TODAY'S TEXTBOOKS

The textbook and supporting materials are the primary means by which social studies is taught in most classrooms. When you consider the questionable quality of many textbooks, the use of textbooks becomes a double-edged sword. Teachers use the textbooks too much and the majority of the textbooks used are mediocre. As a result, students are provided weak educational foundations.

Teachers and school districts rely on textbooks for several reasons. Textbooks appear to present information in a well-organized way; the use of textbooks appears to ensure that certain topics are taught throughout the district; and for busy teachers, it is often easier to follow their textbooks than to plan alternative lessons.

At some point teachers began to assume that they had to use the textbooks because of decisions made by school administrators. This appears to be a false assumption. Shannon (1982) asked teachers why they used textbooks. Seventy-seven percent of the teachers stated that their administrators would not allow them to teach without their textbooks. However, when administrators were asked why teachers relied on textbooks, they expressed a belief that teachers had made deliberate decisions to use textbooks.

Students working with textbook materials. Such practices do not encourage student interaction and create negative attitudes toward social studies.

Photograph by Carmine L. Galasso.

Do teachers need to follow the textbook? Can teachers go beyond the textbook? Do teachers have the authority to set their social studies textbooks aside? After considering the limitations of many textbooks and suggestions for improving social studies instruction in the following sections, you should be able to answer these questions.

Textbook Strengths

Although this section outlines weaknesses within a majority of social studies texts, textbooks are still useful. For example, the information contained in most textbooks is organized and potentially instructive. This can help students learn key points. Second, social studies textbooks have high-quality graphics. They tend also to have attractive page formats and visually appealing illustrations.

Textbook Shortcomings

Social studies textbooks have many weaknesses. To sell their books publishers consider the type of scrutiny they will receive by educators and the public. This contributes to textbook shortcomings described below.

Coverage. By trying to satisfy as many requests as possible, space constraints limit the amount of discussion allotted to each topic. Textbooks therefore contain superficial descriptions of too many topics, a phenomenon referred to as *coverage.*

When teachers rely on the brief textbook descriptions of topics, students only learn about facts and dates. The focus is on trivial details learned for the test, not an understanding and appreciation of the vast richness of social studies topics.

Controversial Topics. Special-interest groups have had a dramatic impact on the quality of children's textbooks. Publishers have responded to many criticisms by deleting potentially objectionable passages and topics. Learning suffers because children are forced to read about dates, places, and events without the opportunity to consider the interesting value conflicts surrounding social studies topics. Larkins, Hawkins, and Gilmore (1987) analyzed a textbook series and reported that while children are required to read about trivial information, "there is not a word about freedom of speech or of the press..." (p. 309). How are children to learn about the Bill of Rights and other important subjects when controversial issues have been deleted from the textbooks?

Poor Organization. Many textbook series are poorly organized. Topics taught at one grade level are not being taught in succeeding grade levels. This array of topics does not support the spiral curriculum notion that concepts should be taught in greater depth at each higher grade level.

Trivial Information. The focus on topics such as family, neighborhood, and community in the primary grades has contributed to the trivial nature of primary-grade social studies textbooks. This scope and sequence format often requires students to study topics they already know, or to spend valuable instructional time studying topics they would normally learn elsewhere. Larkins, Hawkins, and Gilmore (1987) emphasized their concerns about the organizational quality of primary-grade textbooks by stating, "If asked to choose between teaching primary-grade social studies with available texts or eliminating social studies from the K-3 curriculum, we would choose the latter" (p. 299).

Outdated Information. Because of the length of time it takes to publish textbooks, some information is outdated when the textbooks reach the schools. To avoid "dating" the textbooks, current issues are avoided.

Questionable Content. Larkins, Hawkins, and Gilmore (1987) used the word *vacuous* to describe the content presented in many social studies textbooks. Vacuous means empty, pointless, stupid, and inane. They stated that textbooks include information children already know and present information that children would learn without instruction. Further, many textbooks include information and ideas that teachers normally impart without the textbook. Finally, textbooks ask students to read about the activities of others rather than actively involving them in the learning process. For example, they cited an instance where students were asked to read about other children conducting a community study rather than conducting their own study.

Limited Skill Instruction. While numerous skills are listed in the teacher's guide, the skills that are most easily tested were found to receive the most emphasis within the texts. If texts are focusing primarily on skills that are easily tested, you might wonder how much emphasis is given to the development of critical thinking skills.

Textbook publishers acknowledge the importance of reading skill instruction in social studies and state that their series reinforce reading skills. However, the amount of reading skill instruction provided in social studies textbooks is weak. Direct reading skill instruction (suggesting how teachers might help children learn to read the textbooks) is limited. Further, children are required to utilize reading skills that may not have been taught.

Nationalistic Orientation. In an ever-smaller world the political, social, and economic affairs of one country are affected by events and decisions occurring in other countries. In a review of social studies textbooks, Elliott, Nagel, and Woodward (1985) discovered that social studies textbooks used in the United States were dominated by topics related to the United States. According to these authors, international and cross-cultural studies received minimal attention.

Unrealistic Representations of Women and Minorities. During the past few decades textbooks have been criticized for reinforcing stereotypical views of male and female roles. They have also been criticized for excluding the contributions of cultural, racial, and ethnic minorities. Publishers are doing more to include illustrations of women and minorities in nonstereotypical roles.

De Facto Decision Making. As you begin and continue your teaching career you may feel compelled to follow the textbook. By adhering to the textbook you are allowing the publisher to make educational decisions on your behalf. Be careful that you do not allow textbook publishers to exercise control over your teaching.

Are publishers completely to blame? No! Educators have not sent clear messages to the publishers. Further, they often have not critically examined the quality of the textbooks they use. You need to be familiar with these types of problems so you can achieve maximum benefits from using the textbooks.

READABILITY

Readability is a variable affecting the quality of social studies textbooks and social studies instruction. Publishers use readability formulas in an attempt to inform educators that the materials are appropriate for specified grade levels.

The issue of readability extends beyond the use of textbooks. Teachers want to know if their students will be capable of reading other instructional materials. Are supplemental materials, newspaper articles, and excerpts from children's literature books appropriate for children's reading abilities? There are a number of formal and informal readability measures available to teachers.

Limitations of Readability Formulas

Readability measures can help teachers, but they have several limitations. Readability formulas fail to consider the qualitative aspects of written texts such as levels of meaning, children's interests, and children's prior experiences. Parents and teachers alike readily admit that children can read difficult materials when interested in the topic. Similarly, poorly written and uninteresting passages are difficult, even when written well below the children's reading levels.

Readability levels have had a negative impact on the quality of children's social studies textbooks. After an author completes a manuscript it is subjected to a readability analysis. Passages that appear to be too difficult are then modified. This modification process usually results in complex sentences being shortened. Connecting words (*also, but, then, however, therefore*) that help the reader identify relationships are often deleted. Vocabulary terms that have precise meanings are often replaced with more general terms that often confuse rather than clarify concepts. The result of efforts to maintain an appropriate readability level is reading passages that often become more difficult to read and understand.

Reading can expand a child's horizons.

Photograph by Ken Karp.

Suggestions for Using Readability Measures

There are several situations in which you may benefit from using readability formulas. When selecting reading materials, whether textbook materials, supplemental reading materials, primary source materials, or computer software, you need some means of determining the difficulty level of the materials. When you serve on a textbook committee you may also want to consider the readability level of the material as one of the factors in selecting a text.

However, formal means are not the only method and may not be the best way to determine if the materials are appropriate for your students. This section of the chapter offers suggestions for determining readability. The suggestions include formal and informal strategies for determining reading difficulty.

PHAN. The PHAN strategy requires teachers to consider three factors: reference cohesion, explicitness of relationships, and vocabulary difficulty (Clark, 1981). Before analyzing a passage, first divide the reading passage into phrases. After identifying the phrases locate pronouns and their referents. Next, determine the distance (number of words or phrases) between each pronoun and the object to which it refers. The greater the distance between the pronoun and its referent, the more difficult the reading level. The recommended limit between a pronoun and its referent is three phrases. This number is lower for younger children.

After determining the distance between pronouns and their referents, examine the explicitness of the relationships. The explicit relationship is an analysis of the proper use of connective words such as *because, and, but, before, after,* and *therefore.* Some relationships are explicit, others more abstract and implied. After considering the degree of explicitness, ask yourself if your students are capable of understanding the reading passage.

The final analysis in the PHAN procedure is the difficulty level of the vocabulary. As you consider vocabulary difficulty, you should also consider your students' ability levels and their familiarity with the concepts and vocabulary words contained in the passage.

Cloze Procedure. The cloze procedure requires teachers to select a passage and then delete a number of words. A child is then asked to read the passage and supply the missing words. The cloze procedure is not recommended for children prior to grade four.

The number of words between deleted words should decrease as children move to higher grades. For example, you should delete every ninth word for fourth-grade children and delete every fifth word for eighth-grade children. Also, you should not delete proper nouns and dates.

The independent reading level is achieved if the reader correctly replaces at least 57 percent of the original words. The instructional level requires the reader to replace at least 44 percent of the words correctly. You should be most concerned with the instructional level because this is the level at which most teaching occurs.

Correct matching below the 44 percent level indicates that the child is functioning at the frustration level for that particular passage.

Teacher Judgment. Research studies indicate that teacher judgment is a highly reliable means of matching students and reading materials. As you attempt to make judgments about the suitability of reading materials for your students, you should consider the following (Rush, 1985):

- vocabulary difficulty
- sentence complexity
- difficulty of concepts and ideas
- explicit relationships (use of connective words)
- interpretation of graphics (pictures, graphs, maps, charts)

You will find this process helpful when new students are assigned to your classroom. They usually arrive prior to their cumulative folders. In an effort to place these youngsters in appropriate instructional groups, have each new child read portions of text passages. When the passage is completed ask a few literal and inferential comprehension questions. This procedure is a valid means of gaining information about children's reading abilities.

Formally prepared readability measures have limited value, and they actually have a negative impact on students' ability to read textbooks and other written materials. As you consider the appropriateness of materials for your students you will need to make subjective decisions based on your professional judgment. Your professional judgment may be enhanced by using variations of the procedures described in this section. Trust your judgment and select materials because they are appropriate for your children, not because they achieve a certain score on a formal readability scale.

IMPROVING READING IN SOCIAL STUDIES

This section of the chapter provides a variety of specific suggestions that will help your students read and understand social studies materials. The ideas also contribute to improving your students' reading skills because they reinforce reading objectives. While you will find many of these ideas described in your reading methods textbooks, the ideas presented here will provide specific help for social studies.

Modifying the Text

One of your most urgent concerns will be to determine how to help students who have difficulty reading your social studies textbook. This is a common problem because most classrooms have at least a handful of children who cannot read well enough to learn from the text. You may even find a majority of your students experience unnecessary difficulties—text passages may challenge even your best readers. You might try modifying the text in the following ways.

Written Modifications. One means of modifying the text is to delete portions of the text. One teacher simply used a black marker and deleted as many sentences as possible to reduce the amount of text material for her poor readers. Another technique is to use an accent marker to highlight key sentences. Readers may be told to focus their attention on the highlighted sentences as they read the text. A third means of modifying the text is to simply require your less-capable readers to read the paragraphs relating to your objectives. Tangential paragraphs can be skipped.

A fourth modification requires rewriting portions of the text and adding topic sentences. First, read the section of the text you intend to assign to determine if each paragraph has a topic sentence. If a topic sentence is missing you should insert one. If a topic sentence is present, examine it to determine if it is explicit enough for your students. You might identify paragraphs with no topic sentences and allow children to provide appropriate topic sentences.

A final suggestion for modifying the written text is to examine the relationships between pronouns and their antecedents. The distance between pronoun and antecedent should be less than three phrases. If the distance is too great or the referent is not clear, insert the correct term in place of the pronoun.

These suggestions can help children learn from the text and develop a sense of accomplishment. However, they also have several limitations. Because most social studies texts are poorly organized and include superficial coverage of topics, you will need to embellish the concepts developed in the text through alternative methods (teacher explanation, films, discussions, etc.).

Building Readers' Schema

You should provide ample time before assigning reading material to help your students relate the concepts described in the text passage to their schemes. In other words, you will need to take time to help students discover the relationship between the concepts in the text and their own experiences.

Prior to assigning a reading passage you should introduce concepts to the children. Teachers often do this as a vocabulary development exercise. You may present key concepts, ask students to describe their knowledge of the concepts, and then add necessary information. The concept-development techniques described in Chapter 10 are useful for this process.

Reading comprehension is increased when students can relate reading materials to their personal experiences. When children can relate text material to their schemes they can also read at a higher difficulty level.

Modifying Presentation

Another suggestion is to alter the way the textbook is presented to the students. You can read it aloud to them or you can record the passage on an audio cassette.

Children can then listen to the recording at a listening center. As children listen to the tape they can read along in their textbook. By using cassettes they can also return to the listening center and replay the recorded passages as often as necessary to master the information.

If you do not have the time to record the passages you may use parent volunteers to read the material. Accomplished readers, whether from your classroom or a higher grade level, can also record the passages. Poor readers from the upper grades can also be asked to read passages. They should practice the passage and re-record sections they are not pleased with. This will help them improve their reading skills and boost their self-esteem.

Tape recorders and listening centers can be used to help children learn information contained in reading passages.

Photograph by David W. Van Cleaf.

Caution: You should not require children to take turns reading aloud in a large-group setting. When children read aloud in a group setting they are concerned with pronunciation and articulation; they are not concerned with comprehension. Oral reading therefore tends to inhibit comprehension. In addition, when children are expected to take turns reading orally most of the other children do not pay attention. The oral reading process is slow. It overloads the short-term memory process and inhibits transfer to long-term memory. The oral reading process also limits children's ability to identify relationships between ideas. The next time you have an opportunity to observe a classroom in which children take turns reading aloud, watch the behaviors of the children. They will appear restless and bored.

Modifying the means by which the text material is presented may be preferable to deleting sentences and sections of passages. As it is, textbooks tend to provide too little supporting information. Deleting any of the supporting information further limits the students' ability to understand the concepts.

Cooperative Learning

The cooperative learning strategy was briefly described in Chapter 13 as a means of nurturing moral development. It is also an excellent means of helping children gain maximum benefit from text passages.

Cooperative learning is a process in which students are assigned to groups of three or four. Each group usually consists of youngsters from high, average, and low ability levels. The purpose of the heterogeneous mix is to encourage children to help one another. Cooperative learning experiences have been found to contribute to the academic achievement of children from each ability level while nurturing goals related to democratic citizenship.

While there are many variations of cooperative learning, two will be described here. One method is to assign students to their cooperative learning groups. Within their groups the children should decide how to read the assigned passage and how to answer the questions related to the passage. For example, as one child reads, the other group members follow along and listen for information related to the questions. When the passage has been read the group members answer the questions and take time to ensure that each member understands the answers to the questions.

A second cooperative learning strategy is a variation of the student team-learning technique described by Slavin (1986). In this format the teacher assigns a reading passage and three or four questions related to the passage. If there are three questions the teacher assigns three students to each cooperative learning group. If there are four questions, the teacher may assign four students to each cooperative learning group. Children then get into their cooperative learning groups and read the passage. Each member of a cooperative learning group then selects one question to explore in greater detail—to become an expert. Children then regroup into expert groups. If there are three questions there will be three expert groups, one for each question. Each expert group considers, discusses, and answers its assigned question. After the expert groups have developed an expertise about their questions, children re-form into the original cooperative learning groups. Each member then takes time to teach the information related to his or her particular question to the other group members. When all group members understand each question they are ready to be evaluated.

The evaluation process is a little different in cooperative learning. A final grade for each child may be computed by averaging the scores earned by the members in each group and then combining the group score with the individual's personal score. Thus, if a child has a high personal score, but the group's average is low, the child would receive a lower grade. If a child's individual score was low and the group score was high, the child would earn a higher grade. Children quickly learn that their best chances for earning a high grade are to learn the information well and ensure that other members of the group do the same. The grading process is illustrated in Table 14–1.

Table 14–1 Cooperative Learning Grading Format

TEAM MEMBERS	INDIVIDUAL SCORE	GROUP AVERAGE	PROJECT GRADE*
John	94	95.8	189.8
Mary	83	95.8	178.8
Suzy	100	95.8	195.8
Fred	86	95.8	181.8

*To compute the project grade, first add the individual student scores and divide by the number of students in the group. Then place the group mean score (average) in the Group Average column. Then add each child's individual score to the group average score for the child's final grade for the activity.

Source: Slavin, R.E. (1986). *Using student team learning* (3rd ed.). Baltimore, MD: John Hopkins University Center for Social Organization of Schools. Reprinted with permission of Robert Slavin.

In a democratic society individual rights and group responsibilities may conflict. Since we are social beings, we need to develop responsibility to society. But to do this we must also develop the capabilities of each individual. Cooperative learning is a means of nurturing the individual while encouraging children to assume greater responsibility for others. Cooperative learning is also an excellent means of helping poor readers learn information from textbooks.

Graphic Representations

The Piagetian-based Ypsilanti Perry Preschool Project encourages students to represent (illustrate) learning activities as a means of enhancing learning. After youngsters have engaged in a learning experience they are required to represent the activity in some other format. They may draw a picture, construct a model, dictate a story, or enact a skit. The purpose is to encourage students to represent an activity in an alternative way, which requires them to reconsider the concept from a different perspective.

As children consider reading passages they should be encouraged to illustrate the information in an alternative manner. Semantic mapping, nation schema, and "What I Know/Don't Know" are representation activities described in this section. Several variations are also summarized in this section.

Semantic Maps. Semantic maps are a means of helping children illustrate relationships between main and supporting ideas in a passage. Children use circles, squares, lines, and directional arrows to denote relationships between concepts and supporting information.

Figure 14–1 illustrates a semantic map for a reading passage about pioneers. As children read the passage they are required to list key words and ideas. After they read the passage they develop a semantic map that illustrates the relationships between the key words and ideas.

Nation Schema. Ohlhausen and Roller (1986) described a means of graphically representing information that enhances children's conceptual understanding of "nations." According to the authors there are seven key topics related to the study of any country. These topics also appear to underlie studies of communities, neighborhoods, cities, and states. As children begin to study a new political entity they should be asked to consider underlying topics. They should be directed to consider the land and the people. The study of the land can be subdivided into three topics: location, landforms, and climate. The study of people should also be subdivided. Topics related to people include history, culture, economy, and government.

As children study and read they should focus on these subtopics (see Table 14–2). By considering these subtopics as they study new cities, states, or countries, students will develop a stronger schema and will be better able to learn information related to the new political entity.

What I Know/Don't Know. The "What I Know/What I Don't Know" activity has been proposed as a means of guiding and enhancing children's understanding of their reading assignments (Heller, 1986). This activity requires students to think about a concept before they read about it. The teacher should state the concept or topic and provide students with an opportunity to list things they know about the concept in a "What I Know" column. As children read the passage they are encouraged to add ideas they had known but had not listed before reading the passage.

Figure 14–1 A Semantic Map for a Lesson on Pioneers

Source: Adapted from a semantic map ("Ancient Greece") that was submitted as a course requirement by Steve Henry, Northern Hills Junior High School. Reprinted and adapted with permission from Steve Henry.

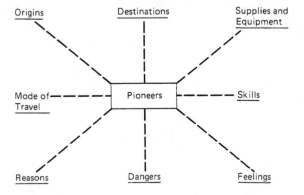

Table 14–2 Nation Schema Guide

I. The Land

A. Location:

B. Landforms:

C. Climate:

II. The People

A. Past:

B. Customs:

C. Economy:

D. Government:

Source: Ohlhausen, M.M., & Roller, C.M. (1986). Teaching students to use a nation schema to learn about countries. *Journal of Reading, 30,* pp. 212–217. Adapted with permission of the International Reading Association.

As children read they can write newly learned information in a second column, "What I learned." A third column, "What I don't know," should be provided so students can list confusing points they encounter as they read. These points can be clarified when they finish reading. Table 14–3 contains a format that will help structure children's thinking.

Table 14–3 What I Know/Don't Know Reading Guide

Reading Purpose:

What I already know:

What I learned from my reading:

What still confuses me:

Source: Heller, M. (1986). How do you know what you know? Metacognitive modeling in the content areas. *Journal of Reading, 29,* pp. 415–422. Adapted with permission of the International Reading Association.

Additional Graphic Representations. Jones, Pierce, and Hunter (1988/1989) described additional formats for illustrating relationships graphically. Flowcharts, family trees, and time lines are a few of the ways teachers can help students examine the structures and relationships presented in textbook descriptions of concepts. Graphic representations not only help children understand ideas but they help synthesize new ideas with existing ideas. Further, representations are a means of actively involving children in the reading and learning process. Several graphic representation formats are presented in Figure 14–2.

You should follow five steps as you use graphic representations. First, help students survey the passage. This will help them identify the structural format of the passage. Most passages follow one of the sequential formats illustrated in Figure 14–2. Second, allow students to predict a possible format for the passage's representation. Display possible graphic representations and take time to explain how each might be used. After students become more familiar with a variety of graphic representations they will more readily select the most appropriate representation. Third, allow children to read the passage. As they read the passage they should modify the representation selected in the second step and add information to blank portions of their representations. Fourth, children should complete their graphic outline using information gleaned both from the reading and from information taken from personal experiences. The final step is to summarize the information outlined on their graphic representation. Summaries can be either written or oral.

Reading-Comprehension Strategies

There are numerous reading-comprehension strategies teachers may find useful. Three such strategies are described in this section.

SQ3R. The SQ3R method is a means of helping children improve their comprehension. *S* requires children to survey the passage before they read it. As they survey the passage they are attempting to get an overview of it and predict the type of information they will encounter. They look through the selected material noting larger words, titles, graphs, and paragraph organization. *Q* requires children to develop questions about the passage. Headings, subheadings, and graphic illustrations should be examined as prompts for children's prereading questions. *3R* requires children to then read, recite, and review the passage.

The SQ3R method provides students with a format that helps them direct their reading. They think about a passage before they read it and therefore read for a specific purpose. Because children are reading for a specific purpose they can focus on relevant information and disregard superfluous information.

DRTA. A variation of SQ3R was proposed by Stauffer (1975). DRTA represents the Directed Reading and Thinking procedure and is recommended for reading relatively short passages. The DRTA procedure requires children

Graphic representations are visual illustrations of verbal statements. Frames are sets of questions or categories that are fundamental to understanding a given topic. Here are shown nine "generic" graphic forms with their corresponding frames. Also given are examples of topics that could be represented by each graphic form. These graphics show at a glance the key parts of the whole and their relations, helping the learner to comprehend text and solve problems.

Spider Map

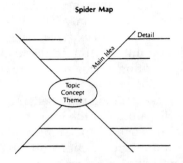

Used to describe a central idea: a thing (a geographic region), process (meiosis), concept (altruism), or proposition with support (experimental drugs should be available to AIDS victims). Key frame questions: What is the central idea? What are its attributes? What are its functions?

Continuum/Scale

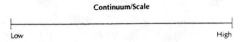

Used for time lines showing historical events or ages (grade levels in school), degrees of something (weight), shades of meaning (Likert scales), or ratings scales (achievement in school). Key frame questions: What is being scaled? What are the end points?

Compare/Contrast Matrix

	Name 1	Name 2
Attribute 1		
Attribute 2		
Attribute 3		

Used to show similarities and differences between two things (people, places, events, ideas, etc.). Key frame questions: What things are being compared? How are they similar? How are they different?

Series of Events Chain

Initiating Event

Event 1

Event 2

Final Outcome

Event 3

Used to describe the stages of something (the life cycle of a primate); the steps in a linear procedure (how to neutralize an acid); a sequence of events (how feudalism led to the formation of nation states); or the goals, actions, and outcomes of a historical figure or character in a novel (the rise and fall of Napoleon). Key frame questions: What is the object, procedure, or initiating event? What are the stages or steps? How do they lead to one another? What is the final outcome?

Problem/Solution Outline

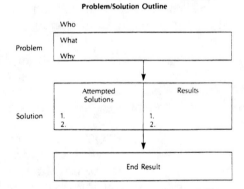

Used to represent a problem, attempted solutions, and results (the national debt). Key frame questions: What was the problem? Who had the problem? Why was it a problem? What attempts were made to solve the problem? Did those attempts succeed?

Figure 14–2 Alternative Graphic Representations

Source: Jones, B.F., Pierce, J. & Hunter, B. (1988/1989). Illustration "Graphic Forms with Corresponding Text Frames," pp. 22–23 from Teaching students to construct graphic representations. *Educational Leadership, 46,* pp. 20–25. Reprinted with permission of the North Central Regional Educational Laboratory (NCREL).

to establish a purpose for their reading. As they identify a purpose they should also make predictions about information, ideas, and perspectives they expect to encounter. Children then read the passage and verify their predictions. As they read, they also attend to information supporting the purpose for which they

Network Tree

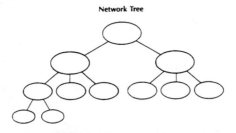

Used to show causal information (causes of poverty), a hierarchy (types of insects), or branching procedures (the circulatory system). Key frame questions: What is the superordinate category? What are the subordinate categories? How are they related? How many levels are there?

Fishbone Map

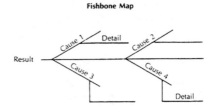

Used to show the causal interaction of a complex event (an election, a nuclear explosion) or complex phenomenon (juvenile delinquency, learning disabilities). Key frame questions: What are the factors that cause X? How do they interrelate? Are the factors that cause X the same as those that cause X to persist?

Human Interaction Outline

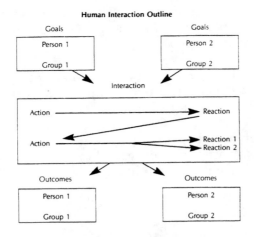

Used to show the nature of an interaction between persons or groups (European settlers and American Indians). Key frame questions: Who are the persons or groups? What were their goals? Did they conflict or cooperate? What was the outcome for each person or group?

Cycle

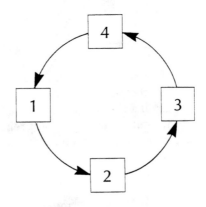

Used to show how a series of events interact to produce a set of results again and again (weather phenomena, cycles of achievement and failure, the life cycle). Key frame questions: What are the critical events in the cycle? How are they related? In what ways are they self-reinforcing?

Figure 14–2 Alternative Graphic Representations (*cont.*)

Source: Jones, B.F., Pierce, J. & Hunter, B. (1988/1989). Illustration "Graphic Forms with Corresponding Text Frames," pp. 22–23 from Teaching students to construct graphic representations. *Educational Leadership, 46,* pp. 20–25. Reprinted with permission of the North Central Regional Educational Laboratory (NCREL).

are reading. Finally, children should be asked to predict what will occur in the following passage.

The DRTA method encourages students to approach reading passages with open and questioning minds. As they approach a passage they should make predictions, but they must be flexible and open enough to alter their predictions.

In a sense, they are using inquiry skills as they read. As with the inquiry process, they identify a purpose (problem), identify hypotheses, collect data, and finally accept or reject their hypotheses.

MULTIPASS. This comprehension strategy was proposed by Schumaker, Deshler, Alley, Warner, and Denton (1982). It requires readers to do three things: survey the passage, sizeup the information in the passage, and sort out the important information.

The survey step is like the survey step in the SQ3R procedure. The size-up step requires children to make a second pass over the material presented in the passage. As they make the second pass they skim the material rather than read the entirety of the text from beginning to end. This enables students to gain the important information in the passage and allows them to avoid reading portions not pertinent to their purpose. Finally, children sort out the important information and test themselves. In this step they review and attempt to master the important points.

Like the previous two comprehension strategies, MULTIPASS provides children with a means of reading for a purpose and focusing on key points. It also indirectly encourages them to learn to skim text materials.

Comprehension Strategies and Cooperative Learning. Montague and Tanner (1987) recommended forming cooperative learning groups based on children's preferred comprehension strategies. They recommended teaching children the three comprehension strategies described in the preceding sections and then assigning them to cooperative learning groups consisting of like-minded children who prefer the same comprehension strategy. This seems like an exciting means of matching children according to their preferred learning styles.

Summarizing

Summarizing is a means of helping students learn key ideas in reading passages. The summarizing process requires the teacher to select a reading passage. As children read the passage they locate topic sentences and main ideas. They then summarize the passage by restating the information and ideas they considered important. Children should also state why they feel the information and ideas are important. After passages have been summarized, the students should have opportunities to discuss their summaries. These discussions will help them reflect on their work and compare their summaries with the summaries of their peers.

Summarizing has two primary benefits. It contributes to the development of critical thinking skills. As children summarize they must actively consider and select appropriate information. Because summarizing eventually requires children to consider the author's perspective, children have repeated opportunities to consider the perspectives of others and to consider the importance of writing for a particular audience.

Using Nontext Materials

Textbooks tend to contain useful but relatively unexciting information. Teachers must therefore use a variety of nontext materials. Social studies instruction can be improved by relying less on the textbook and more on your creative ideas and the use of alternative materials.

The types of alternative reading materials useful for enhancing social studies include children's literature books, newspaper clippings, photographs, and primary sources. Primary sources include firsthand accounts of events such as diary entries, interviews with people who participated in an event, and a variety of documents relating to the event. A few of these alternatives are described below.

Children's Literature. Children's literature is an excellent means of improving instruction. Children's literature incorporates factual information within a well-developed story line. As children read or listen to these stories they gain a sense of the feelings and mood of the people involved in an event. They also learn about the lifestyles of characters involved in the stories. This becomes a concrete reference point because children can relate the lifestyles of characters within a story to present lifestyles. This also adds a richness to social studies topics that is missing from social studies textbooks.

Little House on the Prairie is an excellent resource when studying westward settlement. *Call It Courage* is an excellent resource when studying island cultures.

Children can be encouraged to compare textbook descriptions of an event with the descriptions contained in literature accounts. They can compare the way in which the material is written as well as the accuracy of the event's description.

Primary Sources. Primary sources can be used to enhance social studies and extend the usefulness of the text. Primary sources include interviews with people who experienced an event. They also include diary entries, correspondence between people, court and legislative proceedings, original photographs, and pictures of events and scenes.

Primary sources may be more difficult to read and analyze because of writing style and the readability level. However, children are motivated to learn from primary sources and are willing to exert additional effort. You can reduce the challenges imposed by these materials by typing transcriptions of handwritten documents or reading difficult material to the children.

If you are studying a recent event or a current event you can invite participants in the event to speak to the class. As they describe their experiences they might show and describe artifacts related to the topic. Children should also be encouraged to ask questions.

A picture is worth a thousand words. Pictures and photographs of events and their settings are effective sources because they help students visualize the

Children like examining pictures of far away places.

Photograph courtesy of the United Nations.

people, objects, and surroundings. Today most important events are recorded in photographs and on video-tape. Prior to the invention of photography, artists were commissioned to illustrate important events. Children will develop a better understanding by viewing the pictures than by simply reading textbook accounts. Museums have ample collections of historical pictures and photographs. They can be copied for use in your classroom.

Newspaper and magazine articles can also be studied. While it is exciting for children to examine copies of old newspapers and magazines, these are usually considered secondary sources. A secondary source is best illustrated by a newspaper reporter. The reporter interviews an eyewitness and then reports the information to the readers.

WRITING AND SOCIAL STUDIES

Writing is an important aspect of learning social studies concepts. As children write they are required to reconsider their ideas and reorganize their ideas into an appropriate format. This section has been included in this chapter because of the important link among reading, writing, and learning. However, the section is brief because much of the information presented in other sections of the chapter applies to writing.

Nelms (1987) advocated integrating writing into the social studies. Nelms identified five types of writing that require children actively to process information. These five types of writing serve as suggestions for you as you attempt to integrate writing and social studies. These suggestions will also actively involve your students while enhancing their knowledge of social studies content.

Writing to Inventory Knowledge

This type of writing serves as a means of determining children's knowledge about a topic—a pretest activity. Students are required to indicate what they know about a topic and identify prior experiences with the topic. Nelms provided several ideas for eliciting children's knowledge. Students can brainstorm, participate in journal writing, develop essays, and complete "What I know/What I don't know" activities.

Writing to Initiate Learning

Prior to studying a new topic or reading a new passage, students should list questions they wish to answer, identify hypotheses, and predict outcomes. If students are preparing for an independent study project they would develop a written proposal for the project.

Writing to Consolidate Learning

As students read to learn about a topic they should do a variety of writing activities. They might take notes, outline the sequence of events, list key points, or paraphrase major ideas. Finally, they may be required to summarize passages. Writing to consolidate learning requires children to reconsider and utilize the information they are studying. They relate new information to previous knowledge, identify areas of uncertainty, and consider the author's intent.

Writing to Personalize Learning

This aspect of writing requires students to relate new concepts and information to their experiences. At this level children are writing to develop personal associations with the information. For example, if children were studying another state, they would be required to relate information about that state to their own state. Children might write about similarities and differences in landforms, natural resources, economic activities, climate, and leisure-time activities. They might also identify the benefits of living in both states and how their lifestyles might be altered if they moved to the other state.

Writing to Clarify Thinking

Writing requires students to examine and clarify their thinking. They should therefore be provided numerous opportunities to write about topics and concepts studied in social studies. Children can develop alternative explanations, predict how one change in an event may have altered the outcomes, or write letters to leaders (deceased or living) expressing a certain course of action.

Writing is a means of allowing students to represent their ideas in an alternative format. Writing can be formal or informal. Children can develop paragraphs and long stories or they may write narratives for cartoons. Writing should not be limited to upper-grade students. Kindergarten and first-grade children can also be involved in the writing process. They can list ideas, draw and label pictures, and dictate language-experience stories.

SUMMARY

While textbooks are the primary instructional material used to teach social studies, there are many weaknesses in the quality of the textbooks. Textbooks cover too much information and consequently cannot explore topics in enough depth to relate information to children's schemes. Today's textbooks are also boring. Interesting and controversial issues are excluded because they might offend special-interest groups.

Many textbooks are too difficult for children to read. A storylike narrative thread is missing and topic sentences are either missing or highly inferential. When passages are rewritten to meet readability guidelines, the resulting passages often become more difficult. Natural sentences are shortened and connecting words that help develop relationships between ideas are often deleted.

While this chapter presented other textbook weaknesses, it also set forth suggestions to help you use your school's textbooks and go beyond the limitations of the texts. Consider the needs, interests, and abilities of your students. Then select and adapt reading materials to maximize your students' learning.

SUGGESTED ACTIVITIES

1. Read a portion of a chapter in a child's social studies textbook. First, count the number of concepts included in each paragraph. Determine if each concept is adequately explained for a child at that grade level. Then examine each paragraph to determine the number of paragraphs that have explicit topic sentences, implicit topic sentences, and no topic sentences. Finally, identify a number of pronouns and count the number of phrases between each pronoun and its referent.

2. Copy several paragraphs from a textbook and try the cloze procedure. Delete every fourth, fifth, or sixth word and have an elementary-age child read the passage.

3. Try the three reading comprehension strategies (SQ3R, DRTA and MULTI-PASS) as you read one of your textbooks.

4. Form a study group for your next exam. Try using a cooperative learning format to guide your group's studies.

5. Locate a readability chart in a reading methods textbook. Then use the chart to determine the readability level of several passages in an elementary social studies textbook.

6. Interview several children. Ask them what they like and dislike about their social studies textbooks.

The earth as seen from the moon during the Apollo 11 space flight.

Photograph courtesy of the National Aeronautics and Space Assn. (NASA).

chapter 15

Supporting Themes

Social studies can be the key to unlocking a world of interest.

*(Grace Heckard, social studies method student)**

- describe each of the five topics presented in this chapter
- identify ways you can use the ideas to enhance social studies lessons

*Reprinted with permission of Grace Heckard.

INTRODUCTION

As you continue in your professional career you will be confronted with a number of new and recurring social studies themes. The school day is filled with many instructional demands, often more than you feel you can address. Any additional demands may seem overwhelming. Yet rather than create additional work for you, many of the themes will help you update and enhance your teaching competencies.

This chapter introduces you to five of these themes. They are: multicultural education, global education, law-related education, computers, and critical thinking. The chapter does not present an in-depth analysis of these themes because of space limitations and the relatively greater importance of the other topics presented in this text.

As you continue your professional development you will be exposed to these themes and have opportunities to implement them in your classroom. You will learn more about them through your education courses, school workshops, interactions with peer teachers, and your professional reading. The themes are important, but they do not replace the initial importance of developing effective planning, teaching, and evaluation abilities.

MULTICULTURAL EDUCATION

I recall supervising a student teacher in a multicultural first-grade classroom. During my first visit I noticed that none of the children in the room could be classified as members of America's white middle class. What really made me take notice was that I had difficulty pronouncing many of the children's names. If America is a melting pot of cultures, it was certainly evident in this classroom.

The composition of many American classrooms includes a diversity of cultures. The number of children representing ethnic minorities has increased to the point that in many urban areas minority children have become the majority. With the recent influx of immigrants and refugees, many of these children do not speak English. In addition to children with ethnic and language differences, a growing number of children are now coming to school from an entirely different culture, a culture of poverty. To be an effective teacher you must understand your students and adapt instruction to meet their needs.

Cultural influences affecting behavior include race, social class, gender, religion, and geographic location. Sex-role behaviors, attitudes toward authority figures, means of expressing emotions, and many school behaviors are aspects of our lives influenced by culture.

Children's behaviors in school and their achievement are affected by their culture. Some children begin kindergarten well prepared for the demands of school. Their culture has provided them with positive attitudes toward learning, they have developed an ability to work individually, and they have been immersed in language-rich environments. These cultural influences provide children with many of the attitudes and readiness skills that will help them succeed. Many other children bring different sets of cultural values to school—values that inhibit their ability to succeed in school.

To become an effective teacher you must understand the complex and subtle influences that culture exerts on children. You must also develop an understanding of how culturally induced behaviors and values affect your students' academic and social progress in school. Finally, you must develop the ability to adapt instruction to meet the personal needs of children within your classroom.

If our task is to prepare youngsters so they can solve the problems they will encounter, we must teach them how to work together. We must include multicultural education in the school's curriculum.

Teachers teach a variety of types of students. They must be sensitive to the students' needs.
Photograph by Laimute E. Druskis.

Multicultural Education Goals

Multicultural education is a term used to describe the relationships between culture and education. Multicultural education programs usually have three primary goals. First, they attempt to sensitize teachers to the effects that cultural differences have on children's learning. A second goal is to help children develop pride in their cultural heritage. The third goal is to help all children develop an understanding and appreciation of the contributions made by members of other cultures.

Multicultural education programs profess many of the democratic values and beliefs included in the NCSS Task Force's (1989) scope and sequence

document. For example, children should develop positive attitudes about tolerance, the rights of others, compassion, liberty, dignity, equal opportunity, justice,
freedom of expression, and working for the common good. By helping children
develop an understanding and appreciation of these concepts, children are more
likely to become ideal citizens—much like the "good person" you described in the
eulogy activity in Chapter 1.

The discussion in the following section will help you understand the goals
of multicultural education programs as they relate to the needs of children. Specific
suggestions and activities will be presented.

Teacher Sensitivity. You must be prepared to meet the demands of
teaching children from different cultures. An understanding and an accepting
attitude is your first challenge. Since you have been successful in college you
have demonstrated values and attitudes that may conflict with the values and
attitudes of children whom you will teach. For example, you likely have
middle-class values toward education. Many children from the lower social
classes do not have the same values toward education. They may be in school
because it will help them get a job when they finish high school. Or, they may
be in school because of compulsory attendance laws. When you ask middle-
class children what they will do after high school they usually indicate *the*
college or university they hope to attend. When you ask children from the lower
socioeconomic class, attending college is less likely to be mentioned. Children's
values toward education frequently differ and will have an effect on your own
students' school behaviors.

The differences in values is also illustrated by an activity conducted by a
primary-grade teacher. The teacher asked her students to draw a picture of
what they wanted to do when they became adults. One child left the paper
blank. When asked why the paper was left blank, the child responded that he
was going to be "like my mom and do nothin' " His middle-class teacher was
shocked by this response because she assumed that all children had middle-
class aspirations.

Subtle attitudes affect the way teachers respond to children. Teachers
tend to react positively to students who are like themselves and less positively to those who are perceived as different. These differences may be racial,
religious, gender, or socioeconomic differences. If you understand the possibility of this occurring you can consciously attempt to overcome the limitations of your biases.

It was mentioned earlier that classroom instructional practices in most
elementary schools can be characterized as teacher directed. The teacher
talks to students and then assigns seatwork activities. Students are most
often expected to work individually. Individual work and individual
achievement represent middle-class values. However, many children come
from cultures in which cooperation and collaborative efforts are valued.
These children have difficulty doing their "own" work because they have
been raised to help one another. As a teacher you have demonstrated an

ability to succeed on your own and you may encounter difficulties when you expect that all children work individually.

Sensitivity to the needs of your students is the first step in becoming a professional capable of meeting the diverse needs of all students. While you must be sensitive, you cannot have lower expectations for children because of ethnic, gender, or social class differences. You must maintain high expectations for each and every youngster. Every child can learn, every child can succeed. You should have empathy for children, but do not arbitrarily lower your expectations. Lowering expectations is a form of condescension, discrimination, and prejudice.

Lack of Role Models. The lack of appropriate role models for children from minority cultures is a second problem addressed by multicultural education programs. Children need positive role models if they are to become well-socialized adults. Many positive role models are available for white middle- class children. Unfortunately, our schools have been criticized for not providing enough positive role models for children from minority groups.

The lack of role models occurs at two levels. First, there is a shortage of teachers and administrators representing different minority groups. Further, the number of minority members entering teaching is declining. Thus, minority children are deprived of opportunities to see representatives from their cultural group serving as educators.

The second aspect of the role-model problem emerges from the curriculum materials used in our schools. Curriculum materials have been criticized because they do not include enough references about the contributions made by members of minority cultures. When children study history, they study the contributions of middle- and upper-middle-class white men. Further, curriculum materials usually present concepts from a white middle-class perspective. They fail to relate concepts important to children from nonwhite, non-middle-class cultures. One effect is that children from nonwhite cultures do not have positive role models to emulate. A second effect is that children from a variety of nonwhite, non-middle-class cultures have difficulty understanding the concepts because of the examples used to develop the concepts.

One of the primary purposes of most multicultural education programs is to help children develop this pride. To do this, children need opportunities to see members of their cultural group acting as positive role models. We need to encourage more members of minority groups to become involved in education. We also need to use curriculum materials that present the contributions of individuals from minority groups. If your social studies materials do not include proper representation, you will need to utilize supplementary materials.

Understanding Others. The third goal of multicultural education programs is to help all children develop a respect and appreciation for the rights, welfare, and contributions of individuals from other cultures. Many classrooms have no minority children. To help children develop respect and appreciation for others, you will need to select curriculum materials that portray the contributions of other cultures. You should also adapt the curriculum to include topics and themes that will enhance children's knowledge of other people. For example, when studying Thanksgiving, include the role and contributions of the Indians. If studying the settlement of the frontier, examine the contributions of women, blacks, and Orientals. If studying community helpers in the health professions, include references to female and minority doctors as well as male nurses.

Numerous books have been written about multicultural education. The discussion in this chapter is designed to introduce you to the concept. There is no magic involved in being an effective multicultural teacher. The task is challenging, but rewarding. You must take time to understand the needs and interests of your students, you must work hard to plan effective lessons for them, you must work hard to acknowledge and overcome your own biases, and you must work diligently to include contributions made by people from other cultures.

Teaching Strategies

A knowledge and appreciation of children's cultural differences is not enough to improve your effectiveness. To be effective with children representing a variety of cultures you will need to develop a flexible teaching style. Several useful suggestions are described below.

Sleeter and Grant (1988) suggested that teachers demonstrate variety and flexibility by adapting instruction to meet children's learning styles, adapting instruction to meet children's skill levels, encouraging children to develop critical-thinking skills, and involving children in a variety of cooperative learning activities. They also encouraged teachers to modify the curriculum for children. Curriculum modifications include relating contributions of cultural groups to the concepts you teach, encouraging children to consider alternative views about issues, and relating concepts to children's schemes.

Stone (1986) reviewed research studies related to multicultural education. She concluded that teachers can meet the educational needs of children by involving the children in small group work, cooperative learning activities, and peer-tutoring opportunities. She stated that these types of activities nurture interactions among children, which provide them with more positive views of children from other cultures. She also indicated that in a small-group setting the children have opportunities to master the information in a less stressful environment.

Teaching Activities

The teaching suggestions described above are rather general. There are a number of specific activities you can do with your students that will help them become more understanding and accepting of others. Morrison (1984) suggested a variety of activities for developing multicultural awareness in young children. The first ten suggestions in this section were adapted from Morrison. Children in the primary grades will find them enjoyable and worthwhile. Many of Morrison's activities can be adapted for use with older children. Morrison's ideas are followed by additional suggestions.

Puzzles. You can make puzzles for children by first mounting pictures of people from different cultures on oak tag or cardboard. Then cut the mounted pictures into fairly large pieces. Children can align the pieces in the correct way to reconstruct the pictures. This activity becomes more useful if you select pictures illustrating people from different cultures who are positive role models.

Puppets. Children can make puppets representing people from a variety of cultures. Children can then develop and present puppet plays.

Stamp and Postcard Collections. Children can collect stamps and postcards from different countries. They can also collect stamps illustrating members of minority groups and their contributions. Children can classify the stamps and postcards by cultural group. If no stamps are available for a particular influential person, children can design their own stamps and postcards.

Family Trees. Children can make family trees representing their families and they can make a classroom family tree.

Artifact Collection. Children can bring artifacts representing different cultures to school. They may set aside an area of the classroom for a "cultural museum."

Easy Food Recipes. Children can prepare recipes representing foods from other cultures. Children can consider how foods from other cultures represent the four food groups.

Arts and Crafts. Children can make arts and crafts materials that represent aspects of other cultures. You should provide introductory remarks in which you tell children the cultural significance of the arts and crafts projects.

Songs and Dances. Children will enjoy participating in song and dance activities. Again, take a few moments to help children learn the significance of the songs and dances.

Maps. Make a large world map and place pins in the countries from which children's families emigrated. You may then use yarn or string and connect the countries of origin and the children's current location.

Class Mural. Children can make a class mural depicting positive aspects of cultures studied throughout the year.

Ethnic Graphs.   Children can collect information about the ethnic composition of the school or classroom and graph the data. Children might collect additional information and develop a cultural data base using the computer.

Community Ethnic Histories.   Children can participate in oral history projects in which they collect information about the contributions of different ethnic groups.

Moral Dilemmas.   As you read literature to children you can pause after reading situations in which prejudice or discrimination occur. Ask students to describe why the situations are objectionable and allow them to propose alternate behaviors.

Current Events.   Children can identify news stories (from television, newspapers, or magazines) depicting prejudice or discrimination. Discussion of these situations can follow the moral dilemma or classroom meeting procedures described in Chapter 13.

Phone Book Foods.   Have children look in the Yellow Pages of the telephone book and identify ethnic restaurants. Children can then graph the number of different types of restaurants and locate the restaurants on a city map. They might also assume the roles of commercial real estate developers and identify suitable locations for new ethnic restaurants.

Inquiry.   Children can identify a topic related to multicultural education and conduct an inquiry investigation into the topic. Topics might include events, people, prejudices, contributions, inventions, and neighborhoods. Chapter 9 described the inquiry process.

Contributions Scrapbook.   Children can develop a scrapbook of contributions made by individuals representing other cultures. Topics could include historical figures, scientific contributions, political contributions, and contributions to the social world.

Needs Chart.   Children can identify the manner in which they satisfy their basic needs. They can then collect information about the way other cultures satisfy basic needs and develop a chart to illustrate similarities and differences.

Analyze Children's Television Programs.   Children should watch typical Saturday morning children's TV programs and commercials. They should identify examples of stereotypical behaviors, the number of males and females portrayed, and the types of activities engaged in by the males and females.

Multicultural education can help you recognize and understand the differences contributing to your students' behaviors in school. With an understanding of children's needs and differences you can personalize instruction so each child is taught in the most appropriate way. You can utilize alternative teaching strategies and you can use a variety of curriculum materials. Personalizing instruction and materials will help your students succeed in school and develop a greater sense of pride in themselves. A good multicultural program will help children develop a greater understanding of the contributions made by other cultures. Finally, a good multicultural education program can help you provide the best education for each of your students.

GLOBAL EDUCATION

Global education is a theme focusing on helping children learn to become world citizens. Our world is "shrinking" because of rapid travel, instantaneous communication, and economic interdependence. Rosecrance (1986) indicated that interactions among countries have changed. The world has been transformed from a collection of territorial nations to a collection of countries that have become "trading states." In the past, international relations were largely based on policies of territorial acquisition and territorial protection. The territorial-state concept is being replaced by policies focusing on international trade. In the future the ultimate success or failure of countries may well be their ability to develop interdependent trading relationships with other nations. Members of the European Economic Community (Common Market) have done this, and they are implementing steps to become increasingly more interdependent.

A picture of the earth from Apollo 16 on the moon.

Photograph courtesy of the National Aeronautics and Space Assn. (NASA).

Countries now rely on other nations for trade, economic development, security, and health. What the citizens of one country do often affects people in other countries. Acid rain, nuclear waste, human rights violations, hunger, poverty, disease, natural resource depletion, ozone depletion, the greenhouse effect, terrorism, war, and the arms race are major topics affecting the well-being of every citizen of the world.

Hamilton (1986) illustrated our interdependence using disease as an example. Many people in underdeveloped countries live in unsanitary conditions. Their health is poor, and their resistance to disease is low. Conditions are ripe for the development and spread of diseases such as influenza and AIDS. Hamilton stated that all of the major flu epidemics in the United States originated in other countries. Most of these epidemics originated in regions of abject poverty. People in the developed countries are linked to developing countries in many ways, including disease.

The earth has been compared to a spaceship traveling through the universe. Like a spaceship, the earth has a number of finite resources that must be protected if the inhabitants are to survive. To help protect a spaceship's resources every occupant must share responsibility for the welfare of the craft. To protect the earth's resources, every person on earth must protect the earth's resources. As inhabitants of spaceship earth, we are dependent on one another.

Bickering between countries, isolationist policies, ignorance, and refusal to address issues affecting the planet will lead to a reduced quality of life for everyone. Thus, global education programs have been advocated to help prepare children for their roles as citizens of the world.

Guidelines

Programs designed to help prepare children for a future in which they can function as citizens of the world should include several goals. Global education programs should help children understand that all people in the world are dependent on each other and must be treated as equals. Further, programs should help children realize that they are members of various communities: local, national, and international.

Gibbons and Neuman (1985/1986) identified four themes that should be incorporated into a global education curriculum. The first theme is that we are all global citizens sharing responsibility for our world. The second theme is family membership. We are all members of the human family. We must understand and care for each other. The third theme is stewardship. We share responsibility for managing the earth's resources. The final theme is developing attitudes of peaceful cooperation. We must resolve conflicts and develop our potential through peaceful means.

Teaching Suggestions

Children need opportunities to learn about global interdependence. The following suggestions will help your students develop an understanding of the interdependence between themselves and people in other parts of the world.

Inquiry. Children should identify problems facing them and then investigate the causes of the problems. As children investigate they should attempt to develop solutions that they can implement.

Home Audit. Have students prepare a list of various items in their homes and determine the country in which the items were made (or assembled). Children can organize their findings and make classroom charts and graphs illustrating the origins of household items.

What Would Happen If? Children can select an item produced in another area of the world and predict how their lives would change if the item were no longer available. Natural resources used in the production of other materials, such as crude oil, could also be considered.

Flu Flow. Children can map the movement of a major flu outbreak.

Pen Pals. You might have your students establish pen-pal relationships with youngsters from another country. As children correspond with one another they have opportunities to discover how their lives are similar and how dependent they are on each other.

Word Origins. Many of the words used in one country originated in another country. Children can be assigned words used in their lives and identify the origins of those words. They may then use a map to locate the places from which the words originated.

Children can also do the reverse of this. Many libraries carry foreign-language newspapers. Students could scan these newspapers and locate words originating in their own country.

Balance of Trade. Children could make import- export charts depicting major products imported and exported from their home country. They may also map the origins and destinations of the imports and exports.

Reverse Roles. Select a current or historical event and have children describe the event from the perspective of a person in another country. They may role-play the reversed roles.

International Business. Identify and investigate a business in your community doing business with other countries. Bankers, farm implement dealers, farmers, car dealers, grocers, and restaurant owners are suggested resources.

Children can also identify local companies involved in international business. The companies can then be classified by the type of business conducted and the major countries with which they do business.

International Job Search. Children can explore job opportunities in other countries. They can study the help-wanted section of the classified ads as they identify jobs requiring employees to work with people from other countries. They could then write a want ad for an ideal international employee.

Current Events Bulletin Board. Children could collect articles about international events affecting their lives. These can be posted on a bulletin board.

Solution Posters. Children can identify a problem and develop posters illustrating possible solutions.

The International Pencil. Wolken (1984) described an elementary geography activity requiring children to discover interdependence involved in making a pencil. The manufacturing of pencils requires natural resources, production processes, workers, people, materials, and equipment. A few of the production resources and processes are listed in Table 15–1.

Children can locate the possible sources of natural resources used in the production of a pencil. They can also make a list of occupations involved in pencil production and examine the quality of the workers' lives. Children can do a similar activity for other products.

The world is rapidly changing. People and nations are becoming more interdependent on one another. If a country and its people are to exist successfully, its citizens will need to develop an outlook that a global education can provide.

Table 15–1 Making a Pencil

Natural Resources	Workers
Wood	Loggers
Lead (graphite, clay, candelilla wax)	Miners
Brass (zinc and copper)	Truck drivers
Eraser (pumice, sulfur chloride)	Factory workers
Lacquer (castor oil)	Dock workers
	Sailors
Processes	**Other Support**
Mining	Fuel
Sawmills	Registering ships
Manufacturing	Chainsaws

Source: Wolken, L. (Nov./Dec. 1984). The international pencil: Elementary level unit on global interdependence. *Journal of Geography, 83,* (6), pp. 290–293. Reprinted with permission of the National Council for Geographic Education.

LAW-RELATED EDUCATION

Law-related education (LRE) is a term now being used to describe programs about children's relationships with the law. LRE introduces students to the legal system and the political structure. It teaches them how the law affects them and how they affect the law.

Law-related education has been described as a three-part program that encompasses content, activities, and resources. The content contained in most LRE curricula helps children learn about the foundations of democratic government. Such programs help children learn about government and the principles upon which our legal system is based. Topics include freedom, authority, justice, privacy, equality, and rule of law. Further, children learn about their rights and are encouraged to develop a greater sense of responsibility. As children learn these

Developing responsible citizens is a major goal of social studies and law-related education programs.

Photograph by Marc Anderson.

concepts they study topics that include juvenile law, the role of the police and courts, and their own roles as responsible citizens.

The second aspect of most law related education programs is active child involvement. A number of excellent curriculum guides are available through local and state bar associations and police organizations. Each of these curriculum guides includes activities that actively involve children. As children study the law they role-play, investigate, conduct mock trials, visit courtrooms and police stations, consider moral dilemmas, and engage in lively discussions.

The third aspect of LRE programs is community resources. Law- related education projects are supported by several organizations representing people in the legal profession. Bar associations and police fraternal organizations support LRE programs and have developed a list of people in the community who can present programs to your students. Lawyers, police officers, probation officers, juvenile judges, legislators, and community leaders have been recruited to serve as resources.

Each state has an office and a coordinator for LRE materials and programs within that state. To determine your state's LRE coordinator, contact the American Bar Association Special Committee on Youth Education for Citizenship. The address and telephone number are:

750 N. Lakeshore Drive
Chicago, IL 60611
(312) 988-5725

Participation in an LRE program helps children develop a better understanding of the law and the legal system. Participation can help children develop more positive attitudes about themselves and the ideals of democratic governance.

Law-related education and the supporting materials are exciting for three reasons. First, LRE can be readily integrated into most elementary-school curriculums. If you are a kindergarten teacher studying community helpers you can include the roles of the police, lawmakers, judges, and attorneys. If you are a third- grade teacher studying your city you can study your city's form of government, the role the city plays in supporting its citizens, and the responsibilities of its citizens. Similar topics can be studied as children study their state, the national government, and foreign countries. Regardless of the specific topic, LRE programs emphasize the development of personal responsibility and an attitude of justice.

A second appealing characteristic of LRE projects and materials is that they overcome several of the limitations of the textbooks. LRE materials are designed to involve children actively and to provide time for them to study topics in greater depth. Further, because the topics relate the law to children's lives, youngsters find the materials and activities more motivating.

A final strength is the collaboration occurring between educators and community leaders. LRE programs reflect an impressive level of cooperation between professionals in the legal community and those in the education community. It is gratifying to find a segment of the community interested in actively supporting the work of teachers.

Suggested Activities

The following activities are designed to help you and your students become actively involved in law related education. A more comprehensive set of activities can be obtained through your state's LRE contact person or your local bar association.

Classroom Rules. Perhaps the best way to involve students in the study of law is to involve them in establishing their own classroom rules. Children should be encouraged to discuss the reasons for the rules as well as consequences for breaking the rules. The rules and consequences may be amended when necessary.

Classroom Bill of Rights. Self-governance and legal concepts are based on rights and responsibilities. You can have your students develop a better understanding of rights and responsibilities in society by allowing them to develop a classroom bill of rights and responsibilities. This list may be amended.

Classroom Constitution. The classroom's bill of rights and responsibilities can be made more formal by developing a classroom constitution.

Rule Comparison Chart. Children can make a chart illustrating the different rules required in different settings. For example, they could illustrate "rules for home" and "rules for school." Other sets of rules could relate to recess, lunchroom, church, sporting events, movie theater, and playing with friends.
Older children can chart types of laws made by different political entities. They could compare local, state, national, and international laws.

Comic Collage. Children can collect comics from the newspaper and make collages of comics illustrating characters breaking rules and characters obeying the rules. Children can then select one of the comics in which the character is breaking a rule and restructure the comic so the character follows the rule.

Rights and the Law Charts. Boles (1986) described an activity in which children identify the relationships among disagreements, rights, and laws. She recommended developing a chart with columns for each of these three headings. Children then identify disagreements that they witness, discuss rights involved in each disagreement, and then list or develop laws (rules) that apply to the disagreement.

Citizenship Review. Children should interview people and ask them to describe recent citizenship activities. Citizenship activities include: writing a letter of complaint, paying taxes, obtaining a driver's license, helping a friend or neighbor, voting, or working for a political candidate.

Fairy Tale Trials. The Colorado Department of Education developed a curriculum guide about the U.S. Constitution. The guide suggested conducting trials of characters performing misdeeds in fairy tales (Burns, 1987). Fairy tales can be read, illegal situations discussed, and students can judge the severity of the misdeed. Students might also propose alternatives, determine consequences for the characters, and identify parallel situations in their own lives.

Moral Dilemmas. As you read stories to children and as you encounter current events reports you may encourage children to discuss the dilemmas using the moral dilemma format described in Chapter 13.

Law-related education is a social studies theme that attempts to help children learn their rights and responsibilities as citizens in a democratic society. LRE programs are exciting because they actively involve children as they learn important democratic skills and concepts.

COMPUTERS AND SOCIAL STUDIES

Computers are emerging as an excellent instructional tool for elementary teachers. Social studies teachers can use computers for drill-and-practice activities, tutorials, simulations, and games. Computers can also be used as writing aids and data bases. This section of the chapter briefly describes ways to use computers to enhance social studies instruction.

Drill-and-Practice Exercises

Drill-and-practice computer programs are similar to drill-and-practice worksheets; they help children practice and master skills and information. Most drill-and-practice activities, including computer programs, require children to provide low-level cognitive responses to questions. Most drill-and-practice programs for elementary social studies are related to simple geography concepts such as states, capitals, and map reading.

While the number of good drill-and-practice programs is increasing, children quickly tire of such programs. Rather than purchase expensive software, your money may be better spent on programs that have a wider range of applications.

Tutorials

Tutorials are generally designed to teach skills and concepts to children. Most tutorials focus on economic concepts. However, an increasing number of tutorials are being developed for other social studies concepts. For example, *Unlocking the Map Code* by Rand McNally teaches geographical concepts to students in the upper elementary grades. Well-prepared tutorials can be educational and motivating.

Simulations

Simulations are classroom activities that have parallels with real-life situations. A number of computer simulations have been developed to help children actively participate in social studies.

Computers are excellent tools for the simulation process. A computer simulation can present a problem and allow students to indicate any one of several responses. The computer quickly responds to the children's input and provides them with a series of follow-up problems. *Oregon Trail* is a popular computer simulation. Children assume the roles of pioneers traveling to Oregon by wagon train. They are confronted with challenges and must make decisions that are representative of problems encountered by early pioneers.

A school computer lab. How can you use computers to teach social studies?

Photograph by Laimute E. Druskis.

Simulations are educational and motivating. While helping children learn about a topic, children are also developing problem-solving skills. Refer to Chapter 12 for a more thorough discussion of simulations and their benefits.

Games

More computer games are available for elementary age children than any other form of computer software. Computer games are highly motivating and well written. Further, they have attractive graphics. When an attractive game format is used in conjunction with an educational concept, learning becomes electrifying. Review Chapter 12 for a more detailed description of social studies games.

Writing Aids

Word processing is perhaps the most notable use of the microcomputers used in homes, schools, and offices. People now use computers like typewriters. To use a computer as a typewriter, insert a word-processing program into the computer, turn it on, and follow some relatively simple directions.

Entries can be edited, saved, and printed. Special programs are available to aid in the editing process. Many programs are available that will automatically check for spelling errors. Other programs will check for grammatical errors. There are even programs that will enable you to add graphic illustrations to your written material.

Requiring elementary-age students to type stories and reports into computers has several limitations. Most youngsters this age cannot type. If required to enter stories into a computer they could quickly become overwhelmed by the typing process. If this occurs, students will become frustrated and develop negative attitudes toward computers and the writing process.

Some children may, however, enjoy entering their own material into the computer, and they should be encouraged. Others will not enjoy this task. You can overcome this limitation by having an adult enter the information for them. Children can then use the computer as they edit their written material.

Primary-grade students enjoy typing their names and words they know on typewriters. They can be encouraged to enter words related to a social studies concept into a computer and then have their words printed. Definitions can be added.

While word processing may be too difficult for many younger students, excellent games and tutorials are available to help them learn keyboard skills. After developing basic keyboard skills the children might like to experiment with word processing as they prepare their social studies assignments.

Data Bases

A data base is like a file cabinet, a card file, a recipe book, and an almanac. A data base is an organized collection of facts and information. While business, industry, and government use data bases extensively, many teachers have yet to realize the beneficial uses of computer data bases.

Students in elementary grades can use data bases as part of their social studies classes. They can collect information, enter it into a data base program, and have the computer produce a graph. They can then examine the graph. By collecting different sets of data, students can compare a variety of graphs. While an adult may need to enter data for younger children, these youngsters are actively involved in collecting the data and examining the graphs produced by the computer. Older children can quickly learn to enter the data and print their own graphs.

Collis (1988) described several activities for elementary-school students. Her activities require children to use data base and graphing programs. Several of her ideas are described below.

Primary-grade children can use data base and graphing programs to store and illustrate information about their lives. Children should collect information about themselves. Topics can include month of birth, favorite holiday, number of pets, types of houses in which they live, vacation sites, and vacation activities. The teacher collects the information from each child, develops a data base template (format), and enters the information for each child into the data base.

The teacher can then use the computer to determine the number of children with birthdays in a certain month, the number of those with the same favorite holiday, and the total number of pets owned by class members. As a follow-up activity, Collis suggested printing graphs of the children's data.

As children get older they can begin creating other types of data bases. Collis suggested involving fifth-grade children in developing a data base of presidents. Children should take time to decide the types of data they want to include in the data base. Once they have decided the specific types of data they want to include they can develop a template for entering the data into the data base. For example, children might include the first and last names, date of birth, date of inauguration, number of years in office, home state, and party affiliation. Children can then be assigned a specific president and collect the data on that individual. Once the data have been entered, students can have the data presented in a variety of ways. For example, they could compare the number of Republican and Democrat presidents elected since 1900.

Data bases may be established to reinforce topics presented in the social studies curriculum. Many social studies curriculums are organized along the expanding environment scope and sequence model. Young children study about themselves, their families, and their neighborhoods. Older children study their city, their state, their country, and other countries. Children can be involved in developing data bases at each level. Primary-grade children can develop data bases about their families and neighborhoods. Third-grade children might develop a city data base. Older children might develop data bases for states or countries.

Computers offer promise for creative social studies teachers. The computer is a tool that will allow you to provide your students with alternative activities and materials. Consider the many possible uses of computers and begin integrating their use into your social studies classroom.

CRITICAL THINKING

A recent report titled "Crossroads in American Education" (National Assessment of Educational Progress, 1989) examined changes in the quality of American education in the past twenty years. The report concluded that gains had been made in basic skill instruction, such as performing simple computations and comprehending simple reading passages. However, the report stated that the nation's school children are largely unable to perform tasks requiring them to think and reason, even at moderate difficulty levels.

The report recommended changing the traditional methods used to teach children. Rather than relying excessively on teacher talk, textbooks, and workbooks, teachers must begin actively involving children in learning activities. Such activities should include discussion teams and cooperative learning strategies. Teachers will need to become less authoritarian and children will need to become more actively involved in learning. If our schools are to improve children's thinking and reasoning skills, current instructional practices must be modified.

Several factors have contributed to our children's inability to think critically. In the late 1970s and during the early 1980s there was a renewed emphasis on teaching the basics. An emphasis on higher-level, critical-thinking skills was neglected. A second factor limiting the development of children's critical-thinking skills has been typical teaching methods. Many classroom activities are teacher directed. Children do not need to think. Third, teachers usually test for mastery using low-level, recall questions. Children focus on facts and low-level skills.

The fourth factor relates to the prevailing view of social studies education, which is citizenship transmission. This tradition emphasizes transmitting information and values to children. Children are told what to learn, what to think, and what to value. Little opportunity is provided for youngsters to question the teacher's statements, the content presented, or the values taught.

Children's cognitive and moral development levels are a fifth factor. Elementary-grade children have difficulty challenging authority figures and questioning information presented in textbooks because of developmental limitations.

Teacher-education programs are a sixth factor. If children are to become critical thinkers, preservice and in-service teacher-education programs must provide adequate training in critical thinking. As a result of these limitations, children are not developing critical-thinking abilities.

To remedy this, social studies lessons should challenge children, engage them in analysis of decisions and accepted practices, and encourage them to engage in problem-solving activities.

Characteristics of Critical Thinking

As you continue your professional development you will encounter various descriptions of critical thinking. You may find these descriptions confusing because they tend to use a variety of terms to describe similar concepts.

While there are different critical-thinking models, it is necessary to describe critical thinking within the context of social studies. Social studies is designed to help people develop an increasingly complex, sophisticated, and accurate understanding of their relationship with the social, physical, and spiritual world. The primary method of investigating social science phenomena is inquiry, a variation of the scientific method. A definition of critical thinking must therefore be aligned with the nature of social studies and the inquiry process.

Dewey (1933) provided a useful definition that encompasses both concerns. From Dewey's perspective critical thinking is defined as, "Active, persistent, and careful consideration of any belief or supposed form of knowledge in the light of the grounds that support it and the further conclusions to which it tends..." (p. 33). Critical thinking is an analytical, questioning process by which people consider the assumptions and factual basis of ideas. It is also a process by which people consider the probable implications of particular actions. For social studies educators the inquiry process constitutes critical thinking.

Effective teachers were described as reflective thinkers. They analyzed the effectiveness of their teaching as a means of improving their skills. Business people use critical thinking as they analyze markets and develop appropriate marketing strategies. Effective citizens utilize critical thinking when analyzing political candidates and issues.

Critical thinking (inquiry) is a sophisticated process that relies on two subprocesses: *data-acquisition skills* and *data-evaluation skills*. Data-acquisition skills are the most basic skills and are used repeatedly when children are involved in critical-thinking activities. Data-acquisition skills appropriate in an elementary-school curriculum include observing, collecting, and classifying information. When decisions are needed, people must acquire appropriate information. Elementary-grade children need numerous opportunities to collect information related to problems, concerns, topics of interest, and events from the present and the past.

Data-evaluation skills are used to determine worth and accuracy of information. Data evaluation requires frequent use of higher-level thinking processes including the following:

- determining factual basis
- determining affective contexts (bias, opinions, attitudes, values)
- determining relevance
- analyzing the logical relationships (assumptions and conclusions)
- determining validity (quality of sources, objectivity, technical correctness, currency)

Students in the elementary grades should have opportunities to analyze information, arguments, and statements to determine whether they are based on facts or opinions. They should have opportunities to determine whether information is relevant or irrelevant. They should also have opportunities to identify the parts of an argument, the reasons used in an argument, and the validity of conclusions. Finally, children should evaluate the accuracy of facts and the credibility of the sources.

Table 15–2 illustrates the relationships among the three levels. It also includes a listing of subskills.

Table 15–2 Thinking Skills for Elementary Children

Inquiry

- recognize and define problem
- formulate hypotheses
- consider implications of hypotheses
- test hypotheses
- develop conclusions

Data Evaluation

- determine factual basis
- determine relevance
- analyze logical relationships
- determine affective contexts
- determine validity

Data Acquisition

- observing
- collecting
- classifying

Improving Critical Thinking

The typical instructional routines in elementary classrooms do not contribute to the development of children's critical thinking. Teachers must alter their own views of the educational process if they hope to help children become critical thinkers. They should provide opportunities for children to identify and investigate problems, challenge them with questions related to divergent thinking and higher-level thought processes, and model critical thinking. Critical thinking develops slowly; therefore patience is necessary. There are excellent critical-thinking programs on the market that can help you teach critical thinking.

Maxwell (1987) synthesized a 1985 thinking-skill report developed by Marzano and Hutchins. The resulting eight suggestions, described below, are general guidelines you may find helpful.

Compare. When new information is presented, students should compare the new information with their existing schemes. This ensures that children understand the new information prior to using the information to analyze and solve problems.

Evaluate. Critical thinkers need to learn methods to evaluate information. Children should be taught to ask four questions about information and statements of fact or opinion. Is it unusual? Is it common knowledge? If not common knowledge, what is the proof? If there is no proof, is the statement reliable?

Systematic Problem Solving. Children must develop their problem-solving skills. They should approach problems systematically and follow the steps in the inquiry process.

Guided Imagery. Guided imagery should be used to help teach difficult information. Guided imagery is a mnemonic process in which children imagine the steps, processes, and procedures involved in an event or experience. Many children and teachers develop stories that help them imagine the information. As they imagine an event or experience they should be encouraged to imagine what each of their senses would experience.

Elaboration. The fifth suggestion is to teach students to elaborate. Elaboration requires children to consider additional aspects of a situation. It also requires children to substantiate their statements and embellish their ideas. They appear to be satisfied responding with short, low-level answers. Encouraging them to embellish and substantiate each point will be challenging.

Invent. Children should be encouraged to be inventive. They may invent new products, alternative solutions, or alternative means of advertising products. This is a divergent-thinking process requiring them to use the processes of analysis, synthesis, and evaluation. The projects listed in Chapter 9 provide opportunities for children to be inventive.

Knowledge Base. You must ensure that children know how to perform the required procedures. If you are teaching your students to compare maps and make inferences, they must understand how to read maps. Similarly, if you want your students to analyze information contained on a graph, they must know how to read graphs. If you want students to inquire, you will need to guide them through the inquiry process.

Set Goals. Encourage children to set goals. When children set goals they are likely to learn more quickly and develop a greater sense of achievement. With a sense of what they want to accomplish in a given time frame, children are less likely to dwell on irrelevant information. This has another benefit. Children must analyze information critically to determine its relevance to their own purposes.

Suggestions

The general guidelines presented in the preceding section provide a foundation on which you can develop your ability to nurture critical-thinking skills. This section offers several specific suggestions.

ALERT The ALERT procedure (Allen, Wright, & Laminack, 1988) requires children to examine commercial messages from sources like television, radio, and magazines critically. Commercials use a variety of bold and subtle strategies to convince youngsters to purchase products. Children are naive and easy targets for advertisers. Although inundated with commercials, young people seldom take the time to consider critically the influences of commercials.

ALERT is an acronym representing five steps in the procedure. *Advance organizer* is the first step. The advance organizer serves as an introduction to the activity. During the introduction children are told to listen for key words, identify the product being advertised, and consider special effects used to sell the product. *Listen* is the second step. The children either listen to the commercial, view the commercial or read the commercial, depending on the type of media used. As they preview the commercial they should attempt to identify the key points described during the advance organizer step.

Explain is the third step. Children consider and explain the explicit and implicit messages contained in the commercial. *Restate/read* is the fourth step. Children restate the message of the commercial in their own words. Young children may dictate a language-experience story at this point and then read their stories. *Test/think/talk* is the final step. After viewing and discussing a commercial children may conduct independent tests of the products to determine the validity of the claims made in the commercial. If testing is not feasible, children might interview people who have used the product to determine the validity of claims made in the commercial.

TV vs. Print. Study a television report about a news event. Identify facts and impressions. Compare the TV account with an account presented in a newspaper or news magazine. How are the images and moods different?

Atmosphere. Barell, Liebmann, and Sigel (1988) described a critical-thinking program emphasizing the classroom environment. The environment was designed to foster the development of children's autonomy and concern for others. By encouraging autonomy and concern for others, children became more likely to consider alternative points of view.

The environment also nurtured positive attitudes about the importance of critical thinking, persistence, and cooperation. Within this environment, children were encouraged to develop behaviors related to listening, goal setting, and decision making. Additional concepts present in this environment were self-directed learning, problem solving, a sense of community, and inquiry. Of course, an atmosphere like this can exist only if the teacher has appropriate attitudes and teaching competencies.

Cooperative Learning. Cooperative learning has been described in other chapters in this textbook. Cooperative learning provides children with opportunities to work in small groups on specific tasks. As children interact with one another they present ideas, listen to the ideas of others, and have the freedom to modify their ideas.

Critical thinking is encouraged at two levels. First, teachers can assign problem-solving tasks to cooperative learning groups. As children investigate the problems and solutions they are engaged in critical-thinking activities. At a second level, critical thinking is nurtured as children test their ideas on one another in the relative security of their small peer group. Children are more likely to propose alternative, "risky" ideas in small groups rather than in a large-group setting.

Questioning. The relationship between the types of questions teachers ask and the types of responses children provide was described in Chapters 6 and 11. When children are exposed to teachers who ask a greater proportion of higher-level questions, they are more likely to provide higher-level responses. When teachers utilize the concept of wait time, children have time to formulate more complex responses.

Strategic Thinking. Koch (1989) described strategic thinking as a variation of the inquiry process. Like inquiry, strategic thinking requires children to analyze tasks, plan their work, and use appropriate learning strategies. While inquiry generally requires children to proceed sequentially through the steps, strategic thinking encourages children to begin with any of the steps and proceed through the steps in any order they determine useful.

Concept Attainment. Conceptualizing is an aspect of acquiring and evaluating information. Concept-development strategies described in Chapter 10 reinforce critical thinking. As concepts are presented, children should have opportunities to consider examples and common attributes. Children should also have opportunities to classify the examples and the attributes to discover how concepts are interrelated. Finally, children should consider the value range of the specific attributes. This encourages critical thinking because of the overlapping nature of concepts and their attributes.

Visual Representations. In several sections of this textbook, including Chapter 14, the use of visual representations was recommended. Semantic maps and time lines are examples of visual representations. When teaching concepts, you should give your students opportunities to develop their own means of representing relationships between concepts and information they are studying. As children develop visual representations they must analyze relationships, identify main points, and illustrate how items are related and interrelated.

Metacognitive Strategies. Metacognition is a process by which people monitor and regulate their own thinking processes. For example, as children read a passage they should relate what they are reading to what they know. They should consider what they expect to occur. As children study for tests they should also utilize metacognitive strategies. Studying for a test requiring memorization requires different cognitive strategies from, say, an essay test. Successful learners have a repertoire of thinking strategies and can shift from one strategy to the next when necessary.

Metacognition helps children gain self-control and responsibility for their learning. With a greater sense of control over the learning process, coupled with mastery of several metacognitive strategies, children are better prepared to consider tasks requiring critical thinking.

Current teaching practices must be modified if critical thinking is to be nurtured in schools. The use of a variety of the teaching strategies described in this textbook will enable you to nurture your children's mastery of basic skills and their ability to think critically. This section of the chapter was included to provide you with an overview of critical thinking and ways to encourage your students to become critical thinkers. If you are a child-centered teacher and you ask your students to consider thought-provoking applications of concepts taught in social studies, you will nurture their reasoning and critical-thinking abilities.

SUMMARY

There are many themes vying for inclusion in the social studies curriculum. They will not require you to teach more information or spend more time in an already busy schedule. Rather, these themes are important and should be considered as means of improving your teaching.

Multicultural education, global education, law-related education, computers, and critical thinking are topics that will enhance social studies. You can integrate concepts related to each of these topics into your social studies curriculum and enliven your social studies lessons.

SUGGESTED ACTIVITIES

1. Review the cultural values categories described in Chapter 5. How can the cultural values described by Kluckhohn be used to improve multicultural education programs?

2. Examine the scope and sequence chart in an elementary social studies textbook. Identify topics that would readily allow you to integrate global and law-related education.

3. Call your local bar association or your state's LRE coordinator. Request sample materials, review the materials, and adapt a textbook lesson to include the LRE materials.

4. Modify the international pencil activity and outline a lesson using another commonly used item.

5. Review several computer programs for possible use in social studies. Games, simulations, data bases, and word-processing programs for children should be reviewed. "Mess about" with them to get a good feel for their uses in your classroom.

6. Review the critical-thinking model illustrated in Table 15–2. Examine a portion of the teacher's guide to determine how many of the attributes of critical thinking are reinforced and developed.

7. Review several children's commercials and identify possible ways to use the ALERT procedure. Consider the words and special effects used to sell the products.

8. Describe the relationships between inquiry, concept attainment, discussion, role playing, and simulation activities and the skills involved in critical thinking.

REFERENCES

Allen, E. G., Wright, J. P., & Laminack, L. L. (1988). Using language experience to ALERT pupils' critical thinking skills. *The Reading Teacher, 41,* 904–910.

Andrews, J. L. (1988). Putting America on the map: The voyage of Columbus. *Learning 88, 17,* 64–65.

Armstrong, D. G., & Savage, T. V. (1974). *Who fired that shot?* Unpublished manuscript, Texas A & M University, College Station, TX.

ASCD (1989). *Resolutions 1989.* Available from Association for Supervision and Curriculum Development, Alexandria, VA.

Baker, L., & Van Cleaf, D. W. (1988). Discrepant events: The element of surprise. *Teaching K-8, 19,* 60–62.

Barell, J., Liebmann, R., & Sigel, I. (1988). Fostering thoughtful self-direction in students. *Educational Leadership, 45,* 14–17.

Barr, R. D., Barth, J. L., & Shermis, S. S. (1977). *Defining the social studies.* Arlington, VA: National Council for the Social Studies.

Baumrind, D. (1967). Child care practices anteceding three patterns of preschool behavior. *Genetic Psychology Monographs, 75,* 43–88.

———. (1971). Current patterns of parental authority. *Developmental Psychology Monographs. 4*(1, Pt. 2.).

Bennett, W. J. (1986). *First lessons.* Washington, DC: U.S. Department of Education.

Berliner, D. C. (1984). The half-full glass: A review of research on teaching. In P. Hosford (Ed.), *Using what we know about teaching* (pp. 51–77). Alexandria, VA: Association for Supervision and Curriculum Development.

Bloom, B. S. (1984). The search for methods of group instruction as effective as one-to-one tutoring. *Educational Leadership, 41,* 4–17.

Bloom, B. S., Engelhart, M. D., Furst, E. J., Hill, W. H., & Krathwohl, D. R. (1956). *Taxonomy of educational objectives. The classification of education goals: Handbook 1. Cognitive domain.* New York: Longmans, Green.

Boles, W. (1986). *The Bill of Rights* (Teacher's Guide). Lincoln: Nebraska Committee for the Humanities.

Bredekamp, S., & Shepard, L. (1989). How best to protect children from inappropriate school expectations, practices, and policies. *Young Children, 44,* 14–24.

Brophy, J., & Good, T. L. (1986). Teacher behavior and student achievement. In M. Wittrock (Ed.), *Handbook of research on teaching* (3rd ed.) (pp. 328–375). New York: Macmillan.

Burns, P. (1987). Fairy tales on trial. In *The Constitution: Experiencing democracy.* Denver: Colorado Department of Education.

Clark, C. H. (1981). Assessing comprehensibility: The PHAN System. *The Reading Teacher, 34,* 670–675.

Collis, B. (1988). *Computers, curriculum, and whole- class instruction.* Belmont, CA: Wadsworth.

Cooper, J. D., Warncke, E. W., Ramstad, P. A., & Shipman, D. A. (1979). *The what and how of reading instruction.* Columbus, OH: Chas. E. Merrill.

Dewey, J. (1933). *How we think.* Boston: Heath.

Doyle, W. (1980). *Classroom management.* West Lafayette, IN: Kappa Delta Pi.

Edney, J. J. (1979). The nuts game: A concise common dilemma—An analog. *Environmental Psychology and Nonverbal Behavior, 3,* 252–254.

Elkind, D. (1981a). Child development and the social studies curriculum of the elementary school. *Social Education, 45,* 435–437.

——— (1981b). *The hurried child.* Reading, MA: Addison-Wesley.

Elliott, D. L., Nagel, K. C., & Woodward, A. (1985). Do textbooks belong in elementary social studies? *Educational Leadership, 42,* 22–24.

Ellis, A. K. (1986). *Teaching and learning in elementary social studies* (3rd ed.). Boston: Allyn & Bacon.

Ellis, M. (1985). *What really happened at the Alamo?* Unpublished manuscript, Mansfield, TX.

Erikson, E. (1963). *Childhood and society* (2nd ed.). New York: W.W. Norton & Co., Inc.

Fling, F. (1909). One use of sources in the teaching of history. *History Teacher's Magazine, 1,* 5–7.

Frymier, J. (1977). *Annehurst curriculum classification system.* West Lafayette, IN: Kappa Delta Pi.

Gage, N. L., & Berliner, D. C. (1988). *Educational psychology* (4th ed.). Boston: Houghton Mifflin.

Gagné, R. M. (1965). The learning of concepts. *The School Review, 73,* 187–196.

Gall, M. D. (1970). The use of questions in teaching. *Review of Educational Research, 40,* 707–721.

Geographic Education National Implementation Project (1987). *K-6 geography.* Washington, DC: Geographic Education National Implementation Project.

Giaconia, R. (1987). *Teacher questioning and wait time.* Unpublished doctoral dissertation, Stanford University, Stanford, CA.

Gibbons, M., & Neuman, M. (1985/1986). Creating a curriculum for a global future. *Educational Leadership, 43,* 72–75.

Glasser, W. (1969). *Schools without failure.* New York: Harper & Row.

Goodlad, J. I. (1983). What some schools and classrooms teach. *Educational Leadership, 40,* 8–19.

Hallam, R. (1960). Piaget and the teaching of history. *Educational Research, 12,* 3–12.

Hamilton, J. W. (1986). *Main street America and the third world.* Cabin John, MD: Seven Locks.

Hartoonian, H. M. (1989). Social mathematics. In M. A. Laughlin, H. M. Hartoonian, & N. M. Sanders (Eds.), *From information to decision making* (pp. 51–64). Washington, DC: National Council for the Social Studies.

Hatcher, B. (1983). Putting young cartographers "on the map." *Childhood Education, 59*, 311–315.

Heller, M. (1986). How do you know what you know? Metacognitive modeling in the content areas. *Journal of Reading, 29*, 415–422.

Hendry, C., Lippitt, R., & Zander, A. (1944). Reality practice and educational method. *Psychodrama Monographs, 9*. Ambler, PA: Horsham Foundation.

Herman, W. L. (1983). What should be taught where? *Social Education, 47*, 94–100.

Hohmann, M., Banet, B., & Weikart, D. P. (1979). *Young children in action*. Ypsilanti, MI: The High/Scope Press.

Hunter, M. (1982). *Mastery learning*. El Segundo, CA: TIP Publications.

Hymes, J. L. (1981). *Teaching the child under six* (3rd ed.). Columbus, OH: Chas. E. Merrill.

Jacko, C. M. (1981). *Where do you stand? A simulation risk exercise*. Paper presented at the annual meeting of the Association for Teacher Educators, Dallas, TX.

Jones, B. F., Palincsar, A. S., Ogle, D. S., & Carr, E. G. (1987). Strategic Teaching: A cognitive focus. In B. F. Jones, A. S. Palincsar, D. S. Ogle, & E. G. Carr (Eds.), *Strategic teaching and learning: Cognitive instruction in the content areas* (pp. 33–70). Alexandria, VA: Association for Supervision and Curriculum Development.

Jones, B. F., Pierce, J., & Hunter, B. (1988/1989). Teaching students to construct graphic representations. *Educational Leadership, 46*, 20–25.

Joyce, B., & McKibbin, M. (1982). Teacher growth and school environments. *Educational Leadership, 40*, 36–41.

Joyce, B., & Weil, M. (1986). *Models of teaching* (3rd ed.). Englewood Cliffs, NJ: Prentice Hall.

Kamii, C. (1984). Autonomy: The aim of education envisioned by Piaget. *Phi Delta Kappan, 65*, 410–415.

Kluckhohn, F. (1950). Dominant and substitute profiles of cultural orientations: Their significance for analysis of social stratification. *Social Forces, 28*, 376–393.

Koch, K. A. (1989). Strategic thinking in the social studies. In M. A. Laughlin, H. M. Hartoonian, & N. M. Sanders (Eds.), *From information to decision making*. Washington, DC: National Council for the Social Studies.

Kohlberg, L. (1985). The Just Community approach to moral education in theory and practice. In M. W. Berkowitz & F. Oser (Eds.), *Moral education: Theory and application* (pp. 27–87). Hillsdale, NJ: Lawrence Erlbaum.

Kolb, D. A. (1976). *Learning style inventory: Technical manual*. Boston: McBer.

Krawetz, M. (1984). *Self-esteem Passport*. New York: Holt, Rinehart & Winston.

Larkins, A. G., Hawkins, M. L., & Gilmore, A. (1987). Trivial and nonformative content of elementary social studies: A review of primary texts in four series. *Theory and Research in Social Education, 15*, 299–311.

Levstik, J. (1986). Teaching history: A definitional and developmental dilemma. In V. Atwood (Ed.), *Elementary school social studies* (pp. 68–84). Washington, DC: National Council for the Social Studies.

Lord, F. E. (1941). A study of spatial orientation of children. *Journal of Educational Research, 34*, 481–505.

Manzo, A. V. (1985). Expansion modules for the ReQuest, CAT, GRP, and REAP reading/study procedures. *Journal of Reading, 28*, 498–502.

Martin, R. J., & Van Cleaf, D. W. (1983). Language arts students improve writing skills. *Catalyst for Change, 12*, 17–18.

Marzano, R. J., & Arredondo, D. E. (1986). *Tactics for thinking.* Alexandria, VA: Association for Supervision and Curriculum Development.

Marzollo, J. (1988). Do worksheets work? *Parents Magazine, 63*, 108–112.

Maxwell, L. (1987). Eight pointers on teaching children to think. *Research in Brief.* Washington, DC: Office of Educational Research and Improvement, U.S. Department of Education.

McGraw-Hill. (1986). *Our nation, our world—The success series (2nd ed.). New York: McGraw-Hill.*

McKinney, C. W., Larkins, A. G., Ford, M. J., & Davis, J. C. (1983). The effectiveness of three methods of teaching social studies concepts to fourth-grade students: An aptitude- treatment interaction study. *American Educational Research Journal, 20*, 663–670.

Merrill, M. D., & Tennyson, R. D. (1977). *Teaching concepts: An instructional design guide.* Englewood Cliffs, NJ: Educational Technology Publications.

Messick, R. G., & Chapin, J. R. (1989). Using data in elementary social studies programs. In M. A. Laughlin, H. M. Hartoonian, & N. M. Sanders (Eds.), *From information to decision making* (pp. 11–18). Washington, DC: National Council for the Social Studies.

Montague, M., & Tanner, M. L. (1987). Reading strategy groups for content area instruction. *Journal of Reading, 30*, 716–725.

Morrison, G. S. (1984). *Early childhood education today* (3rd ed.). Columbus, OH: Chas. E. Merrill.

Muir, S. P. (1979). Testing a case for inquiry social studies in the elementary school. *Social Education, 43*, 385–387.

———. (1985). Understanding and improving students' map reading skills. *The Elementary School Journal, 86*, 207–216.

Muir, S. P., & Frazee, B. M. (1986). A developmental perspective. *Social Education, 50*, 199–203.

National Assessment of Educational Progress (1989). *Crossroads in American education.* Princeton, NJ: Educational Testing Service.

NCSS Task Force on Scope and Sequence (1989). In search of a scope and sequence for social studies. *Social Education, 53*, 376–387.

Nelms, B. (1987). Response and responsibility: Reading, writing, and social studies. *The Elementary School Journal, 87*, 571–589.

Nuffield Foundation. (1967). *Pictorial representation.* New York: John Wiley.

Ohlhausen, M. M., & Roller, C. M. (1986). Teaching students to use a nation schema to learn about countries. *Journal of Reading, 30*, 212–217.

Orlich, D. C., Harder, R. J., Callahan, R. C., Kravas, C. H., Kauchak, D. P., Pendergrass, R. A., & Keogh, A. J. (1985). *Teaching strategies.* (2nd ed.). Lexington, MA: Heath.

Parker, W. C. (1984). Developing teachers' decision making. *Journal of Experimental Education, 52*, 220–226.

Pattison, W. D. (1966). Territory, learner and map. *The Elementary School Journal, 67*, 146–153.

Piaget, J. (1965, originally published 1932). *The moral judgement of the child. New York: The Free Press.*

Project SPAN (1982). *The current state of the social studies: A report of Project SPAN.* Boulder, CO: Social Science Education Consortium.

Raths, L., Harmin, M., & Simon, S. (1986). *Values and teaching. Columbus, OH: Chas. E. Merrill.*

Redfield, D. L., & Rousseau, E. W. (1981). A meta-analysis of experimental research on teacher questioning behavior. *Review of Educational Research, 51*, 237–245.

Reinhartz, J., & Van Cleaf, D. W. (1986). *Teach-practice-apply: The TPA Instructional Model, K-8.* Washington, DC: National Education Association.

Roberts, N., Friel, S., & Ladenburg, T. (1988). *Computers and the social studies.* Menlo Park, CA: Addison-Wesley.

Rosecrance, R. (1986). *The rise of the trading state: Commerce and conquest in the modern world.* New York: Basic Books.

Ross, D., D., & Kyle, D. W. (1987). Helping preservice teachers learn to use teacher effectiveness research. *Journal of Teacher Education, 38,* 40–44.

Roueche, J. E., & Baker, G. A. (1986). *Profiling excellence in America's schools.* Arlington, VA: American Association of School Administrators.

Rousseau, J. J. (1974, originally published 1762). *Emile.* (S. E. Frost, Jr. Ed., R. L. Archer, Trans.). New York: Baum

Rowe, M. B. (1974). Wait-time and rewards as instructional variables, their influence on language, logic and fate control: Part 1. Wait-time, *Journal of Research in Science Teaching, 11,* 81–94.

Ruggiero, V. R. (1988). *Teaching thinking across the curriculum.* New York: Harper & Row.

Rush, R. T. (1985). Assessing readability: Formulas and alternatives. *The Reading Teacher, 39,* 274–283.

Ryan, F. L. (1980). *The social studies sourcebook.* Boston: Allyn & Bacon.

Schaps, E., Solomon, D., & Watson, M. (1985/1986). A program that combines character development and academic achievement. *Educational Leadership, 43,* 32–35.

Schumaker, J., Deshler, D., Alley, G., Warner, M., & Denton, P. (1982). MULTIPASS: A learning strategy for improving reading comprehension. *Learning Disability Quarterly, 5,* 295–304.

Shaftel, F. R., & Shaftel, G. (1982). *Role playing in the curriculum* (2nd ed.). Englewood Cliffs, NJ: Prentice Hall.

Shannon, P. (1982). Some subjective reasons for teachers' reliance on commercial reading materials. *The Reading Teacher, 35,* 884–889.

Shoop, M. (1987). Reading aloud to students: Questioning strategies to listening comprehension. *Reading Horizons, 27,* 127–137.

Shulman, L. S. (1987a). Knowledge and teaching: Foundations of the new reform. *Harvard Educational Review, 57,* 1–22.

———. (1987b). *National board certification: Why and how?* Paper presented at the annual meeting of the National Council for the Social Studies, Dallas, TX.

Simon, S. B., Howe, L. W., & Kirschenbaum, H. (1978). *Values clarification.* (rev. ed.). New York: Hart.

Slavin, R. E. (1986). *Using student team learning* (3rd ed.). Baltimore, MD: Johns Hopkins University Center for Social Organization of Schools.

Sleeter, C. E., & Grant, C. A. (1988). *Making choices for multicultural education.* Columbus, OH: Chas. E. Merrill.

Smith, R. J., & Barrett, T. C. (1979). *Teaching reading in the middle school* (2nd ed.). Reading, MA: Addison-Wesley.

Snyder, M. (1987). Valentine maps and metaphors. *Learning 87, 16,* 33.

Stauffer, R. (1975). *Directing the reading-thinking process.* New York: Harper & Row.

Stone, L. (1986). International and multicultural education. In V. Atwood (Ed.). *Elementary school social studies: Research as a guide to practice* (pp. 34–54). Washington, DC: National Council for the Social Studies.

Taba, H. (1967). *Teacher's handbook for elementary social studies.* Palo Alto, CA: Addison-Wesley.

Texas Education Agency (1987). Chapter 75 in *The State Board of Education rules for curriculum.* Austin, TX: Texas Education Agency.

Thomas, A., & Chess, S. (1977). *Temperament and development.* New York: Brunner/Mazel.

Thornton, S. J., & Vukelich, R. (1988). Effects of children's understanding of time concepts on historical understanding. *Theory and Research in Social Education, 16,* 69–82.

Van Cleaf, D. W. (1979). *A comparison of parents' attitudes with those of kindergarten teachers and principals concerning kindergarten objectives and preferences relating to behaviorist and cognitive transactionist methods.* Unpublished doctoral dissertation, University of Nebraska.

———. (1981). Strengthening map skills through orienteering. *Social Education, 45,* 462–463.

———. (1984). Guiding student inquiry. *The Social Studies, 75,* 109–111.

———. (1985). The environment as a data source: Map activities for young children. *Social Education, 49,* 145–146.

———. (1986). *Teaching elementary social studies: Supplemental materials.* Unpublished manuscript, Washburn University, Topeka.

Van Cleaf, D. W., & Martin, R. J. (1982). Piaget's model of moral development. *Capstone Journal of Education, 3,* 20–29.

Van Cleaf, D. W., & Schkade, L. (1987). Student teacher learning styles: Another dimension of reform. *Teacher Education and Practice, 4,* 25–34.

———. (1989). Brain hemisphere preferences of student teachers with selected academic majors. *Teacher Education and Practice, 5,* 39–44.

Wales, C. E., Nardi, A. H., & Stager, R. A. (1987). *Thinking skills: Making a choice.* Morgantown: Center for Guided Design, West Virginia University.

Wheeler, R. (1980). Salute to the classroom teacher #1: Betty Grey and Susan Semchak. *Social Education, 44,* 40–41.

Wixson, K. K. (1983). Questions about text: What you ask about is what children learn. *The Reading Teacher, 37,* 287–293.

Wolken, L. (1984). The international pencil: Elementary level unit on global interdependence. *Journal of Geography, 83,* 290–293.

Wynne, E. A., & Walberg, H. J. (1985/1986). The complementary goals of character development and academic excellence. *Educational Leadership, 43,* 15–18.

Zevin, J. (1969). Mystery island, *Today's Education, 58,* 42–43.

Index

Academic learning time, 53–54
Accommodation, 72
Activities, teaching and learning, defined, 73–74
  personalizing instruction, 111–12
Adaptation, 72
Affective development, 238
Affective learning, 240, 242
Alamo, Battle, 199–200, 204, 205, 207–11
Allen, Elizabeth G., 354
Alley, Gordon, 324
American Bar Association Committee on Youth Education for Citizenship, 344
Analyzing data, 193
Andrews, Julia L., 157
Anthropology and the social studies, 37
Anticipatory set, 76
Armstrong, David G., 199
Arredondo, Daisy E., 219, 227, 228, 229
Articulation, curriculum, 27
Assimilation, 72
Association for Supervision and Curriculum Development, 286
Attitudes, 288
Attitudes toward social studies, 2

Attitudinal surveys, 128–30
Attributes, 215, 221, 226
Attribute value, 215, 224, 226
Authoritarian parents, 105, 294, 295. *See also* Parenting styles.
Authoritative parents, 104–5, 293, 294. *See also* Parenting styles.

Baker, George A., 59
Baker, Lyle, 303
Banet, B., 112
Barell, John, 354
Barr, Robert D., 12, 13, 18
Barrett, Thomas, 239
Barth, James L., 12, 13, 18
Baumrind, Diana, 104, 293–95
Behaviorism
  described, 5–6
  programs, 68
  teaching practices, 20–21
Beliefs, 288
Bennett, William J., 40, 41
Berliner, David, 52, 54, 105, 123
Birthday News, 204, 205
Bloom, Benjamin, 6, 78
Boles, Wilma, 345
Bredekamp, Sue, 126
Brophy, Jere E., 53, 55

Burns, P., 346

Callahan, Richard C., 240, 241
Carr, Eileen G., 133
Cavett, Dorcas, 160
Chapin, June R., 155
Character, 12, 286. *See also* Moral development.
Checklists
  evaluation, 130–31
  questioning, 248
Chess, Stella, 104
Child-centered learning, 7–8, 222, 230
Children's literature, 325
Citizenship education, 37–38
  activities, 43
Civics. *See* Citizenship education.
Clarity, instructional, 55
Clark, Charles H., 313
Classification, 102
Classroom complexities, 50–51
Classroom management, 16, 54, 97, 293. *See also* Moral development.
Classroom meetings, 135–36, 302
Closure, 74
Cloze procedure, 313–14

Cognitive developmental psychology
  described, 6–8
  programs, 68
  teaching practices, 20–21
Cognitively Oriented Curriculum, 80–82, 112
Collis, B., 349
Colorado Department of Education, 346
Compass rose, 150
Comprehension, effective teaching, 58
Comprehension, reading
  evaluative, 239, 240
  inferential, 239, 240
  literal, 239, 240
Computers
  data bases, 348–49
  drill and practice exercises, 346
  games, 271–75, 348
  managing children, 273
  simulations, 271–74, 347–48
  tutorials, 346–47
  uses, 346–49
  word processing, 348
Concept attainment strategy, 223–25, 355
Concept pattern strategy, 227–28
Concepts, 35, 36, 45–46
  attributes, 214, 215. See also Attributes.
  attribute value, 215. See also Attribute value.
  benefits, 216–18
  communication, 216–17
  deductive teaching, 219–22
  defined, 35, 214
  examples, 215
  inductive teaching, 219, 222–28
  student achievement, 216
  teaching strategies, 88–89, 219–28
  types, 214
Conclusions, research, 194–95
Concrete operational thought, 102–3
Consequences. See Natural consequences.
Content decisions, 108–9
Content teaching, 190, 193
Controversial topics, 310
Cooper, J. David, 78
Cooperation, 237, 266, 273

Cooperative learning
  appropriate environment, 54–55
  critical thinking, 354–55
  reading, 317–18, 324
Coordinates, map, 152
Coverage, 310
Critical attributes. See Attributes.
Critical thinking, 190, 237, 240, 242, 273, 287, 311, 324, 350–56
  activities, 353–56
  characteristics, 350–52
  definition, 351
  inhibiting practices, 350
  suggestions, 352–53
Crossroads in American Education, 350
Cultural perspectives, 97–100
Culture, school, 106–7
Current events, 136, 249, 258, 338
Curriculum
  adapting, 47
  described, 24, 101
  formal, 24–25
  fragmentation, 308
  guides, 70
  hidden, 25
  materials, 110–11, 335, 336

Data bases, computer, 348–49
Data-acquisition skills, 351, 352
Data-evaluation skills, 351–52
Davis, Jo Ann, 269
Decenter, 291
Democratic values and beliefs, 28, 29, 333
Denton, Pegi, 324
Dependent variable, 173
Deshler, Donald, 324
Developmental psychology. See Cognitive developmental psychology.
Devil's advocate, 252
Dewey, John, 10, 351
Diaries. See Journals.
Direct instruction, 6
Discrepant events, 303
Discussion Risk activity, 136–37
Discussions, 234, 235, 248–52
  comparative, 249–50
  guided, 89–90, 226–27, 251
  open ended, 249
  social problem solving, 250

  starters, 252
Disequilibration, 296, 299, 303
Divergent thinking 352, 353
Doyle, Walter, 50–51, 54

Economics, 199
Economics and the social studies, 38
Edney, Julian J., 266, 267
Effective teaching
  characteristics, 69
  practices, 52–57
Egocentric thought, 102, 291
Elevation, maps, 148–49
Elkind, David, 6, 17, 26, 96
Elliott, David L., 311
Ellis, Arthur K., 159
Ellis, Marianna, 199, 200, 207, 211
Engaged time, 53
Enthusiasm, 56
Erikson, Eric, 3–4, 103, 105
Erikson's psychosocial stages, 3–4, 103
Ethics, 286
European Economic Community, 339
Evaluation, 74, 121, 122–23
  effective teaching practices, 56–57
  formative, 120, 123
  limitations, 123–26
  purposes, 119–21
  questioning, 235–36, 248
  summative, 120, 123
Examples
  nonexamples, 215
  positive, 215
Expanding environment curriculum, 33–34, 36, 349
Expectations, teacher, 54
Extension activities, 74
Extrapolation, 181

Fact file, 201
Facts, 46, 217
Feedback, 57
Feuerstein, Reuven, 6
Field trips, 198
Flexibility, teacher, 58, 86, 272
Fling, F., 205

Formal operational thought, 102–3
Foxfire project, 203
Frazee, Bruce M., 148, 153
Freedom, 18
Friel, Susan, 271
Frymier, Jack, 72, 95, 111

Gage, N. L., 105, 123
Gagné, Robert M., 220–21
Gall, Meredith D., 242
Games, 256, 257, 269–71
  benefits, 269
  computer, 274–75, 348
  guidelines, 270–71
  limitations, 269–70
Gandhi, Mohandas, 292
Gender differences and learning, 105–6
Generalizations, 36, 45–46, 218–19
  strategies, 228–29
Gent, Ruth, 299
Geography and the social studies 38, 43–45
  activities, 45, 195, 196, 342
  themes, 43–44
Giaconia, Rose M., 243
Gilmore, Allison, 310, 311
Glasser, William, 135–36, 249, 250, 302
Global education 339–42
  activities, 340–42
  goals, 340
Goals, 70–71
Good, Thomas L., 53, 55
Goodlad, John I., 18
Grades, 57, 123
Grant, Carl A., 336
Graphic representations, 318–21, 322–23. See also Representations, graphic.
Graphs
  axes, 173
  bar, 168, 173, 175, 177–79
  bead, 170
  circle, 175, 182–83
  climographs, 182
  common errors, 183–86
  computers, 349
  defined, 168
  developmental stages, 168–74
  histographs, 177
  line, 168, 175, 179–82

people, 169, 170
picture, 174, 175–77
rudimentary, 169
variable, quantity, 168, 174
variable, time, 168, 174
Gray, Betty, 268
Grid lines, 155
Grouping students, 110, 113, 120, 151, 195, 200, 201, 266
Groups, small, 267, 273

Hallam, Roy, 41, 42
Hamilton, John M., 340
Hansen, Susan, 299
Harder, Robert J., 240, 241
Harmin, Merrill, 300
Hartoonian, H. Michael, 187
Hatcher, Barbara, 147
Hawkins, Michael, L., 310, 311
Heckard, Grace, 331
Heller, Mary F., 319, 320
Hemisphere specialization. See Learning style.
Hendry, Charles E., 258
Henry, Marguerite, 268
Henry, Steve, 134, 135, 319
Herman, Wayne, 37–40
Hidden curriculum, 123
High-level thinking, 190, 351, 352
High stakes testing, 126
History and the social studies, 38–39, 40–42, 205
  activities, 42, 197, 198
  role playing, 261, 263
Hohmann, Mary, 112
Howe, Leland, W., 262, 263, 300, 301, 302
Hunter, Barbara, 321, 322–23
Hunter, Madeline, 6, 71, 77
Hurried Child, The, 17
Hutchins, C. L., 352
Hymes, James L., Jr., 17
Hypotheses, 191–92

Inculcation, values, 9, 13
Independent study, 113, 202, 327. See also Investigations, mini.
Independent variable, 173
Individualizing instruction, 112–13. See also Personalizing instruction.

Inquest, 251
Inquiry, 14, 15, 324
  activities, 92–93, 194–203, 338
  benefits, 190
  collecting data, 192–93
  critical thinking, 351–52, 355
  problem statement, 191–92
  projects, 194
  role playing, 260
  simulations, 266
  steps, 191–94, 204–5
  students' role, 190
  teachers' role, 190, 201
Integration, concept development, 217, 218
International Pencil, 342
Interpersonal skills, 59, 237
Interpolation, 181
Interviews, 203
Investigations, mini, 200–2, 204, 205

Jacko, Carol M., 136
Jones, Beau Fly, 133, 321, 322–23
Journals, 133
Joyce, Bruce, 49, 60–61, 215, 216, 223, 265, 299
Just Community, 296–97

Kamii, Constance, 285, 297
Kauchak, Donald P., 240, 241
Keogh, Andrew J., 240, 241
King, Martin Luther, Jr., 291, 292
Kirschenbaum, Howard, 262, 263, 300, 301, 302
Kluckhohn, Florence, 97, 98, 106, 356
Kniep, Willard M., 15
Knowledge and the social studies, 28
Koch, Kathryn A., 355
Kohlberg, Lawrence, 6, 288–89, 296
  stages of moral development, 288–89
Kolb, David, 100, 107
Kravas, Constance, 240, 241
Krawetz, M., 301
Ku Klux Klan, 288
Kyle, Diane W., 57–58

Labeling children, 97, 126
Ladenburg, Thomas, 271

Laminack, Lester L., 354
Language, concepts, 216–17
Language experience stories, 133–34, 328
Larkins, A. Guy, 310, 311
Latitude, 156
Law-related education, 343–46
  activities, 345–46
  goals, 343–44
Learning centers, 80–81, 113
Learning environment, 54–55, 245–46
Learning styles, 73, 100–2, 324
  cerebral learning style, 101–2
  left-brain learning style, 101–2
  limbic learning style, 101–2
  right brain learning style, 101–2
Lectures, 220, 236
Levstik, Linda S., 41
Lexington, Battle, 199, 263
Liebmann, Rosemarie, 354
Lippitt, Ronald, 258
Log of Christopher Columbus, The, 157
Longitude, 156
Lord, Francis E., 150

McGraw Hill, 34
McKibbin, Michael, 60–61
Make Way for Ducklings, 75, 77, 80
Manzo, Anthony V., 251
Map projections, 164
Map reading
  cautions, 164
  comparing maps and making inferences, 161–64, 196
  defined, 144
  directions, 149–52
  distance, 157–59
  location, 152–57
  orienting, 149–52
  problems, 142–44
  scale, 157–59
  skills 144–46
  symbols, 146–49
Marien, Joanne, 307
Martin, Rita J., 197, 290
Marzano, Robert J., 219, 227, 228, 229, 352
Marzollo, Jean, 307
Mastery learning, 6, 76, 78

Materials, teaching, 72–73. *See also* Curriculum materials.
  non-text, 325–26
Mathematics
  consumer, 199
  social, 187
Maxwell, Laurie, 352
Measurement, 121–22. *See also* Evaluation.
Mediator, teacher's role, 26
Mental structures, 45
Merrill, M. David, 221, 222
Merrill-Tennyson strategy, 221–22
Messick, Rosemary G., 155
Metacognition, 225, 355–56
Misty of Chincoteague, 268
Monitoring, 56
Montague, Marjorie, 324
Montessori, Maria, 80
Montessori programs, 68
Moral development, 260
  activities, 293–304
  adult's role, 295–98
  autonomous morality, 290, 292
  classroom responsibilities, 304
  critical thinking, 350
  heteronomous morality, 290–91
  Kohlberg's stages, 289
  moral realism, 290, 291–92
  parenting/teaching styles, 293–95
  Piaget's model, 289–92
  premoral stage, 290
  transitional stage, 292
Moral dilemmas, 91, 258, 260, 288–89, 338, 346
  procedure, 298–99
  sample lesson, 91
Moral education. *See* Moral development.
Moral reasoning, 289
Morality, 287–88. *See also* Moral development.
Morrison, George S., 336, 337
Motivation, 59
Multicultural education, 111, 311, 332–39
  activities, 336–38
  goals, 333–36
  materials, 335
  teaching strategies, 336

Muir, Sharon Pray, 148, 152, 153, 159, 190
Mystery Island, 164, 195–96, 204

NAACP, 288
Nagel, Kathleen Carter, 311
Nardi, Anne H., 268, 279, 283
Nation schema, 319, 320
National Assessment of Educational Progress, 350
National Council for the Social Studies, 62
National Council for the Social Studies Task Force on Scope and Sequence, 15, 27, 29, 30–31, 32, 33, 34, 144, 145, 152, 164, 168, 288, 333
Natural consequences, 297–98
Needs, 195
Nelms, Ben F., 326, 327
Newspaper Birthday activity, 197–98
Newspapers, 197, 198, 252
Newspapers in Education, 73
Nuffield Foundation, 168, 172
Nuts game, 266–67

Objectives, 70–71
  behavioral, 71
  instructional, 71
Observation, personal, 193
Ogle, Donna S., 133
Ohlhausen, Marilyn M., 319, 320
Omnivores, 60
One-to-one correspondence, 169, 170, 171, 183
Oral history, 198, 202–3, 204, 205
Orienteering, 157
Orlich, Donald C., 240, 241

Pacific rim, 33
Pacing, 53, 56, 120
Palincsar, Annemarie S., 133
Parenting styles, 104–5
  authoritarian, 105, 294–95
  authoritative, 104–5, 293–94
  permissive, 104, 294, 295